Shugo Chara!

7

PEACH-PIT

Translated by
Satsuki Yamashita

Adapted by
Nunzio DeFilippis and Christina Weir

Lettered by
North Market Street Graphics

KC
KODANSHA
COMICS
K

A Kodansha Comics Trade Paperback Original.

Shugo Chara! volume 7 copyright © 2008 PEACH-PIT
English translation copyright © 2009, 2013 PEACH-PIT

Published in the United States by Kodansha Comics, an imprint of Kodansha USA Publishing, LLC., New York.

Publication rights for this English edition arranged through Kodansha Ltd., Tokyo.

First published in Japan in 2008 by Kodansha Ltd., Tokyo.

ISBN 978-1-61262-346-7

Original cover design by Akiko Omo.

Printed in the United States of America.

www.kodanshacomics.com

9 8 7 6 5 4 3 2

Translator: Satsuki Yamashita
Adapter: Nunzio DeFilippis and Christina Weir.
Lettering: North Market Street Graphics

Contents

Honorifics Explained

Throughout the Kodansha Comics books, you will find Japanese honorifics left intact in the translations. For those not familiar with how the Japanese use honorifics and, more important, how they differ from American honorifics, we present this brief overview.

Politeness has always been a critical facet of Japanese culture. Ever since the feudal era, when Japan was a highly stratified society, use of honorifics—which can be defined as polite speech that indicates relationship or status—has played an essential role in the Japanese language. When addressing someone in Japanese, an honorific usually takes the form of a suffix attached to one's name (example: "Asuna-san"), is used as a title at the end of one's name, or appears in place of the name itself (example: "Negi-sensei," or simply "Sensei!").

Honorifics can be expressions of respect or endearment. In the context of manga and anime, honorifics give insight into the nature of the relationship between characters. Many English translations leave out these important honorifics and therefore distort the feel of the original Japanese. Because Japanese honorifics contain nuances that English honorifics lack, it is our policy at Kodansha Comics not to translate them. Here, instead, is a guide to some of the honorifics you may encounter in Kodansha Comics books.

-san: This is the most common honorific and is equivalent to Mr., Miss, Ms., Mrs. It is the all-purpose honorific and can be used in any situation where politeness is required.

-sama: This is one level higher than "-san" and is used to confer great respect.

-dono: This comes from the word "tono," which means "lord." It is an even higher level than "-sama" and confers utmost respect.

-kun: This suffix is used at the end of boys' names to express familiarity or endearment. It is also sometimes used by men among friends, or when addressing someone younger or of a lower station.

v

-chan:	This is used to express endearment, mostly toward girls. It is also used for little boys, pets, and even among lovers. It gives a sense of childish cuteness.
Bozu:	This is an informal way to refer to a boy, similar to the English terms "kid" and "squirt."
Sempai/ Senpai:	This title suggests that the addressee is one's senior in a group or organization. It is most often used in a school setting, where underclassmen refer to their upperclassmen as "sempai." It can also be used in the workplace, such as when a newer employee addresses an employee who has seniority in the company.
Kohai:	This is the opposite of "sempai" and is used toward underclassmen in school or newcomers in the workplace. It connotes that the addressee is of a lower station.
Sensei:	Literally meaning "one who has come before," this title is used for teachers, doctors, or masters of any profession or art.
-[blank]:	This is usually forgotten in these lists, but it is perhaps the most significant difference between Japanese and English. The lack of honorific means that the speaker has permission to address the person in a very intimate way. Usually, only family, spouses, or very close friends have this kind of permission. Known as *yobisute,* it can be gratifying when someone who has earned the intimacy starts to call one by one's name without an honorific. But when that intimacy hasn't been earned, it can be very insulting.

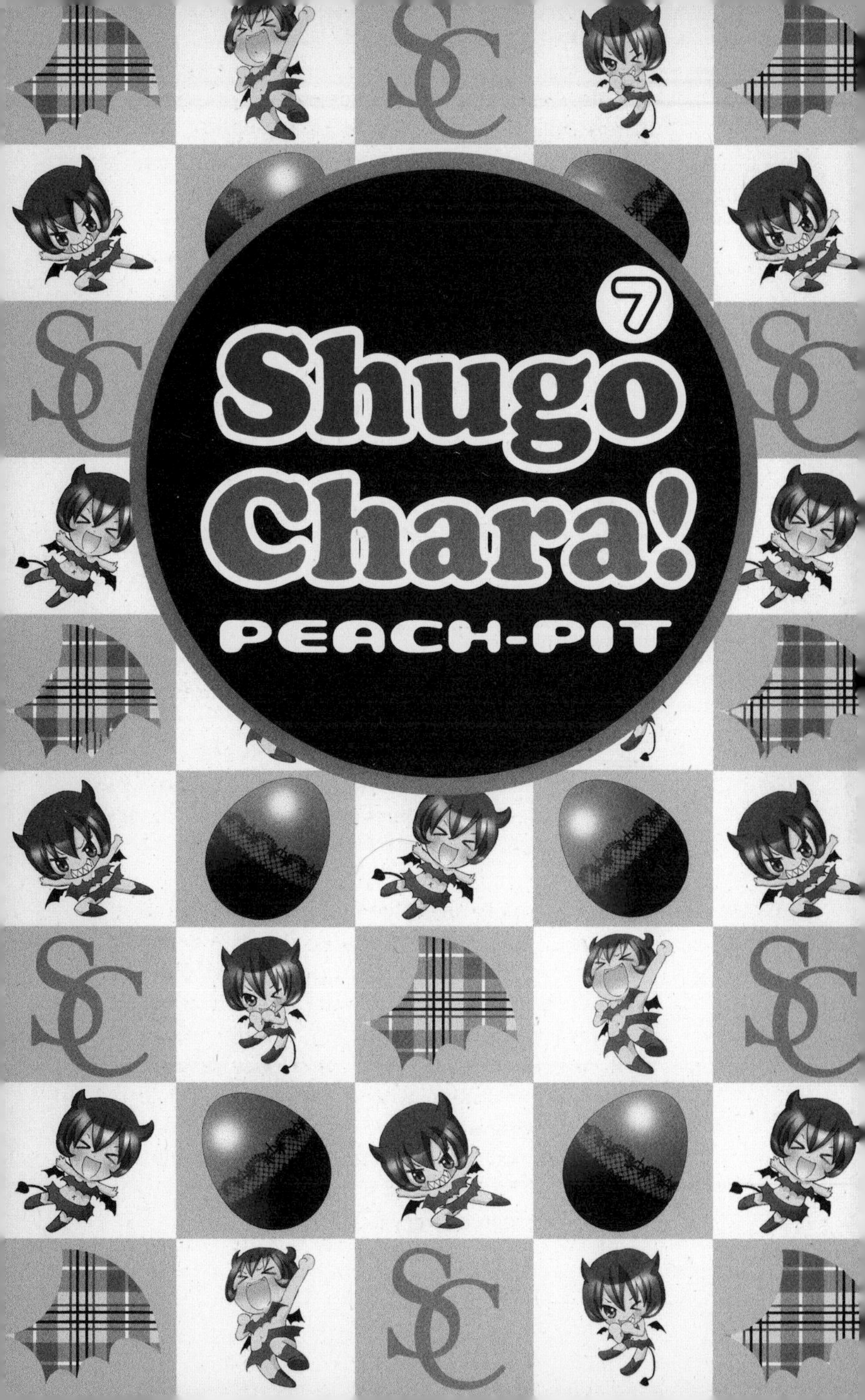
7
Shugo Chara!
PEACH-PIT

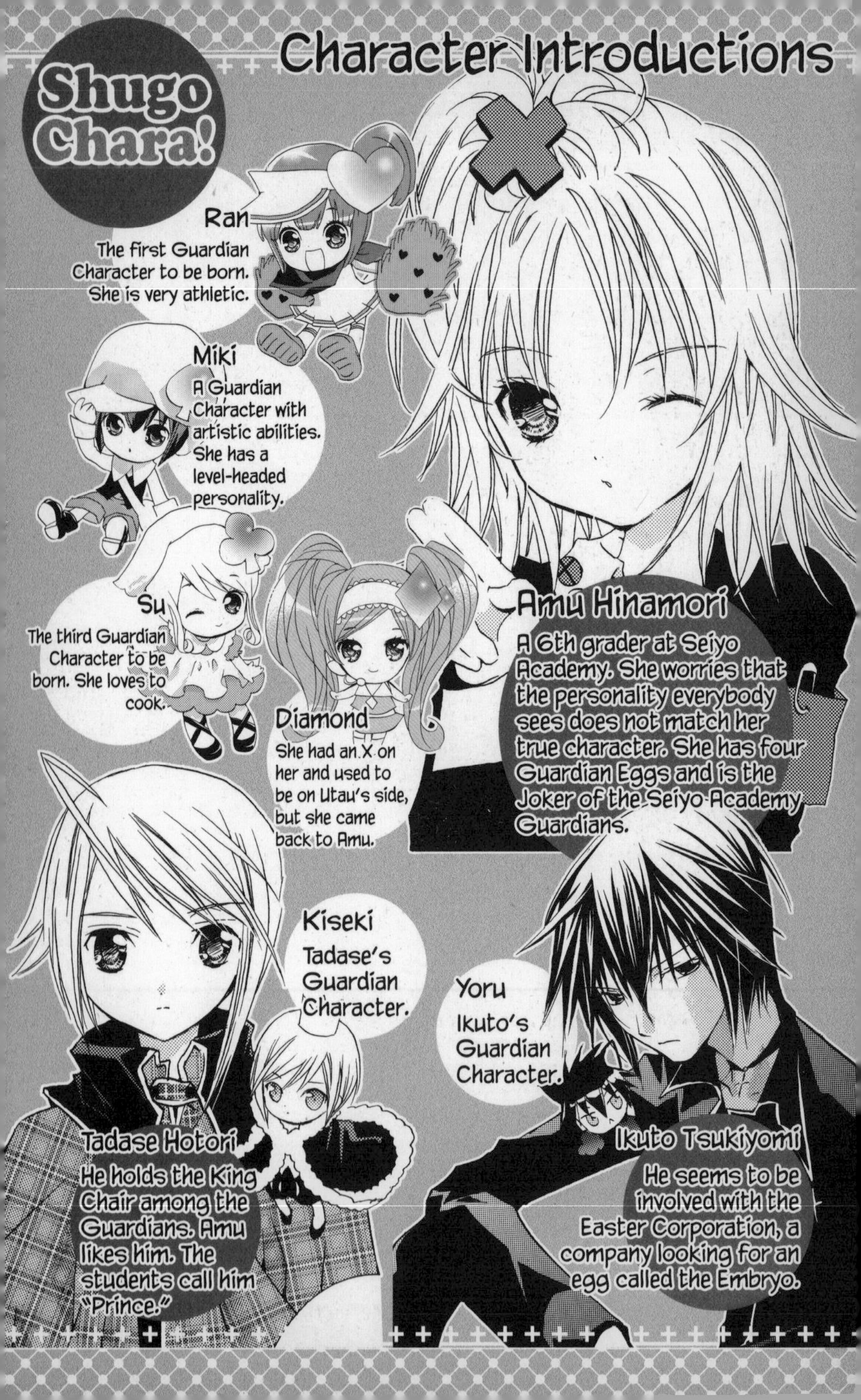
Character Introductions
Shugo Chara!
Ran
The first Guardian Character to be born. She is very athletic.
Miki
A Guardian Character with artistic abilities. She has a level-headed personality.
Su
The third Guardian Character to be born. She loves to cook.
Diamond
She had an X on her and used to be on Utau's side, but she came back to Amu.
Amu Hinamori
A 6th grader at Seiyo Academy. She worries that the personality everybody sees does not match her true character. She has four Guardian Eggs and is the Joker of the Seiyo Academy Guardians.
Kiseki
Tadase's Guardian Character.
Yoru
Ikuto's Guardian Character.
Tadase Hotori
He holds the King Chair among the Guardians. Amu likes him. The students call him "Prince."
Ikuto Tsukiyomi
He seems to be involved with the Easter Corporation, a company looking for an egg called the Embryo.

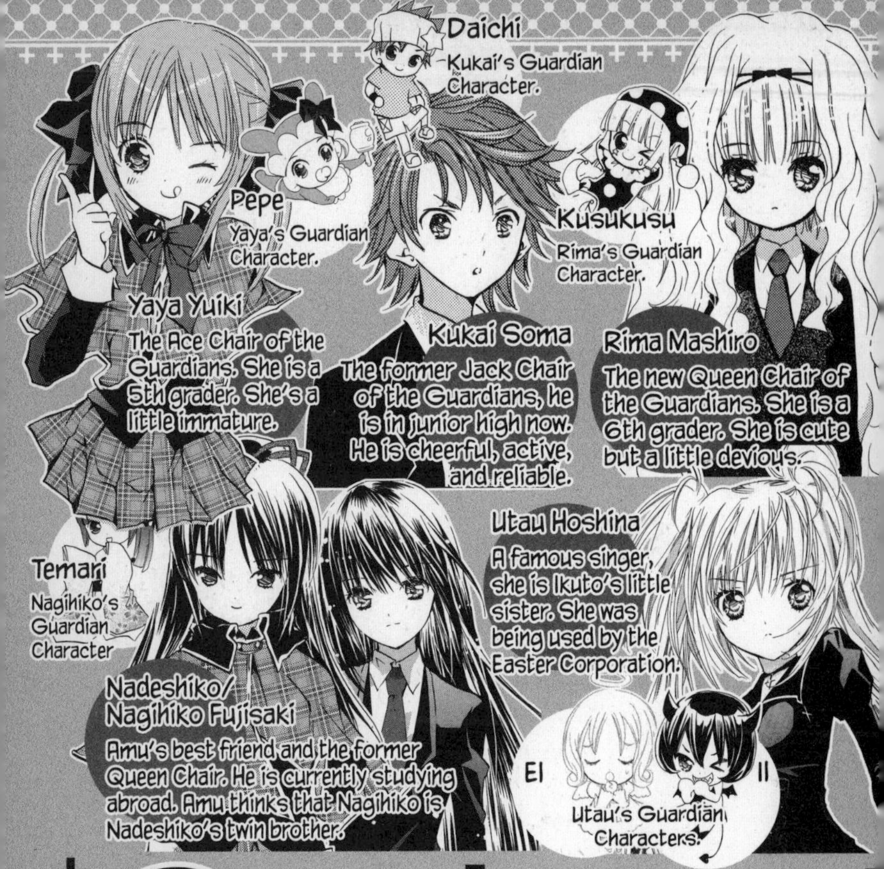
Daichi
Kukai's Guardian Character.
Kusukusu
Rima's Guardian Character.
Pepe
Yaya's Guardian Character.
Rima Mashiro
The new Queen Chair of the Guardians. She is a 6th grader. She is cute but a little devious.
Kukai Soma
The former Jack Chair of the Guardians, he is in junior high now. He is cheerful, active, and reliable.
Yaya Yuiki
The Ace Chair of the Guardians. She is a 5th grader. She's a little immature.
Utau Hoshina
A famous singer, she is Ikuto's little sister. She was being used by the Easter Corporation.
Temari
Nagihiko's Guardian Character
Nadeshiko/ Nagihiko Fujisaki
Amu's best friend and the former Queen Chair. He is currently studying abroad. Amu thinks that Nagihiko is Nadeshiko's twin brother.
Il
El
Utau's Guardian Characters.

The Story So Far

● Amu comes across as cool. But that isn't who she really is. Deep inside, she is shy and a little cynical. One day, she wished she could be more true to herself, and the next day she found three eggs in her bed!

Ran, Miki, and Su hatched from the eggs. They are Amu's "Guardian Characters." They say that they are Amu's "true selves," and when Amu Character Changes with them, she can become good at sports, art, or cooking! Soon after they hatched, Amu found herself recruited to become one of the Guardians at Seiyo Academy. Since then, she's become good friends with the other students who have Guardian Characters.

● The Joker's job is to find Heart's Eggs with X's and save them. But it seems that the Easter Corporation is looking for an egg called the Embryo, and is collecting X Eggs. Amu's fourth Egg had an X on it...

● Amu and her friends were able to stop the Black Diamonds Plan. The X on Diamond came off and she returned to Amu. But afterward, Kairi, the new Jack Chair, moved away. Amu is now on her winter break...

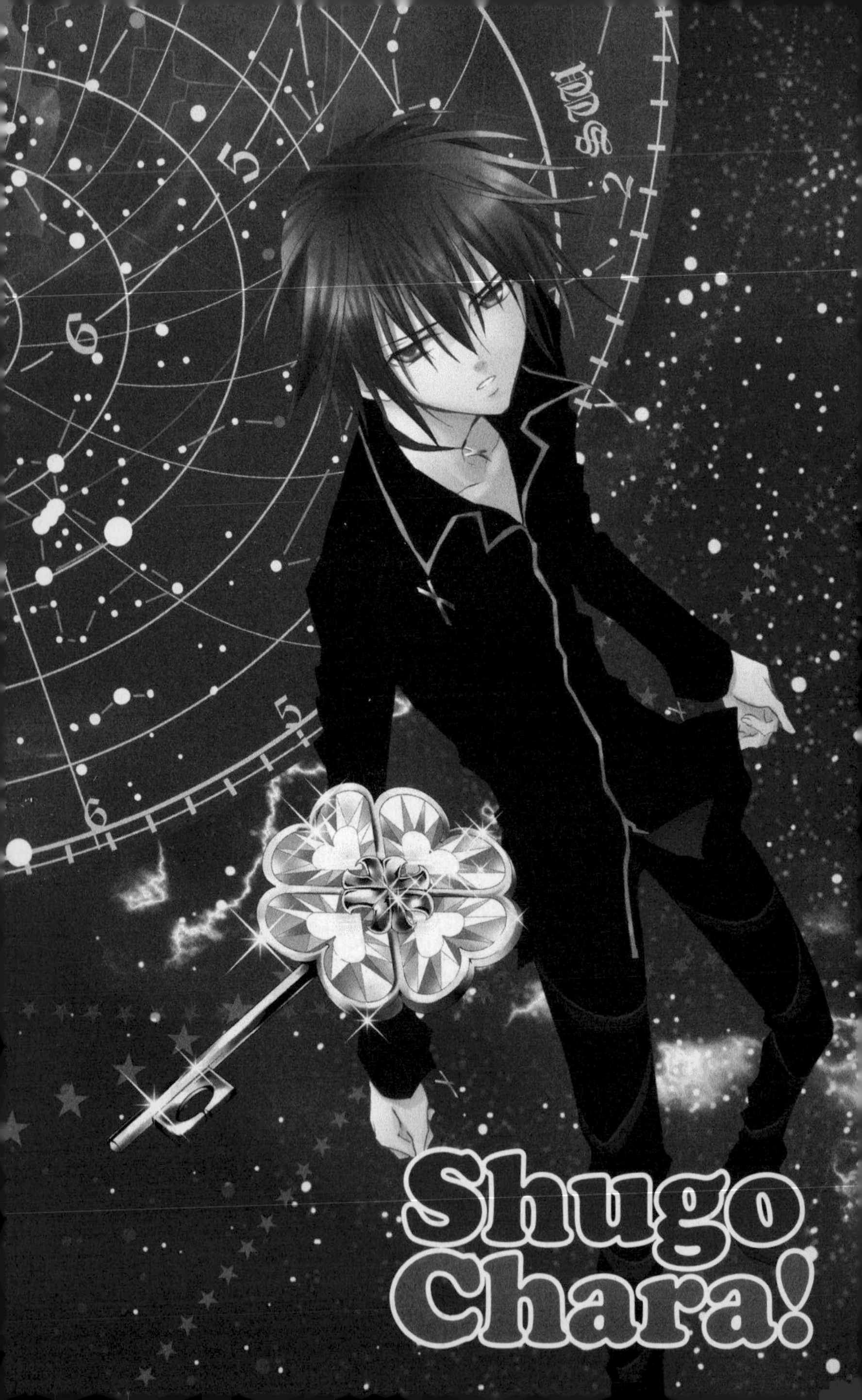
Shugo
Chara!

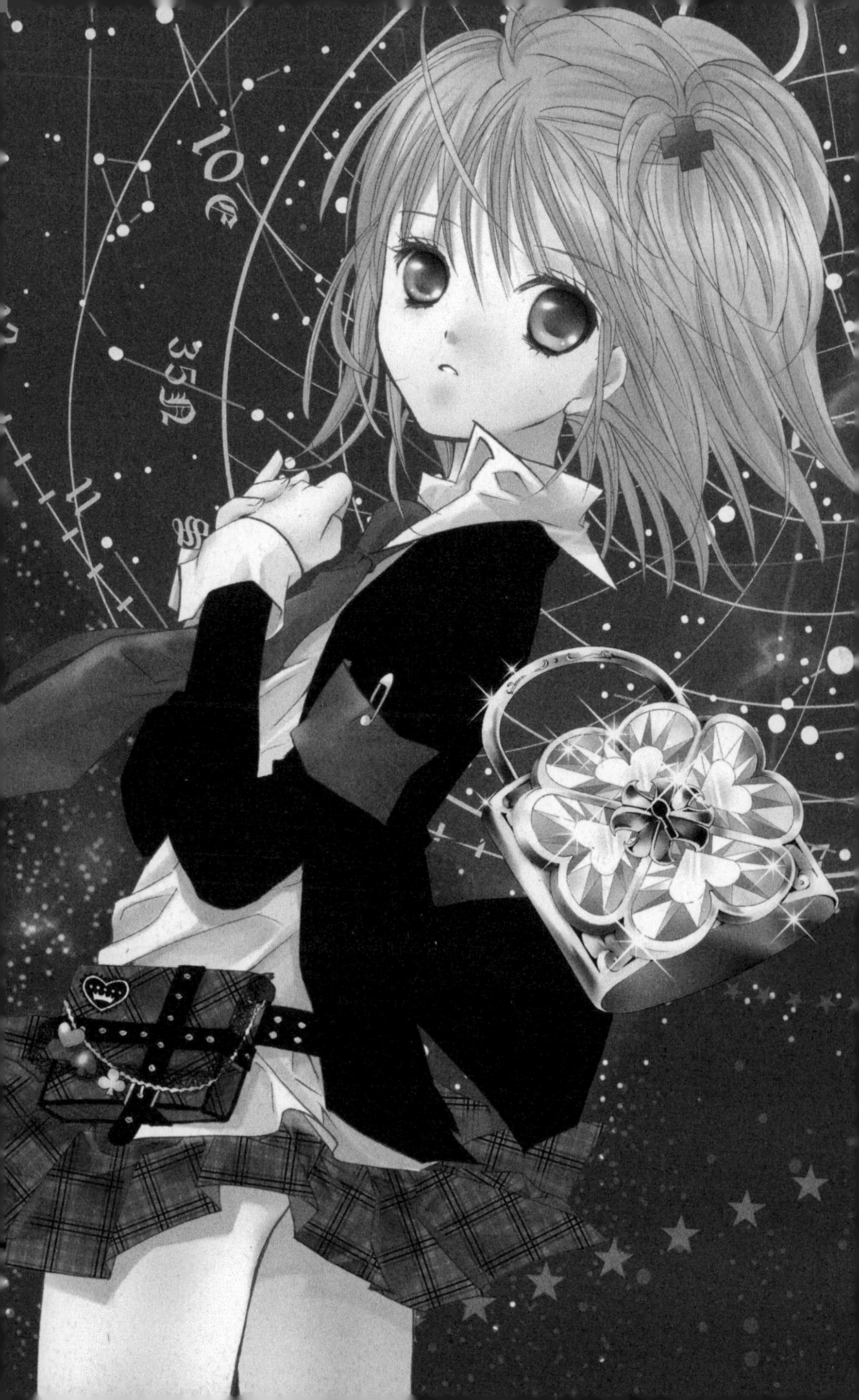

Shugo Chara!

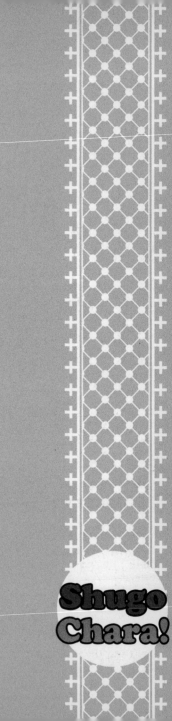

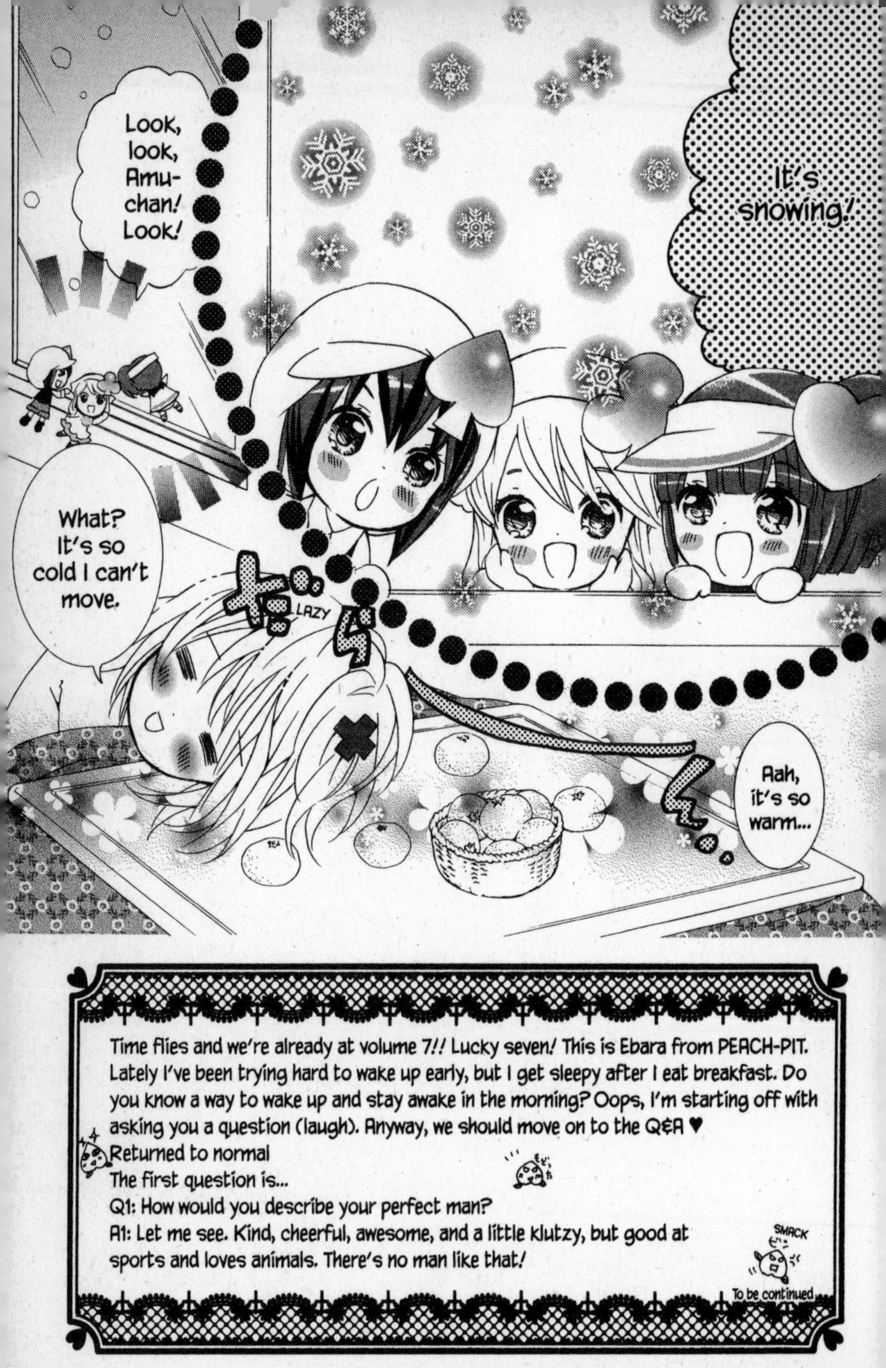
It's snowing!
Look, look, Amu-chan! Look!
What? It's so cold I can't move.
LAZY
Aah, it's so warm...

Time flies and we're already at volume 7!! Lucky seven! This is Ebara from PEACH-PIT. Lately I've been trying hard to wake up early, but I get sleepy after I eat breakfast. Do you know a way to wake up and stay awake in the morning? Oops, I'm starting off with asking you a question (laugh). Anyway, we should move on to the Q&A ♥

Returned to normal

The first question is...

Q1: How would you describe your perfect man?

A1: Let me see. Kind, cheerful, awesome, and a little klutzy, but good at sports and loves animals. There's no man like that!

SMACK

To be continued

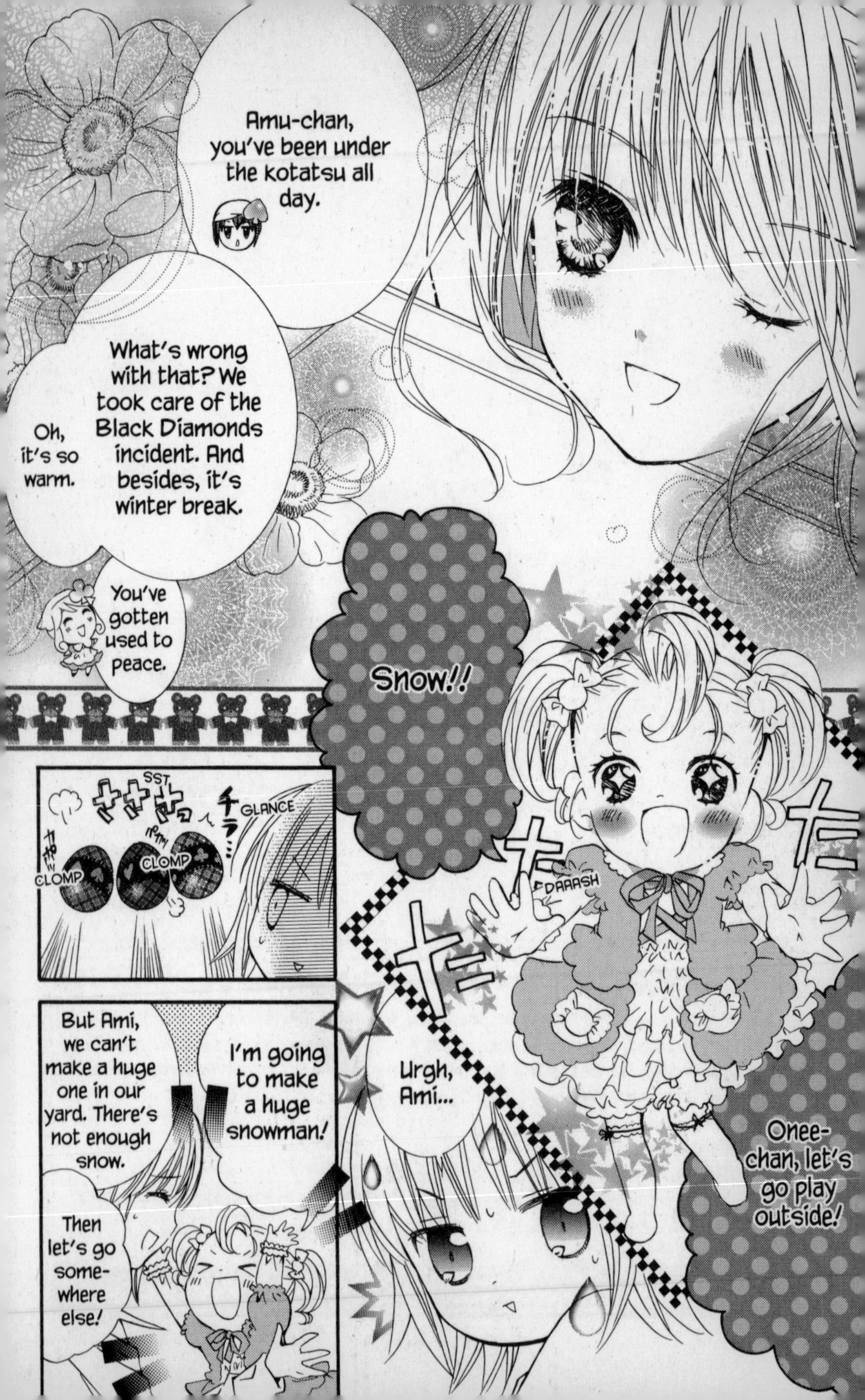

Amu-chan, you've been under the kotatsu all day.
What's wrong with that? We took care of the Black Diamonds incident. And besides, it's winter break.
Oh, it's so warm.
You've gotten used to peace.
Snow!!
DAAASH
Onee-chan, let's go play outside!
Urgh, Ami...
SST
GLANCE
CLOMP
CLOMP
I'm going to make a huge snowman!
But Ami, we can't make a huge one in our yard. There's not enough snow.
Then let's go somewhere else!

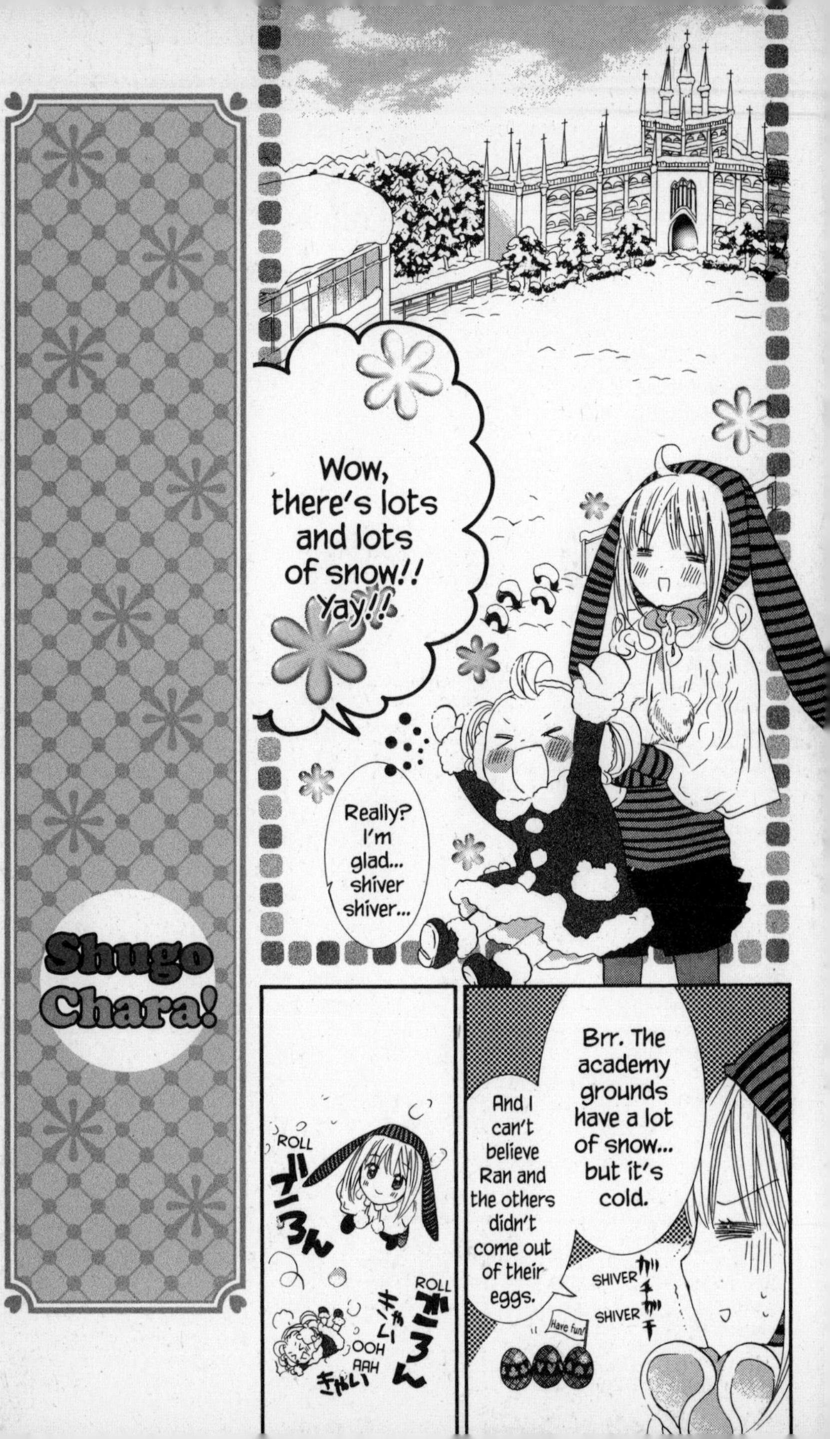
Wow, there's lots and lots of snow!! Yay!!
Really? I'm glad... shiver shiver...
Brr. The academy grounds have a lot of snow... but it's cold.
And I can't believe Ran and the others didn't come out of their eggs.
SHIVER
SHIVER
Have fun!
ROLL
ROLL
OOH
AAH

Shugo Chara!

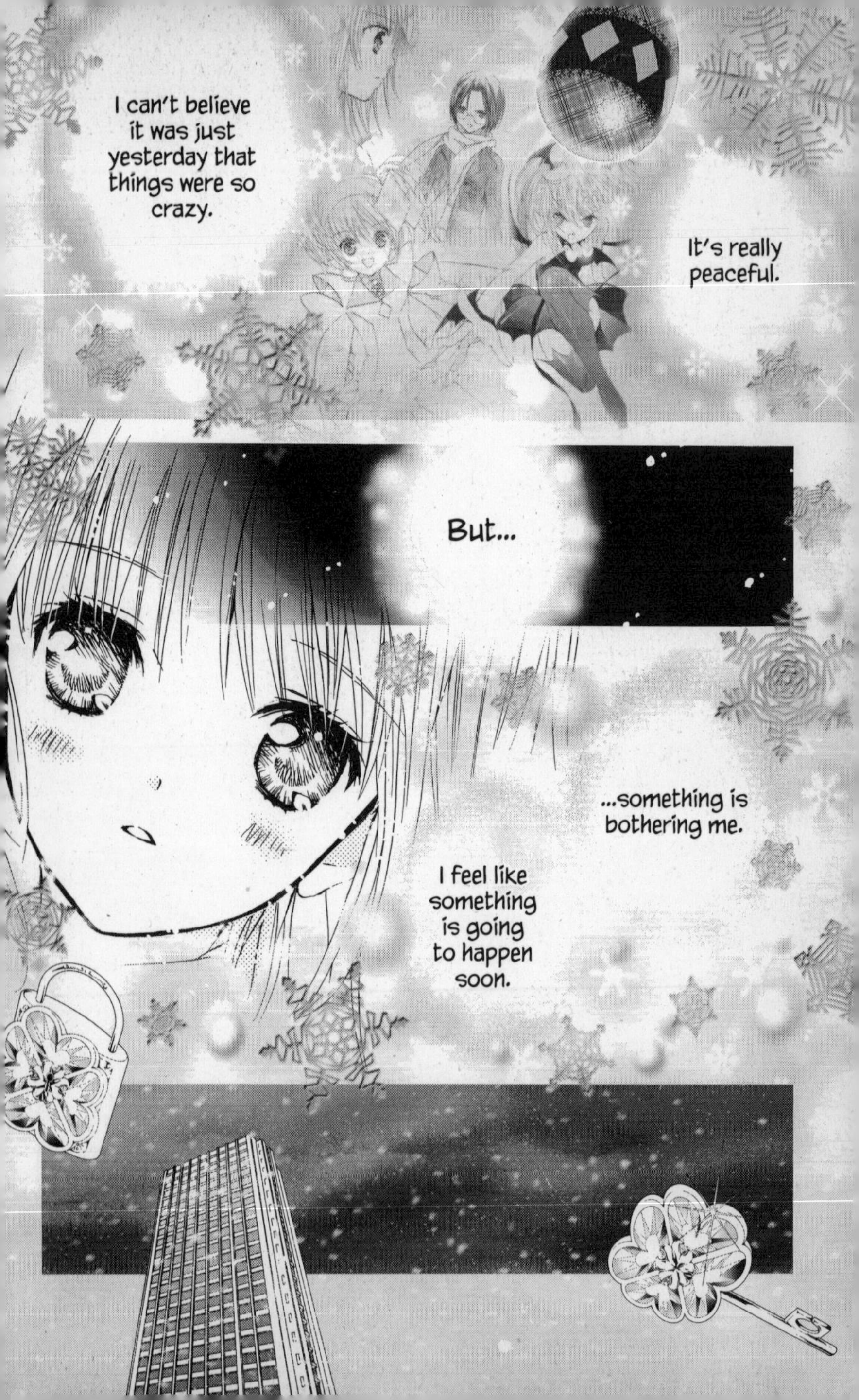
It's really peaceful.
I can't believe it was just yesterday that things were so crazy.
But...
...something is bothering me.
I feel like something is going to happen soon.

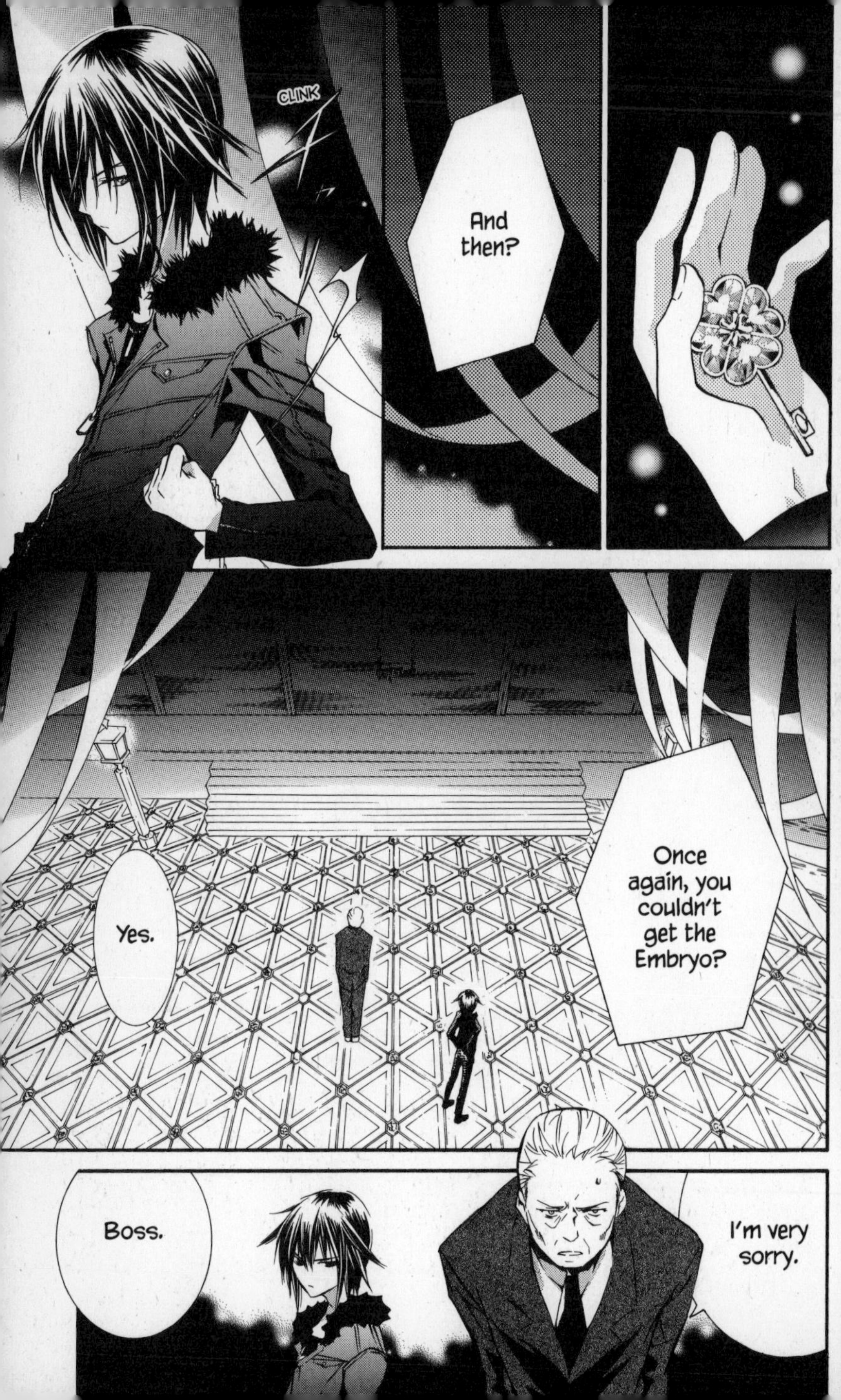
And then?
CLINK
Once again, you couldn't get the Embryo?
Yes.
I'm very sorry.
Boss.

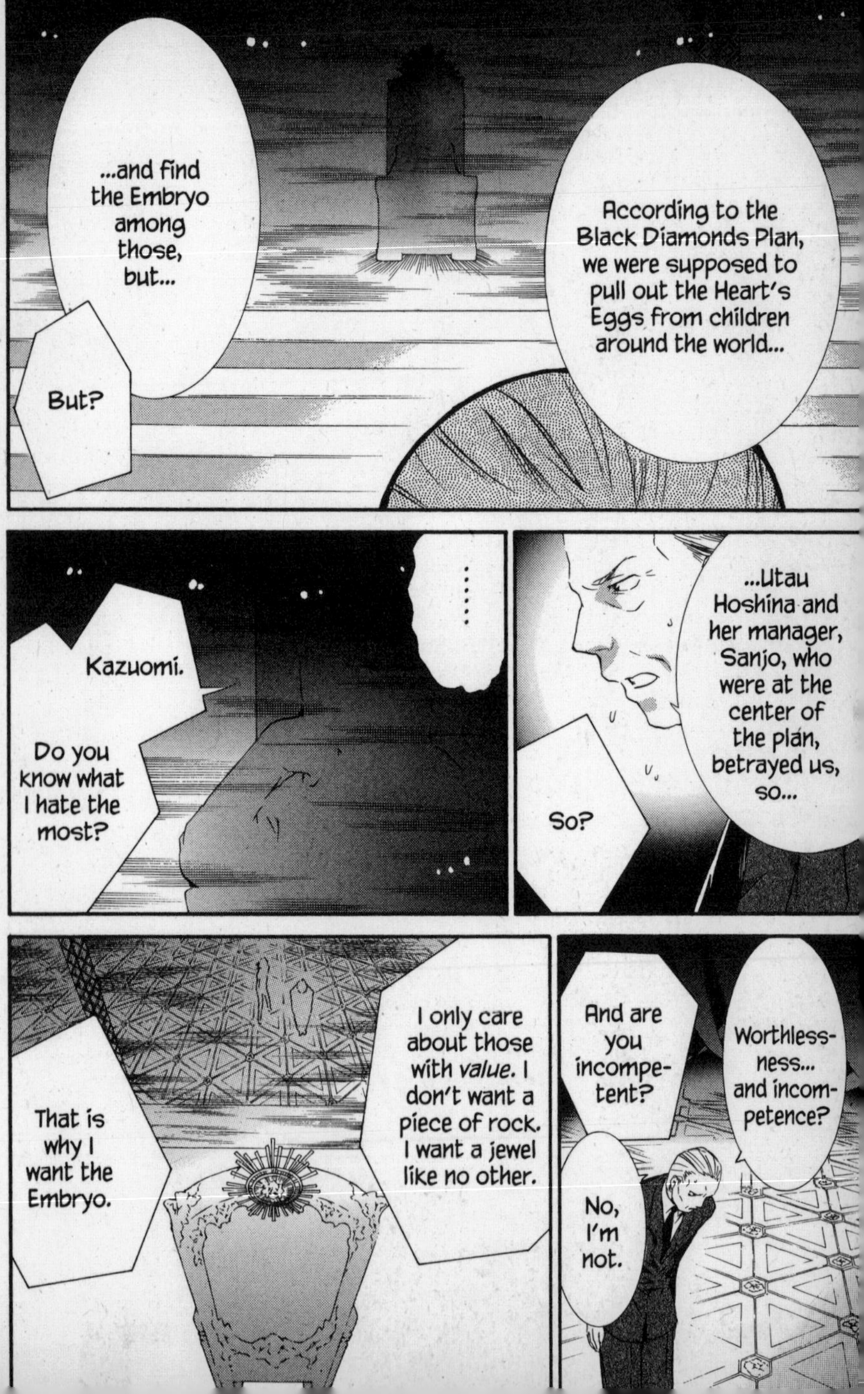
According to the Black Diamonds Plan, we were supposed to pull out the Heart's Eggs from children around the world...
...and find the Embryo among those, but...
But?
...Utau Hoshina and her manager, Sanjo, who were at the center of the plan, betrayed us, so...
So?
......
Kazuomi.
Do you know what I hate the most?
Worthlessness... and incompetence?
And are you incompetent?
No, I'm not.
I only care about those with *value*. I don't want a piece of rock. I want a jewel like no other.
That is why I want the Embryo.

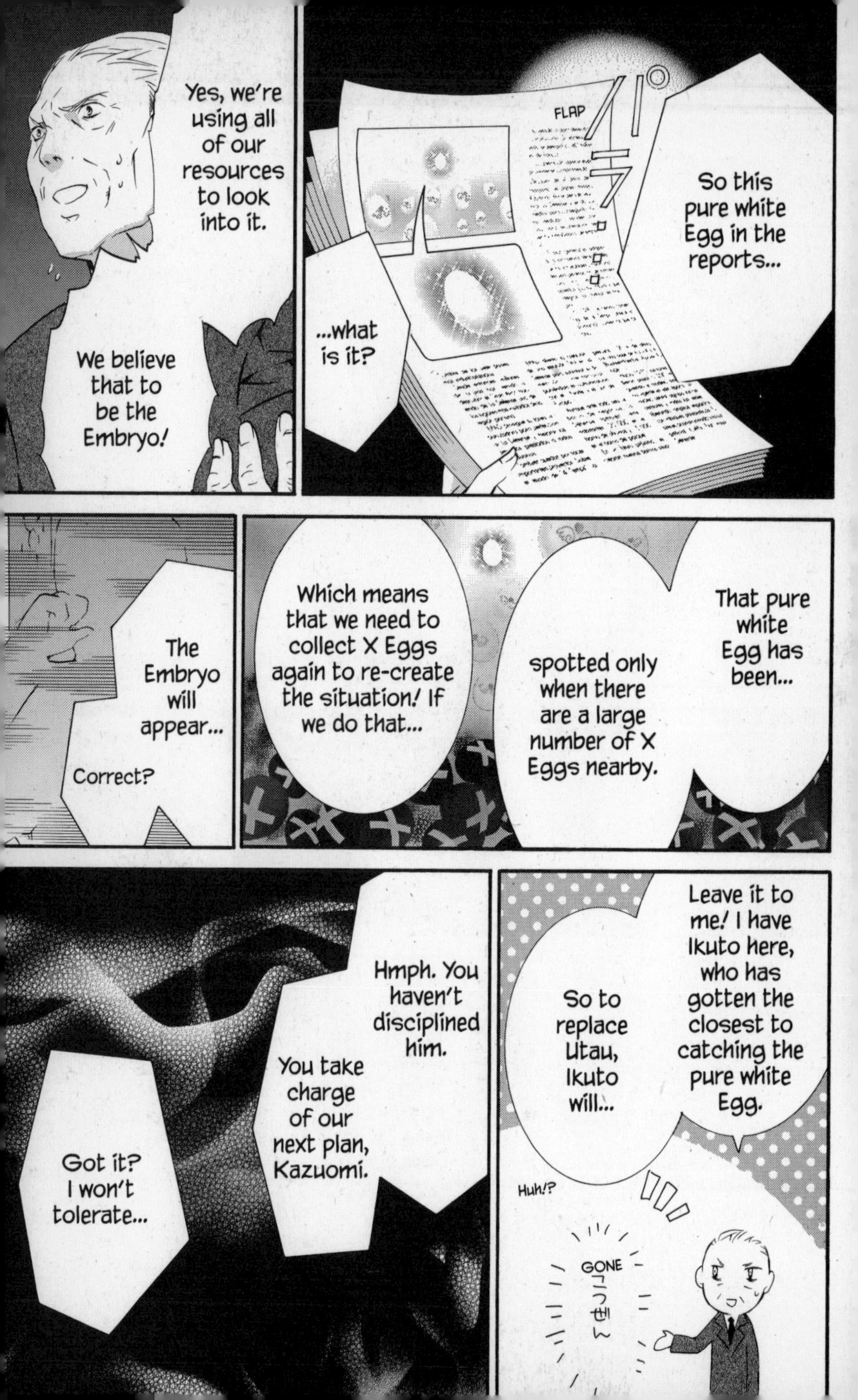
FLAP
So this pure white Egg in the reports...
...what is it?
Yes, we're using all of our resources to look into it.
We believe that to be the Embryo!
That pure white Egg has been...
spotted only when there are a large number of X Eggs nearby.
Which means that we need to collect X Eggs again to re-create the situation! If we do that...
The Embryo will appear...
Correct?
Leave it to me! I have Ikuto here, who has gotten the closest to catching the pure white Egg.
So to replace Utau, Ikuto will...
Huh!?
GONE
Hmph. You haven't disciplined him.
You take charge of our next plan, Kazuomi.
Got it? I won't tolerate...

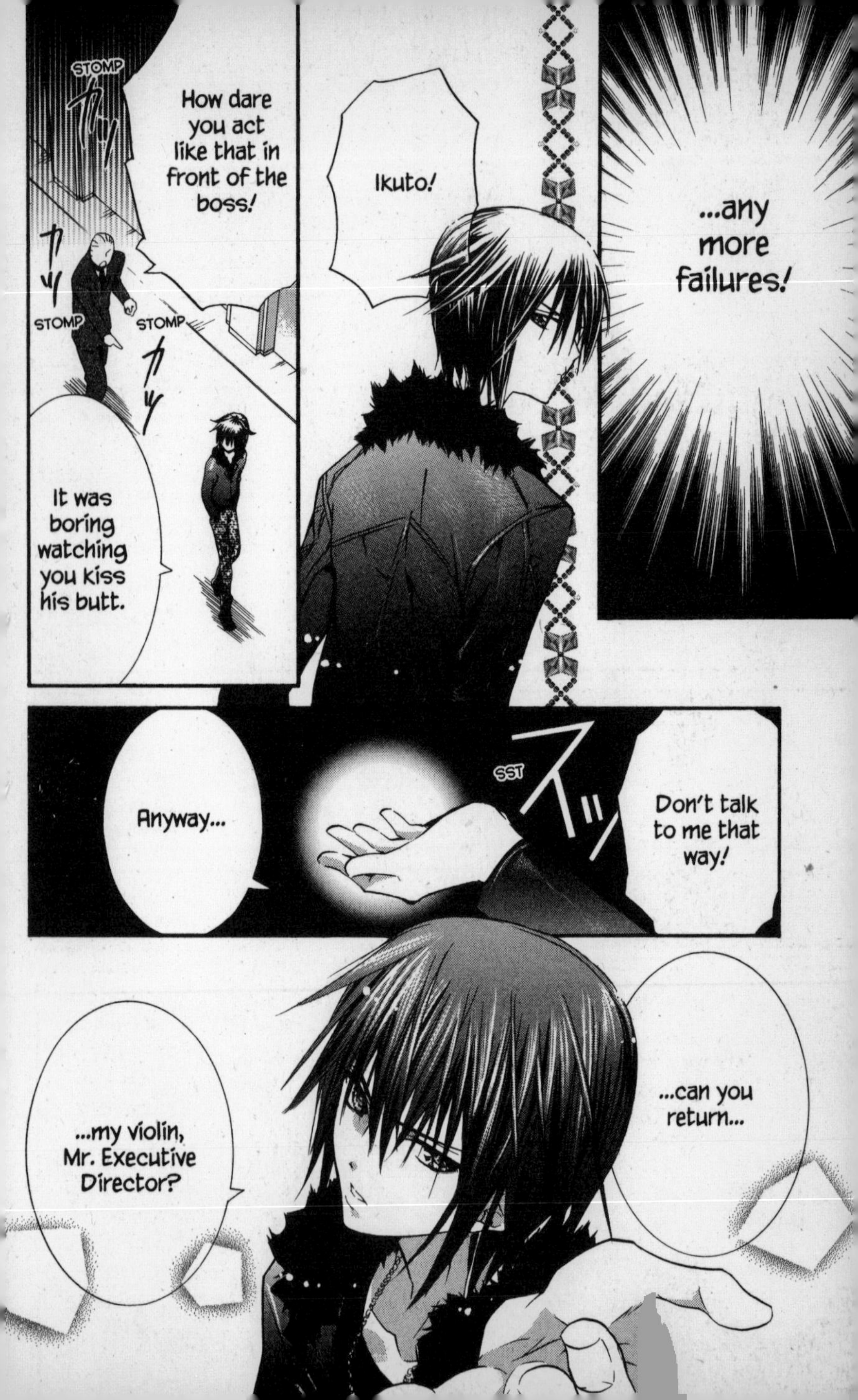
...any more failures!
Ikuto!
STOMP
How dare you act like that in front of the boss!
STOMP
STOMP
It was boring watching you kiss his butt.
Don't talk to me that way!
SST
Anyway...
...can you return...
...my violin, Mr. Executive Director?

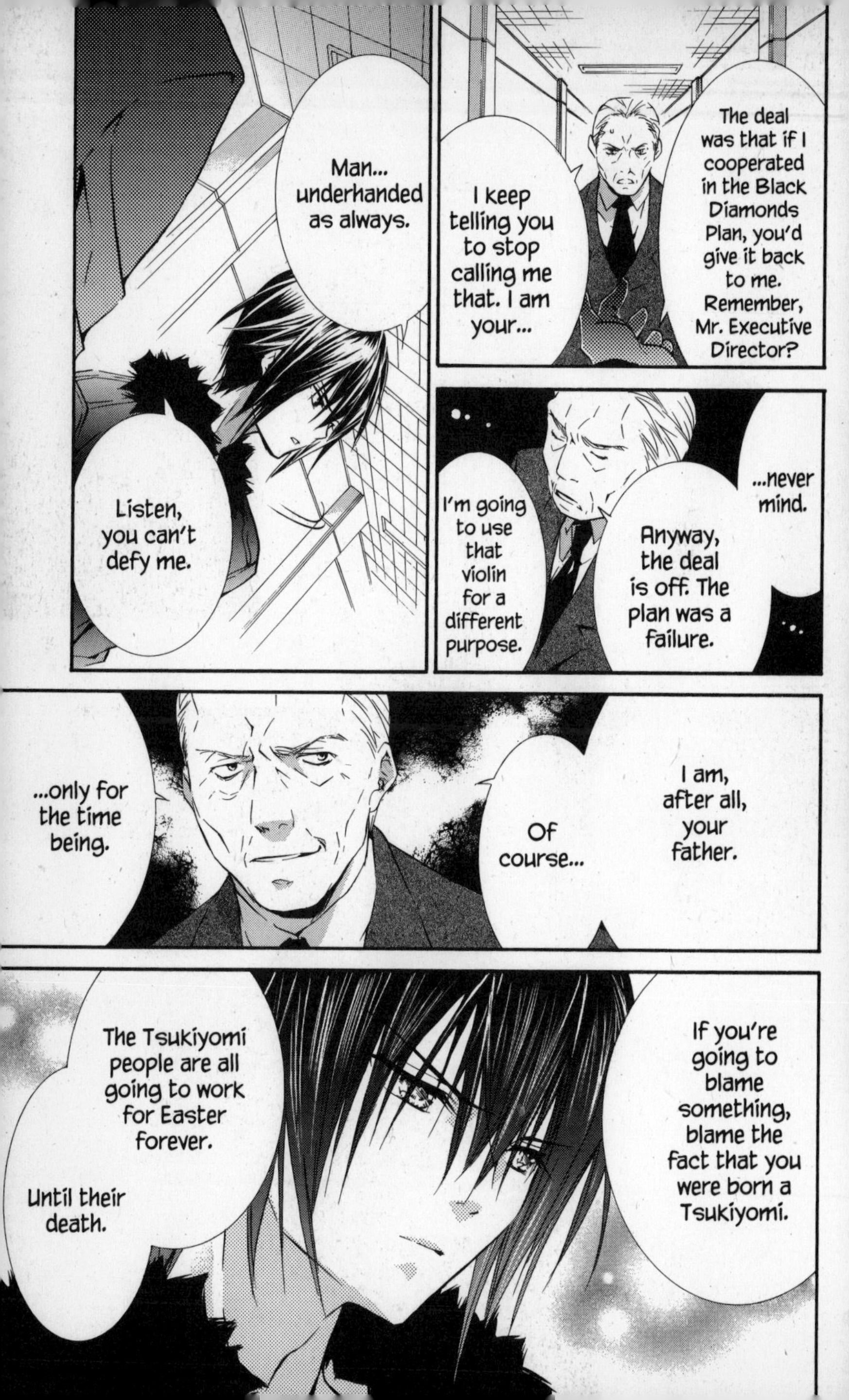
The deal was that if I cooperated in the Black Diamonds Plan, you'd give it back to me. Remember, Mr. Executive Director?
I keep telling you to stop calling me that. I am your...
...never mind.
Anyway, the deal is off. The plan was a failure.
I'm going to use that violin for a different purpose.
Man... underhanded as always.
Listen, you can't defy me.
I am, after all, your father.
Of course...
...only for the time being.
If you're going to blame something, blame the fact that you were born a Tsukiyomi.
The Tsukiyomi people are all going to work for Easter forever.
Until their death.

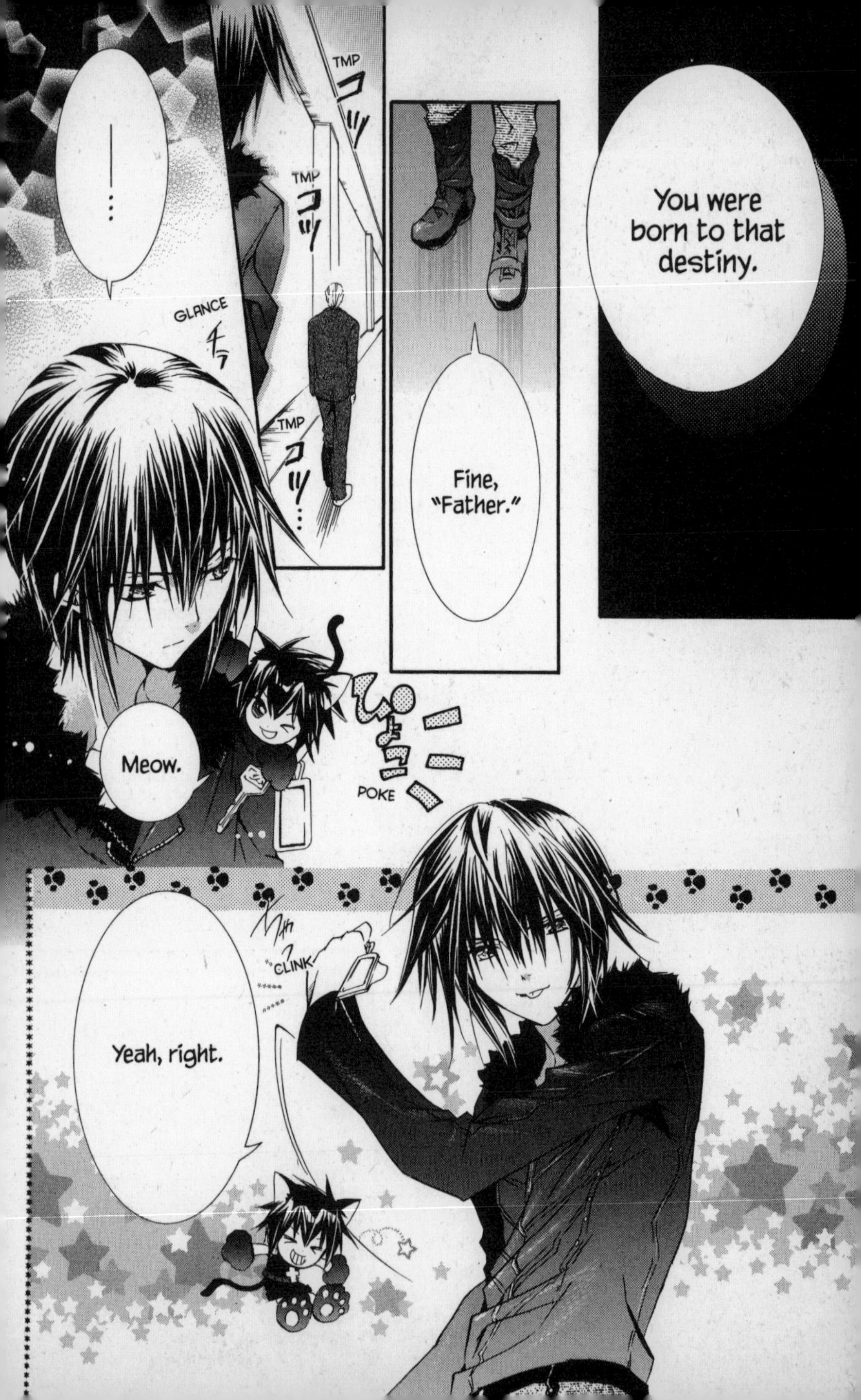
You were born to that destiny.
Fine, "Father."
TMP
TMP
TMP
—...
GLANCE
Meow.
POKE
CLINK
Yeah, right.

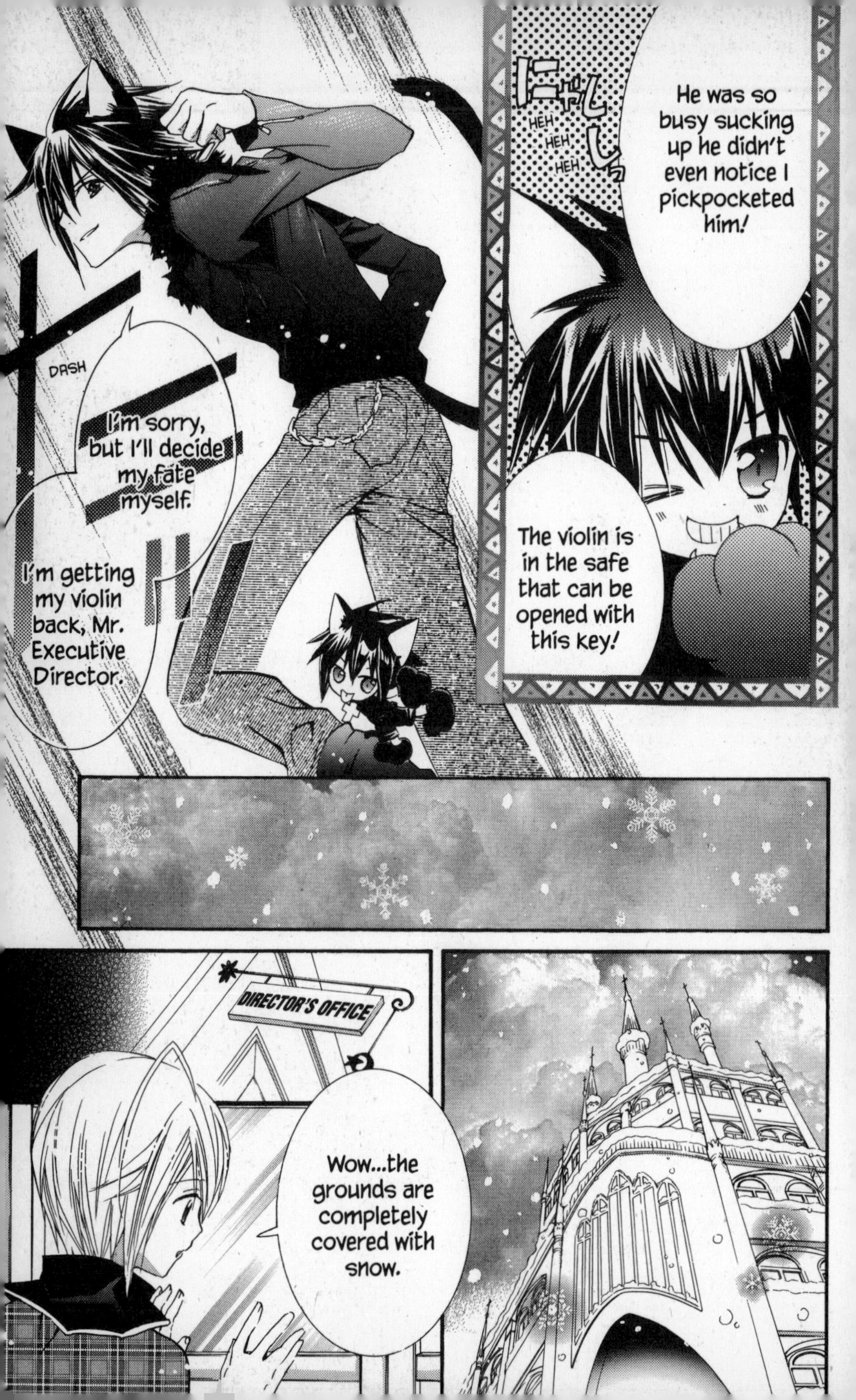
HEH HEH HEH
He was so busy sucking up he didn't even notice I pickpocketed him!
The violin is in the safe that can be opened with this key!
DASH
I'm sorry, but I'll decide my fate myself.
I'm getting my violin back, Mr. Executive Director.
DIRECTOR'S OFFICE
Wow...the grounds are completely covered with snow.

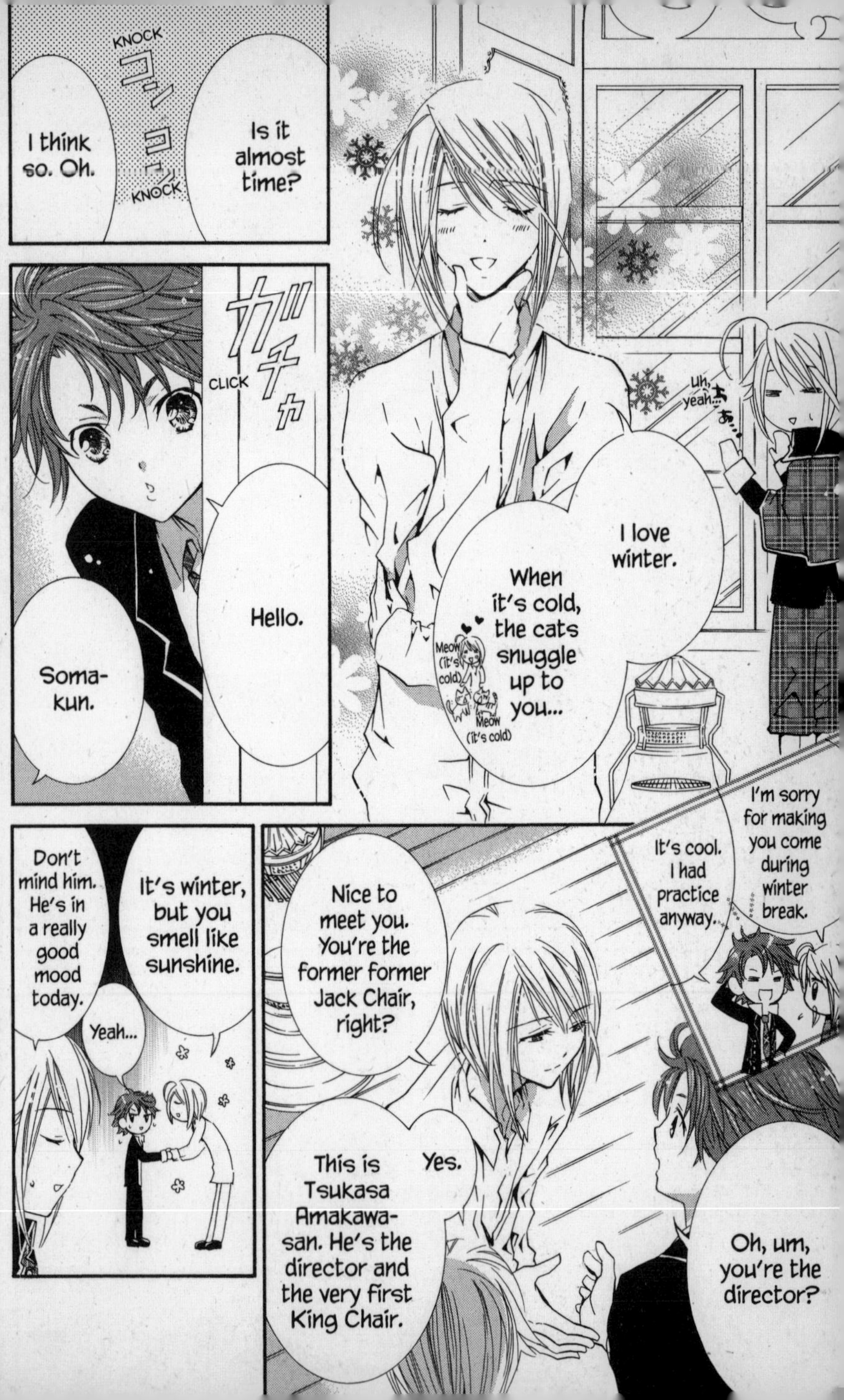

Uh, yeah...
I love winter.
When it's cold, the cats snuggle up to you...
Meow (it's cold)
Meow (it's cold)
Is it almost time?
KNOCK
KNOCK
I think so. Oh.
CLICK
Hello.
Soma-kun.
I'm sorry for making you come during winter break.
It's cool. I had practice anyway.
Nice to meet you. You're the former former Jack Chair, right?
Oh, um, you're the director?
Yes.
This is Tsukasa Amakawa-san. He's the director and the very first King Chair.
It's winter, but you smell like sunshine.
Don't mind him. He's in a really good mood today.
Yeah...

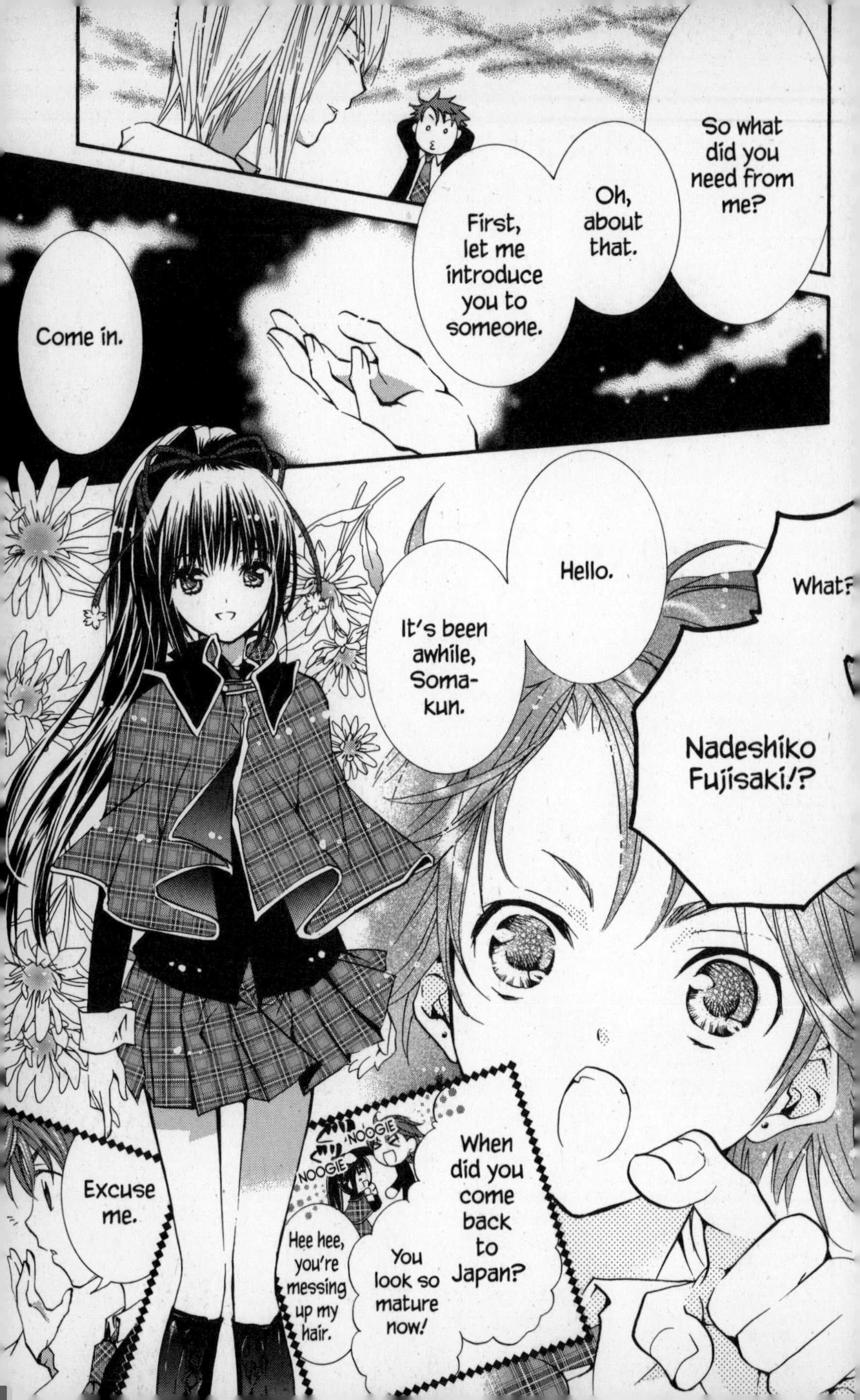
So what did you need from me?
Oh, about that.
First, let me introduce you to someone.
Come in.
Hello.
It's been awhile, Soma-kun.
What?
Nadeshiko Fujisaki!?
When did you come back to Japan?
You look so mature now!
NOOGIE
NOOGIE
Hee hee, you're messing up my hair.
Excuse me.

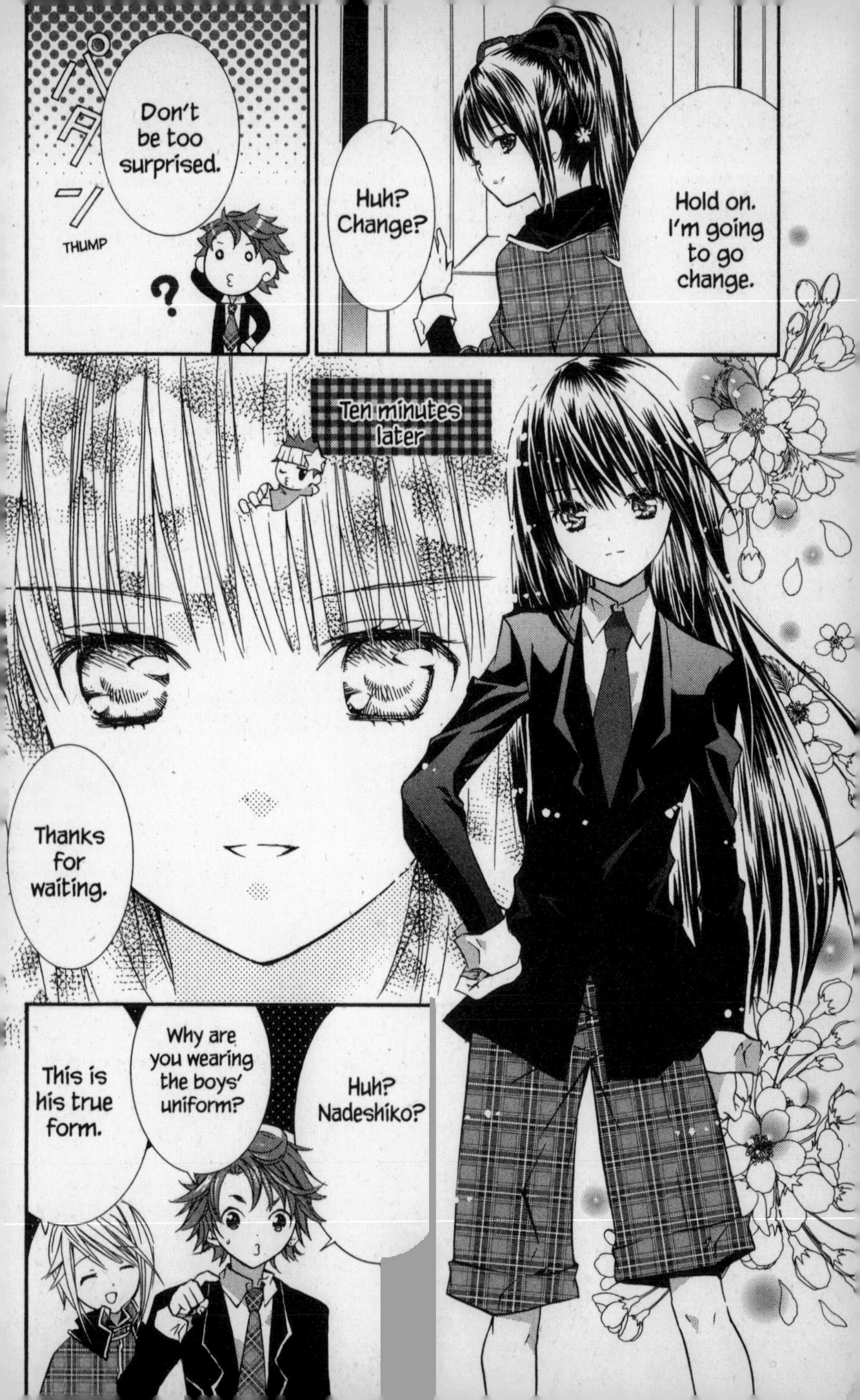
Hold on. I'm going to go change.
Huh? Change?
Don't be too surprised.
THUMP
Ten minutes later
Thanks for waiting.
Huh? Nadeshiko?
Why are you wearing the boys' uniform?
This is his true form.

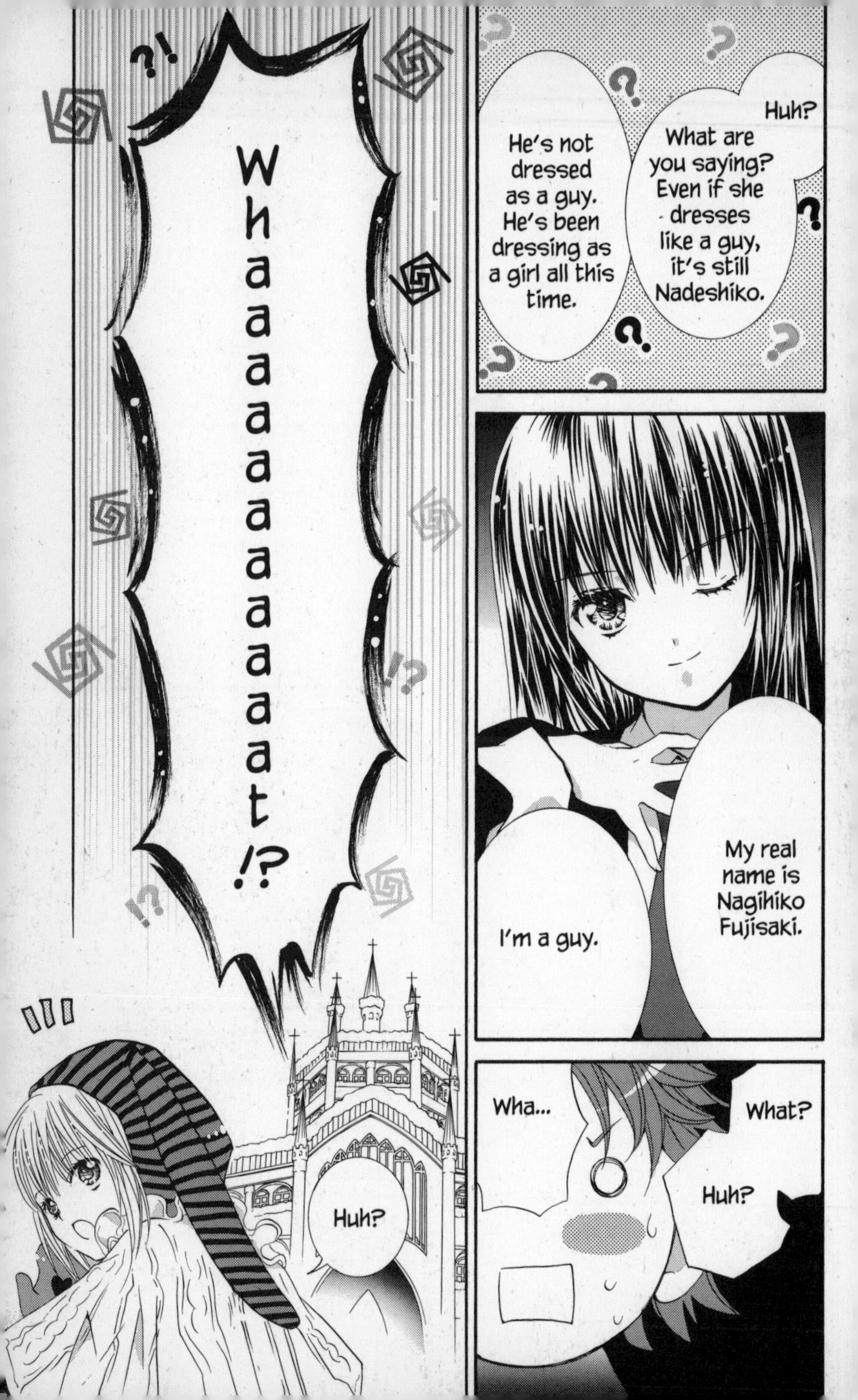
Huh?
What are you saying? Even if she dresses like a guy, it's still Nadeshiko.
He's not dressed as a guy. He's been dressing as a girl all this time.
My real name is Nagihiko Fujisaki.
I'm a guy.
What?
Wha...
Huh?
Whaaaaaaaaaaat!?
Huh?

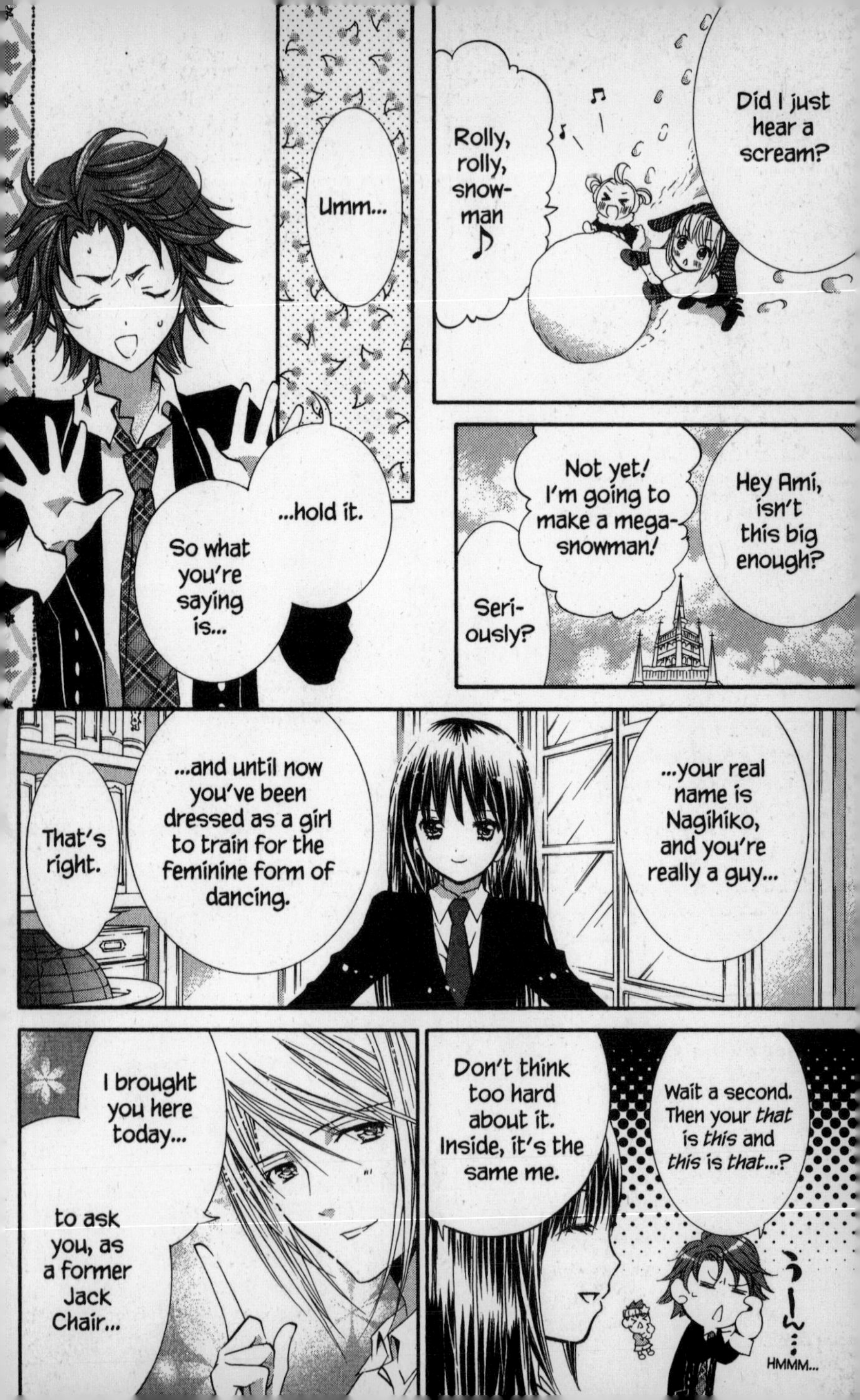

Did I just hear a scream?
Rolly, rolly, snow-man ♪
Hey Ami, isn't this big enough?
Not yet! I'm going to make a mega-snowman!
Seri-ously?
Umm...
...hold it.
So what you're saying is...
...your real name is Nagihiko, and you're really a guy...
...and until now you've been dressed as a girl to train for the feminine form of dancing.
That's right.
Wait a second. Then your *that* is *this* and *this* is *that*...?
Don't think too hard about it. Inside, it's the same me.
HMMM...
I brought you here today...
to ask you, as a former Jack Chair...

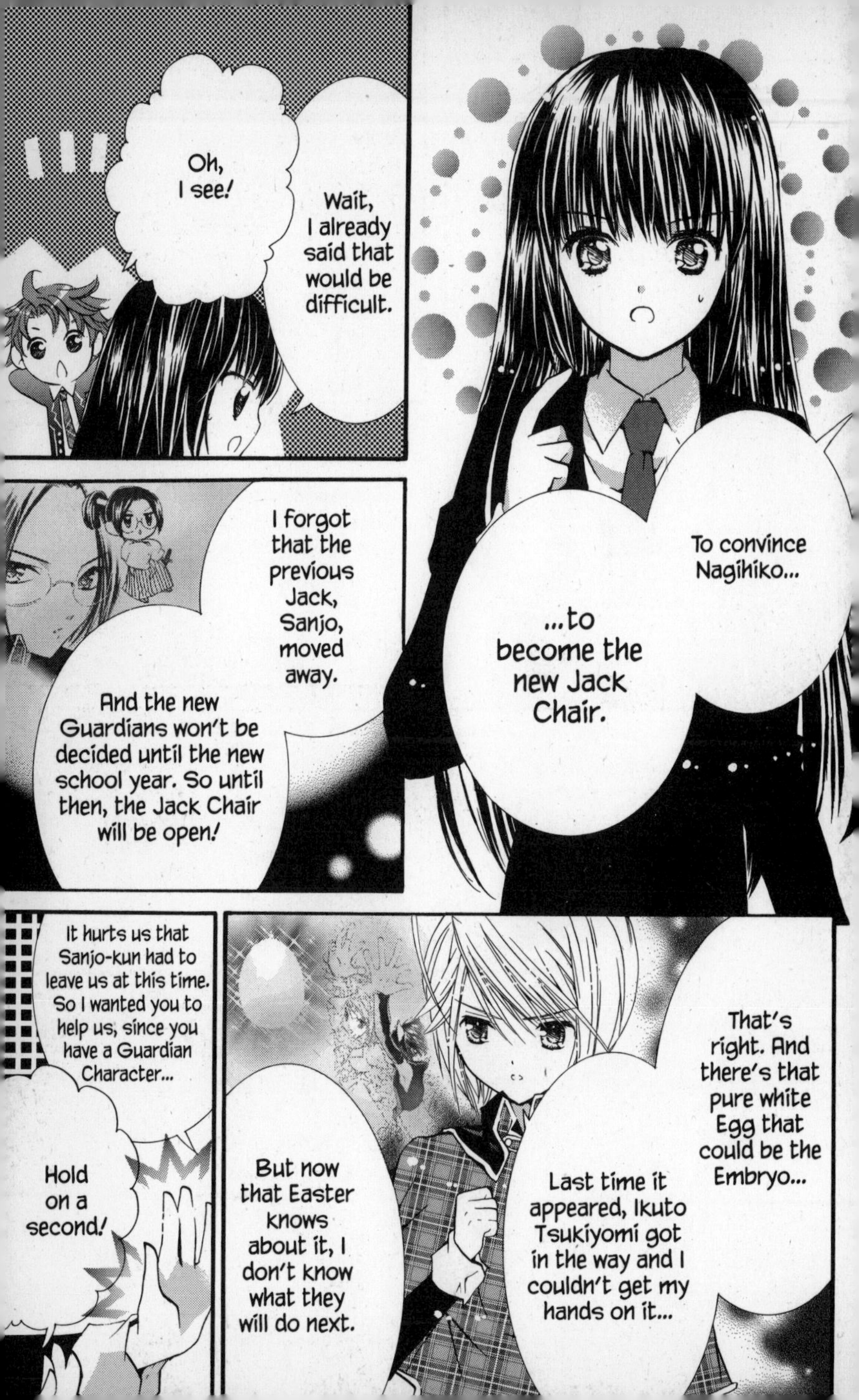

To convince Nagihiko...
...to become the new Jack Chair.
Wait, I already said that would be difficult.
Oh, I see!
I forgot that the previous Jack, Sanjo, moved away.
And the new Guardians won't be decided until the new school year. So until then, the Jack Chair will be open!
That's right. And there's that pure white Egg that could be the Embryo...
Last time it appeared, Ikuto Tsukiyomi got in the way and I couldn't get my hands on it...
But now that Easter knows about it, I don't know what they will do next.
It hurts us that Sanjo-kun had to leave us at this time. So I wanted you to help us, since you have a Guardian Character...
Hold on a second!

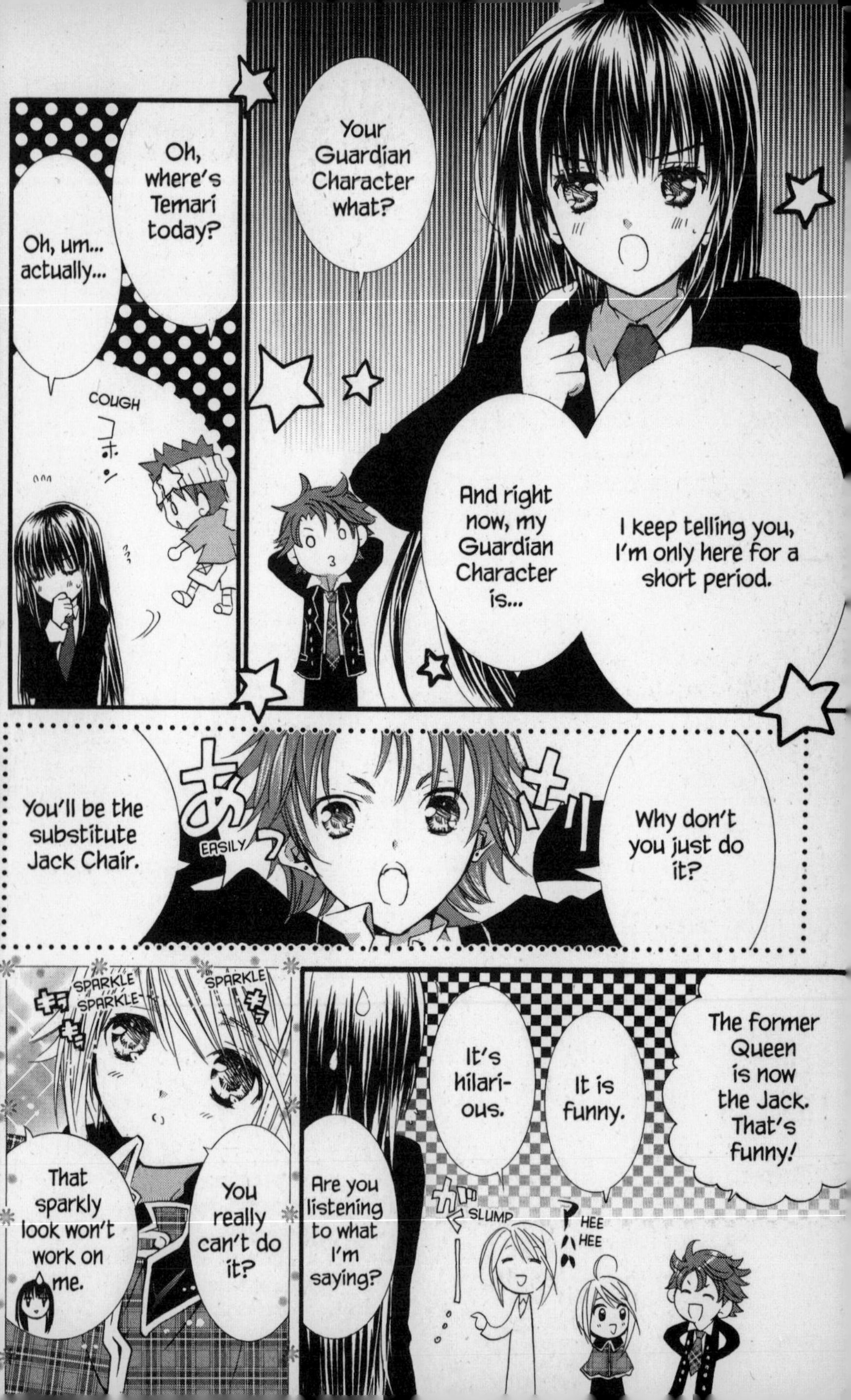
Your Guardian Character what?
I keep telling you, I'm only here for a short period.
And right now, my Guardian Character is...
Oh, where's Temari today?
Oh, um... actually...
COUGH
Why don't you just do it?
EASILY
You'll be the substitute Jack Chair.
The former Queen is now the Jack. That's funny!
It is funny.
It's hilari-ous.
Are you listening to what I'm saying?
HEE HEE
SLUMP
SPARKLE
SPARKLE SPARKLE
You really can't do it?
That sparkly look won't work on me.

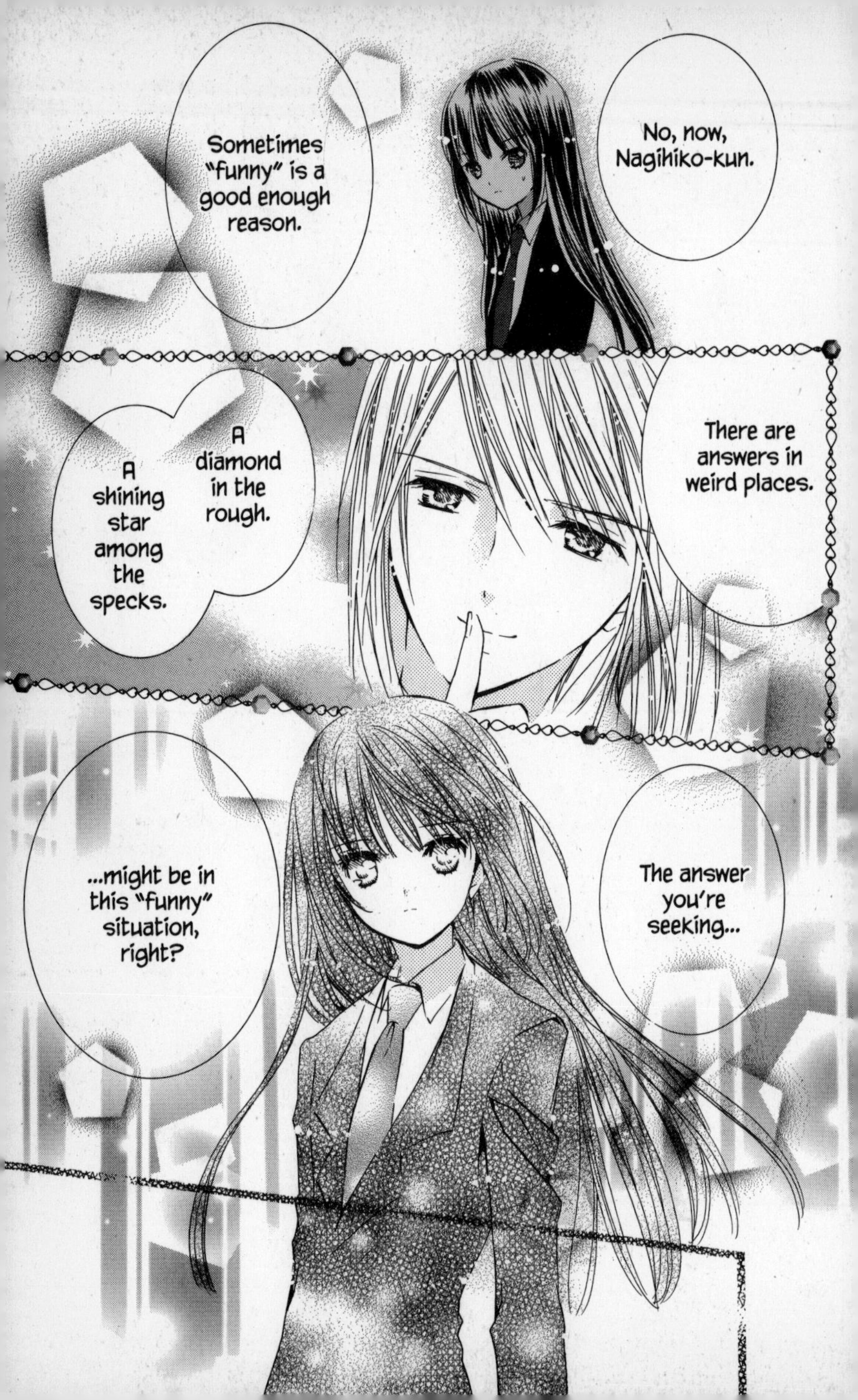
No, now, Nagihiko-kun.
Sometimes "funny" is a good enough reason.
There are answers in weird places.
A diamond in the rough.
A shining star among the specks.
The answer you're seeking...
...might be in this "funny" situation, right?

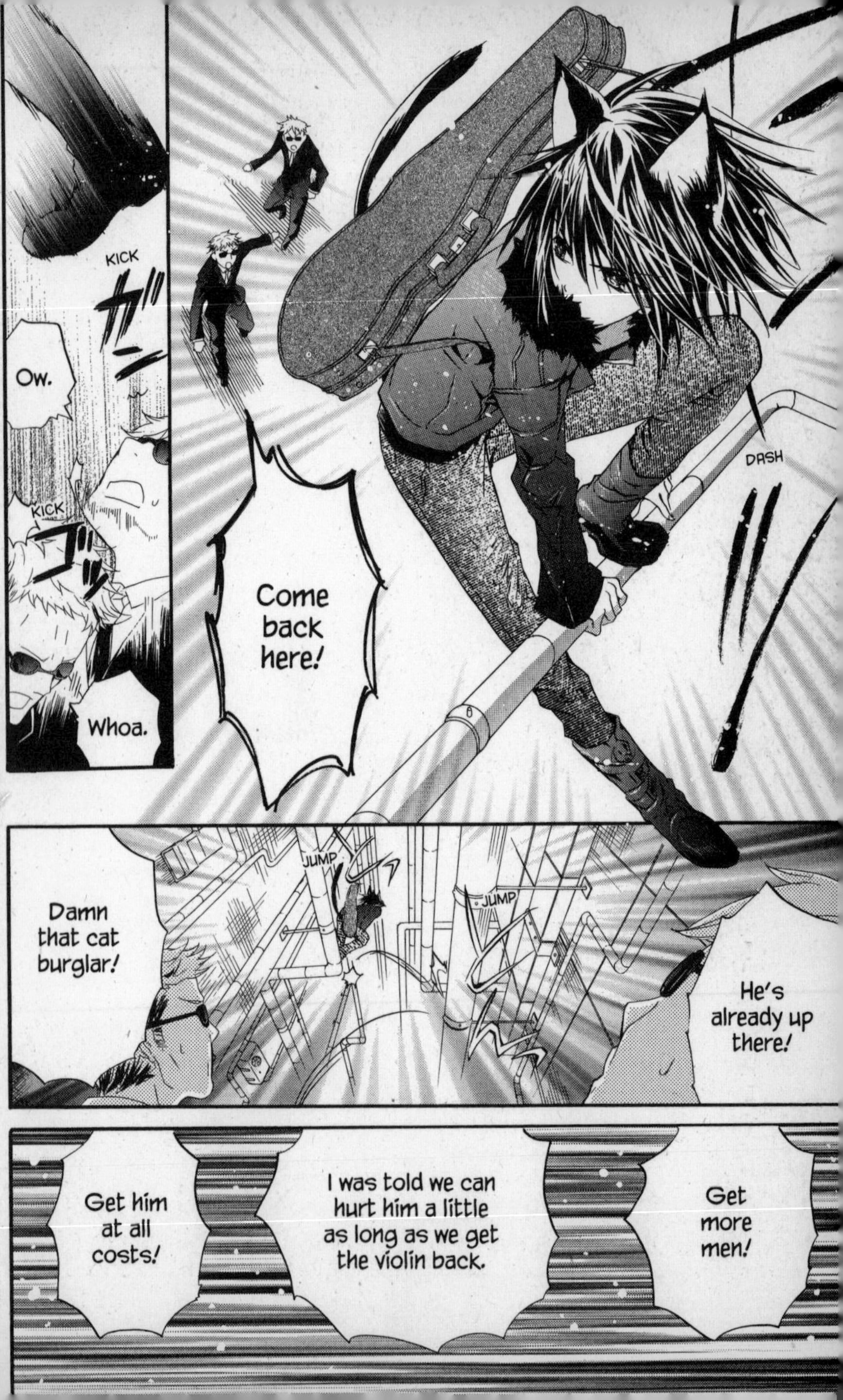
DASH
Come back here!
KICK
Ow.
KICK
Whoa.
He's already up there!
JUMP
JUMP
Damn that cat burglar!
Get more men!
I was told we can hurt him a little as long as we get the violin back.
Get him at all costs!

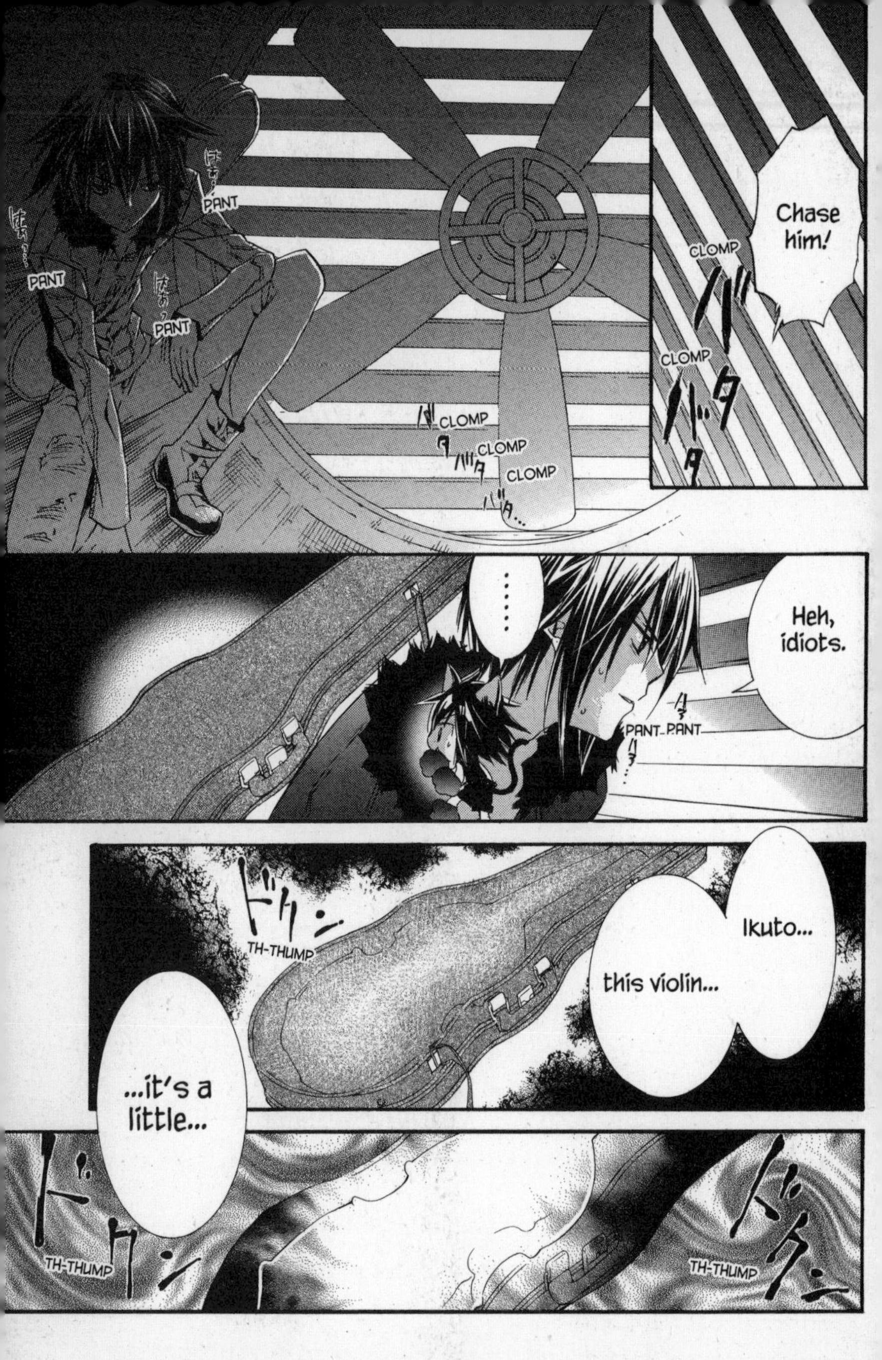
Chase him!
CLOMP
CLOMP
PANT
PANT
PANT
CLOMP
CLOMP
CLOMP
Heh, idiots.
PANT PANT
......
Ikuto...
this violin...
TH-THUMP
...it's a little...
TH-THUMP
TH-THUMP

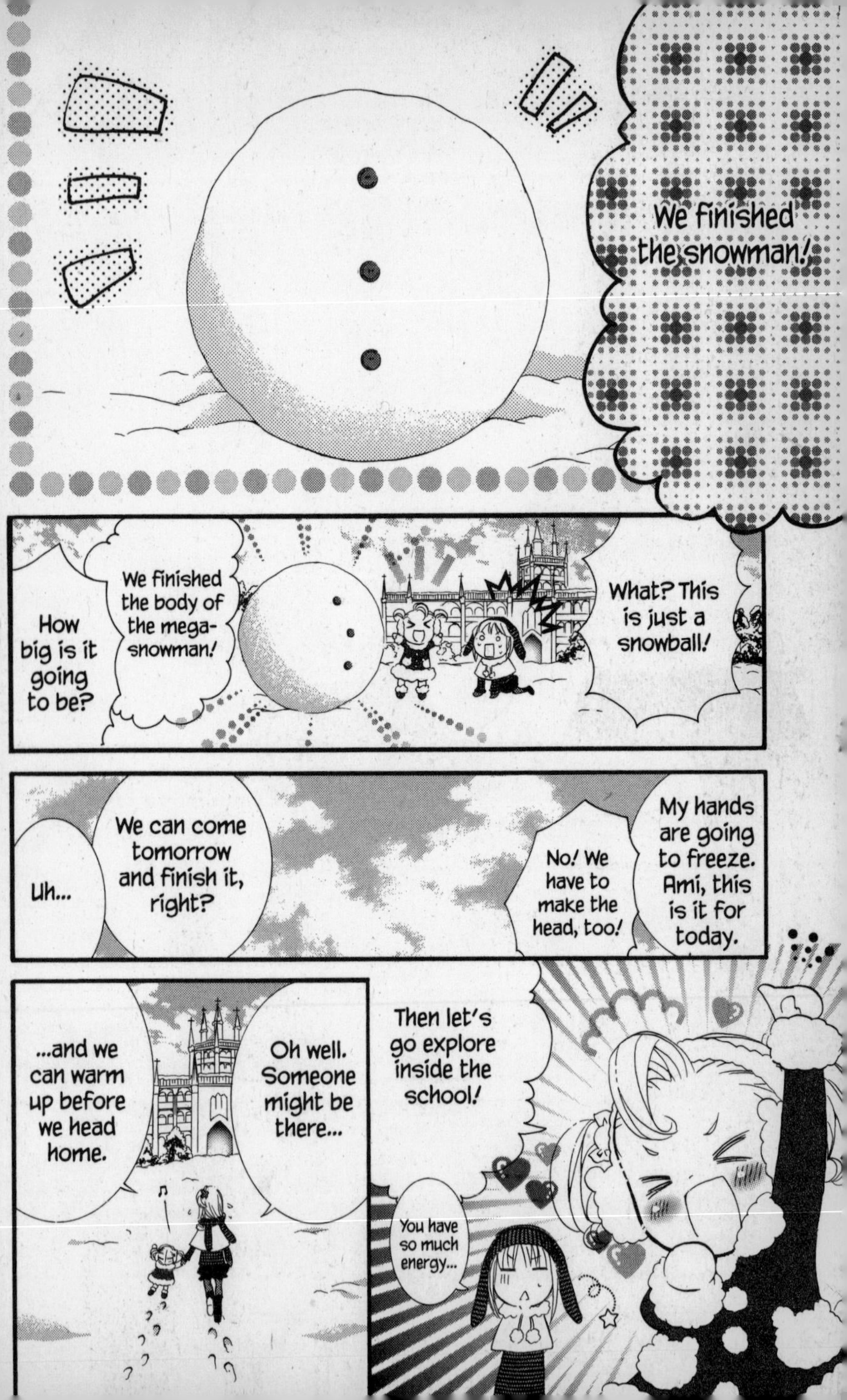
We finished the snowman!
What? This is just a snowball!
We finished the body of the mega-snowman!
How big is it going to be?
My hands are going to freeze. Ami, this is it for today.
No! We have to make the head, too!
We can come tomorrow and finish it, right?
Uh...
Then let's go explore inside the school!
You have so much energy...
Oh well. Someone might be there...
...and we can warm up before we head home.

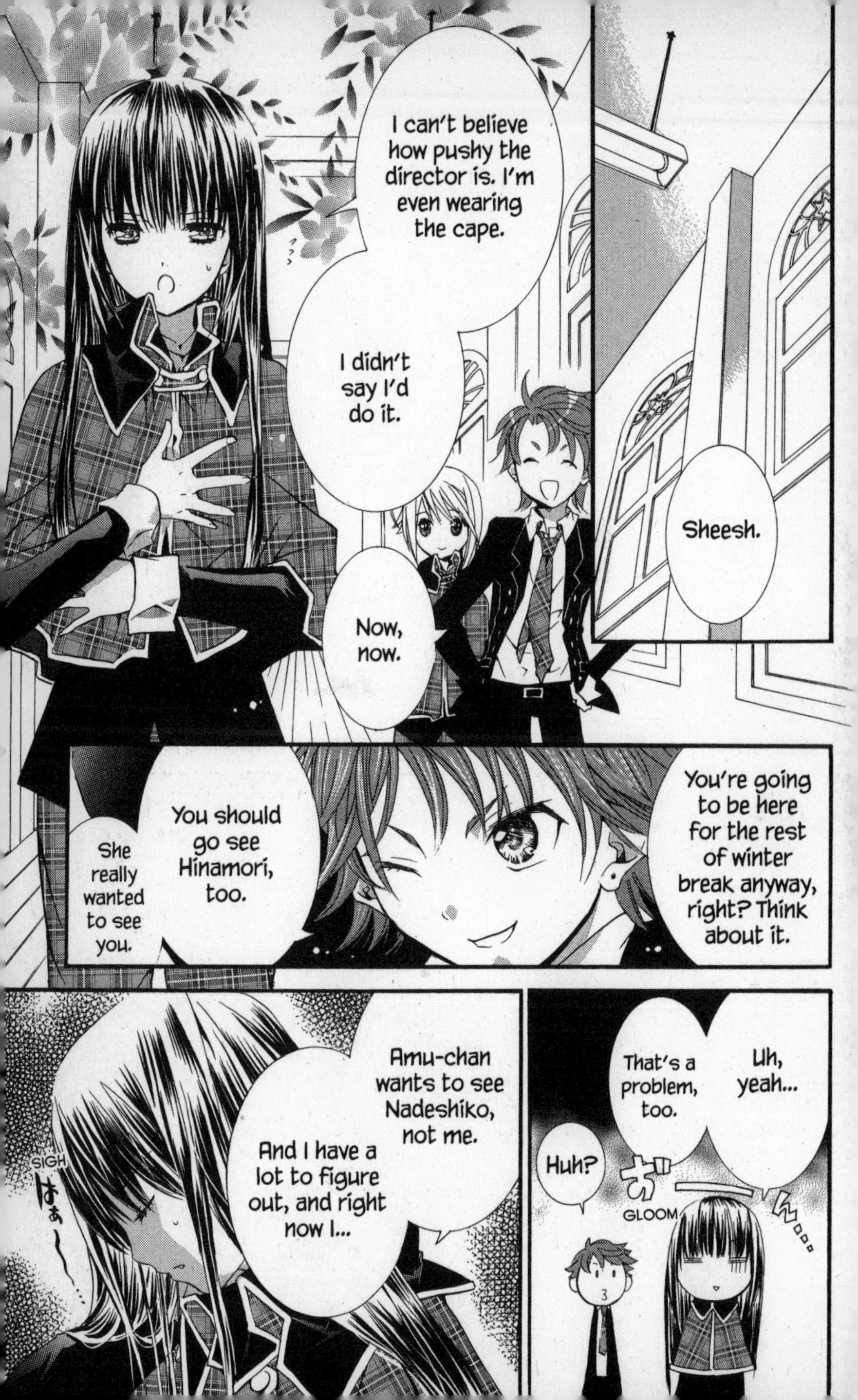
Sheesh.
I can't believe how pushy the director is. I'm even wearing the cape.
I didn't say I'd do it.
Now, now.
You're going to be here for the rest of winter break anyway, right? Think about it.
You should go see Hinamori, too.
She really wanted to see you.
Uh, yeah...
That's a problem, too.
Huh?
GLOOM
Amu-chan wants to see Nadeshiko, not me.
And I have a lot to figure out, and right now I...
SIGH

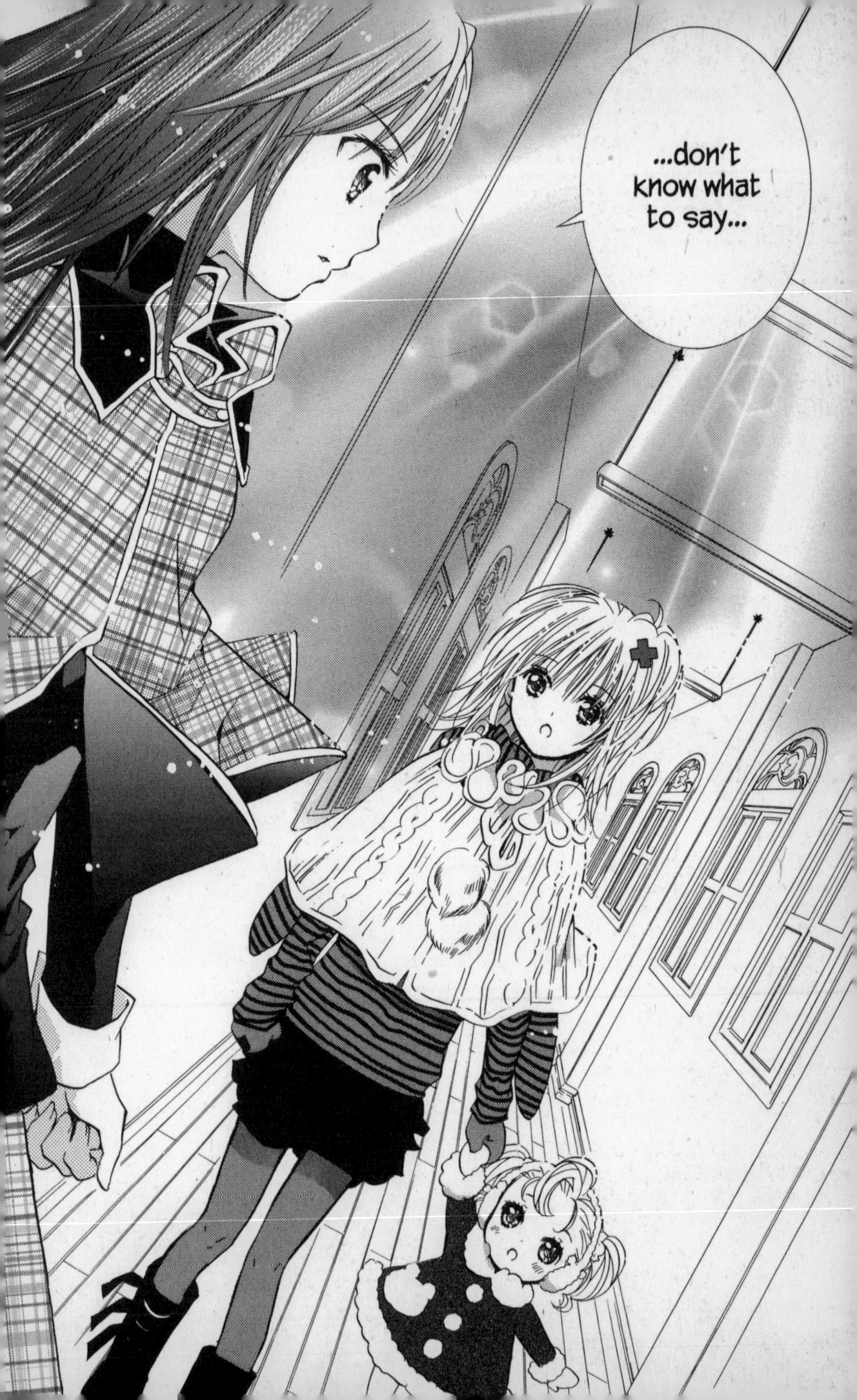
...don't know what to say...

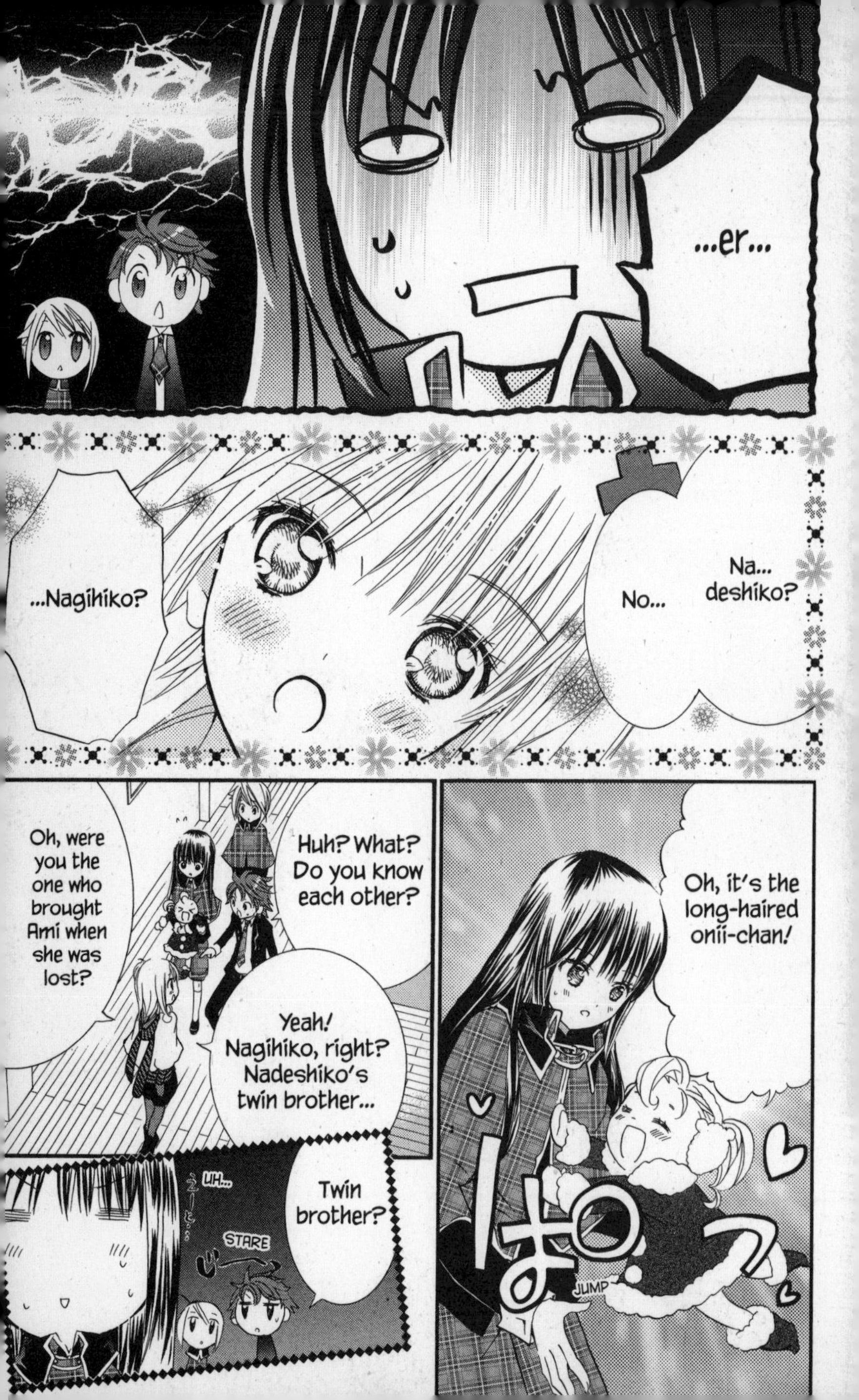
...er...
No... Na... deshiko?
...Nagihiko?
Oh, it's the long-haired onii-chan!
JUMP
Huh? What? Do you know each other?
Oh, were you the one who brought Ami when she was lost?
Yeah! Nagihiko, right? Nadeshiko's twin brother...
Twin brother?
UH...
STARE

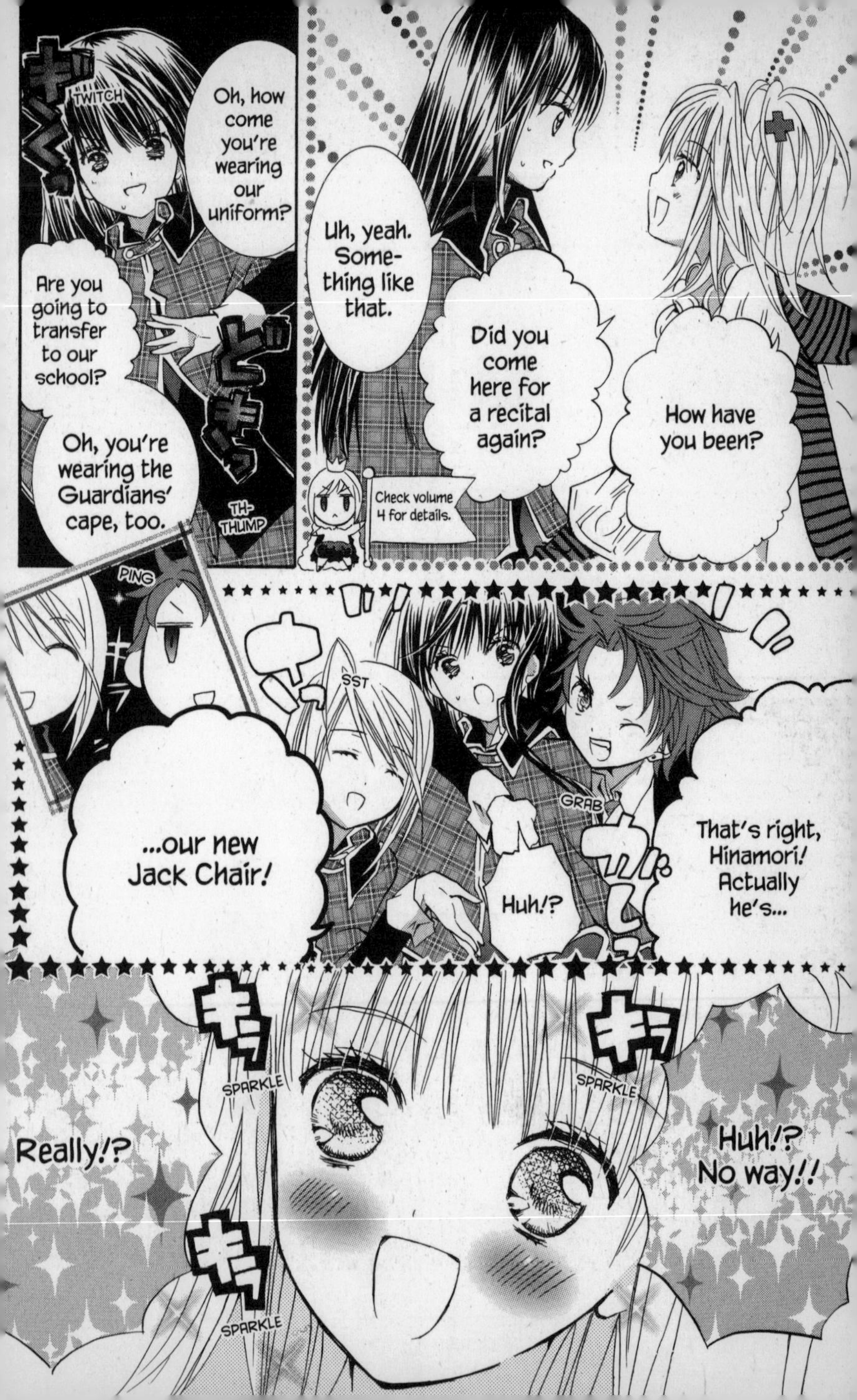
How have you been?
Did you come here for a recital again?
Uh, yeah. Some-thing like that.
Check volume 4 for details.
Oh, how come you're wearing our uniform?
TWITCH
Are you going to transfer to our school?
TH-THUMP
Oh, you're wearing the Guardians' cape, too.
That's right, Hinamori! Actually he's...
GRAB
Huh!?
SST
...our new Jack Chair!
PING
Huh!? No way!!
SPARKLE
SPARKLE
SPARKLE
Really!?

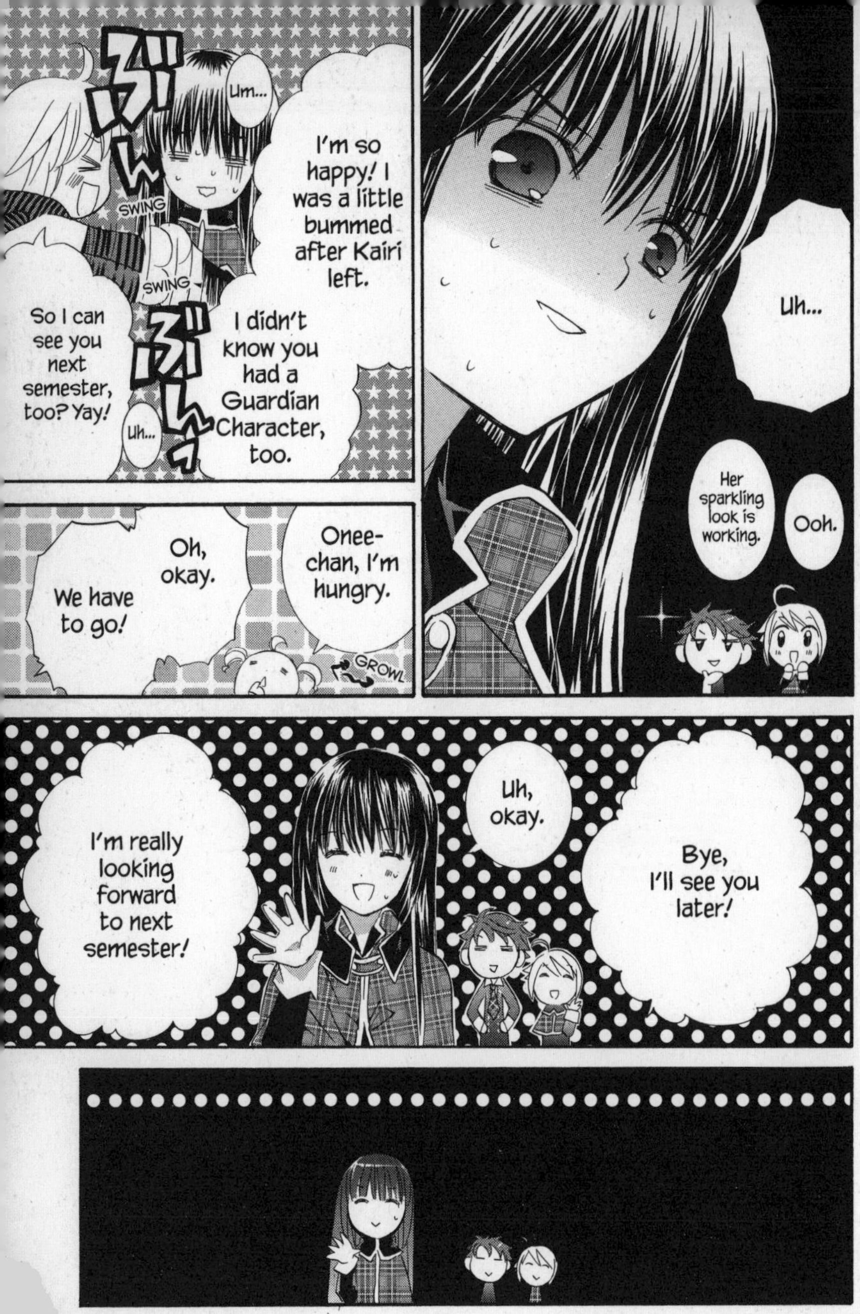
Uh...
Ooh.
Her sparkling look is working.
Um...
I'm so happy! I was a little bummed after Kairi left.
SWING
SWING
I didn't know you had a Guardian Character, too.
So I can see you next semester, too? Yay!
Uh...
Onee-chan, I'm hungry.
GROWL
Oh, okay.
We have to go!
Bye, I'll see you later!
Uh, okay.
I'm really looking forward to next semester!

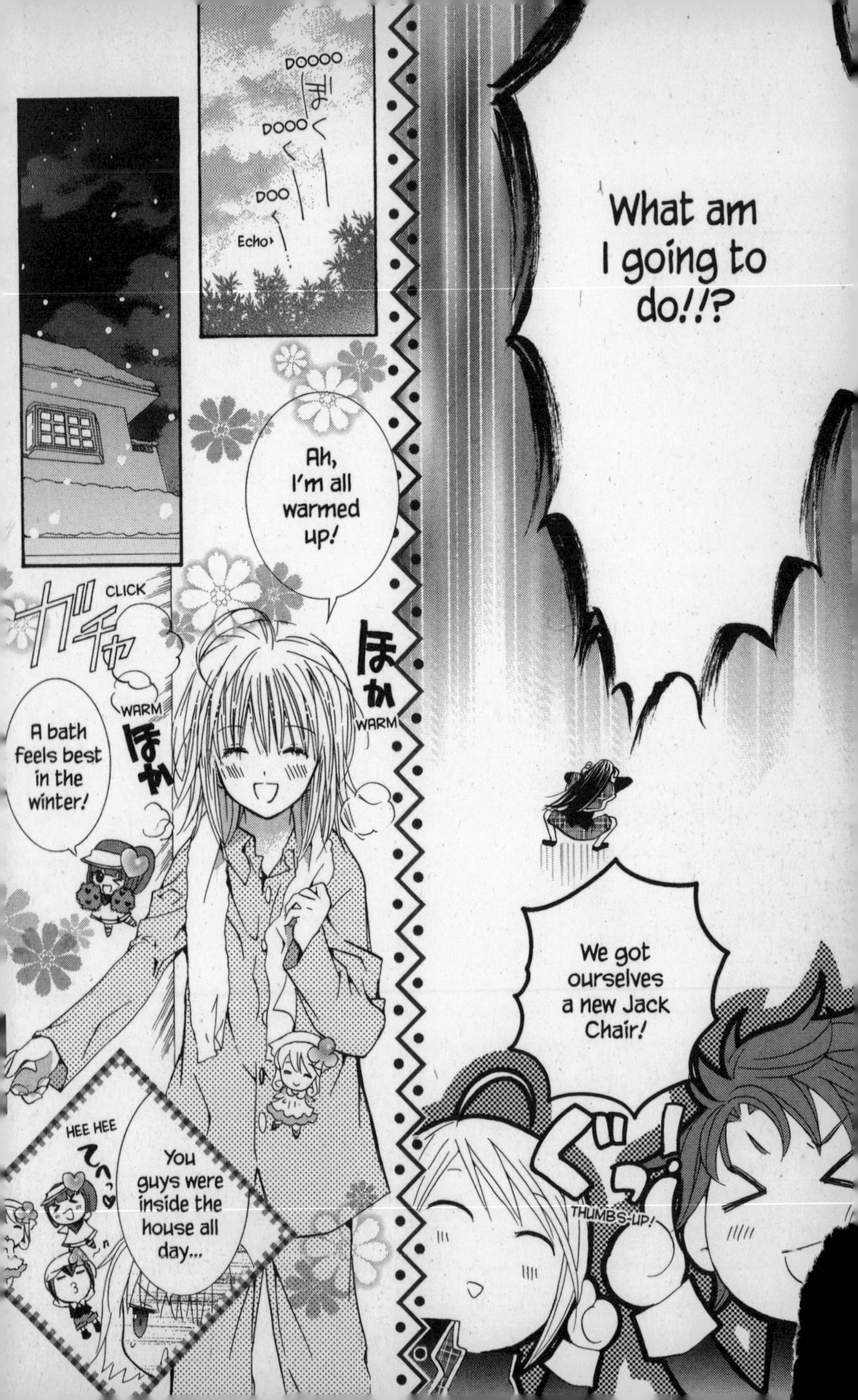
What am I going to do!!?
We got ourselves a new Jack Chair!
THUMBS-UP!
DOOOO
DOOO
DOO
Echo
Ah, I'm all warmed up!
WARM
CLICK
WARM
A bath feels best in the winter!
HEE HEE
You guys were inside the house all day...

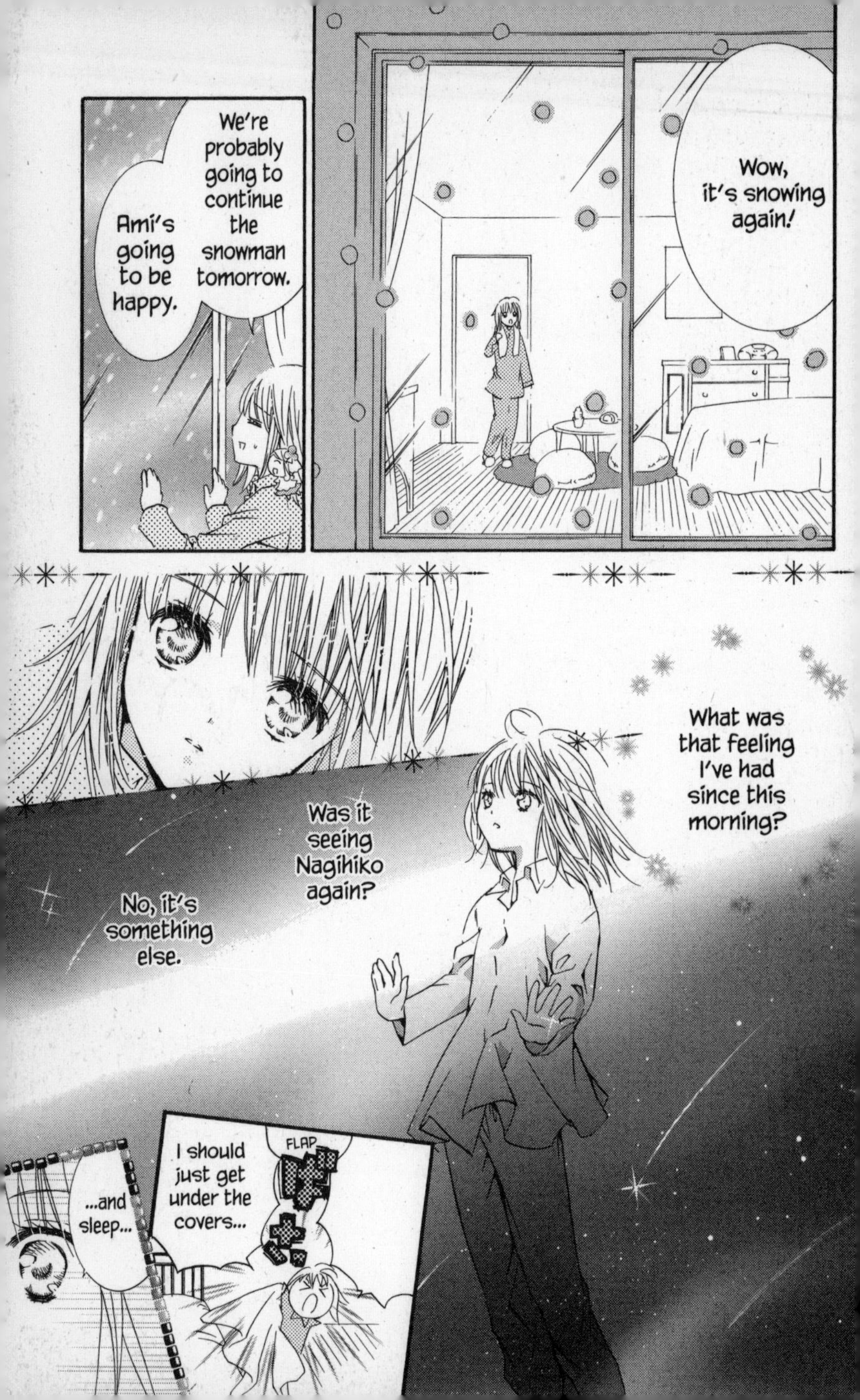
Wow, it's snowing again!
We're probably going to continue the snowman tomorrow.
Ami's going to be happy.
What was that feeling I've had since this morning?
Was it seeing Nagihiko again?
No, it's something else.
FLAP
I should just get under the covers...
...and sleep...

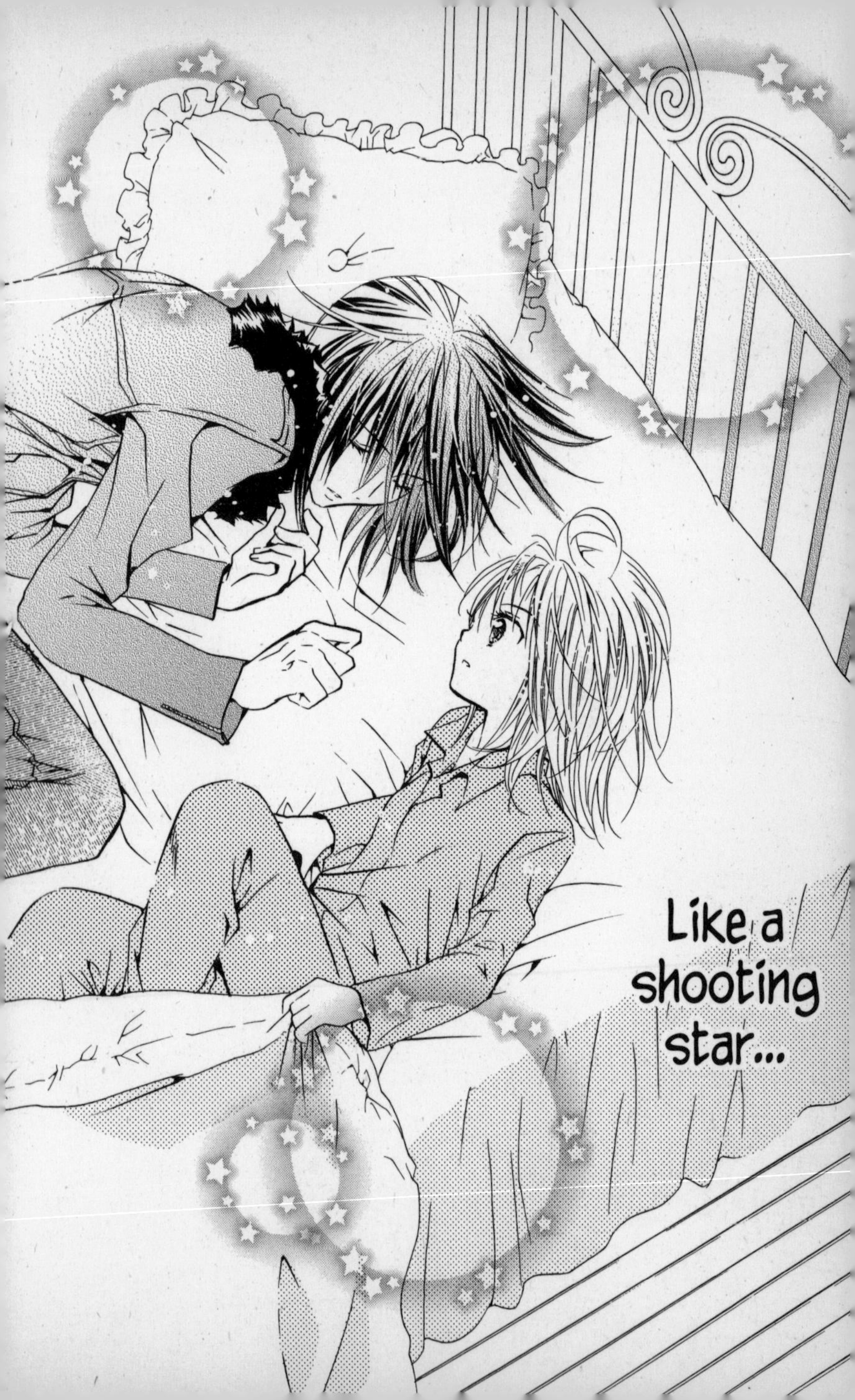
Like a shooting star...

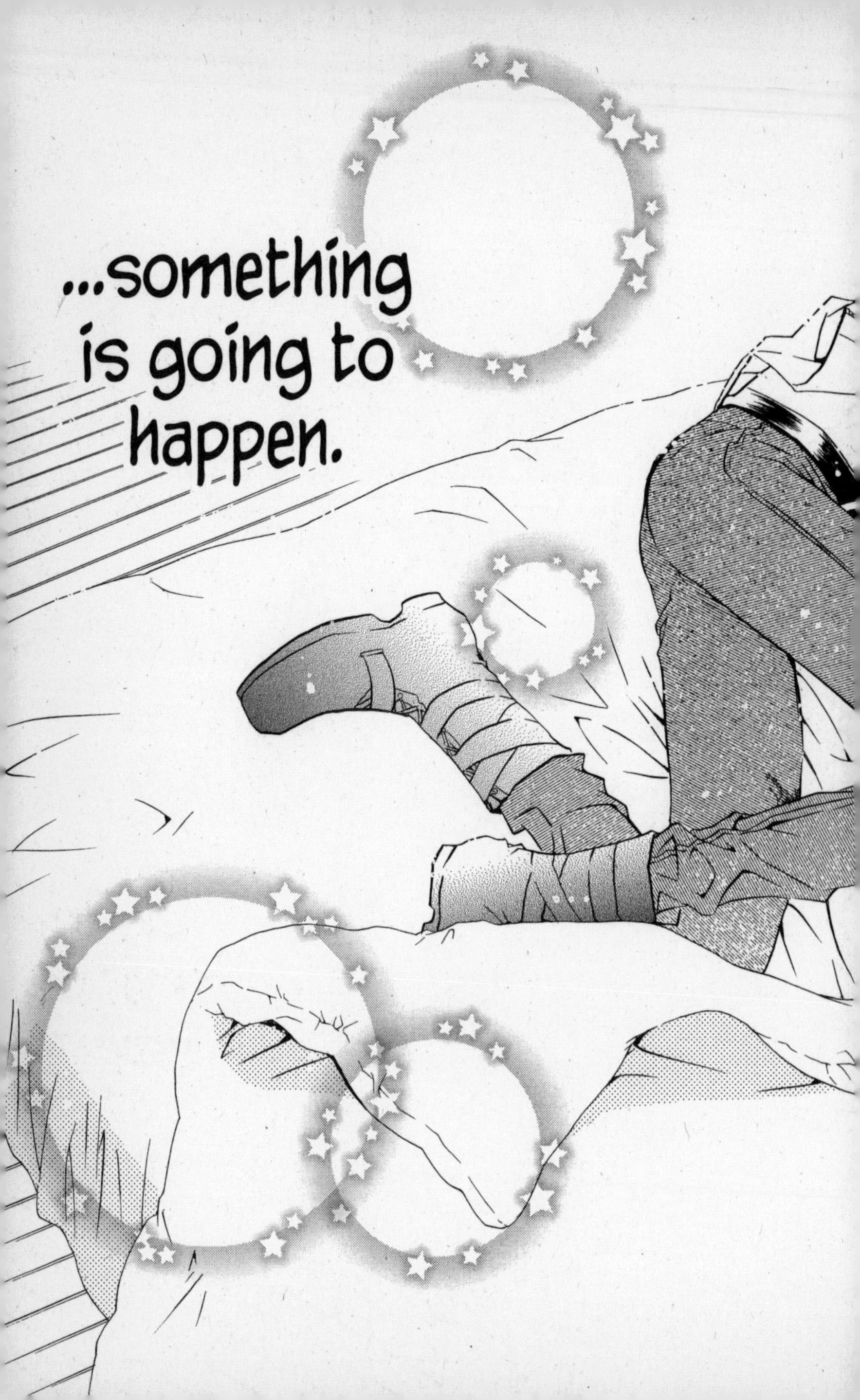
...something is going to happen.

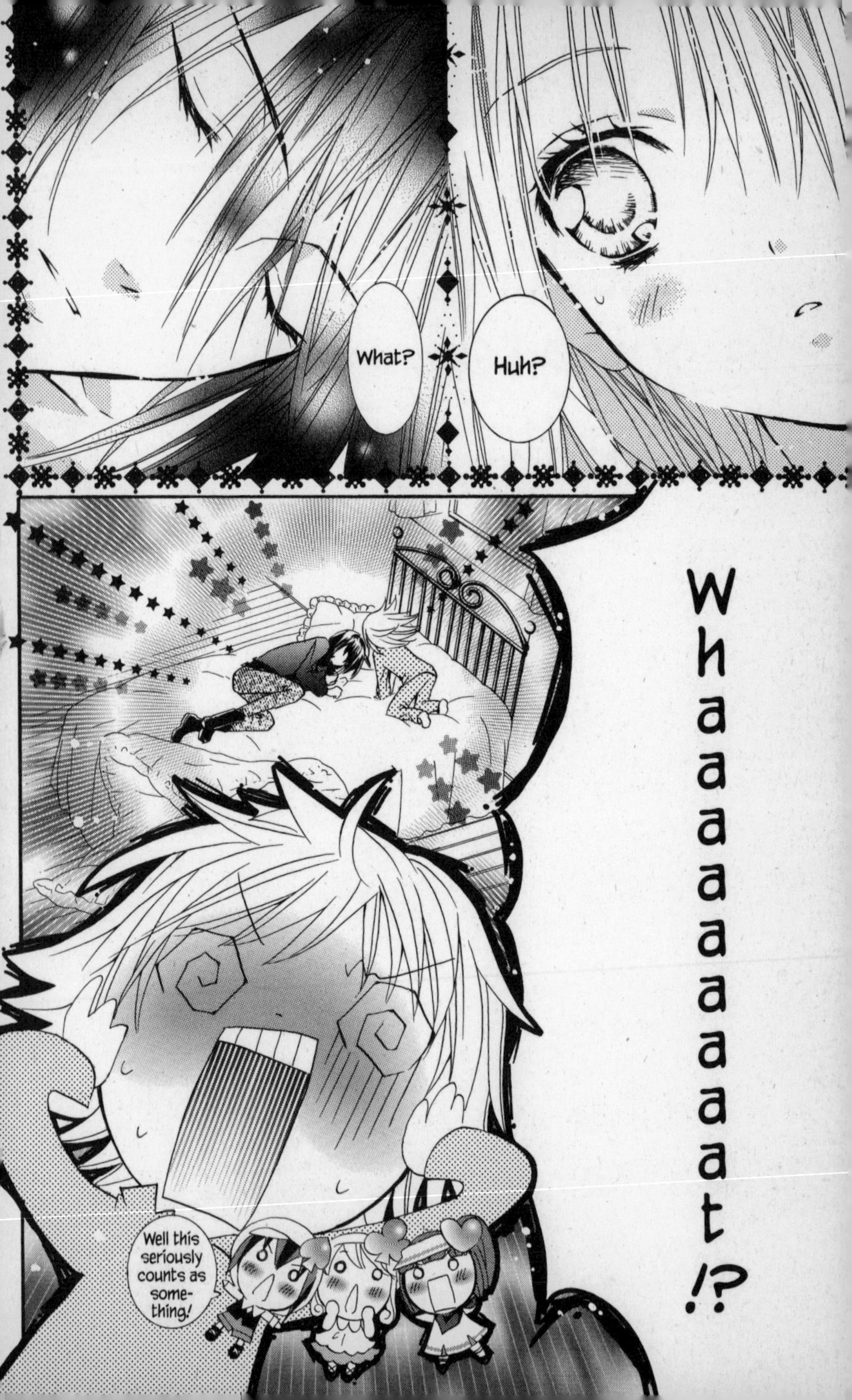
Huh?
What?
Whaaaaaaat!?
Well this seriously counts as some-thing!

Shugo Chara!

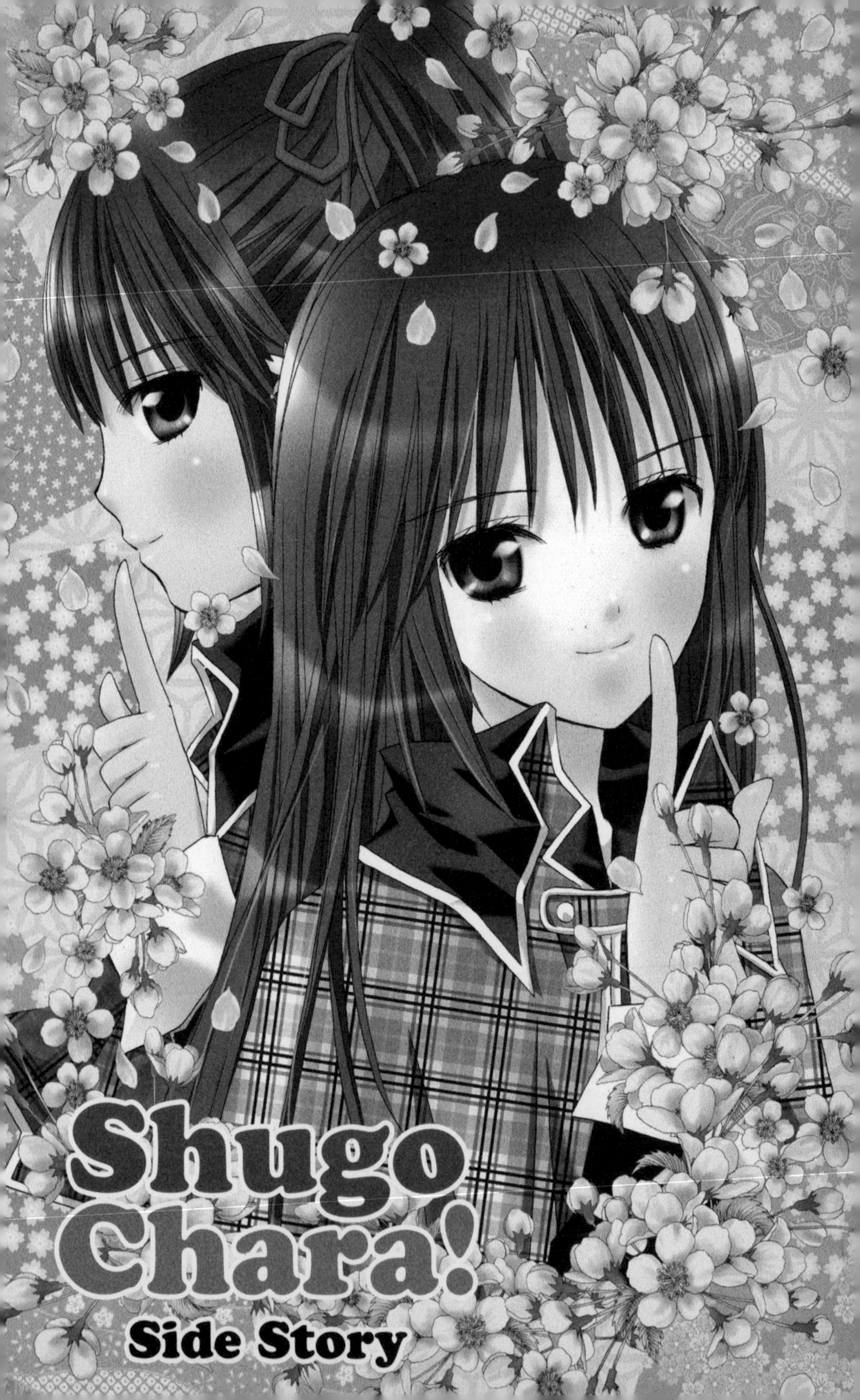
Shugo Chara!
Side Story

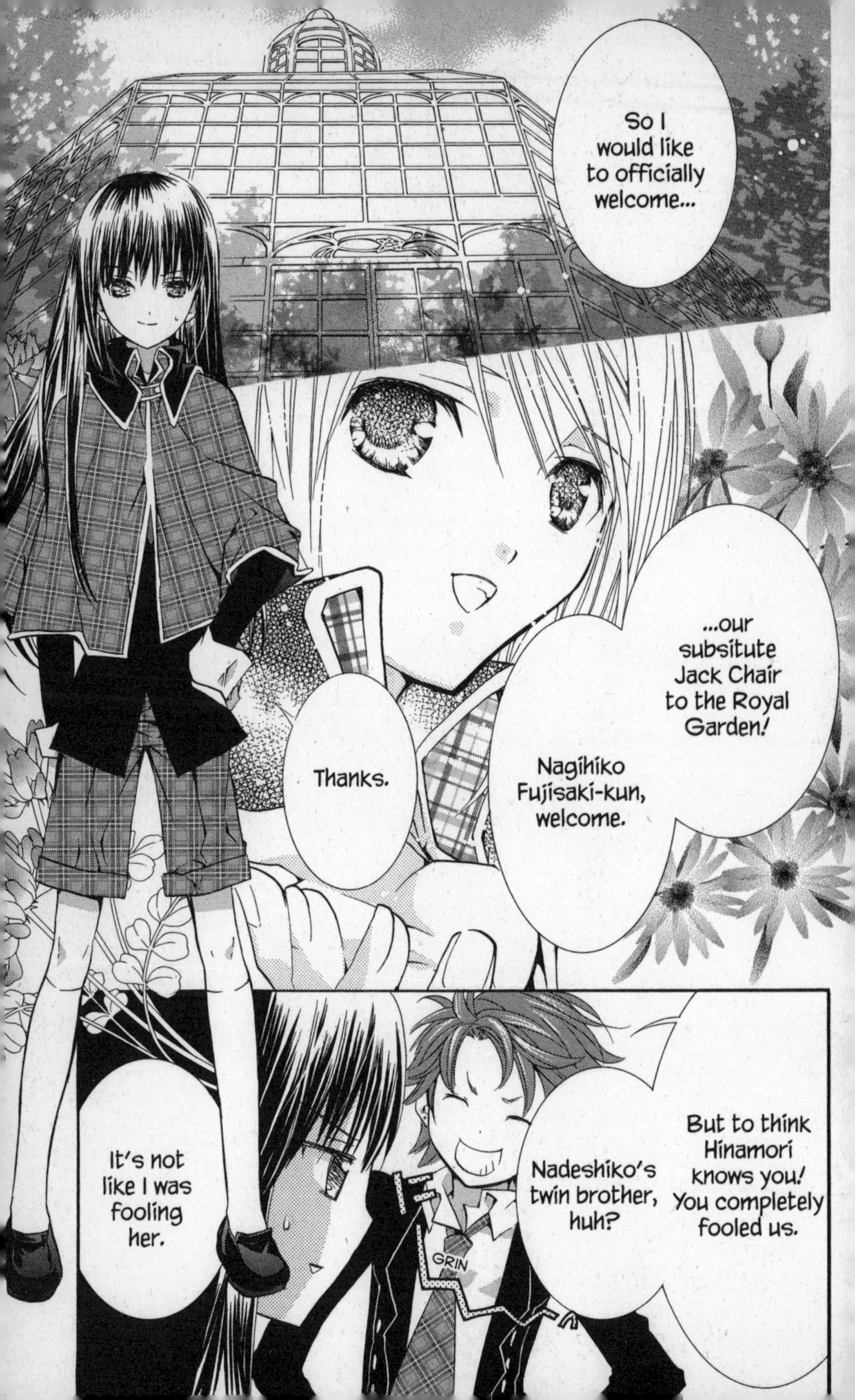
So I would like to officially welcome...
...our subsitute Jack Chair to the Royal Garden!
Nagihiko Fujisaki-kun, welcome.
Thanks.
But to think Hinamori knows you! You completely fooled us.
Nadeshiko's twin brother, huh?
GRIN
It's not like I was fooling her.

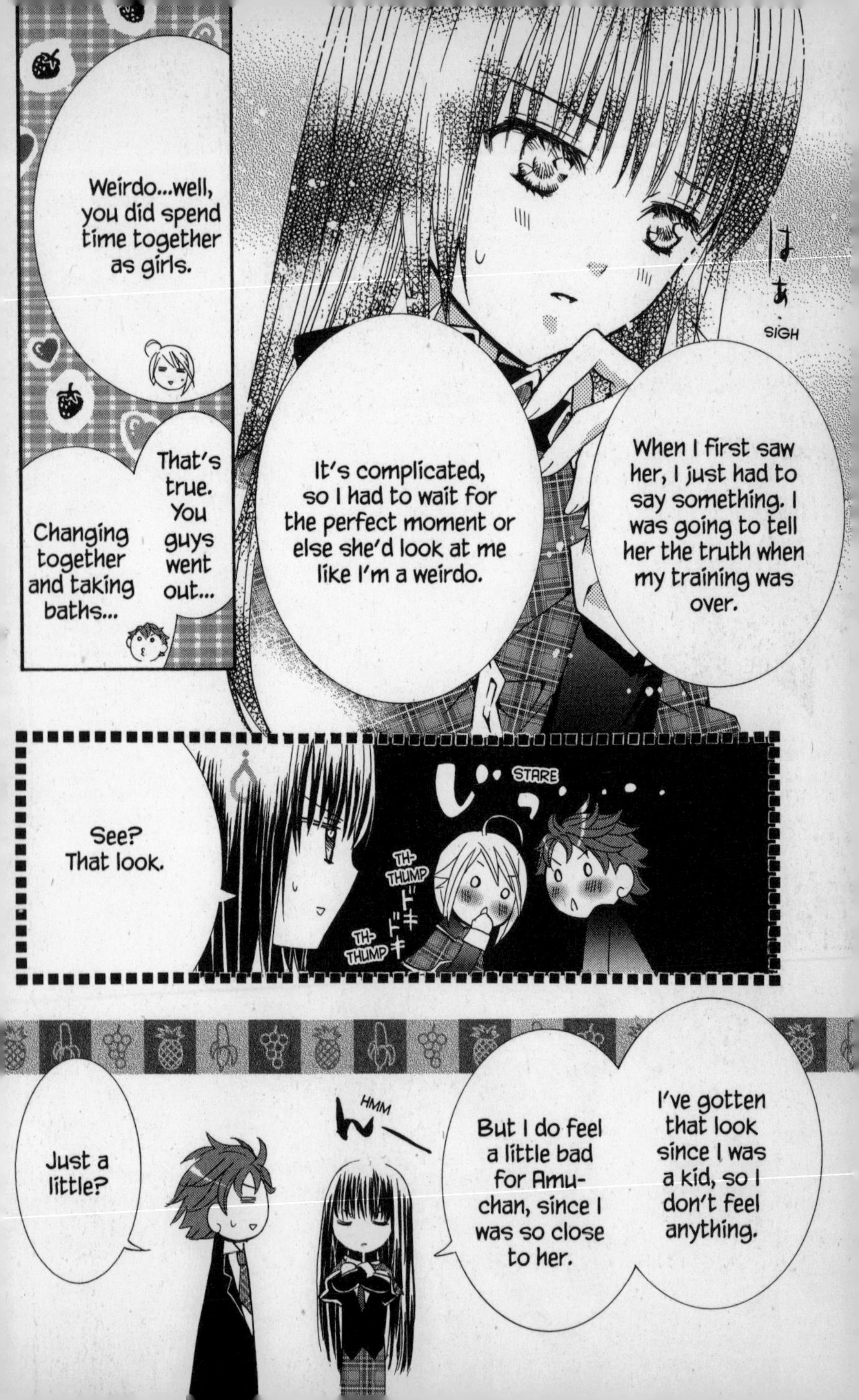
はぁ
SIGH
When I first saw her, I just had to say something. I was going to tell her the truth when my training was over.
It's complicated, so I had to wait for the perfect moment or else she'd look at me like I'm a weirdo.
Weirdo...well, you did spend time together as girls.
That's true. You guys went out...
Changing together and taking baths...
じっ
STARE
ドキドキ
TH-THUMP
TH-THUMP
See? That look.
I've gotten that look since I was a kid, so I don't feel anything.
But I do feel a little bad for Amu-chan, since I was so close to her.
ん—
HMM
Just a little?

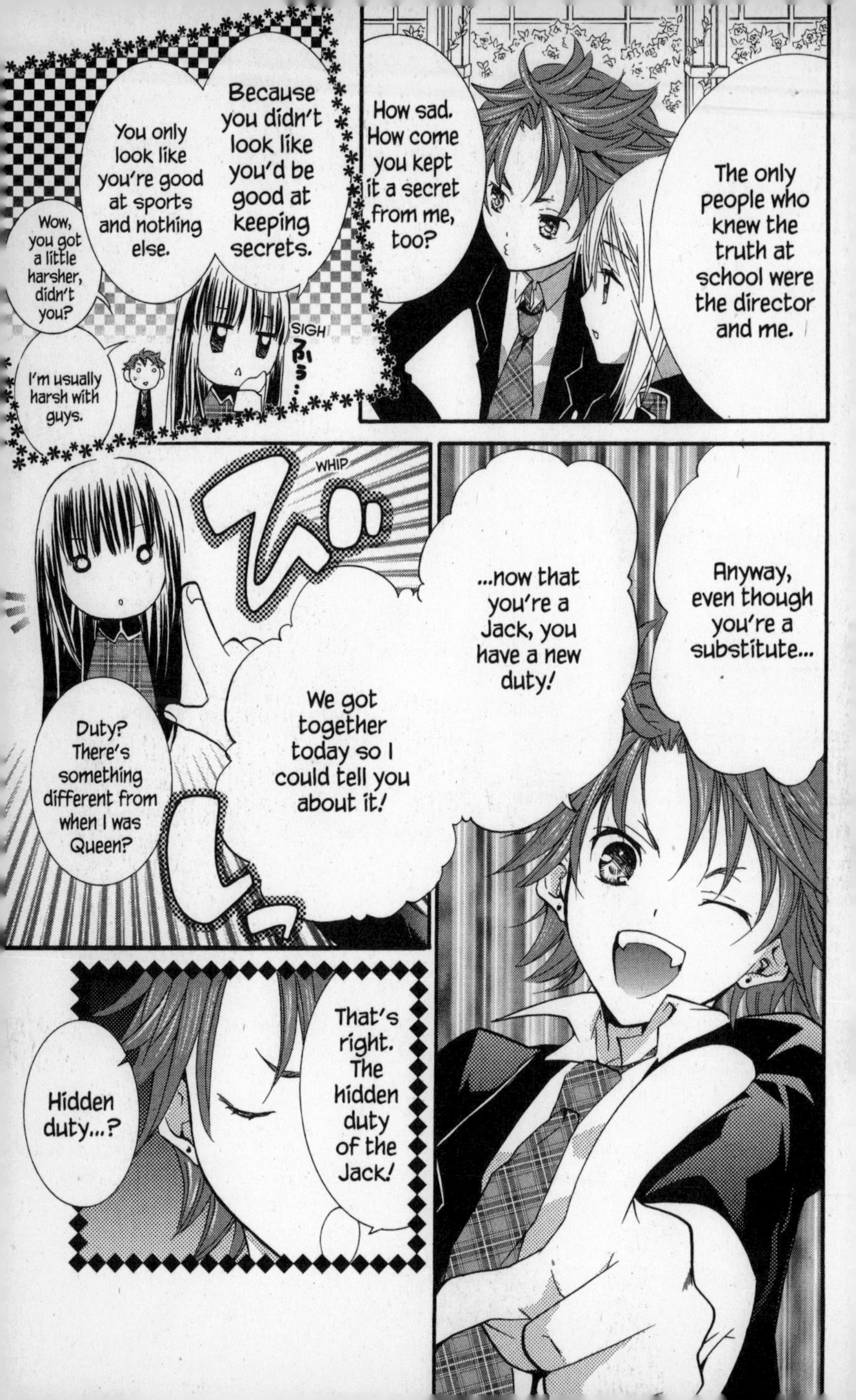
The only people who knew the truth at school were the director and me.
How sad. How come you kept it a secret from me, too?
Because you didn't look like you'd be good at keeping secrets.
You only look like you're good at sports and nothing else.
SIGH
Wow, you got a little harsher, didn't you?
I'm usually harsh with guys.
Anyway, even though you're a substitute...
...now that you're a Jack, you have a new duty!
WHIP
We got together today so I could tell you about it!
Duty? There's something different from when I was Queen?
That's right. The hidden duty of the Jack!
Hidden duty...?

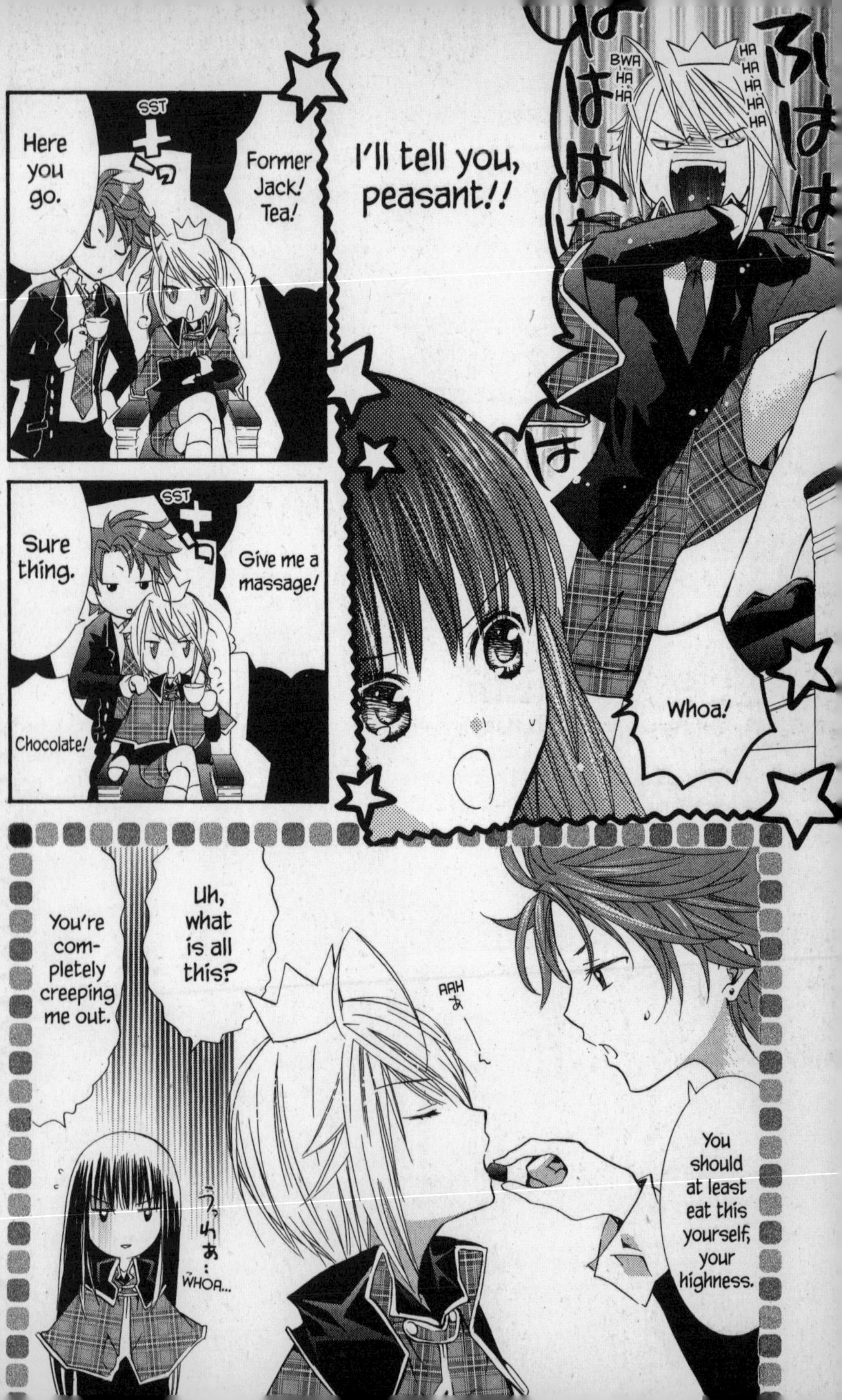
BWA HA HA HA
HA HA HA HA HA
I'll tell you, peasant!!
Whoa!
SST
Former Jack! Tea!
Here you go.
SST
Give me a massage!
Chocolate!
Sure thing.
You should at least eat this yourself, your highness.
AAH
WHOA...
Uh, what is all this?
You're com-pletely creeping me out.

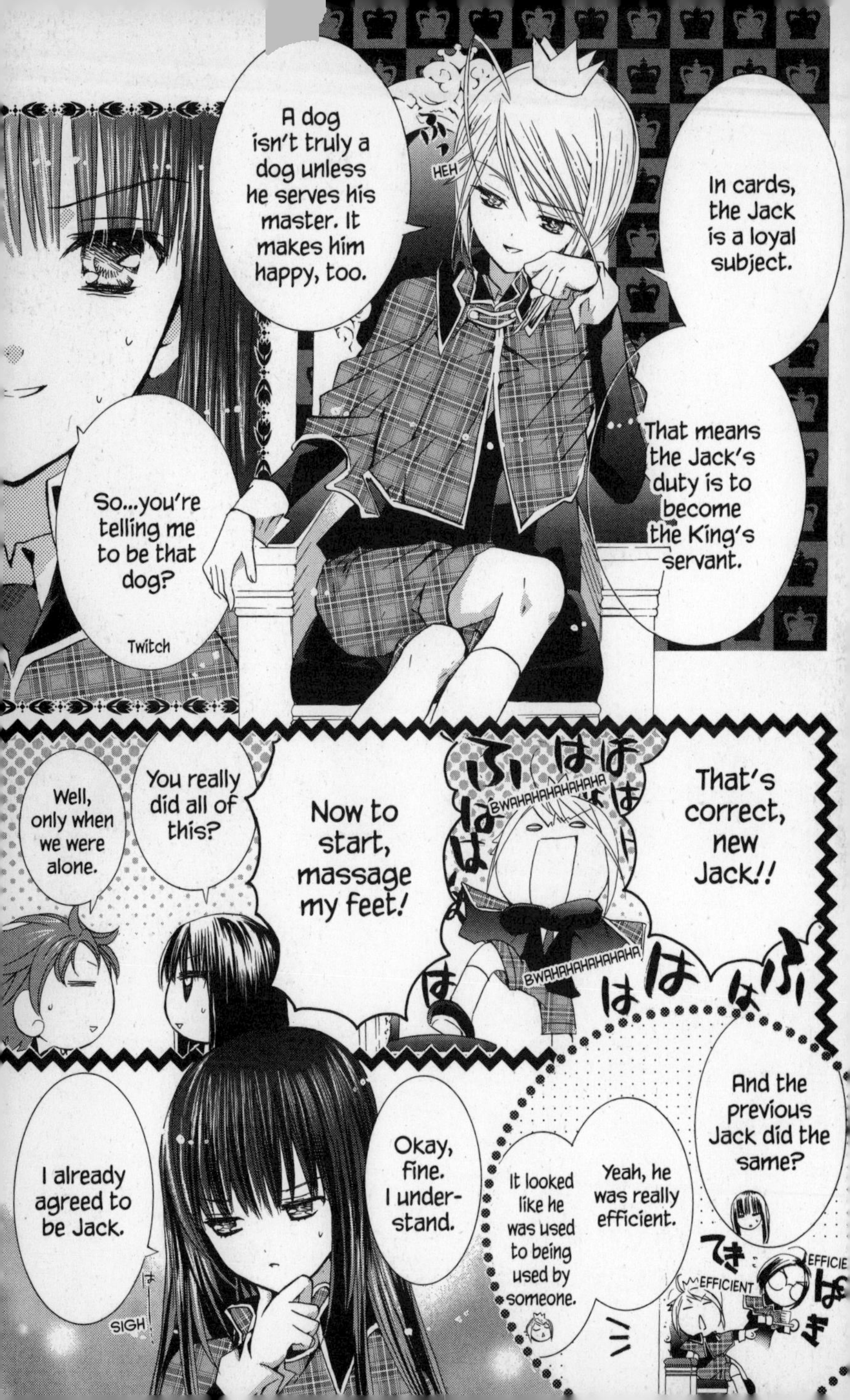
In cards, the Jack is a loyal subject.
That means the Jack's duty is to become the King's servant.
HEH
A dog isn't truly a dog unless he serves his master. It makes him happy, too.
So...you're telling me to be that dog?
Twitch
That's correct, new Jack!!
BWAHAHAHAHAHAHA
BWAHAHAHAHAHAHA
Now to start, massage my feet!
You really did all of this?
Well, only when we were alone.
And the previous Jack did the same?
Yeah, he was really efficient.
EFFICIENT
EFFICIE
It looked like he was used to being used by someone.
Okay, fine. I understand.
I already agreed to be Jack.
SIGH

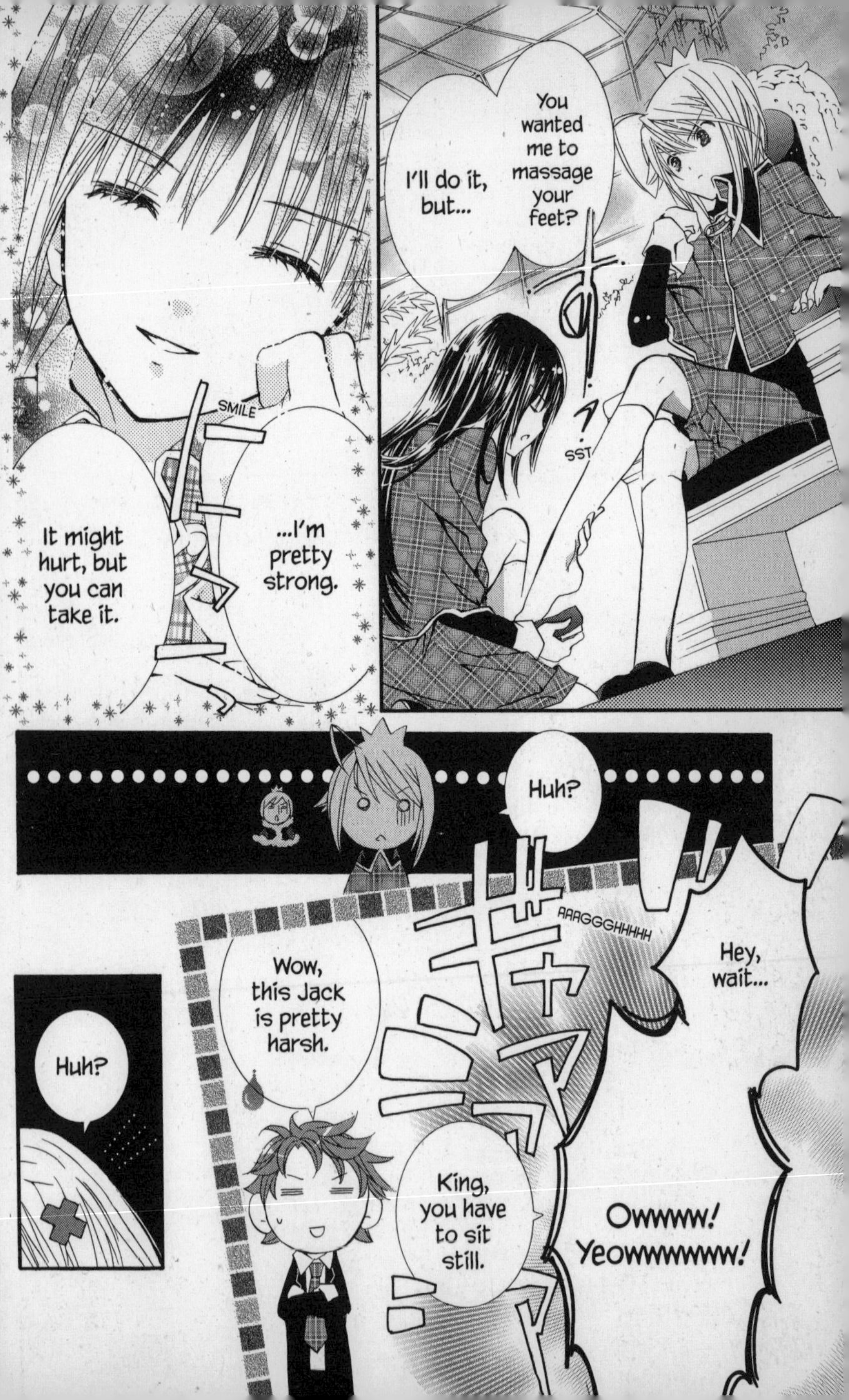
You wanted me to massage your feet?
I'll do it, but...
SST
SMILE
...I'm pretty strong.
It might hurt, but you can take it.
Huh?
Hey, wait...
AAAGGGHHHHH
Owwww! Yeowwwwww!
King, you have to sit still.
Wow, this Jack is pretty harsh.
Huh?

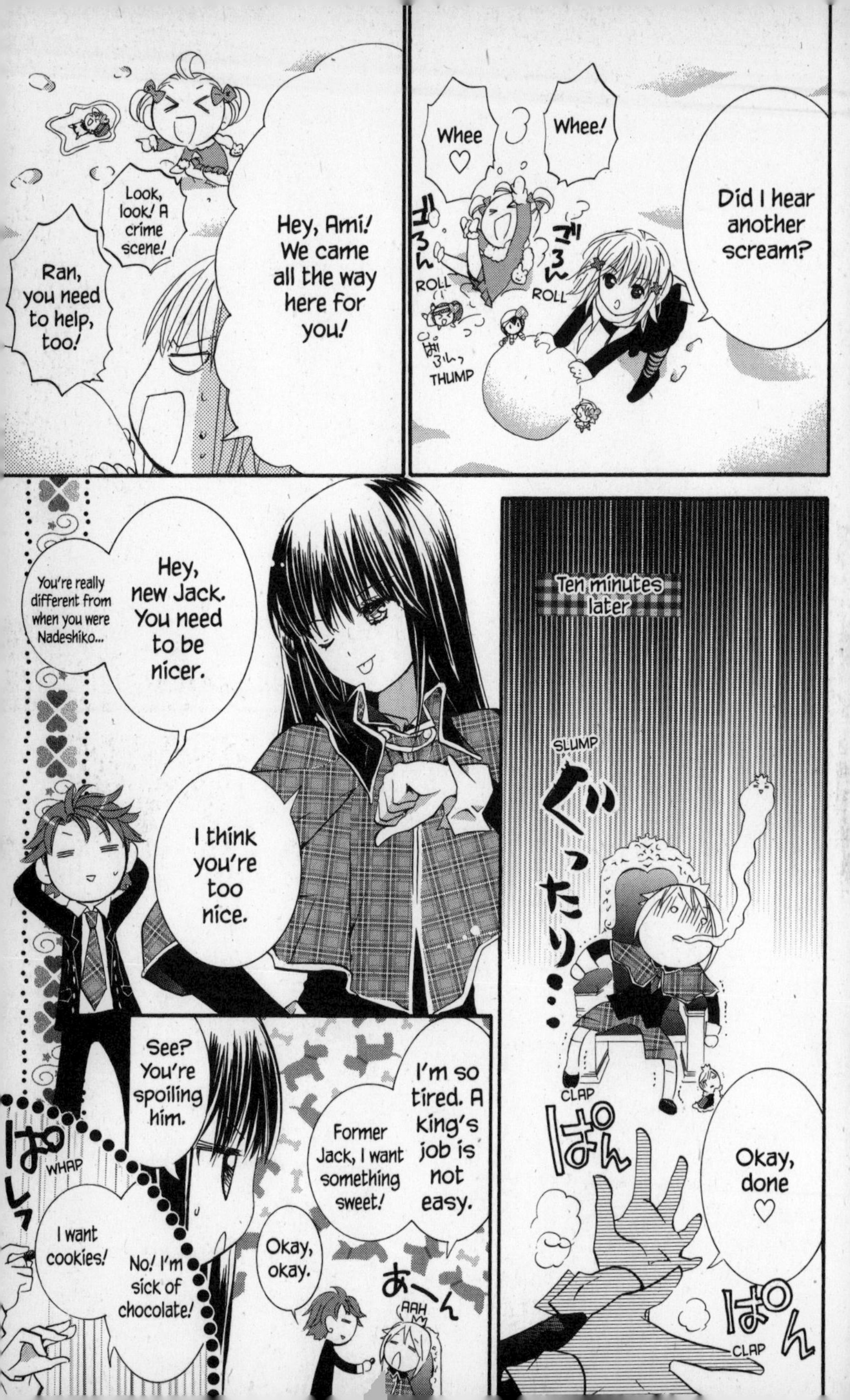
Did I hear another scream?
Whee!
ごろん ROLL
Whee ♡
ごろん ROLL
ぼふんっ THUMP
Hey, Ami! We came all the way here for you!
Look, look! A crime scene!
Ran, you need to help, too!
Ten minutes later
ぐったり… SLUMP
Okay, done ♡
ぱん CLAP
ぱん CLAP
Hey, new Jack. You need to be nicer.
You're really different from when you were Nadeshiko...
I think you're too nice.
I'm so tired. A king's job is not easy.
Former Jack, I want something sweet!
See? You're spoiling him.
Okay, okay.
あ～ん AAH
No! I'm sick of chocolate!
I want cookies!
ぱしっ WHAP

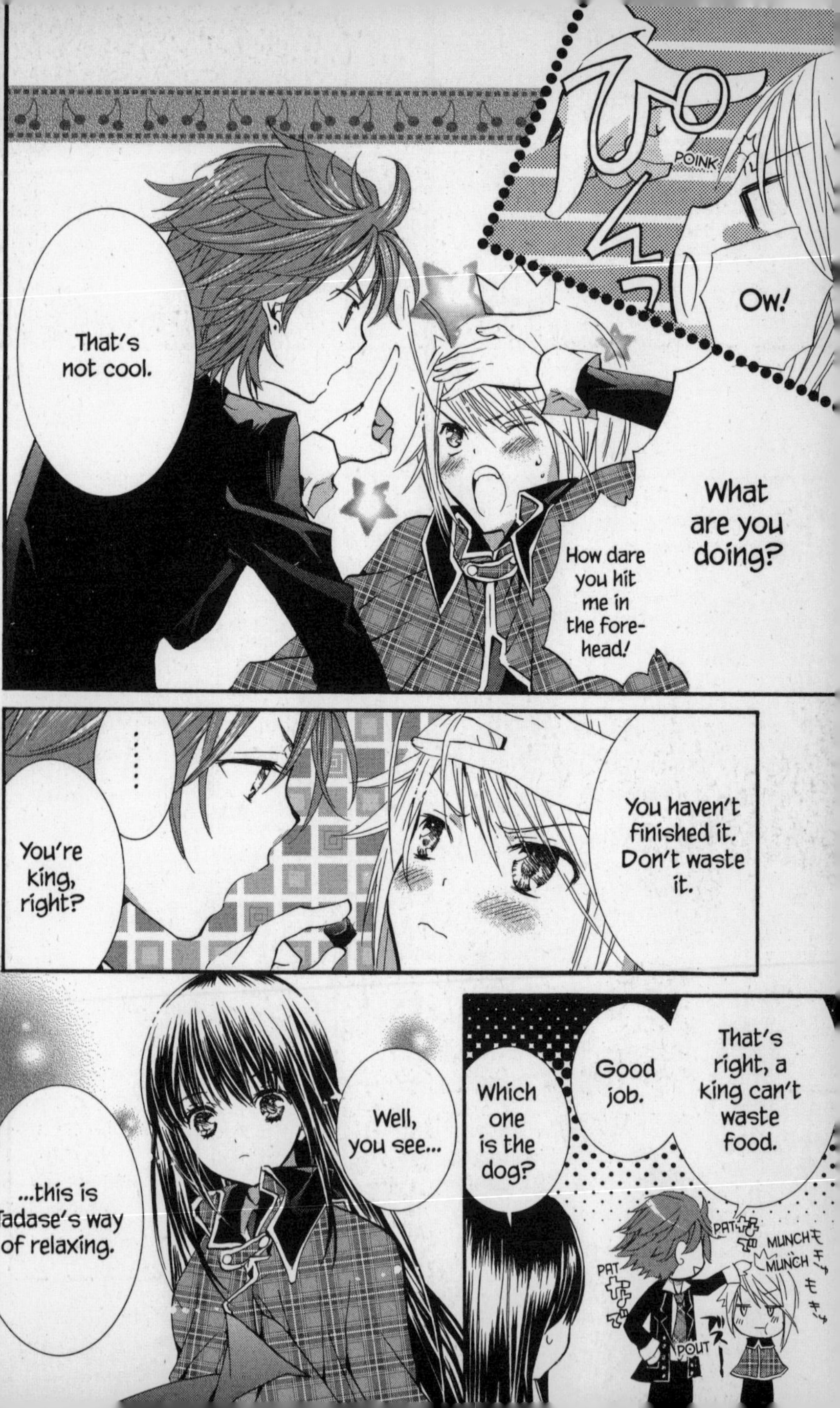
POINK
Ow!
What are you doing?
How dare you hit me in the fore-head!
That's not cool.
You haven't finished it. Don't waste it.
......
You're king, right?
That's right, a king can't waste food.
Good job.
Which one is the dog?
PAT
MUNCH
MUNCH
PAT
POUT
Well, you see...
...this is Tadase's way of relaxing.

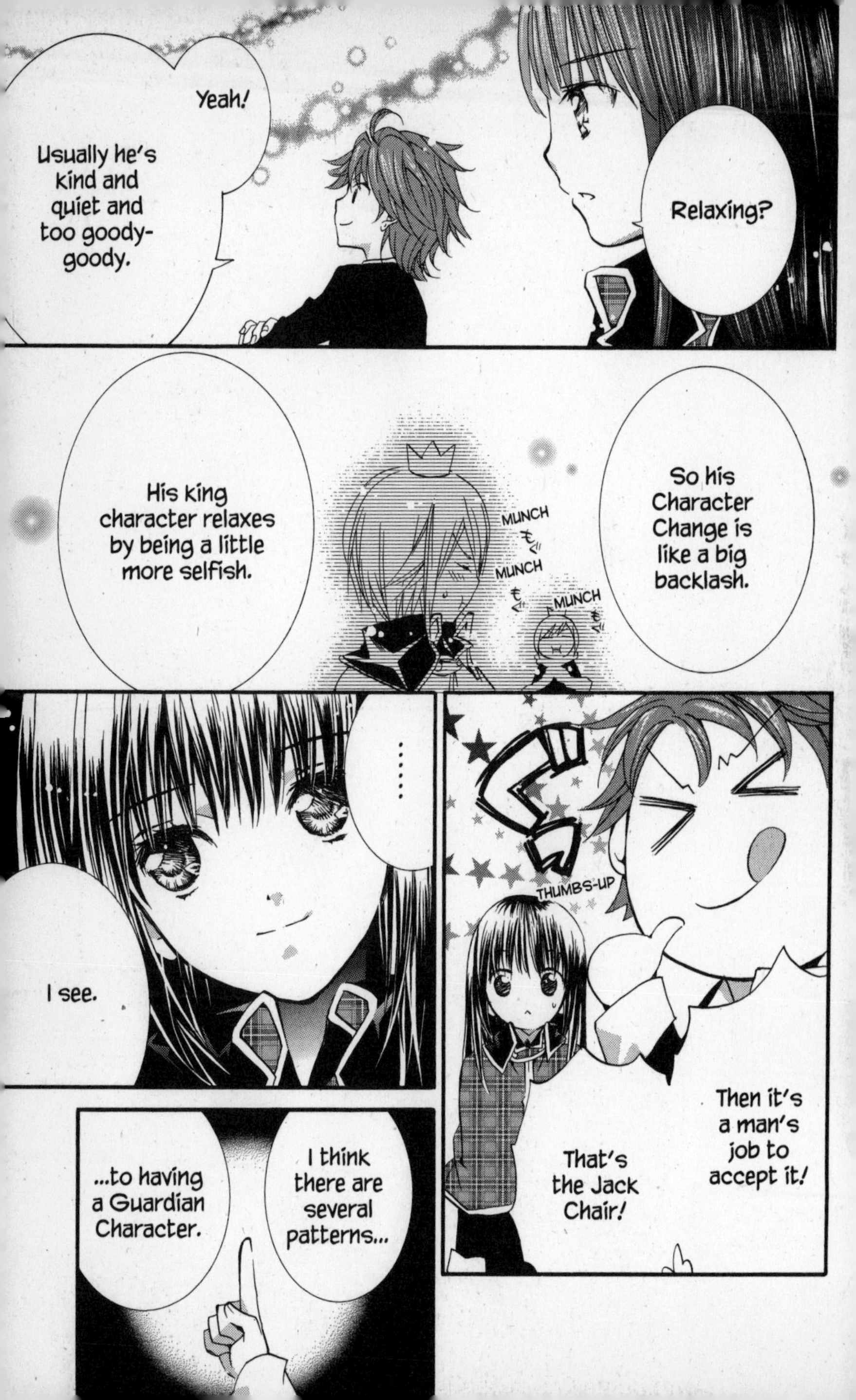
Relaxing?
Yeah!
Usually he's kind and quiet and too goody-goody.
So his Character Change is like a big backlash.
MUNCH
MUNCH
MUNCH
His king character relaxes by being a little more selfish.
THUMBS-UP
Then it's a man's job to accept it!
That's the Jack Chair!
......
I see.
I think there are several patterns...
...to having a Guardian Character.

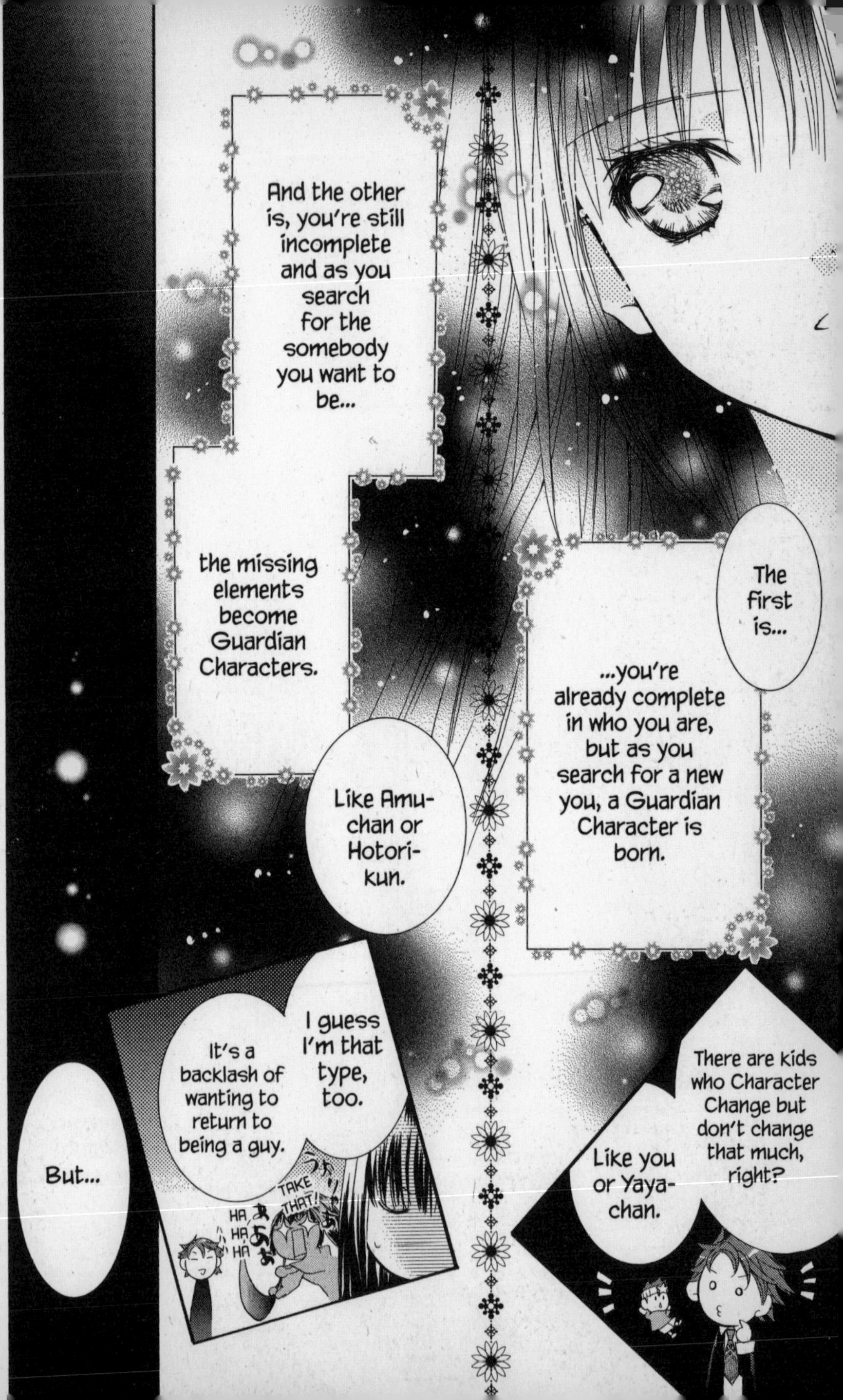
The first is...
...you're already complete in who you are, but as you search for a new you, a Guardian Character is born.
And the other is, you're still incomplete and as you search for the somebody you want to be...
the missing elements become Guardian Characters.
Like Amu-chan or Hotori-kun.
There are kids who Character Change but don't change that much, right?
Like you or Yaya-chan.
I guess I'm that type, too.
It's a backlash of wanting to return to being a guy.
TAKE THAT!
HA HA HA
But...

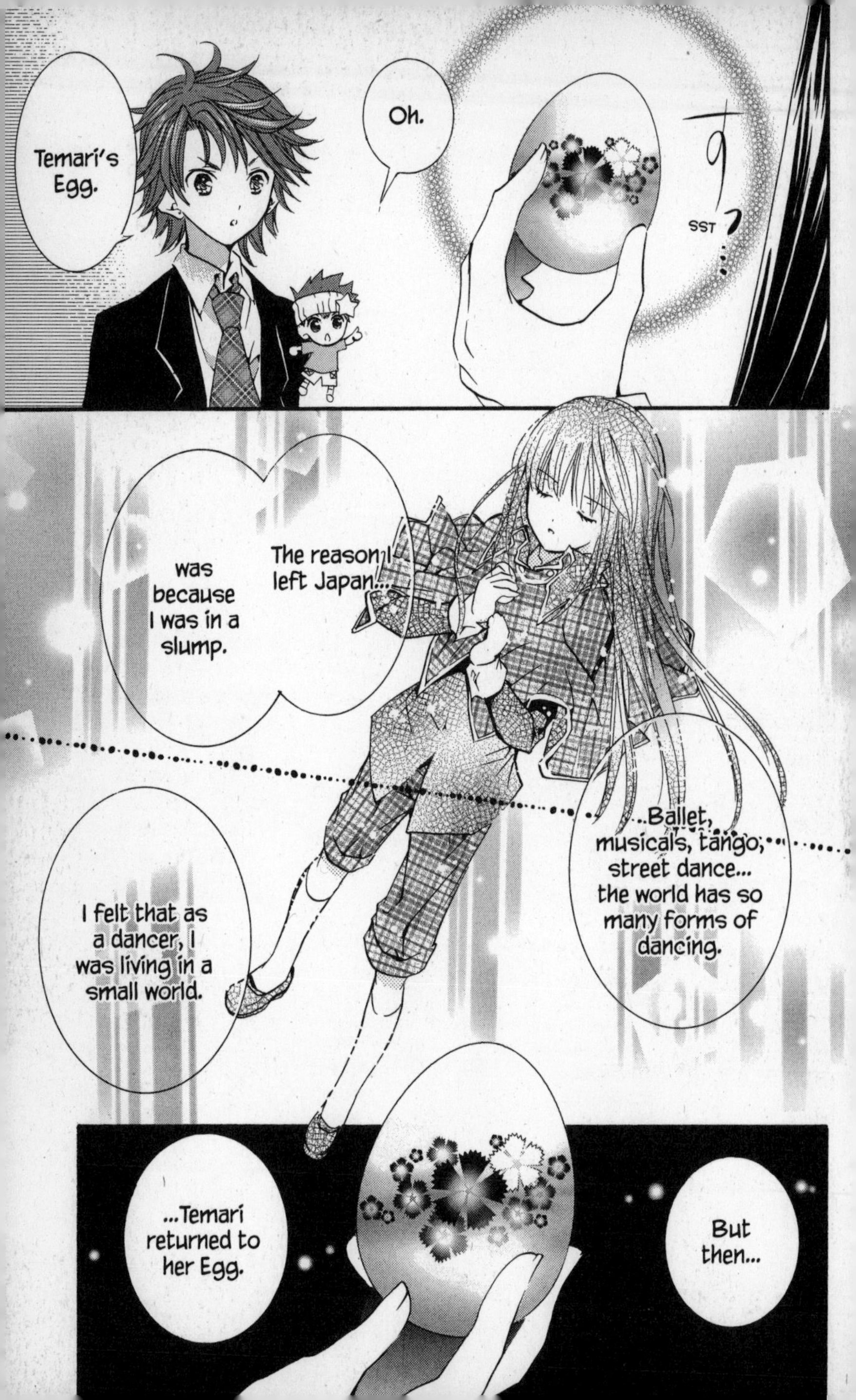
SST
Oh.
Temari's Egg.
The reason I left Japan...
was because I was in a slump.
...Ballet, musicals, tango, street dance... the world has so many forms of dancing.
I felt that as a dancer, I was living in a small world.
But then...
...Temari returned to her Egg.

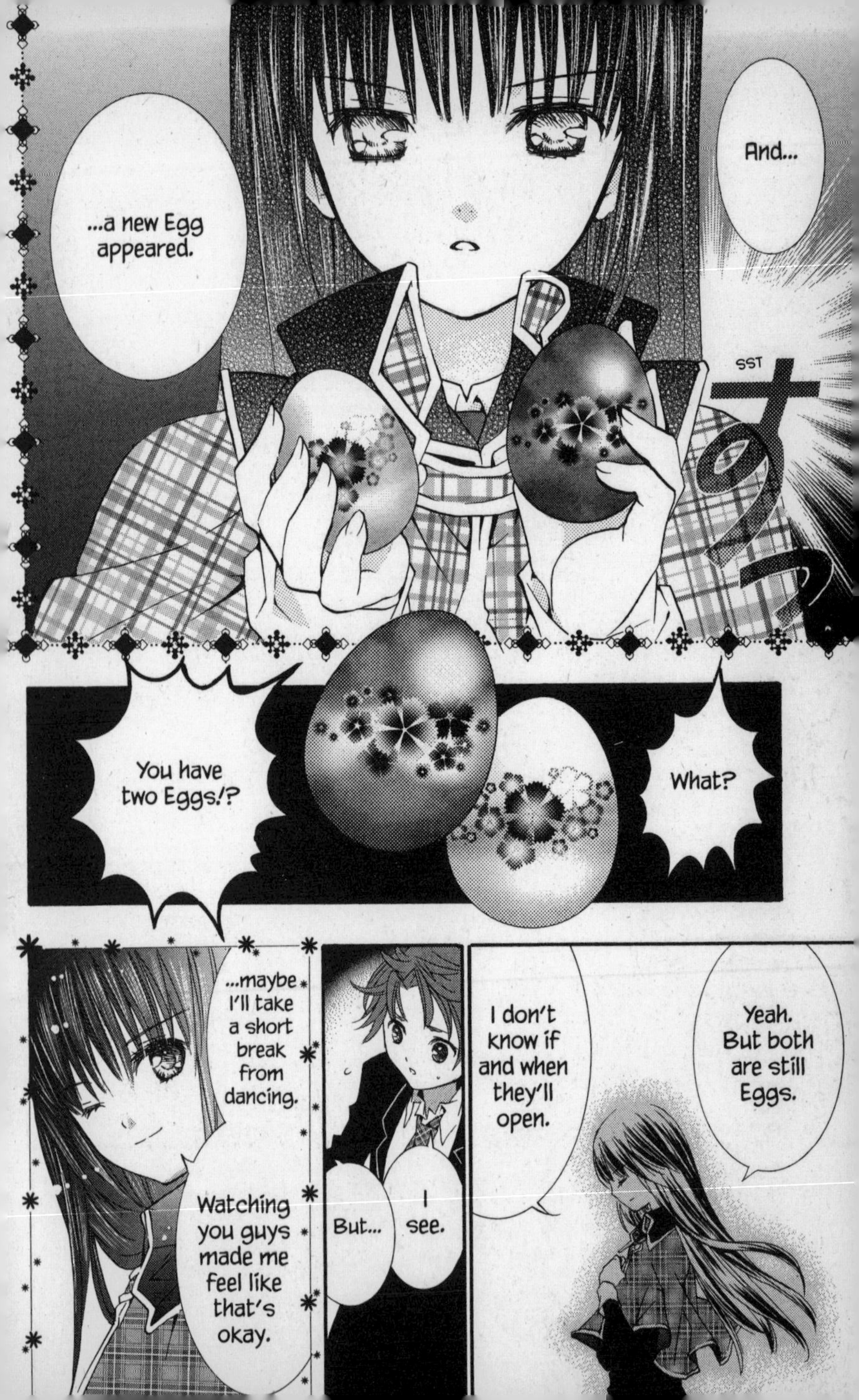
And...
...a new Egg appeared.
SST
What?
You have two Eggs!?
Yeah. But both are still Eggs.
I don't know if and when they'll open.
I see.
But...
...maybe I'll take a short break from dancing.
Watching you guys made me feel like that's okay.

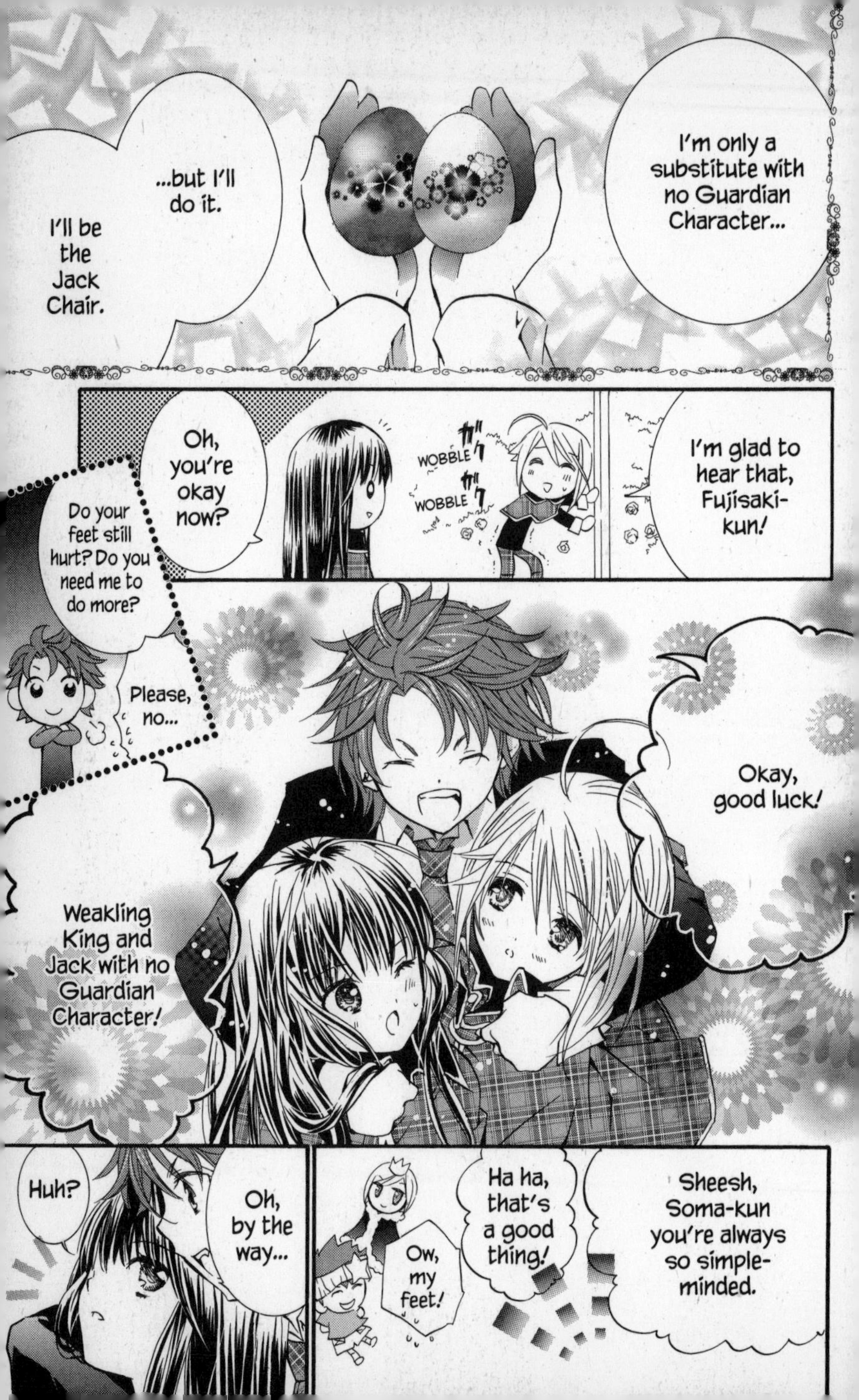

I'm only a substitute with no Guardian Character...
...but I'll do it.
I'll be the Jack Chair.
I'm glad to hear that, Fujisaki-kun!
WOBBLE
WOBBLE
Oh, you're okay now?
Okay, good luck!
Do your feet still hurt? Do you need me to do more?
Please, no...
Weakling King and Jack with no Guardian Character!
Sheesh, Soma-kun you're always so simple-minded.
Ha ha, that's a good thing!
Ow, my feet!
Oh, by the way...
Huh?

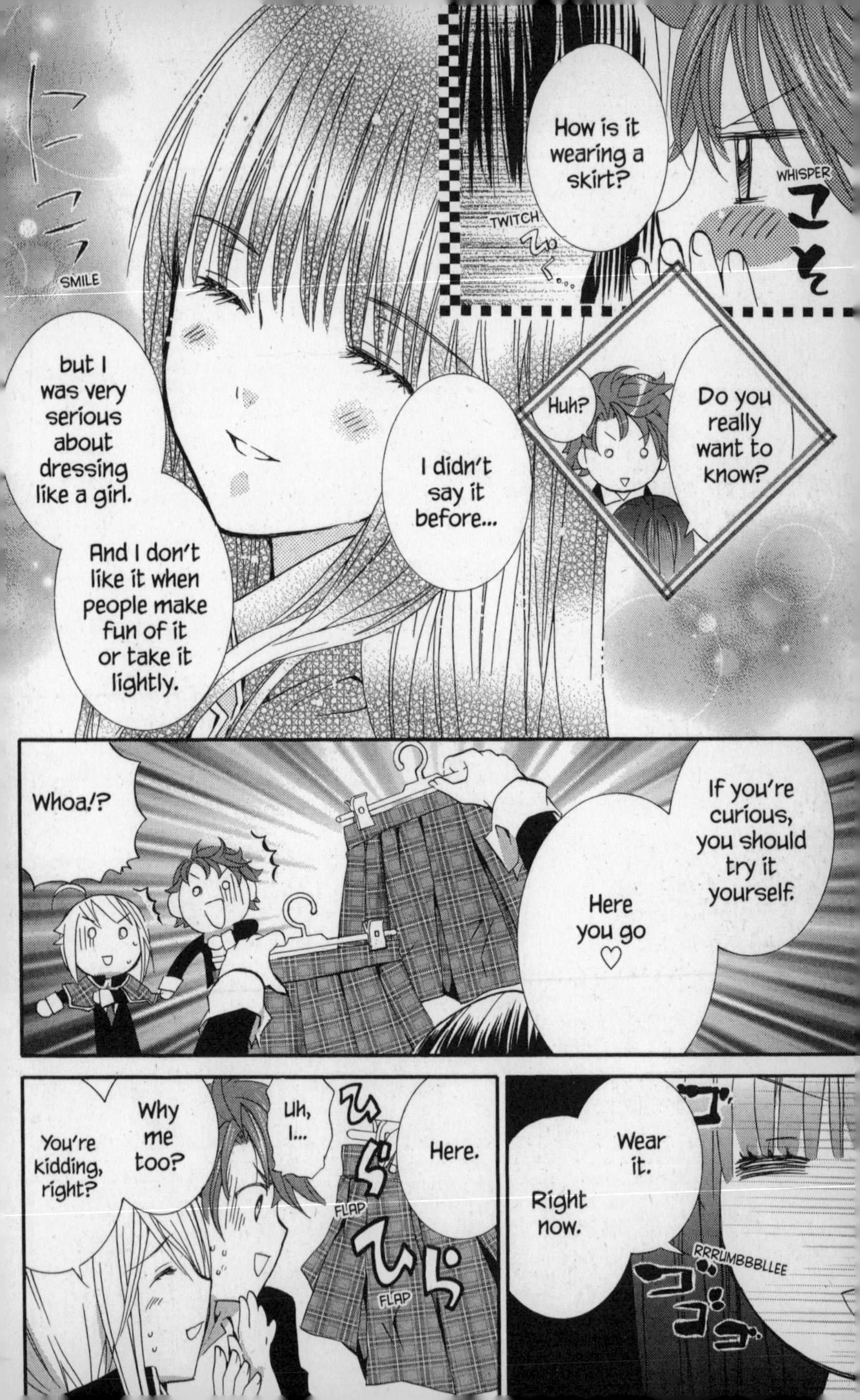
WHISPER
How is it wearing a skirt?
TWITCH
Do you really want to know?
Huh?
I didn't say it before...
but I was very serious about dressing like a girl.
And I don't like it when people make fun of it or take it lightly.
SMILE
If you're curious, you should try it yourself.
Here you go ♡
Whoa!?
Wear it.
Right now.
RRRUMBBBLLEE
Here.
FLAP
FLAP
Uh, I...
Why me too?
You're kidding, right?

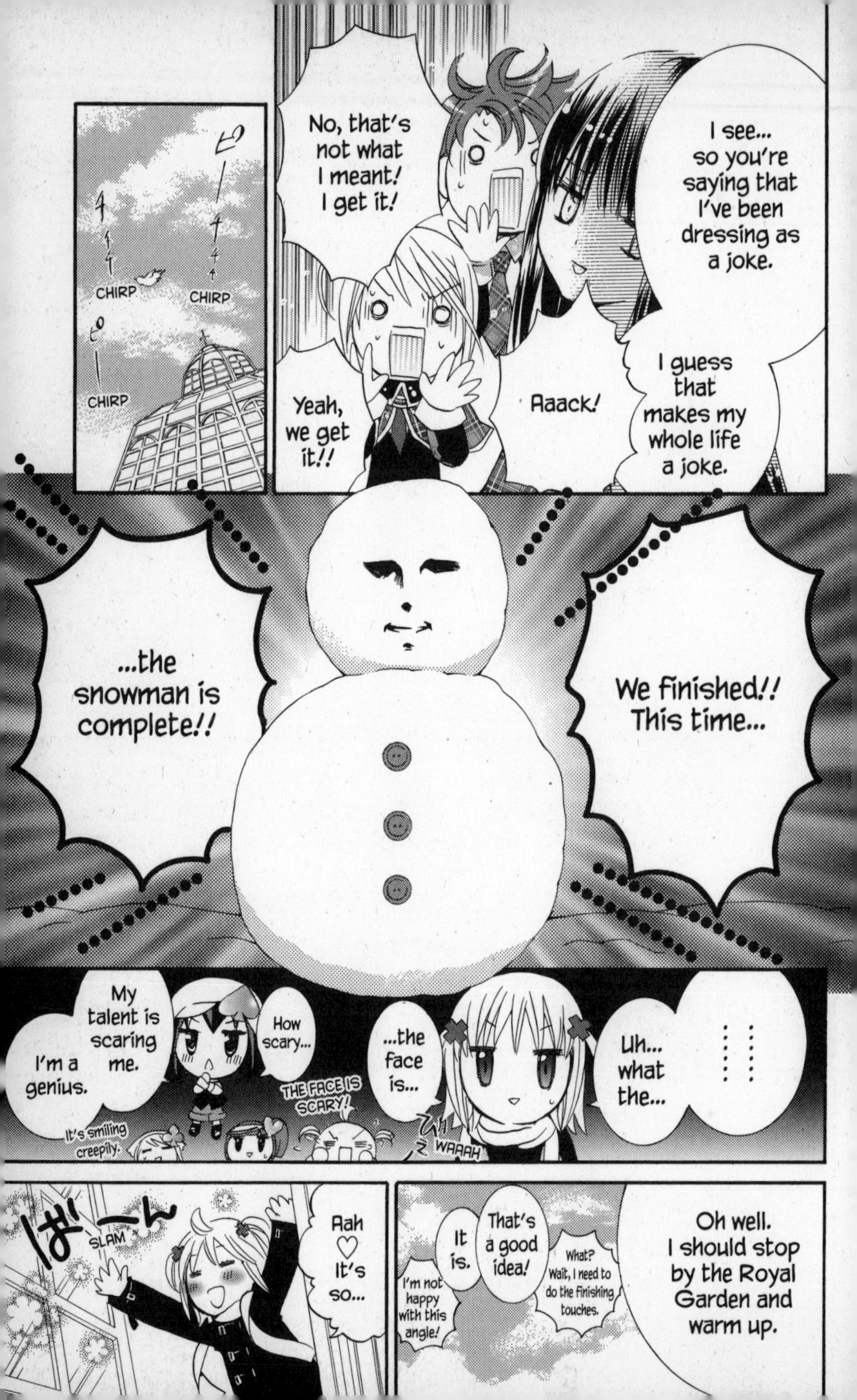
I see... so you're saying that I've been dressing as a joke.
No, that's not what I meant! I get it!
I guess that makes my whole life a joke.
Aaack!
Yeah, we get it!!
CHIRP
CHIRP
CHIRP
We finished!! This time...
...the snowman is complete!!
......
Uh... what the...
...the face is...
WAAAH
THE FACE IS SCARY!
How scary...
My talent is scaring me.
I'm a genius.
It's smiling creepily.
Oh well. I should stop by the Royal Garden and warm up.
What? Wait, I need to do the finishing touches.
That's a good idea!
It is.
I'm not happy with this angle!
Aah ♡ It's so...
SLAM

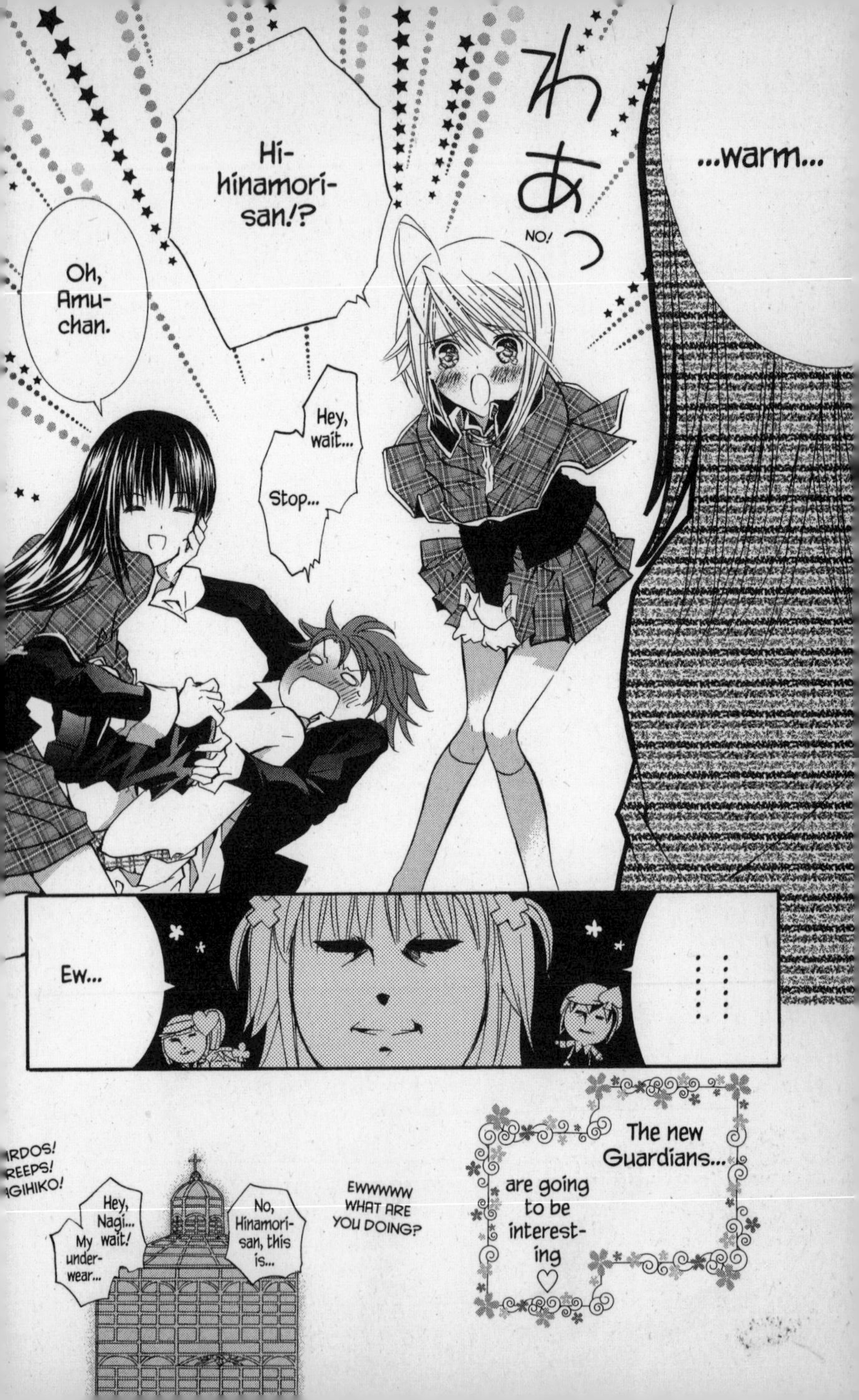
...warm...
わあっ
NO!
Hi-hinamori-san!?
Oh, Amu-chan.
Hey, wait...
Stop...
......
Ew...
The new Guardians...
are going to be interesting ♡
EWWWWW WHAT ARE YOU DOING?
No, Hinamori-san, this is...
Hey, Nagi... wait!
My underwear...
RDOS!
REEPS!
GIHIKO!

Shugo
Chara!

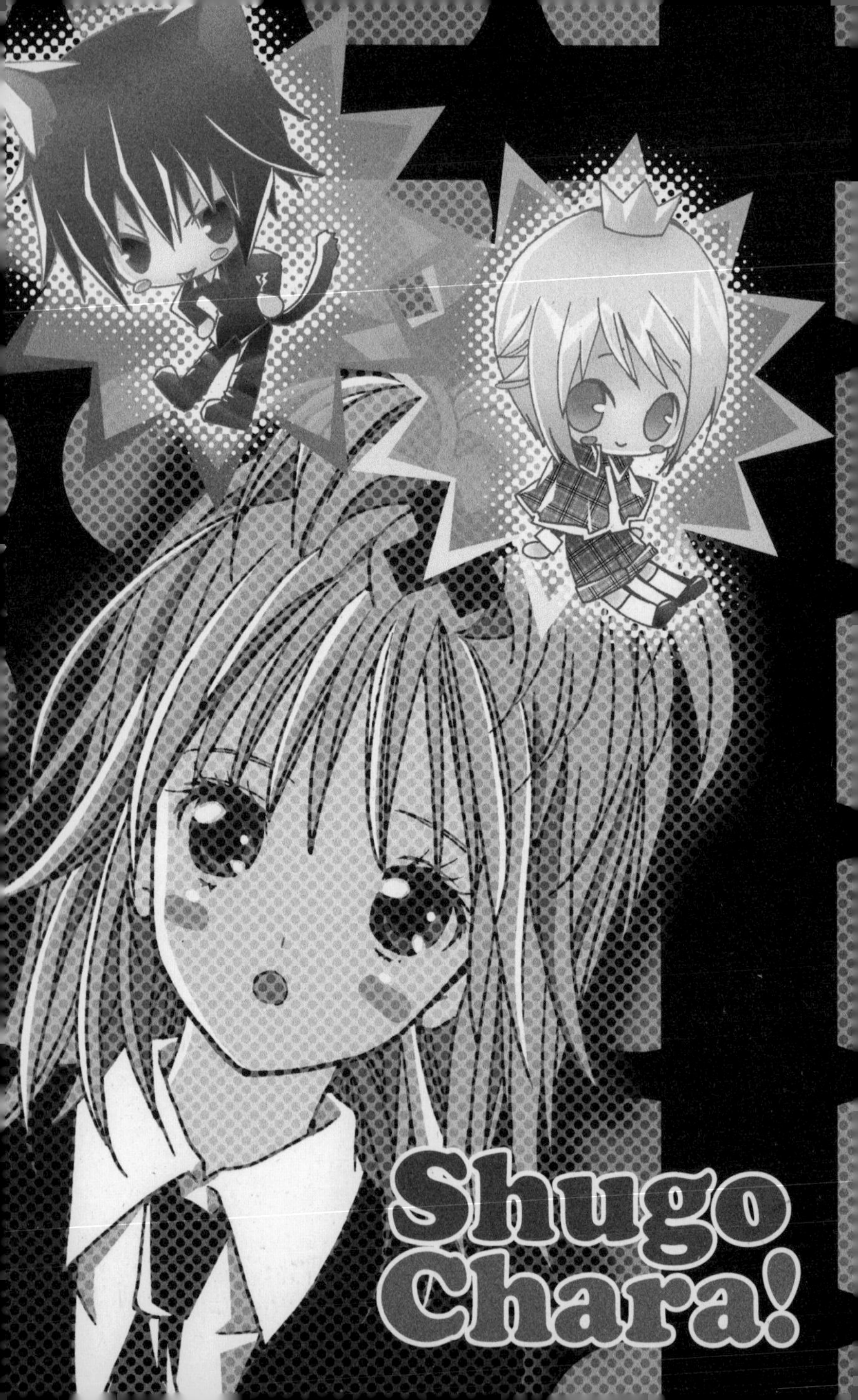
Shugo
Chara!

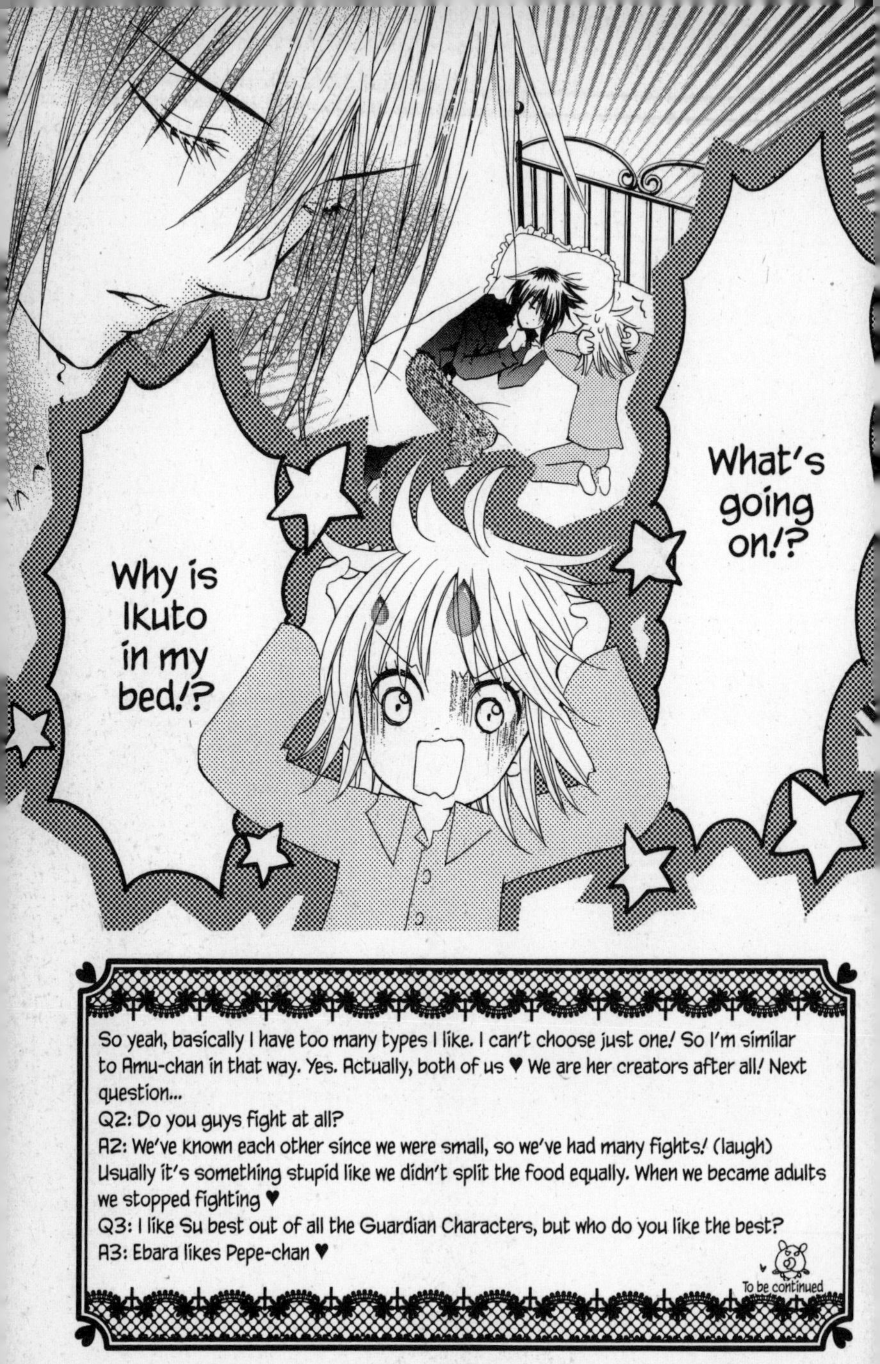
What's going on!?
Why is Ikuto in my bed!?

So yeah, basically I have too many types I like. I can't choose just one! So I'm similar to Amu-chan in that way. Yes. Actually, both of us ♥ We are her creators after all! Next question...

Q2: Do you guys fight at all?

A2: We've known each other since we were small, so we've had many fights! (laugh) Usually it's something stupid like we didn't split the food equally. When we became adults we stopped fighting ♥

Q3: I like Su best out of all the Guardian Characters, but who do you like the best?

A3: Ebara likes Pepe-chan ♥

To be continued

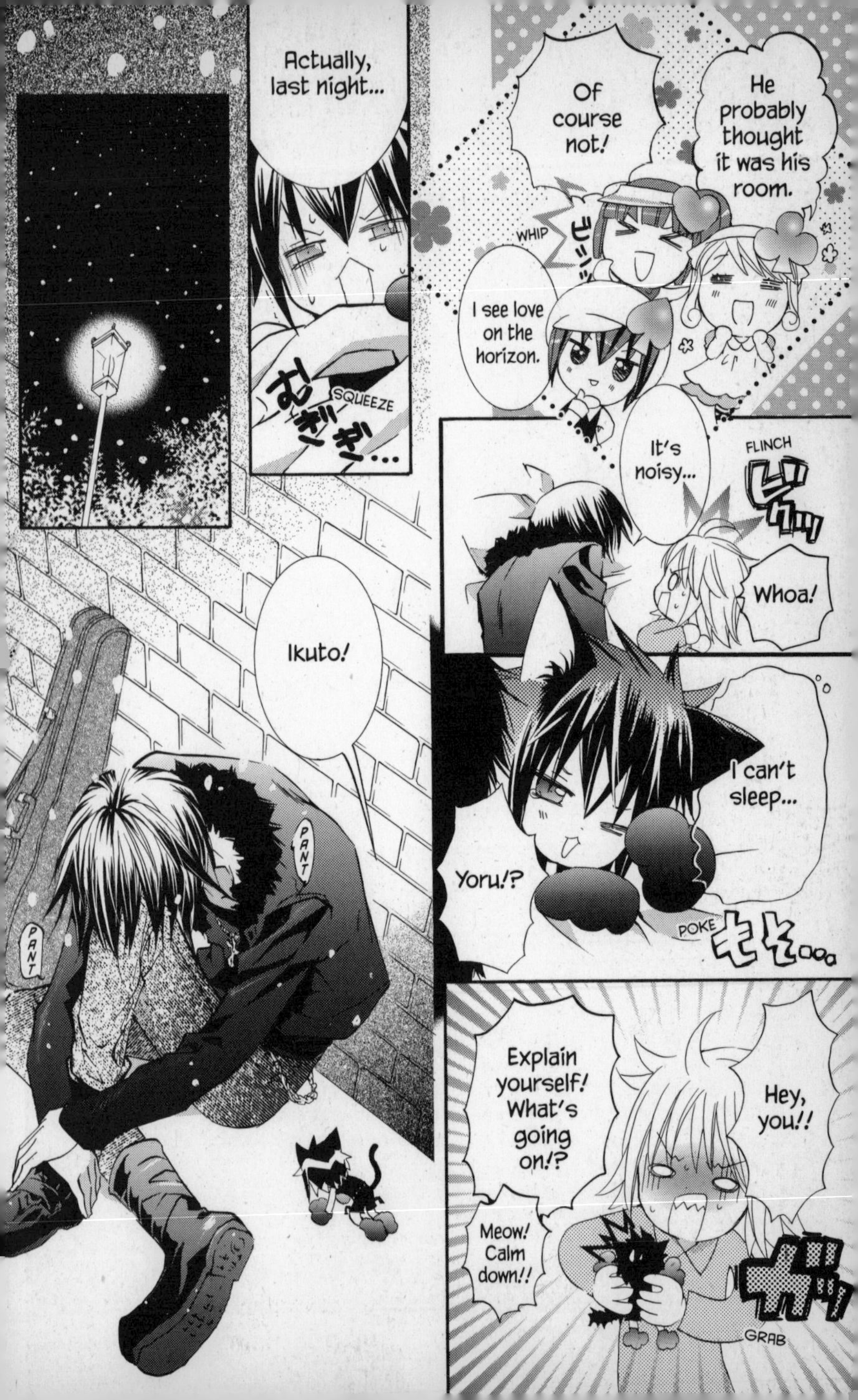

He probably thought it was his room.
Of course not!
WHIP
I see love on the horizon.
FLINCH
It's noisy...
Whoa!
I can't sleep...
Yoru!?
POKE
Hey, you!!
Explain yourself! What's going on!?
GRAB
Meow! Calm down!!
Actually, last night...
SQUEEZE
Ikuto!
PANT
PANT

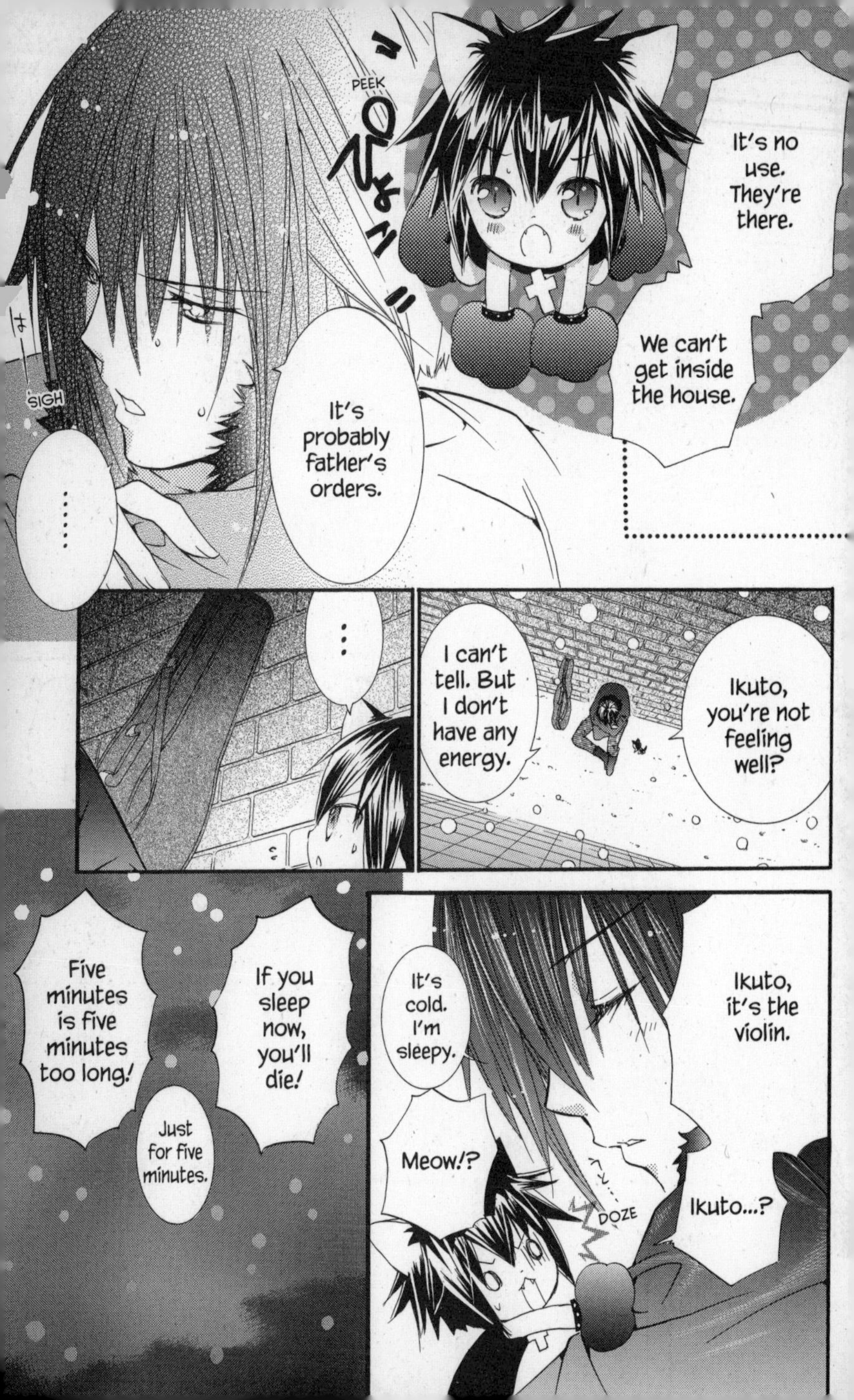

It's no use. They're there.
We can't get inside the house.
PEEK
It's probably father's orders.
SIGH
......
Ikuto, you're not feeling well?
I can't tell. But I don't have any energy.
...
Ikuto, it's the violin.
It's cold. I'm sleepy.
Ikuto...?
DOZE
Meow!?
If you sleep now, you'll die!
Five minutes is five minutes too long!
Just for five minutes.

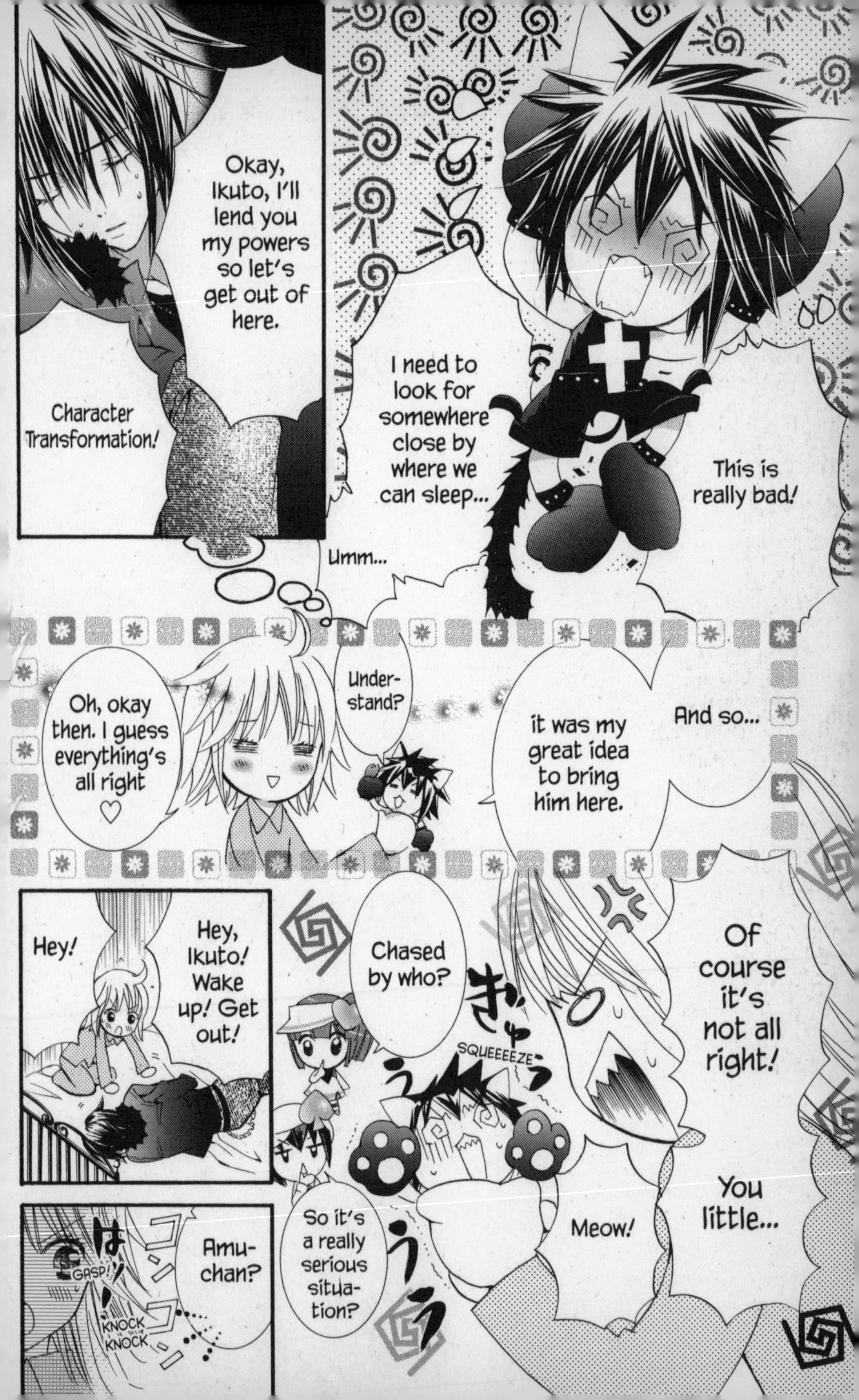

This is really bad!
I need to look for somewhere close by where we can sleep...
Okay, Ikuto, I'll lend you my powers so let's get out of here.
Character Transformation!
Umm...
And so...
it was my great idea to bring him here.
Understand?
Oh, okay then. I guess everything's all right ♡
Of course it's not all right!
You little...
SQUEEEEZE
Meow!
Chased by who?
So it's a really serious situation?
Hey, Ikuto! Wake up! Get out!
Hey!
Amu-chan?
GASP!
KNOCK KNOCK

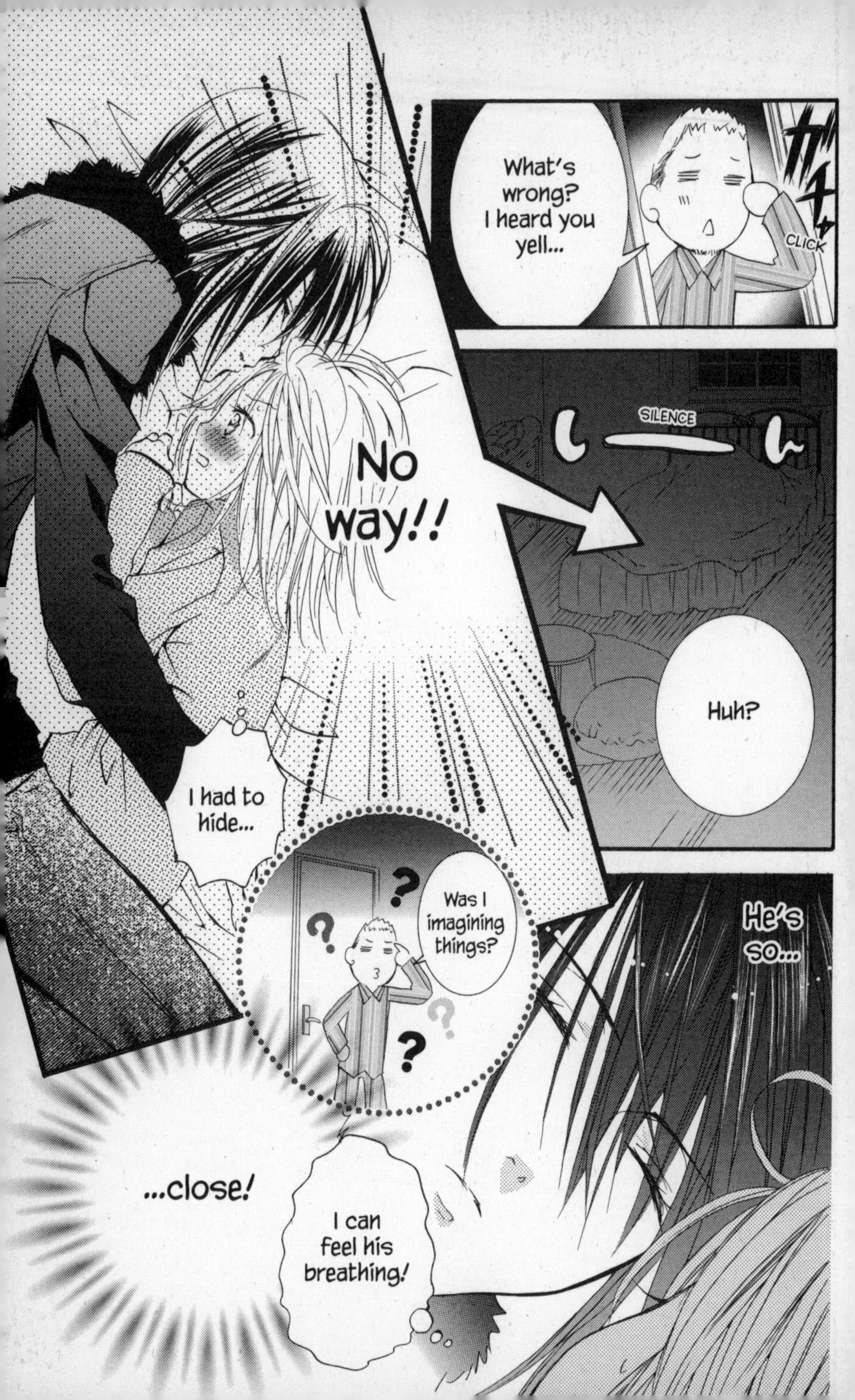
What's wrong? I heard you yell...
CLICK
SILENCE
Huh?
No way!!
I had to hide...
Was I imagining things?
He's so...
...close!
I can feel his breathing!

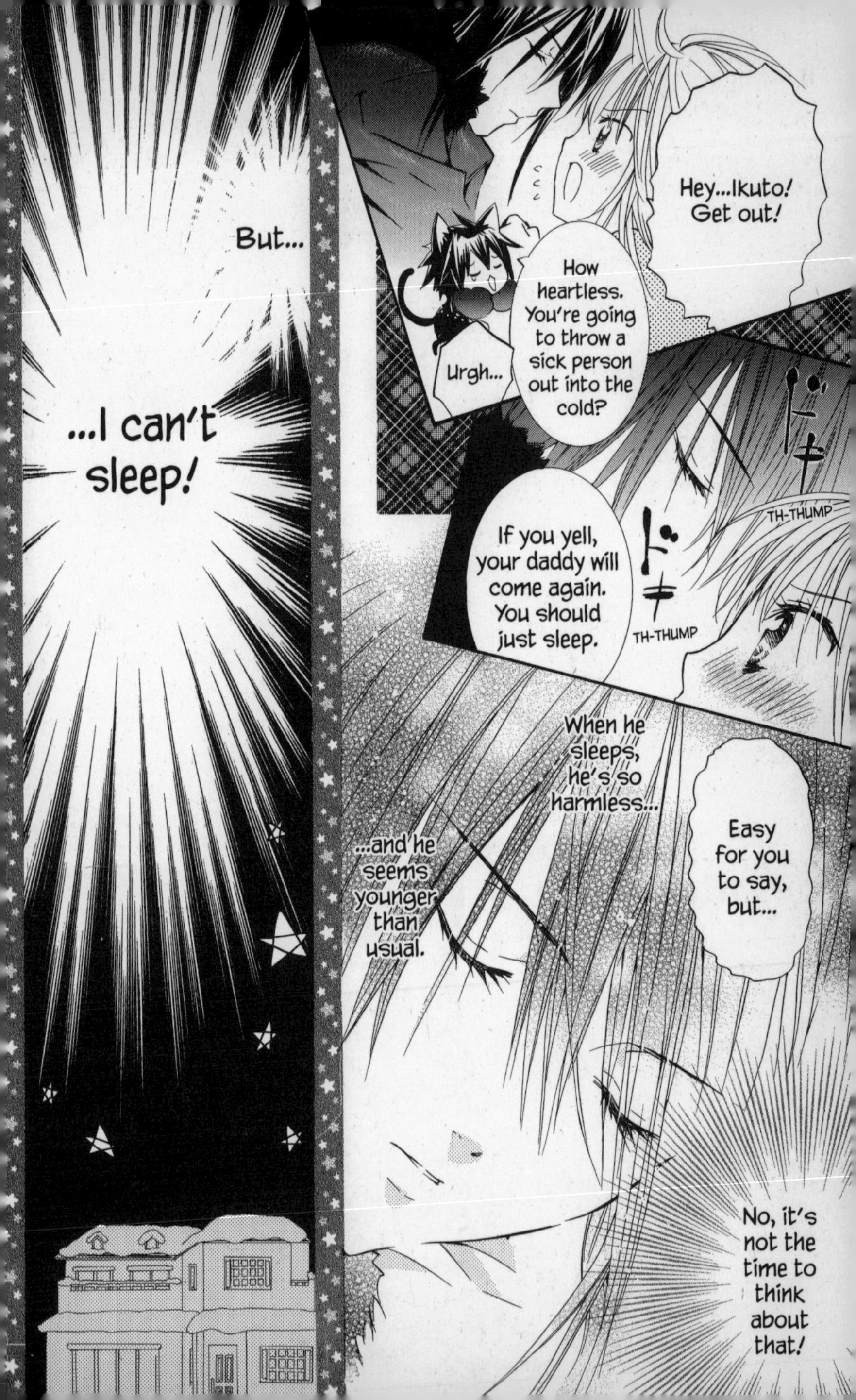

Hey...Ikuto! Get out!
How heartless. You're going to throw a sick person out into the cold?
Urgh...
ドキ
TH-THUMP
ドキ
TH-THUMP
If you yell, your daddy will come again. You should just sleep.
Easy for you to say, but...
When he sleeps, he's so harmless...
...and he seems younger than usual.
No, it's not the time to think about that!
But...
...I can't sleep!

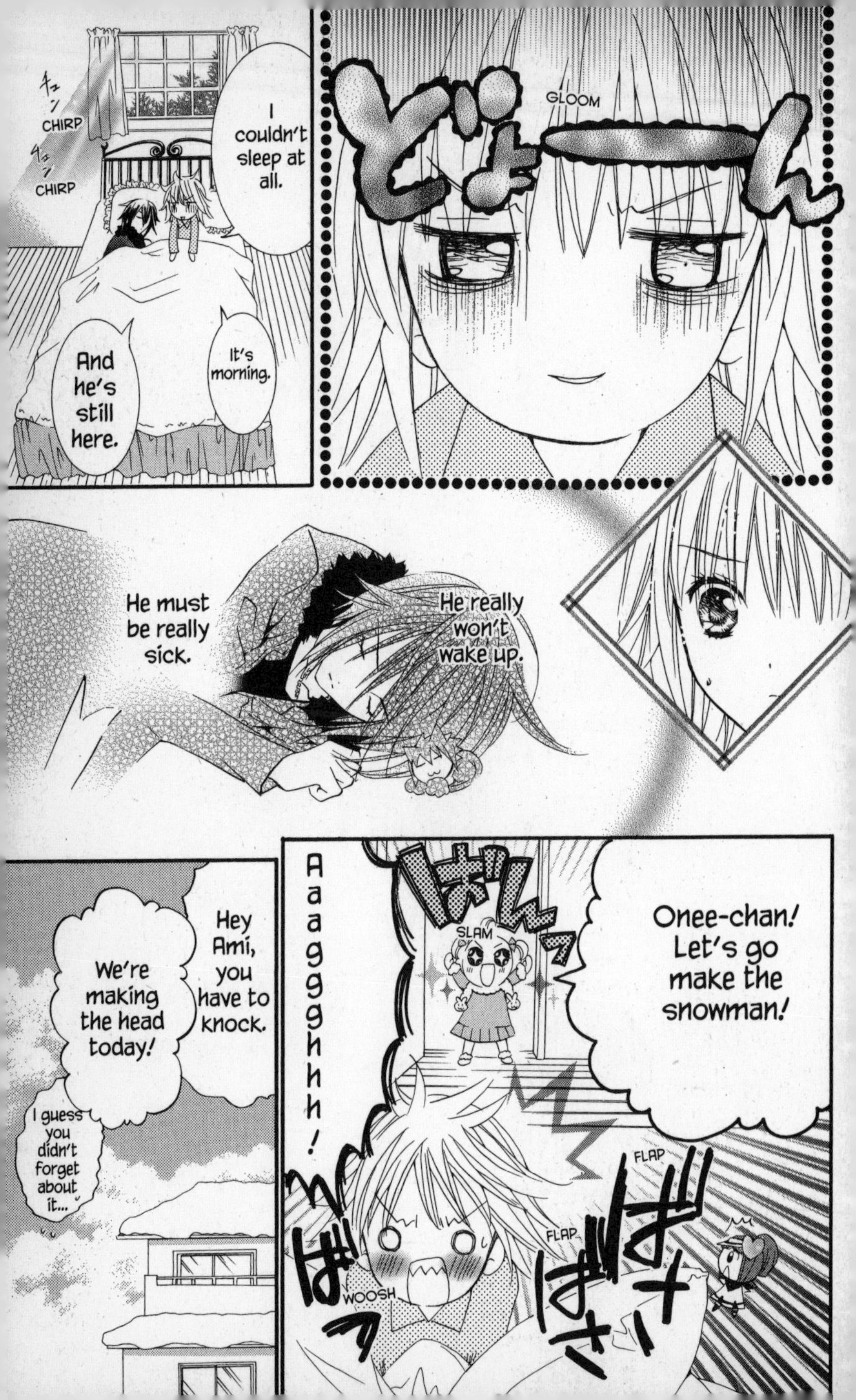
どよーん
GLOOM
チュン
CHIRP
チュン
CHIRP
I couldn't sleep at all.
It's morning.
And he's still here.
He really won't wake up.
He must be really sick.
Onee-chan! Let's go make the snowman!
SLAM
Aaaggghhhh!
FLAP
FLAP
WOOSH
Hey Ami, you have to knock.
We're making the head today!
I guess you didn't forget about it...

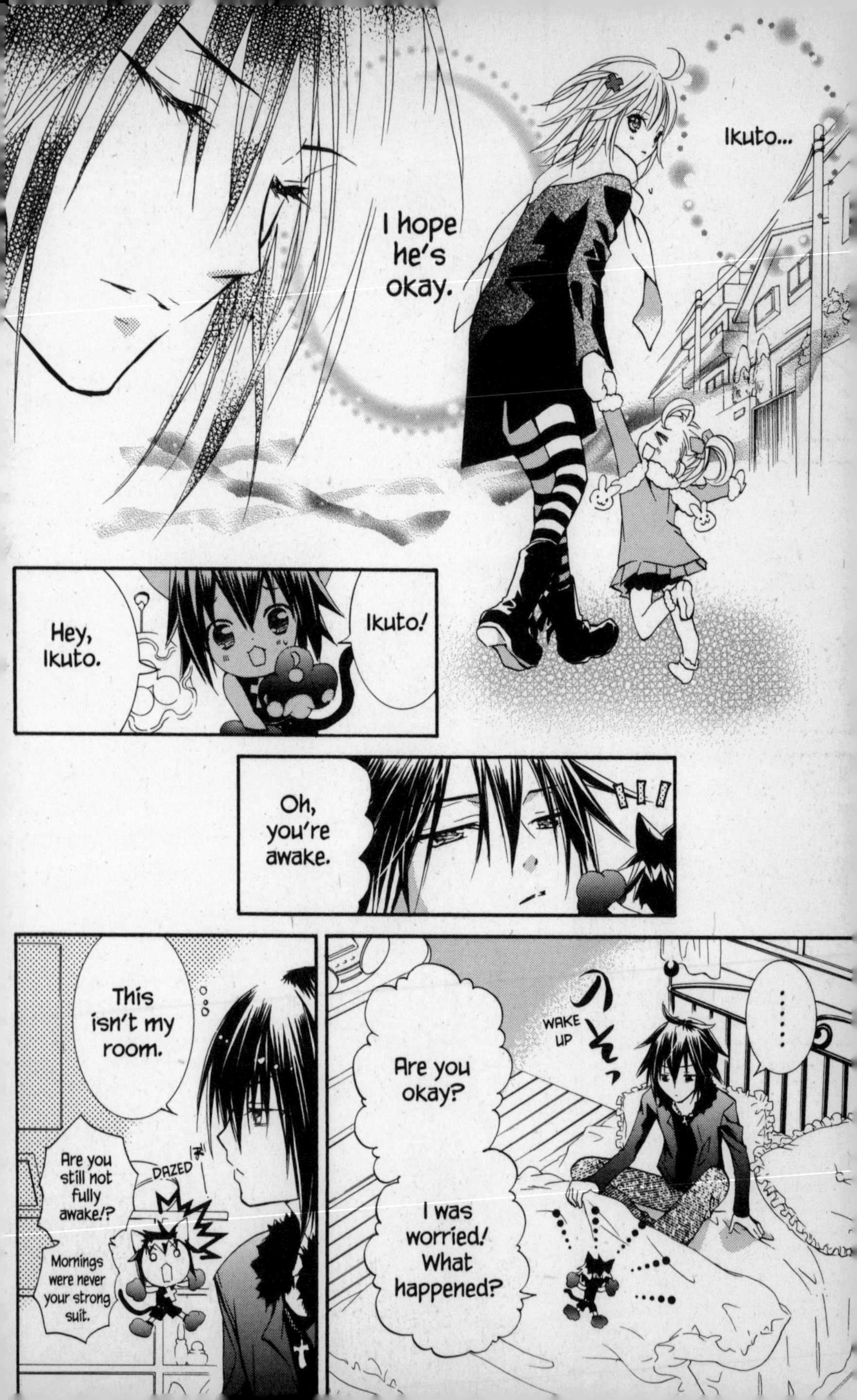
Ikuto...
I hope he's okay.
Ikuto!
Hey, Ikuto.
Oh, you're awake.
......
WAKE UP
Are you okay?
I was worried! What happened?
This isn't my room.
DAZED
Are you still not fully awake!?
Mornings were never your strong suit.

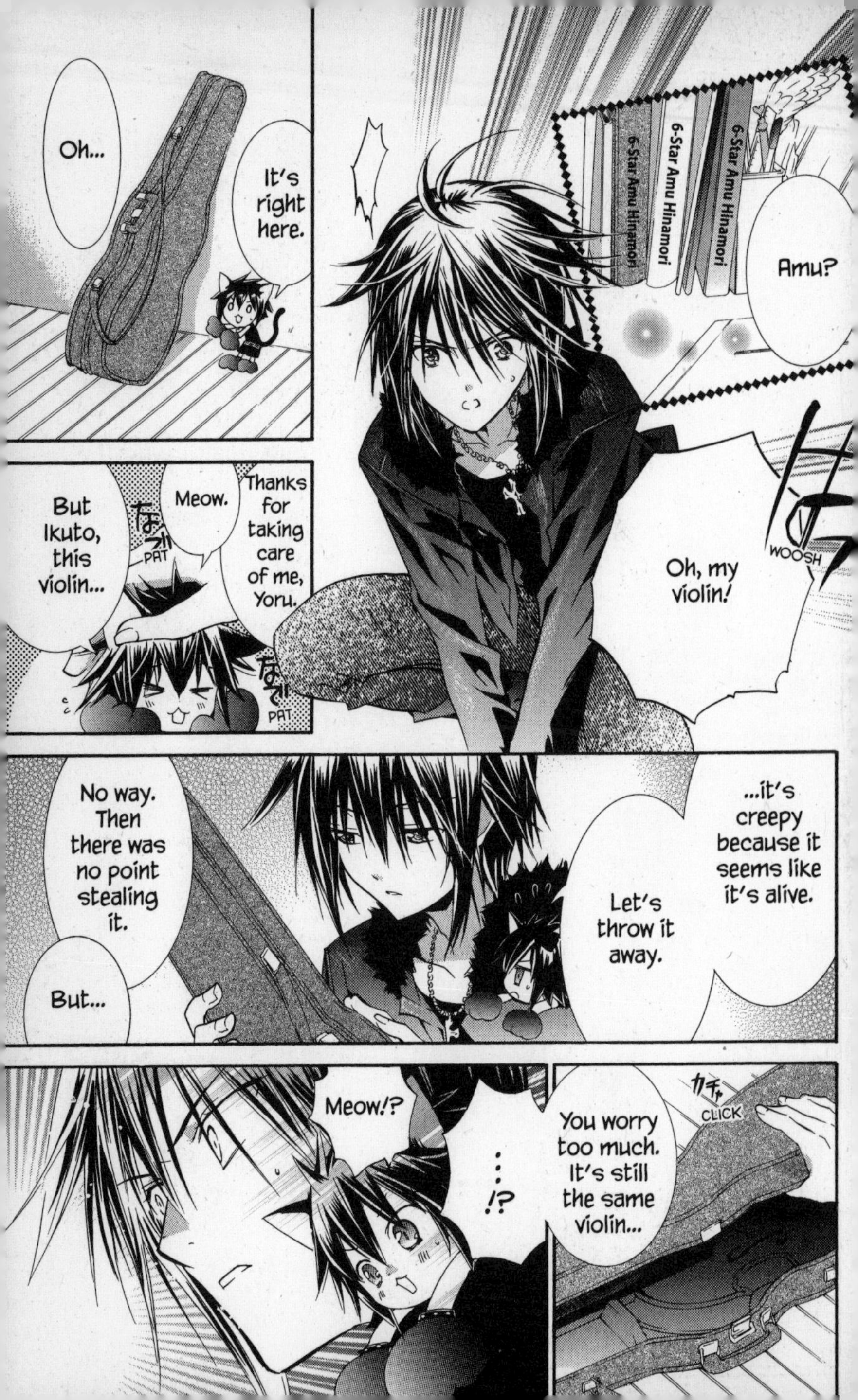

Amu?
6-Star Amu Hinamori
6-Star Amu Hinamori
6-Star Amu Hinamori
WOOSH
Oh, my violin!
It's right here.
Oh...
Thanks for taking care of me, Yoru.
Meow.
PAT
But Ikuto, this violin...
PAT
...it's creepy because it seems like it's alive.
Let's throw it away.
No way. Then there was no point stealing it.
But...
CLICK
You worry too much. It's still the same violin...
...!?
Meow!?

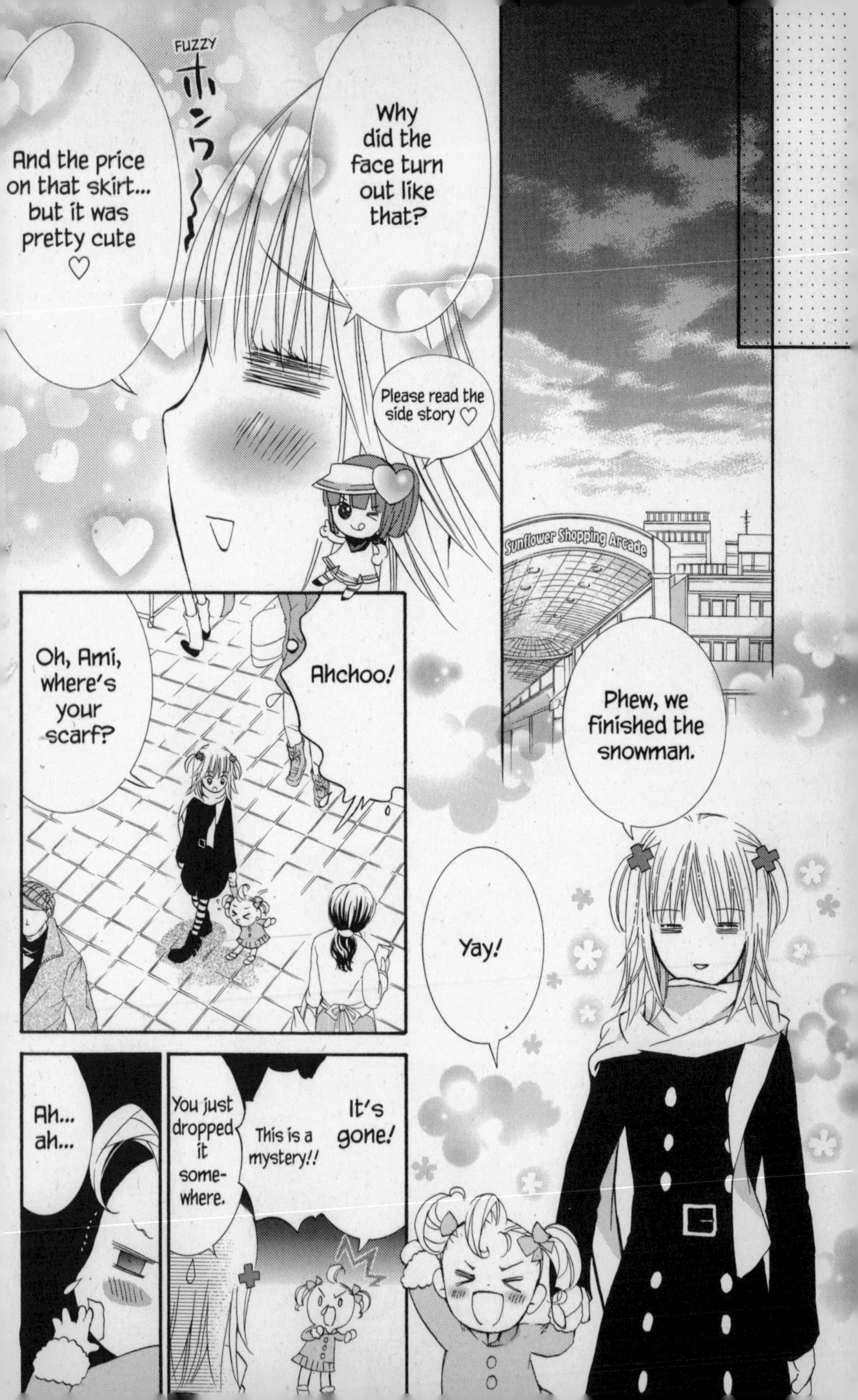
Sunflower Shopping Arcade
Phew, we finished the snowman.
Yay!
Why did the face turn out like that?
FUZZY
ホンワ〜
And the price on that skirt... but it was pretty cute ♡
Please read the side story ♡
Ahchoo!
Oh, Ami, where's your scarf?
It's gone!
This is a mystery!!
You just dropped it some-where.
Ah... ah...

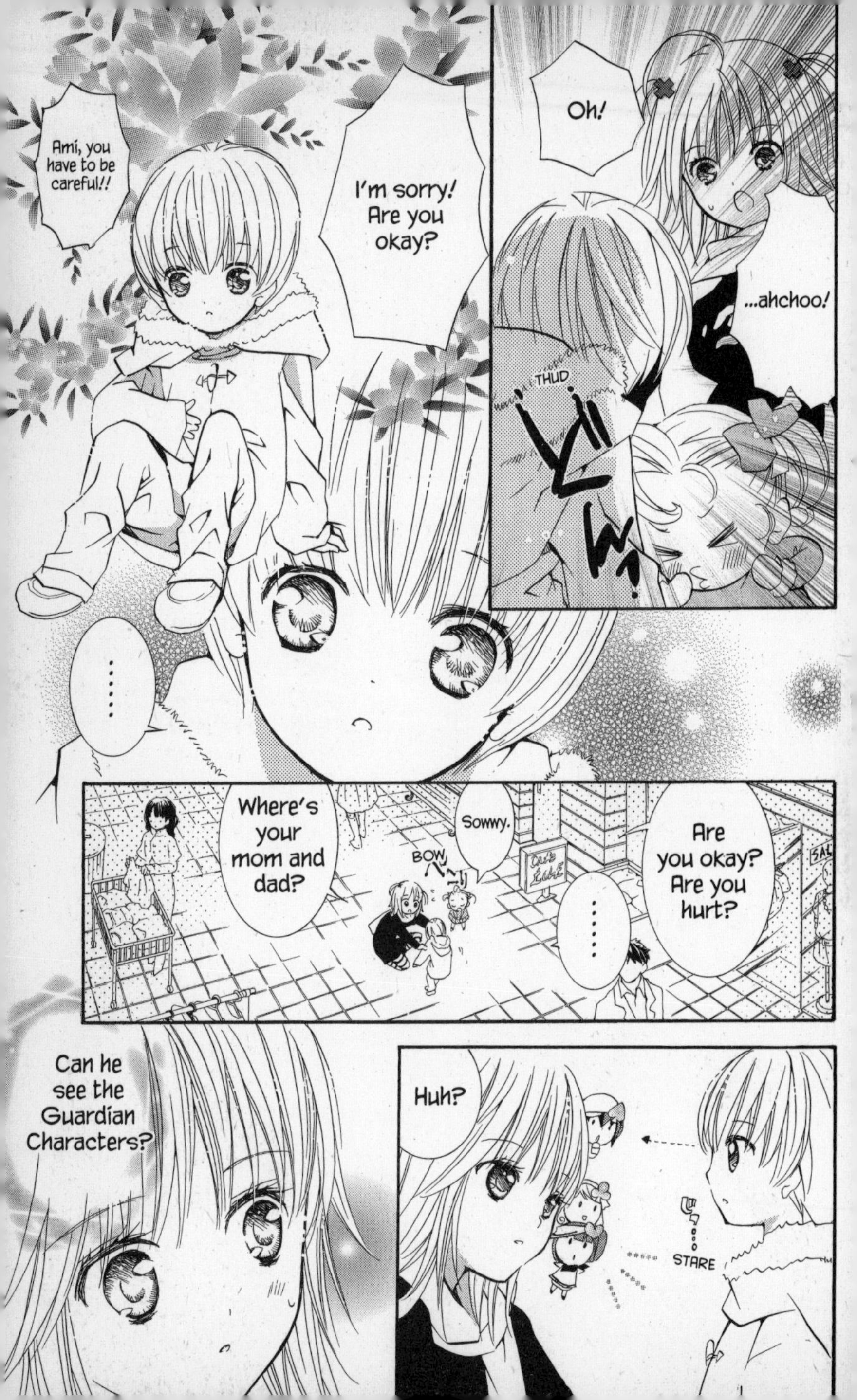
Oh!
...ahchoo!
THUD
I'm sorry! Are you okay?
Ami, you have to be careful!!
......
Are you okay? Are you hurt?
......
Sowwy.
BOW
Where's your mom and dad?
Huh?
STARE
Can he see the Guardian Characters?

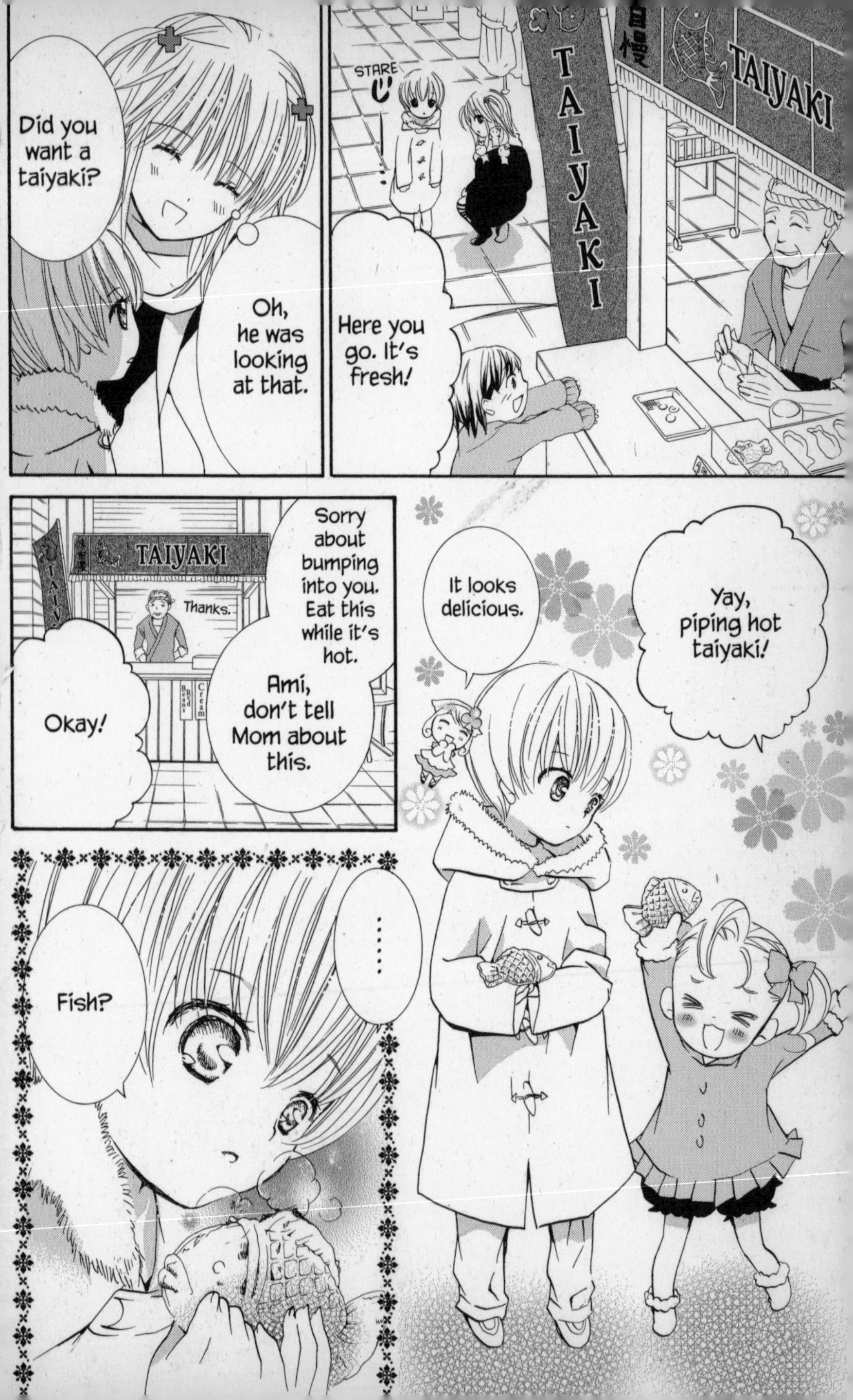
TAIYAKI
TAIYAKI
STARE
Here you go. It's fresh!
Oh, he was looking at that.
Did you want a taiyaki?
Yay, piping hot taiyaki!
It looks delicious.
Sorry about bumping into you. Eat this while it's hot.
TAIYAKI
Thanks.
Ami, don't tell Mom about this.
Cream
Red Beans
Okay!
......
Fish?

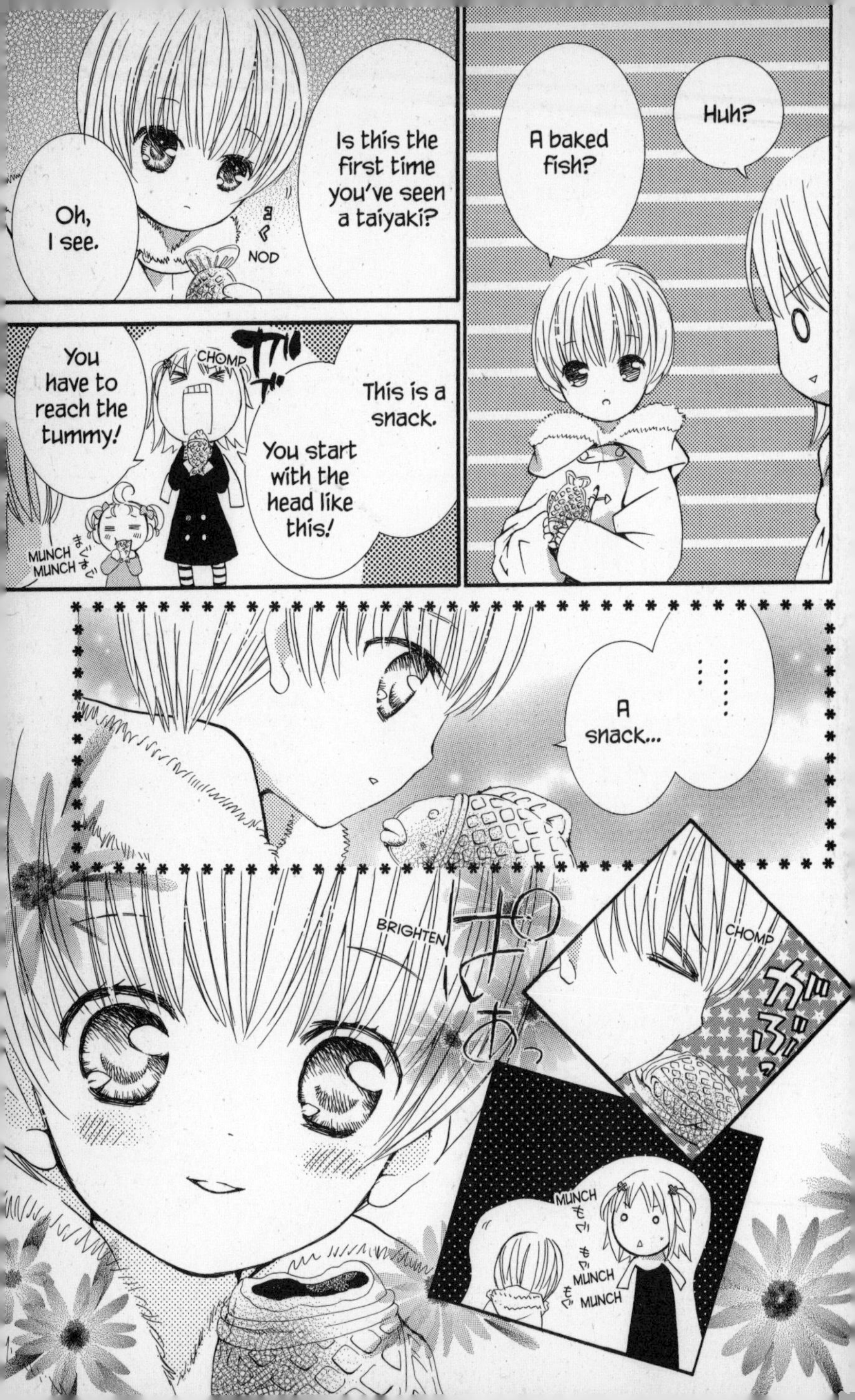
Huh?
A baked fish?
Is this the first time you've seen a taiyaki?
Oh, I see.
NOD
This is a snack.
You start with the head like this!
CHOMP
You have to reach the tummy!
MUNCH MUNCH
......
A snack...
CHOMP
MUNCH
MUNCH
MUNCH
BRIGHTEN

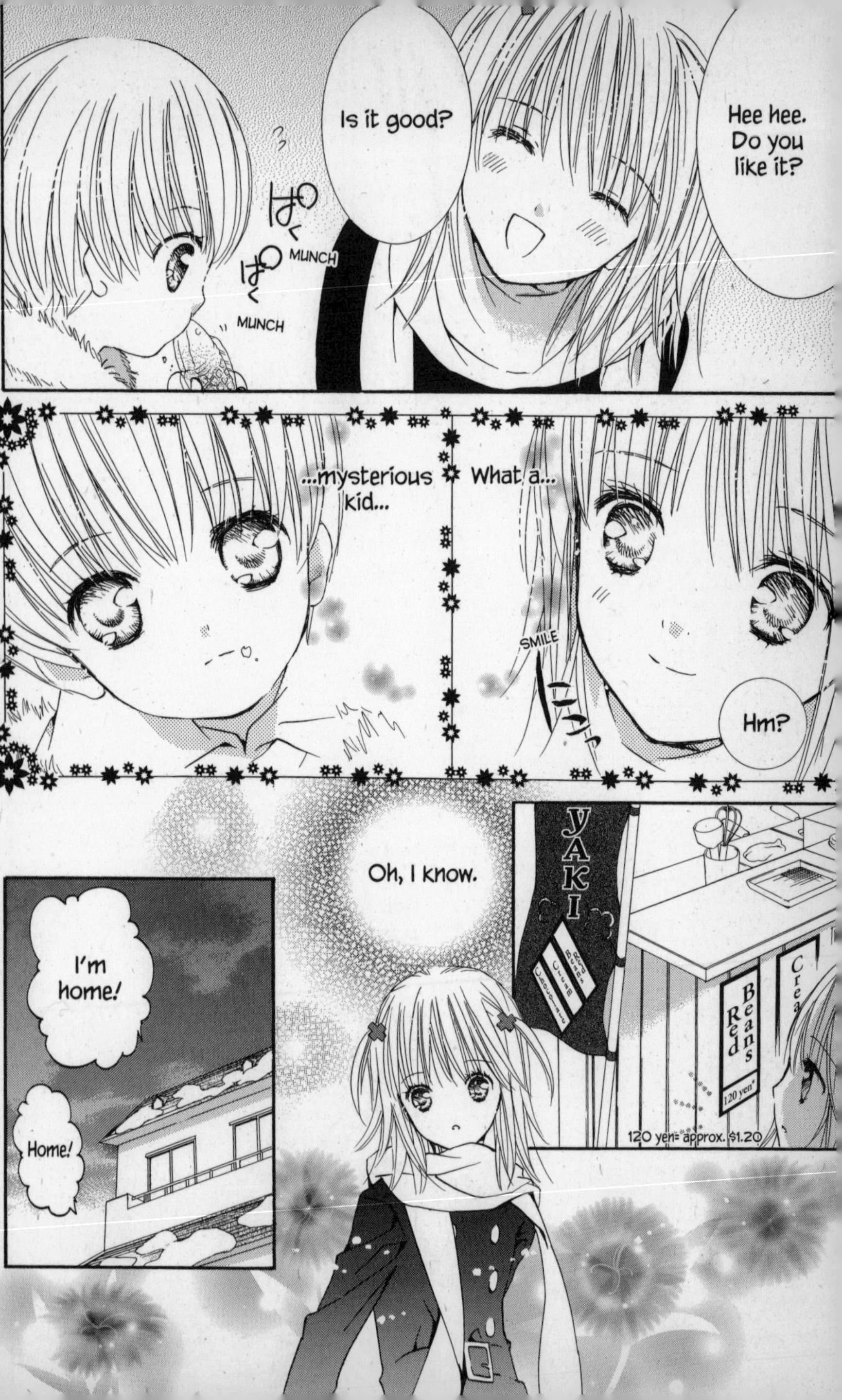
Hee hee. Do you like it?
Is it good?
ぱく
MUNCH
ぱく
MUNCH
What a...
SMILE
Hm?
...mysterious kid...
YAKI
Crea
Red Beans
120 yen*
120 yen= approx. $1.20
Oh, I know.
I'm home!
Home!

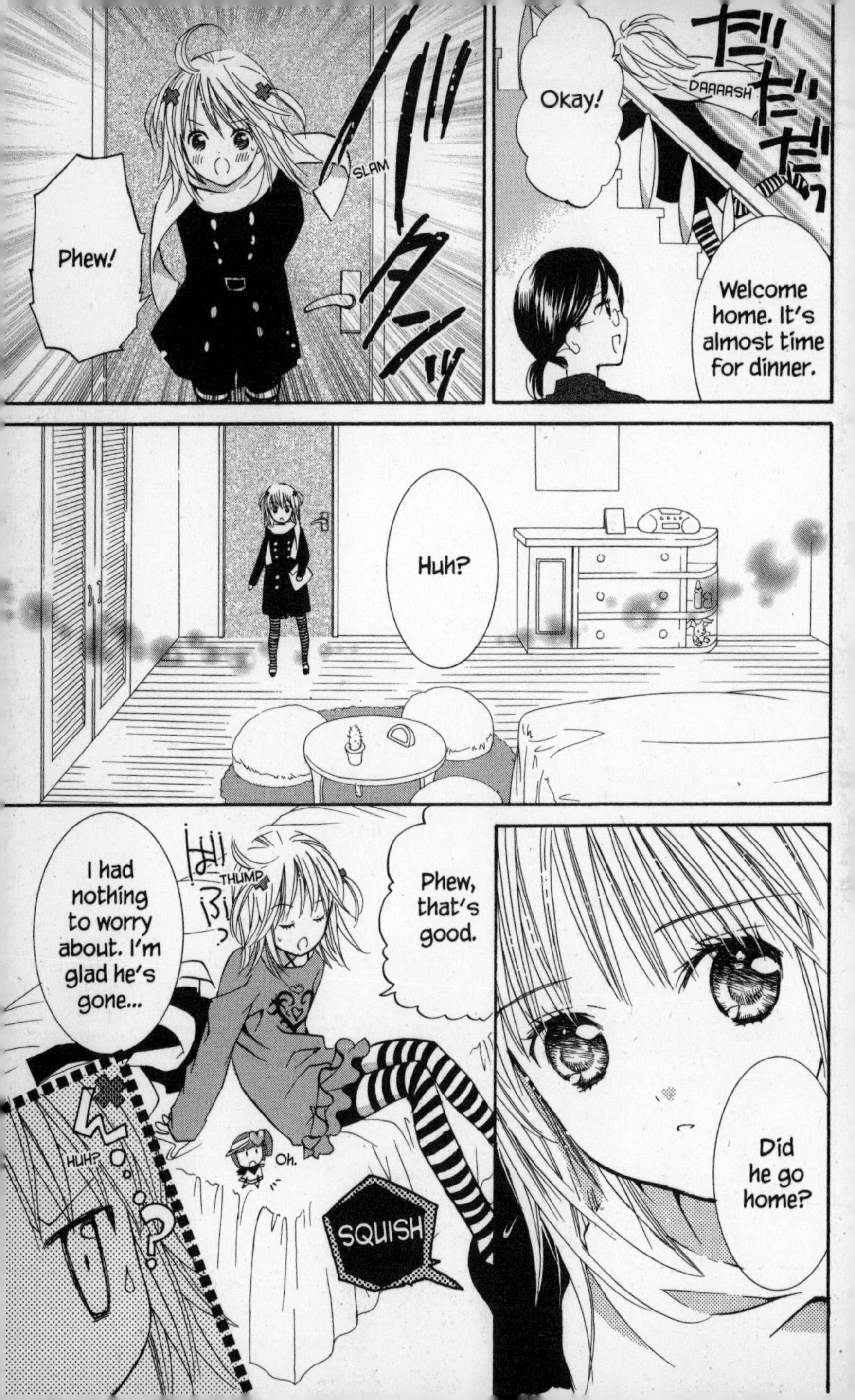

だだだっ
DAAAASH
Okay!
Welcome home. It's almost time for dinner.
バタンッ
SLAM
Phew!
Huh?
Did he go home?
Phew, that's good.
THUMP
I had nothing to worry about. I'm glad he's gone...
SQUISH
Oh.
HUH?

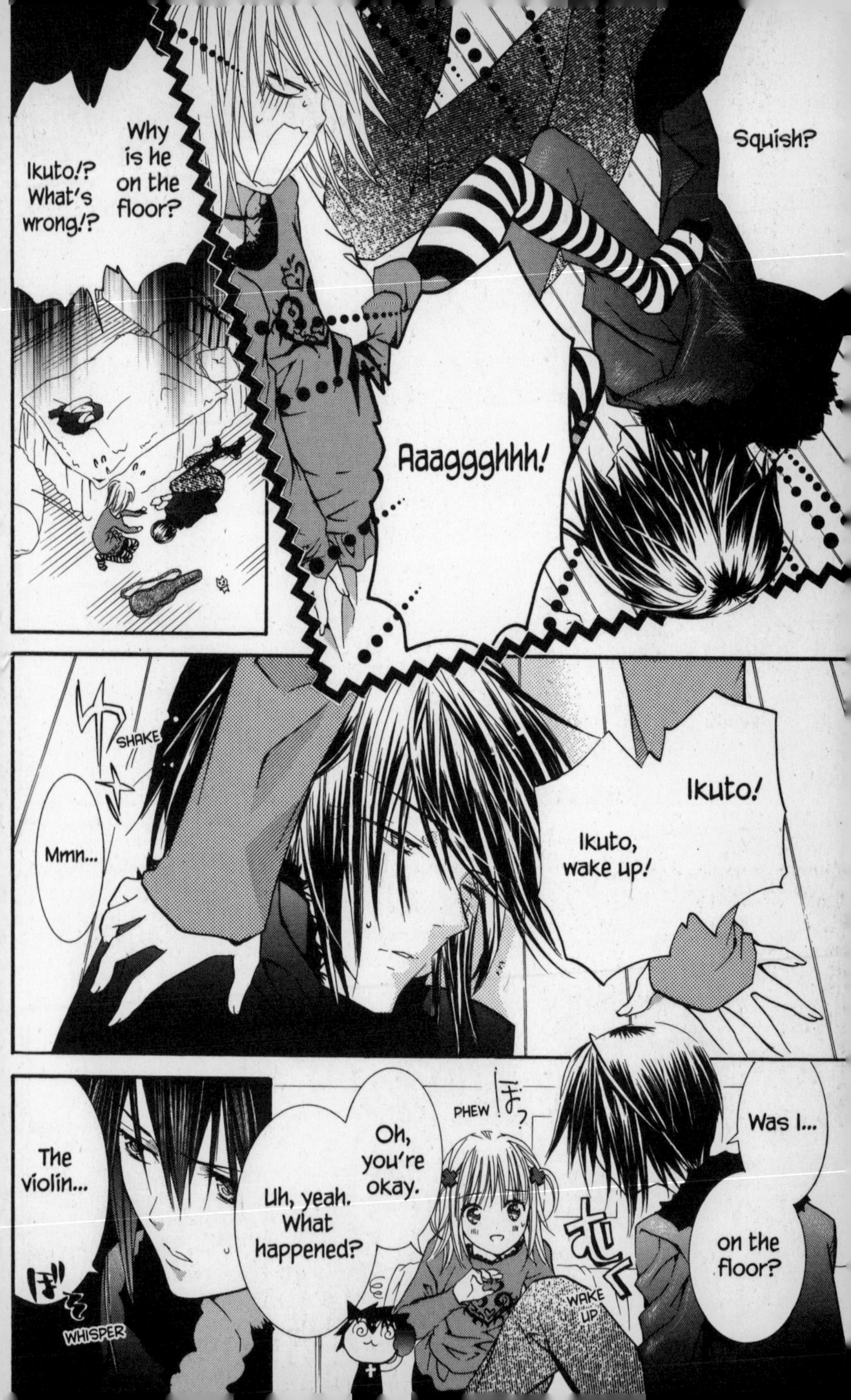
Squish?
Aaaggghhh!
Why is he on the floor?
Ikuto!? What's wrong!?
Ikuto!
Ikuto, wake up!
SHAKE
Mmn...
Was I...
on the floor?
PHEW
Oh, you're okay.
Uh, yeah. What happened?
WAKE UP
The violin...
WHISPER

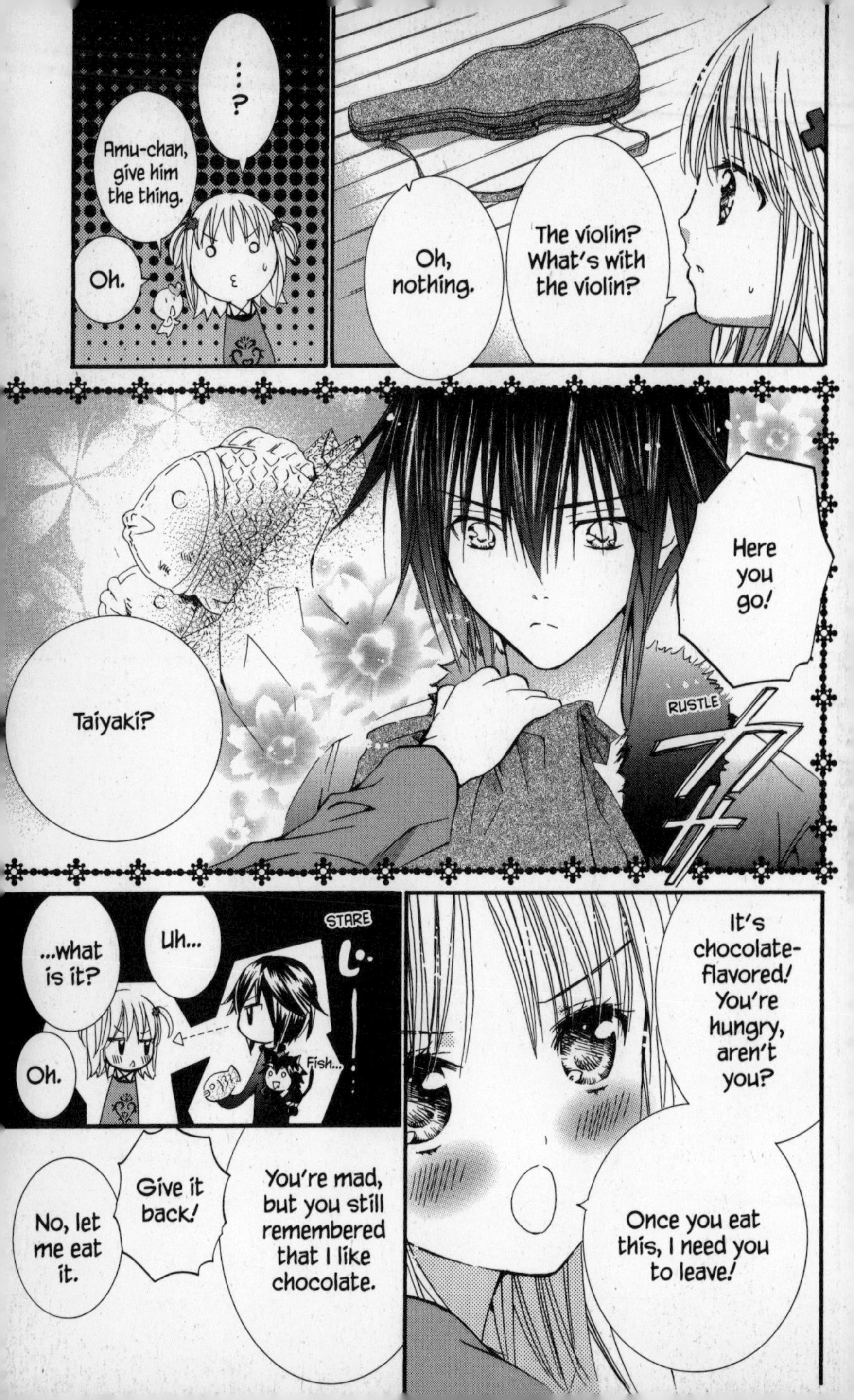
The violin? What's with the violin?
Oh, nothing.
...?
Amu-chan, give him the thing.
Oh.
Here you go!
RUSTLE
Taiyaki?
It's chocolate-flavored! You're hungry, aren't you?
Once you eat this, I need you to leave!
STARE
Uh...
...what is it?
Fish...
Oh.
You're mad, but you still remembered that I like chocolate.
Give it back!
No, let me eat it.

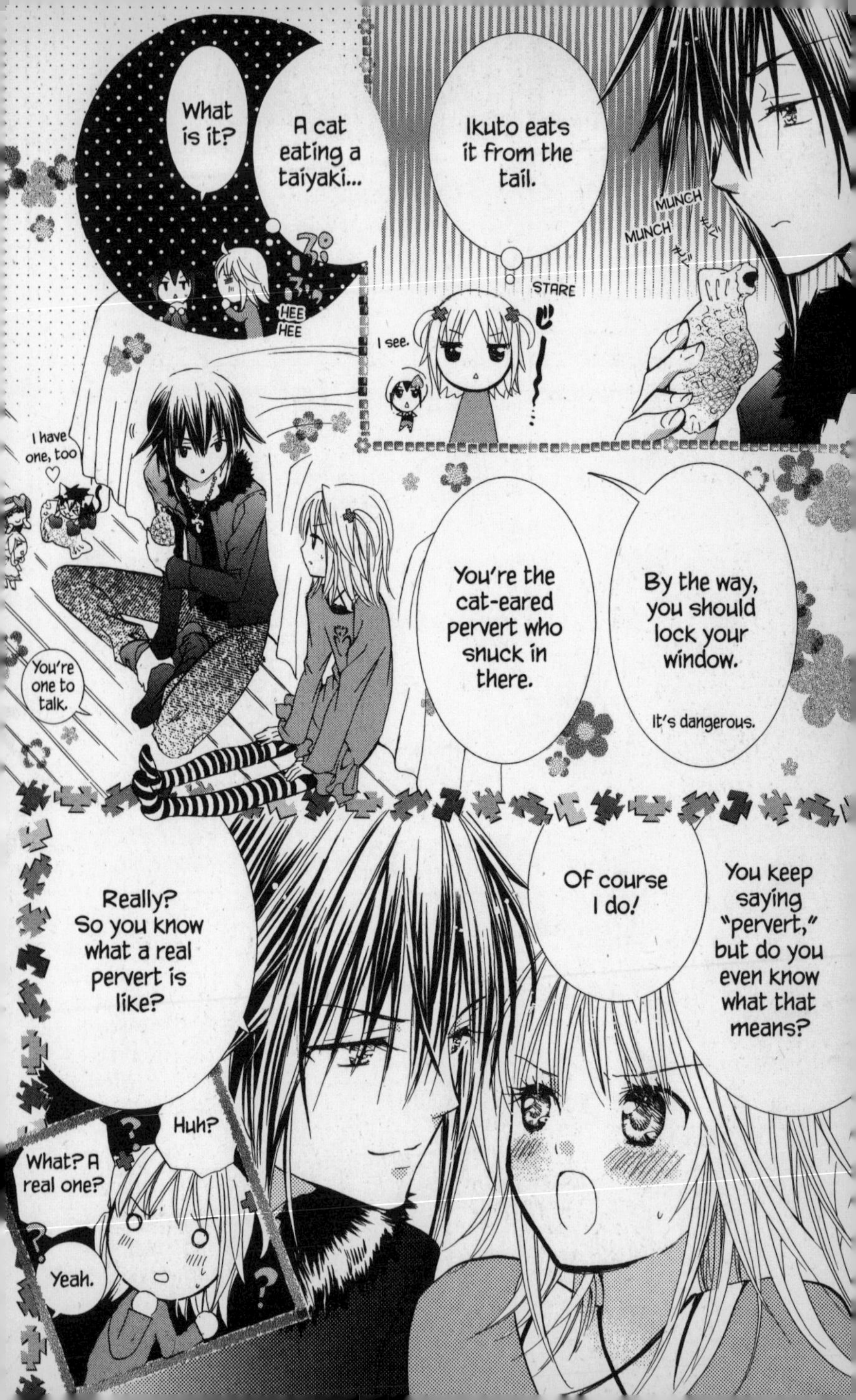
MUNCH
MUNCH
Ikuto eats it from the tail.
STARE
I see.
A cat eating a taiyaki...
What is it?
HEE HEE
By the way, you should lock your window.
It's dangerous.
You're the cat-eared pervert who snuck in there.
I have one, too ♡
You're one to talk.
You keep saying "pervert," but do you even know what that means?
Of course I do!
Really? So you know what a real pervert is like?
Huh?
What? A real one?
Yeah.

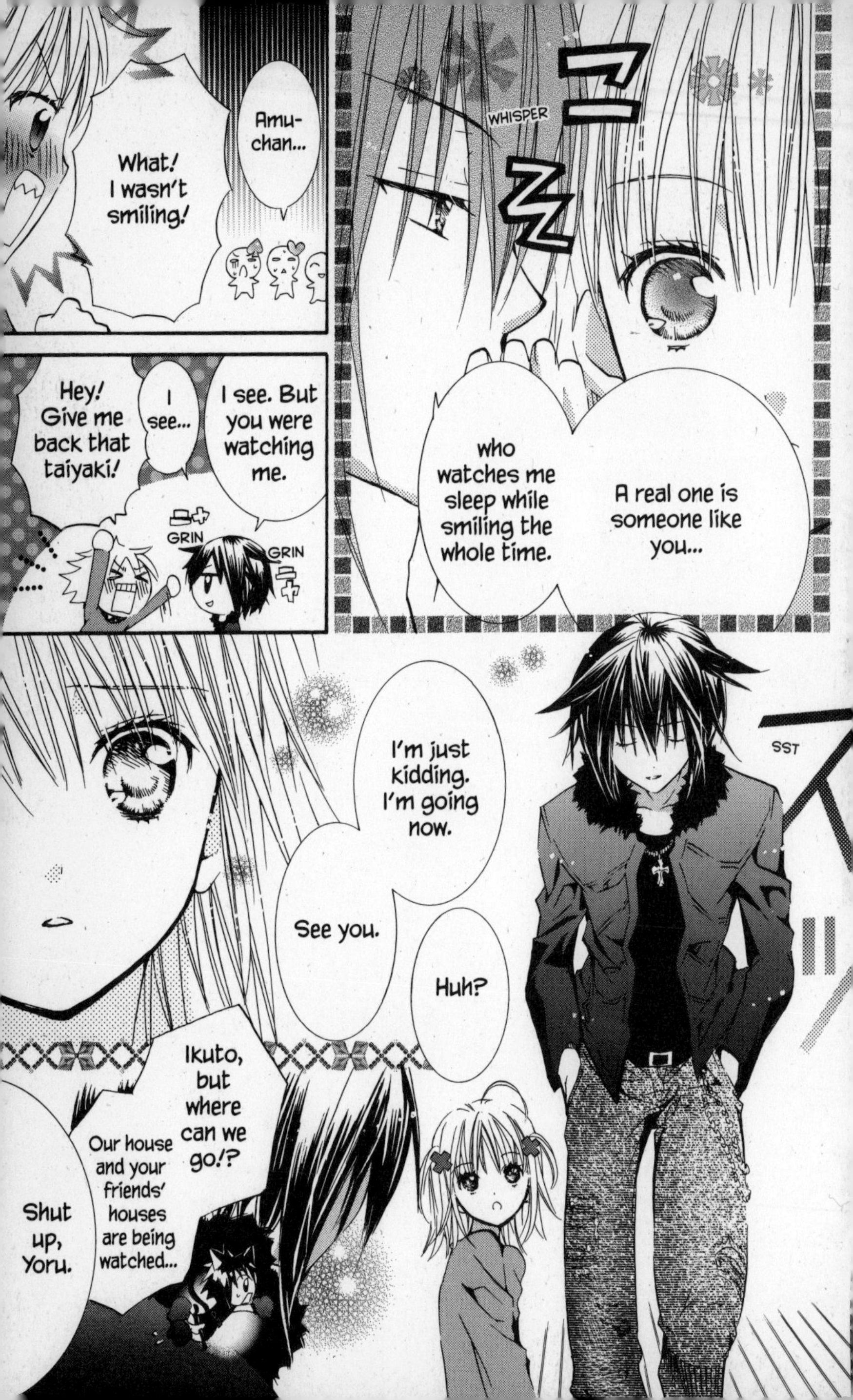
WHISPER
A real one is someone like you...
who watches me sleep while smiling the whole time.
Amu-chan...
What! I wasn't smiling!
I see. But you were watching me.
I see...
Hey! Give me back that taiyaki!
GRIN
GRIN
SST
I'm just kidding. I'm going now.
See you.
Huh?
Ikuto, but where can we go!?
Our house and your friends' houses are being watched...
Shut up, Yoru.

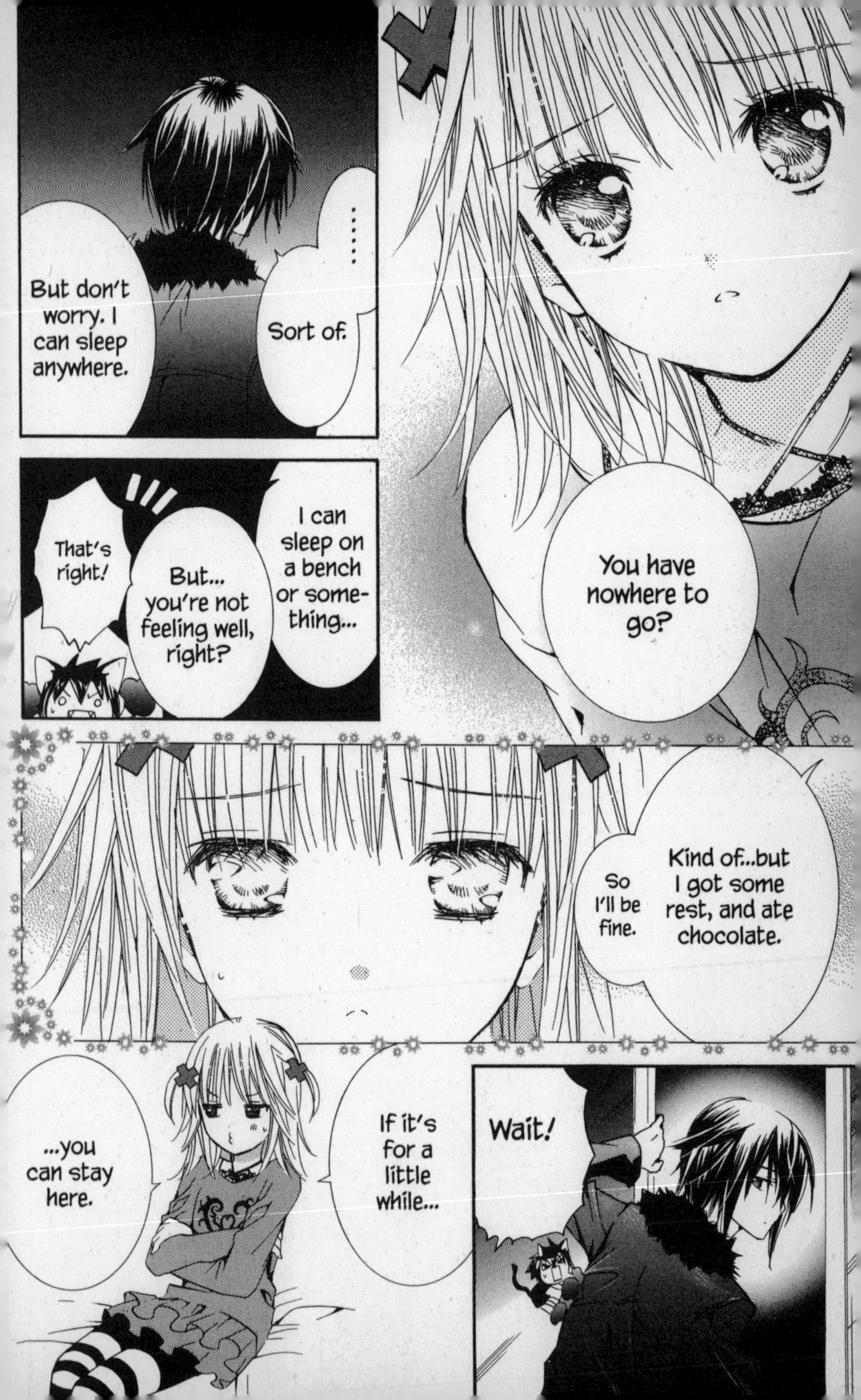
You have nowhere to go?
Sort of.
But don't worry. I can sleep anywhere.
I can sleep on a bench or something...
But... you're not feeling well, right?
That's right!
Kind of...but I got some rest, and ate chocolate.
So I'll be fine.
Wait!
If it's for a little while...
...you can stay here.

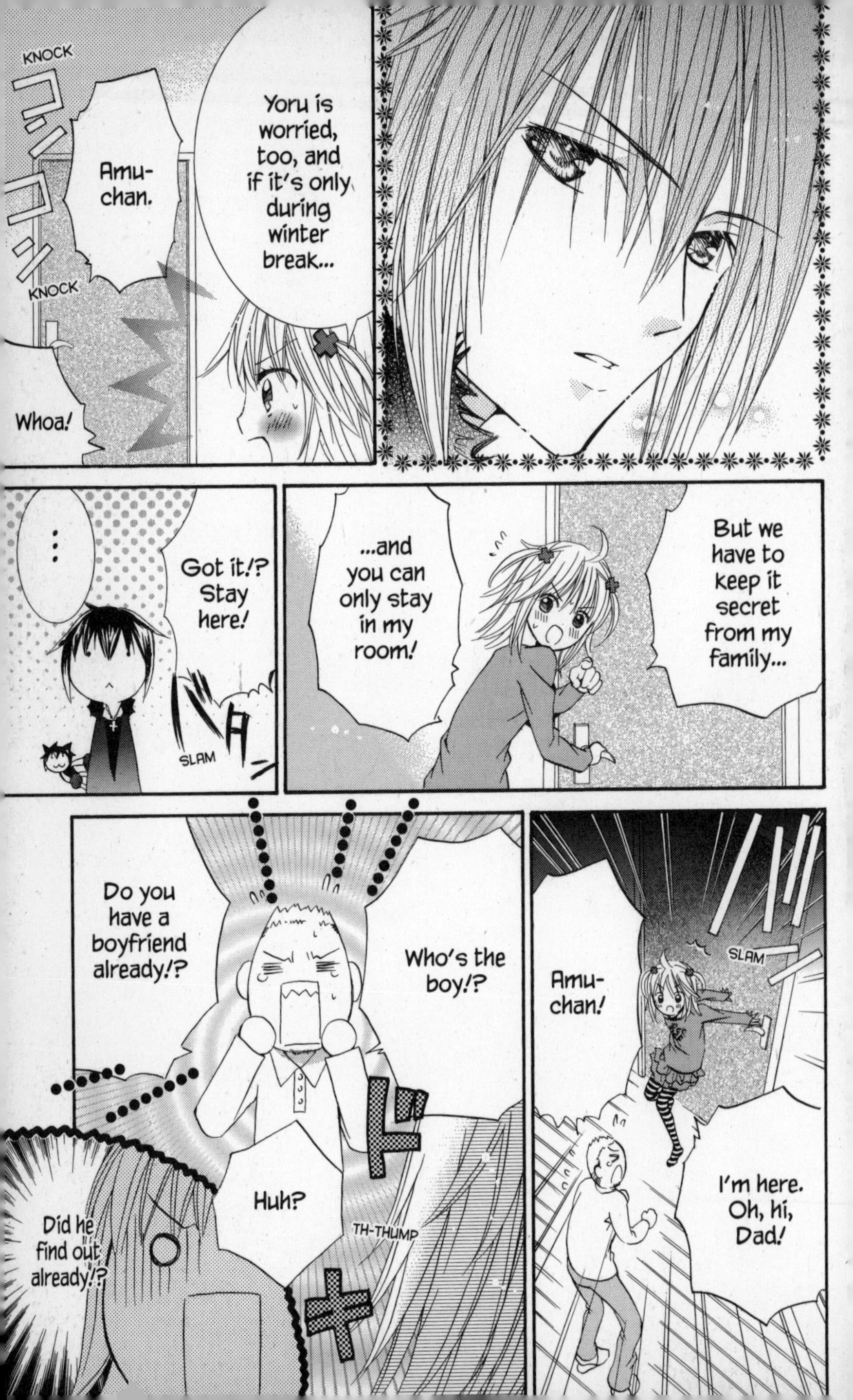
Yoru is worried, too, and if it's only during winter break...
KNOCK
Amu-chan.
KNOCK
Whoa!
But we have to keep it secret from my family...
...and you can only stay in my room!
Got it!? Stay here!
...
SLAM
SLAM
Amu-chan!
I'm here. Oh, hi, Dad!
Who's the boy!?
Do you have a boyfriend already!?
Huh?
TH-THUMP
Did he find out already!?

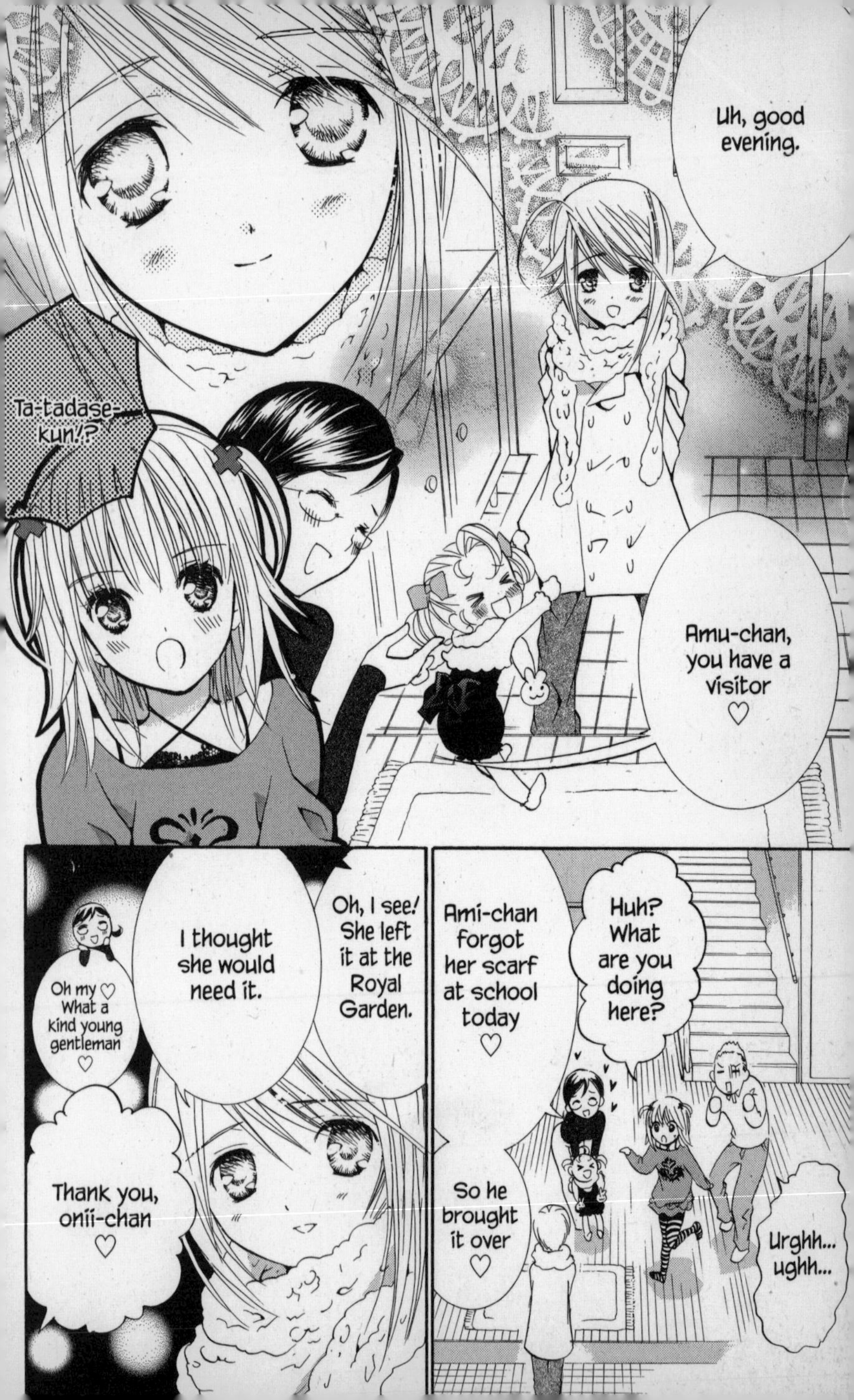
Uh, good evening.
Amu-chan, you have a visitor ♡
Ta-tadase-kun!?
Huh? What are you doing here?
Ami-chan forgot her scarf at school today ♡
So he brought it over ♡
Urghh... ughh...
Oh, I see! She left it at the Royal Garden.
I thought she would need it.
Oh my ♡ What a kind young gentleman ♡
Thank you, onii-chan ♡

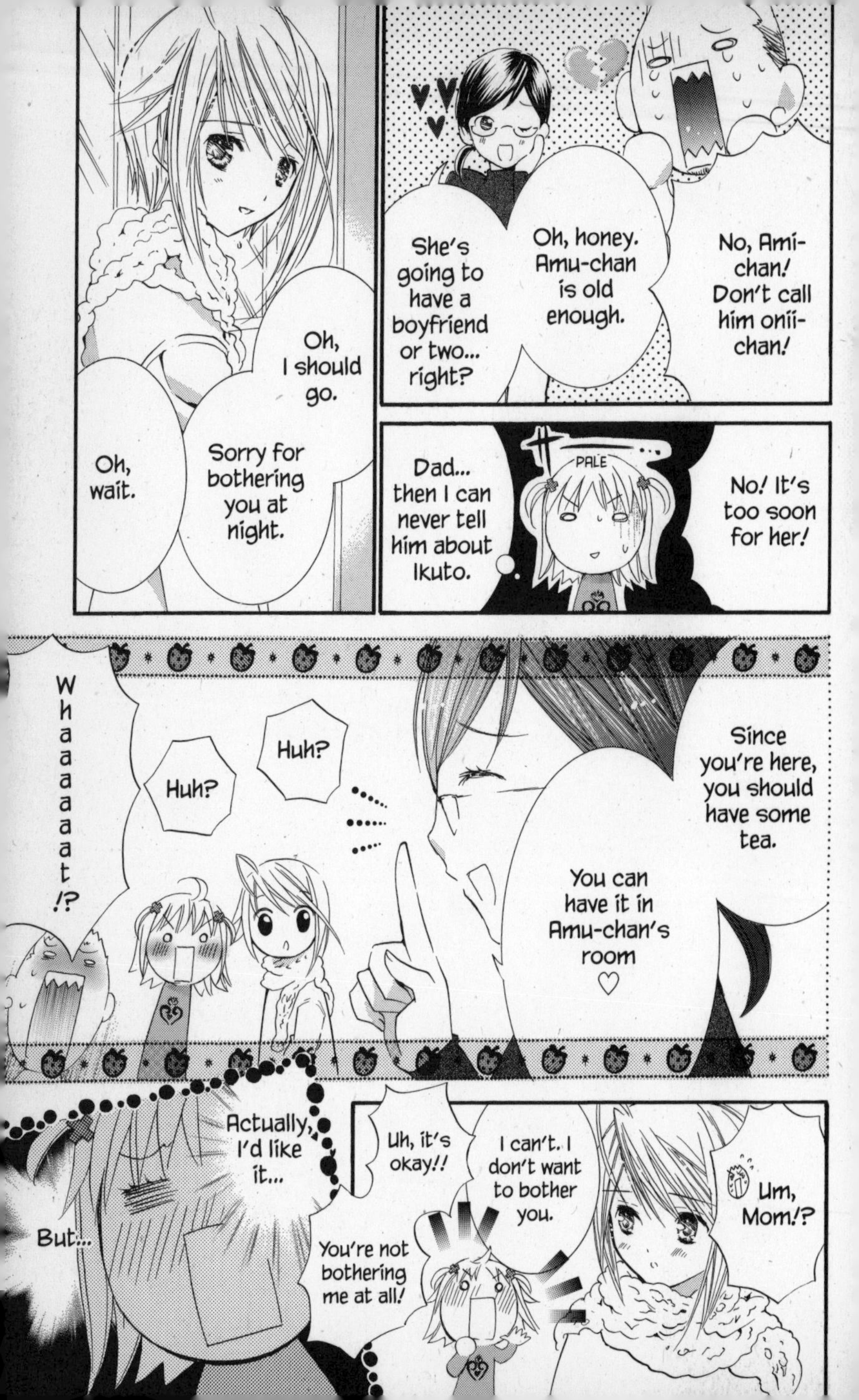
No, Ami-chan! Don't call him onii-chan!
Oh, honey. Amu-chan is old enough.
She's going to have a boyfriend or two... right?
No! It's too soon for her!
PALE
Dad... then I can never tell him about Ikuto.
Oh, I should go.
Sorry for bothering you at night.
Oh, wait.
Since you're here, you should have some tea.
You can have it in Amu-chan's room ♡
......
Huh?
Huh?
Whaaaaaat!?
Um, Mom!?
I can't. I don't want to bother you.
Uh, it's okay!!
You're not bothering me at all!
Actually, I'd like it...
But...

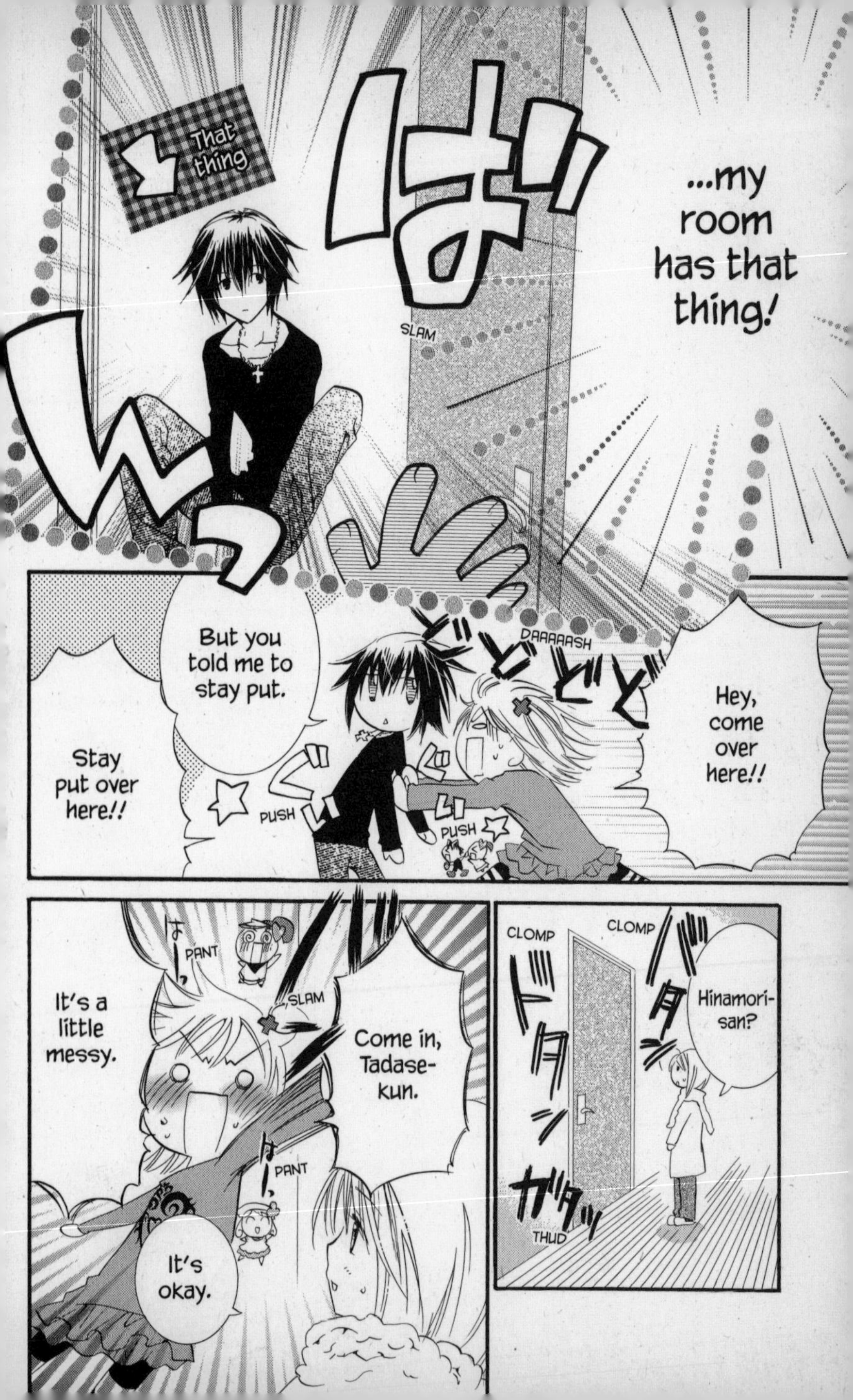
...my room has that thing!
SLAM
That thing
Hey, come over here!!
DAAAAASH
But you told me to stay put.
PUSH
PUSH
Stay put over here!!
CLOMP
CLOMP
Hinamori-san?
THUD
Come in, Tadase-kun.
SLAM
PANT
It's a little messy.
PANT
It's okay.

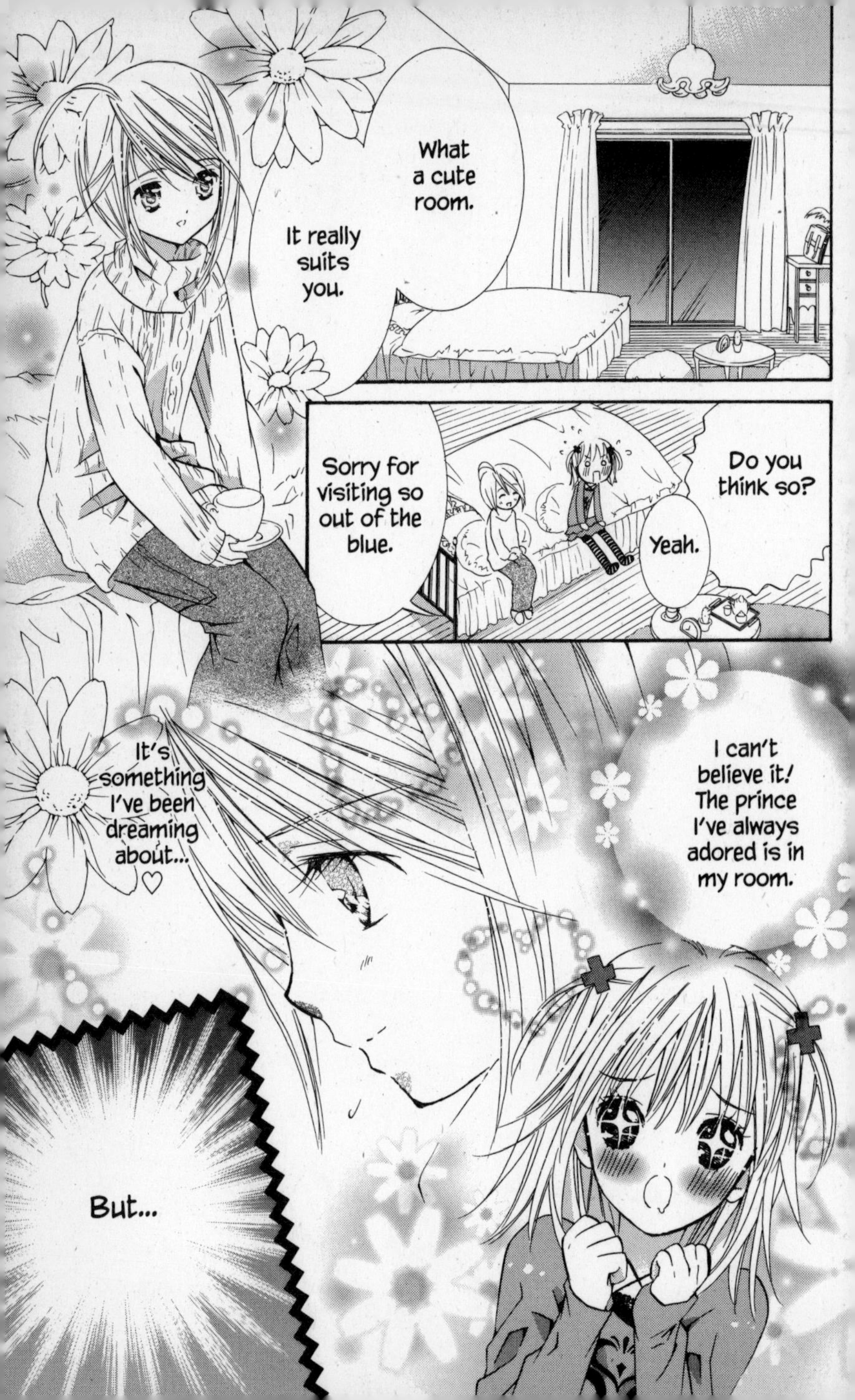
What a cute room.
It really suits you.
Do you think so?
Yeah.
Sorry for visiting so out of the blue.
I can't believe it! The prince I've always adored is in my room.
It's something I've been dreaming about... ♡
But...

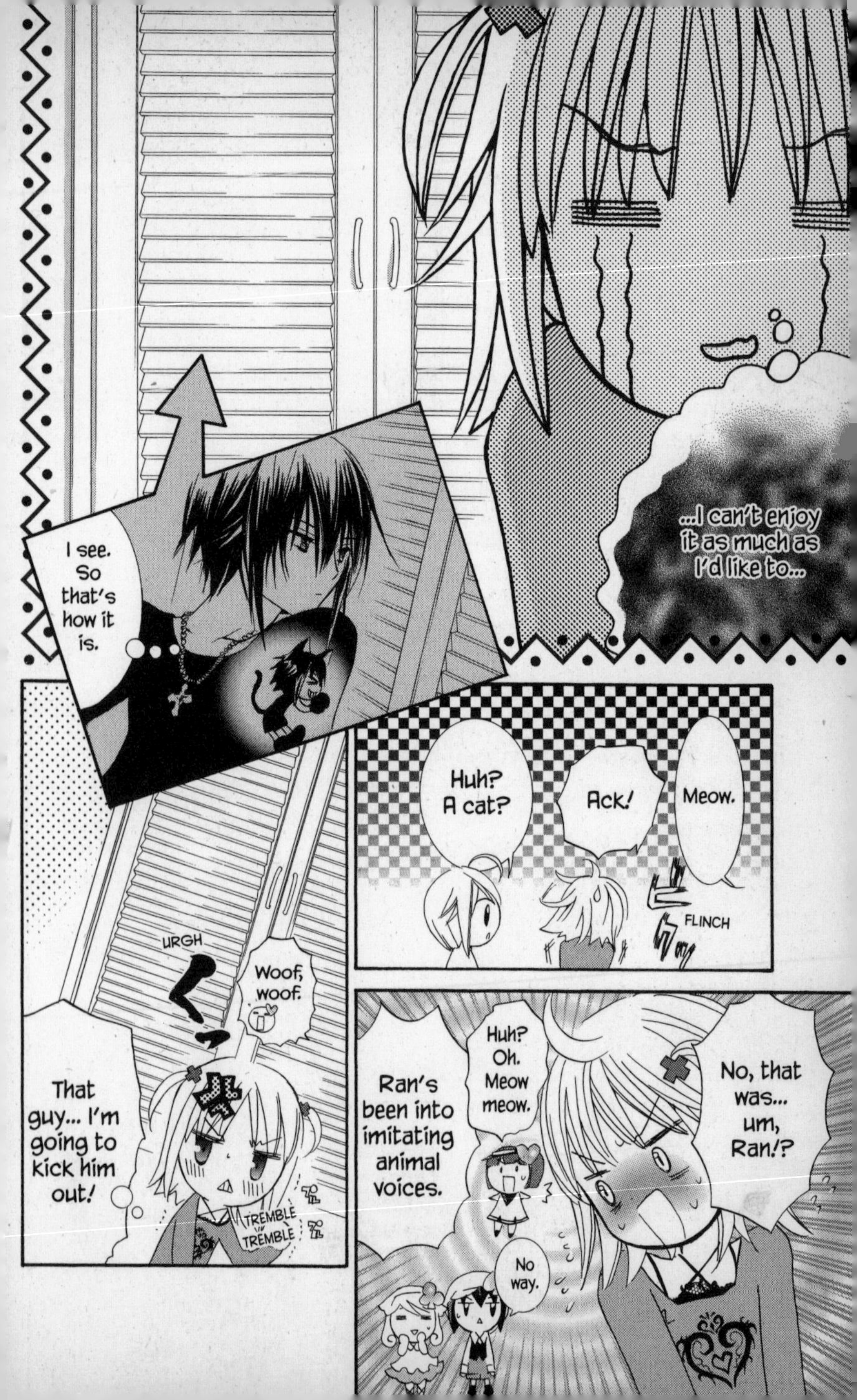
...I can't enjoy it as much as I'd like to...
I see. So that's how it is.
Meow.
Ack!
Huh? A cat?
FLINCH
No, that was... um, Ran!?
Huh? Oh. Meow meow.
Ran's been into imitating animal voices.
No way.
Woof, woof.
URGH
That guy... I'm going to kick him out!
TREMBLE TREMBLE

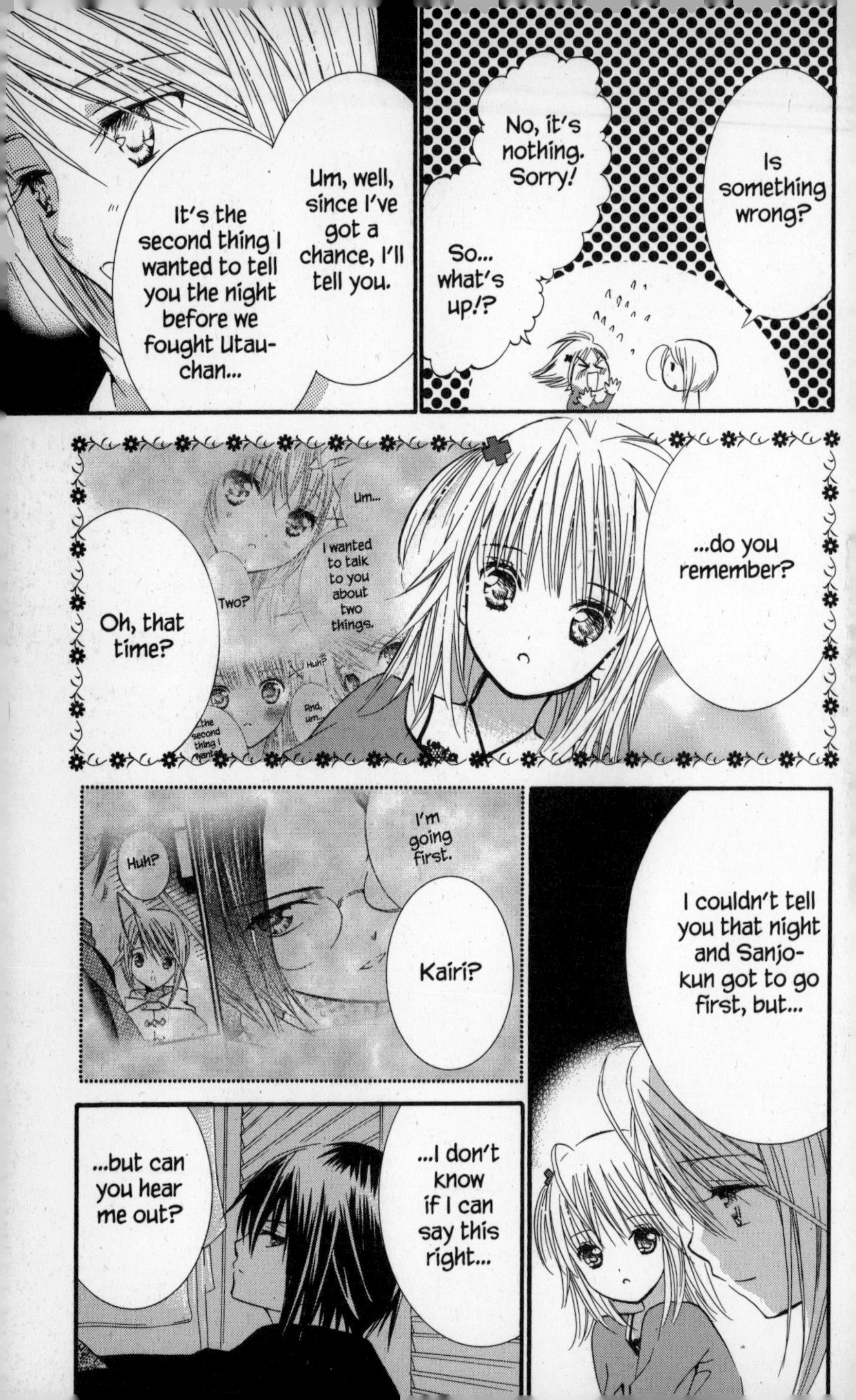
Is something wrong?
No, it's nothing. Sorry!
So... what's up!?
Um, well, since I've got a chance, I'll tell you.
It's the second thing I wanted to tell you the night before we fought Utau-chan...
...do you remember?
Um...
I wanted to talk to you about two things.
Two?
Huh?
And, um...
...the second thing I
Oh, that time?
I couldn't tell you that night and Sanjo-kun got to go first, but...
I'm going first.
Huh?
Kairi?
...I don't know if I can say this right...
...but can you hear me out?

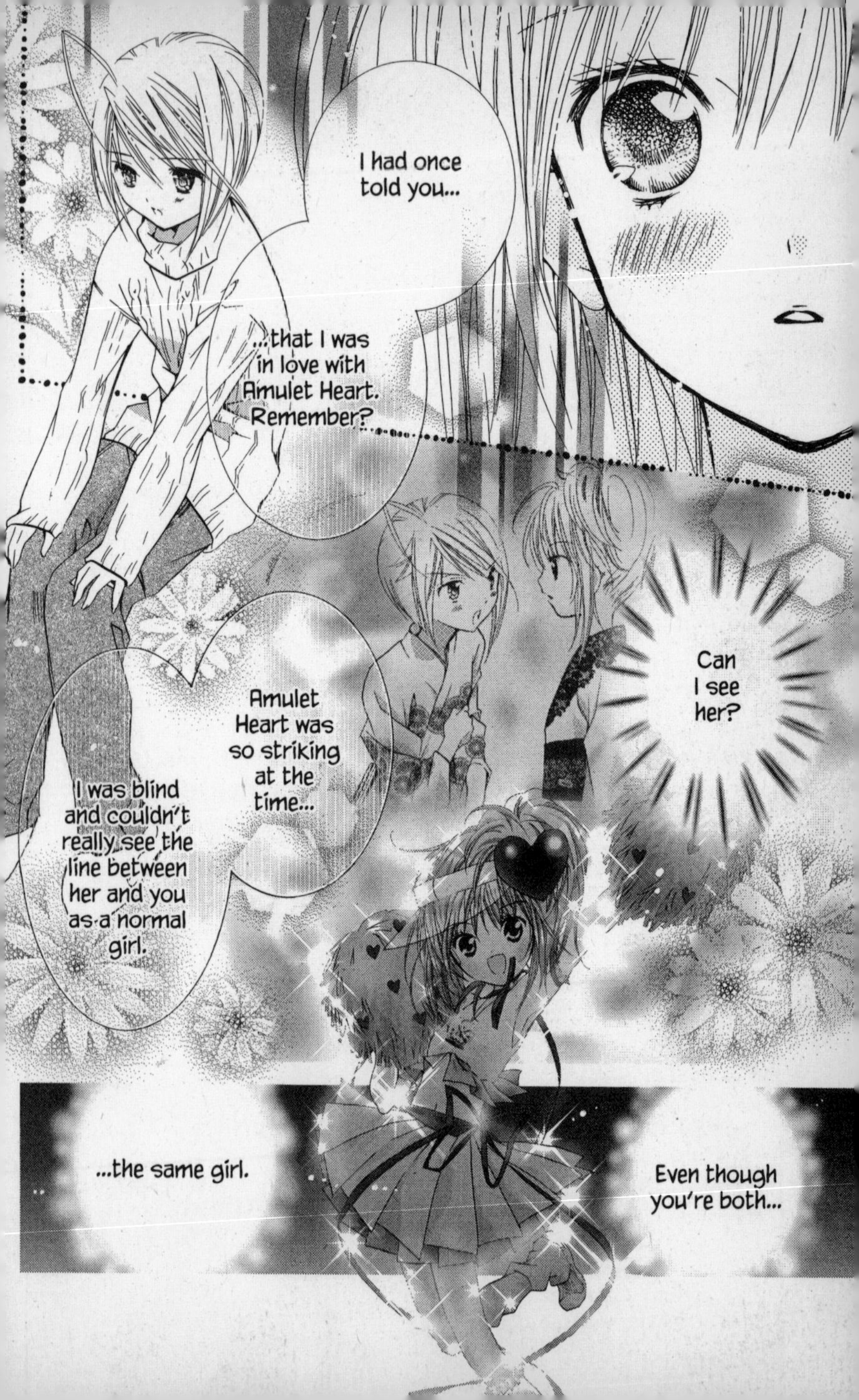
I had once told you...
...that I was in love with Amulet Heart. Remember?
Can I see her?
Amulet Heart was so striking at the time...
I was blind and couldn't really see the line between her and you as a normal girl.
Even though you're both...
...the same girl.

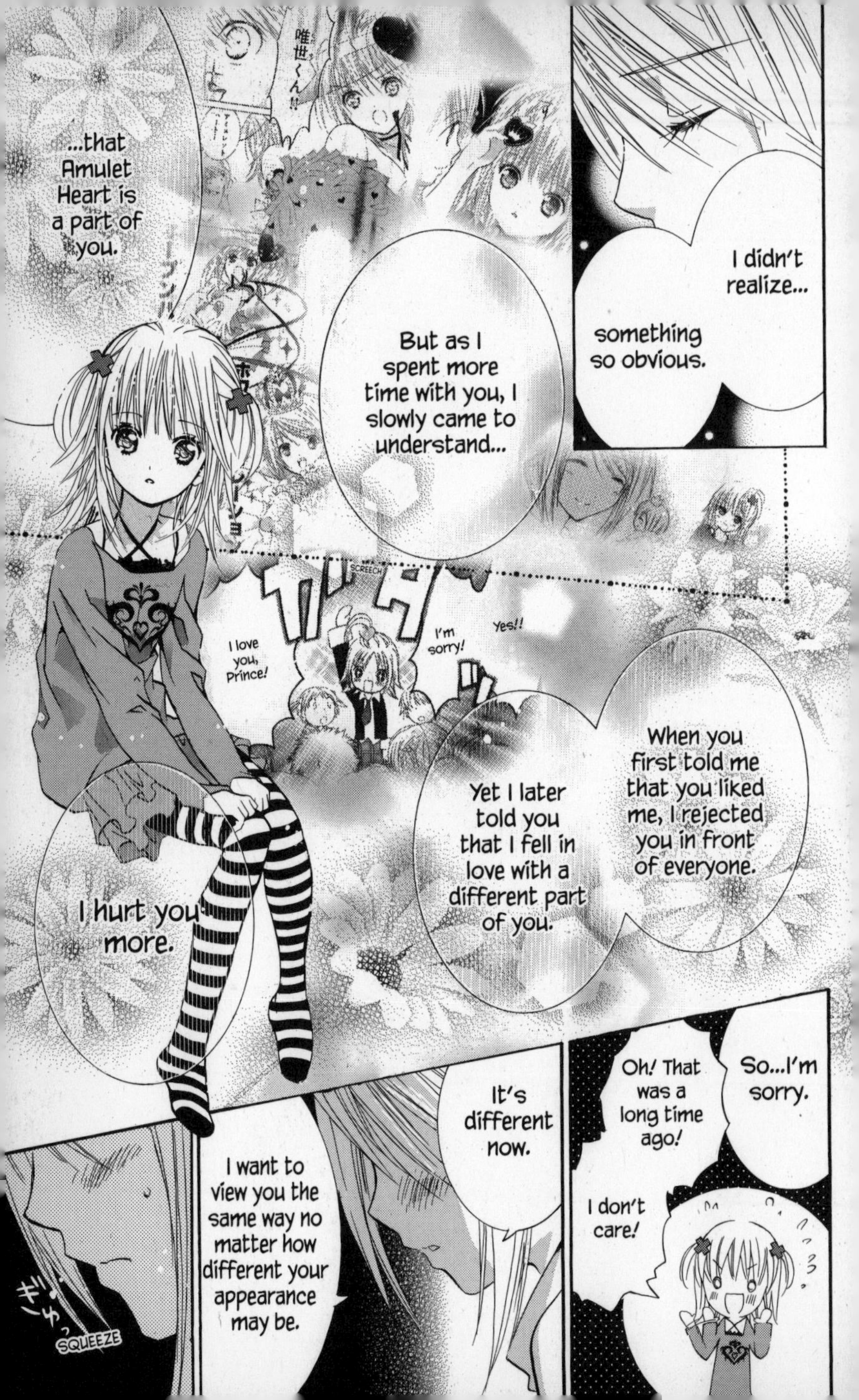
I didn't realize...
something so obvious.
But as I spent more time with you, I slowly came to understand...
...that Amulet Heart is a part of you.
唯世くん!!
SCREECH
Yes!!
I'm sorry!
I love you, Prince!
When you first told me that you liked me, I rejected you in front of everyone.
Yet I later told you that I fell in love with a different part of you.
I hurt you more.
So...I'm sorry.
Oh! That was a long time ago!
I don't care!
It's different now.
I want to view you the same way no matter how different your appearance may be.
SQUEEZE

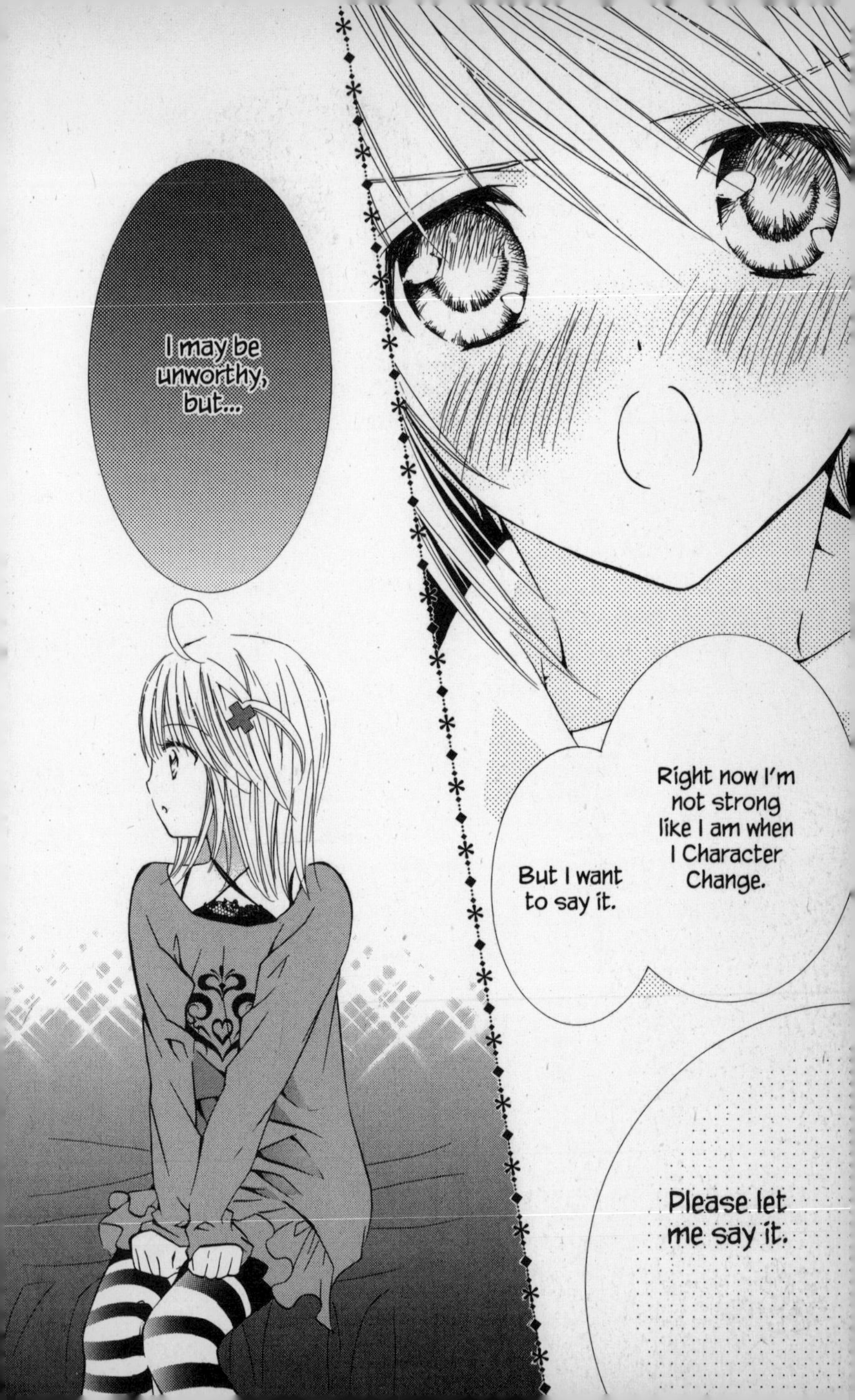
Right now I'm not strong like I am when I Character Change.
But I want to say it.
Please let me say it.
I may be unworthy, but...

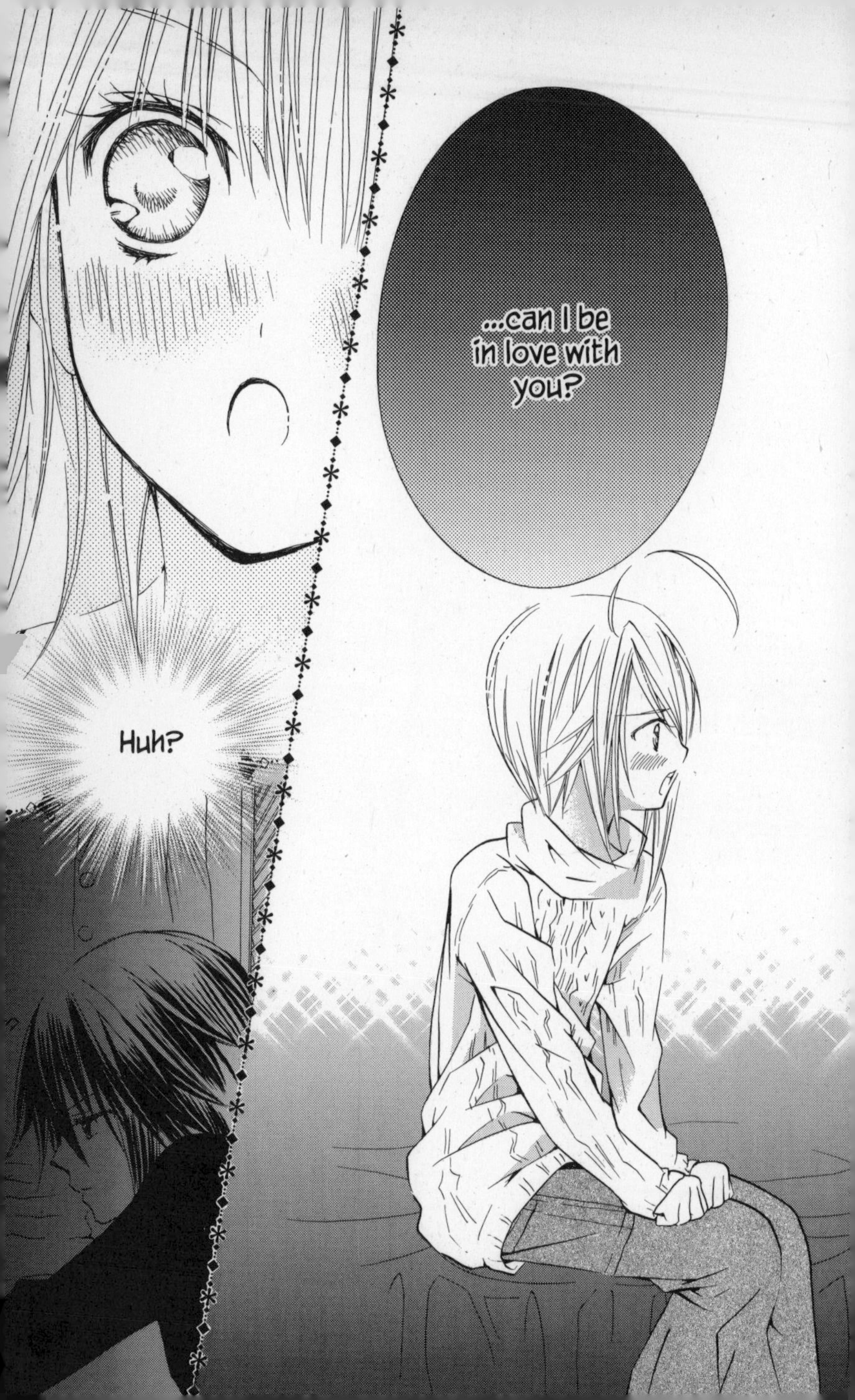
...can I be in love with you?
Huh?

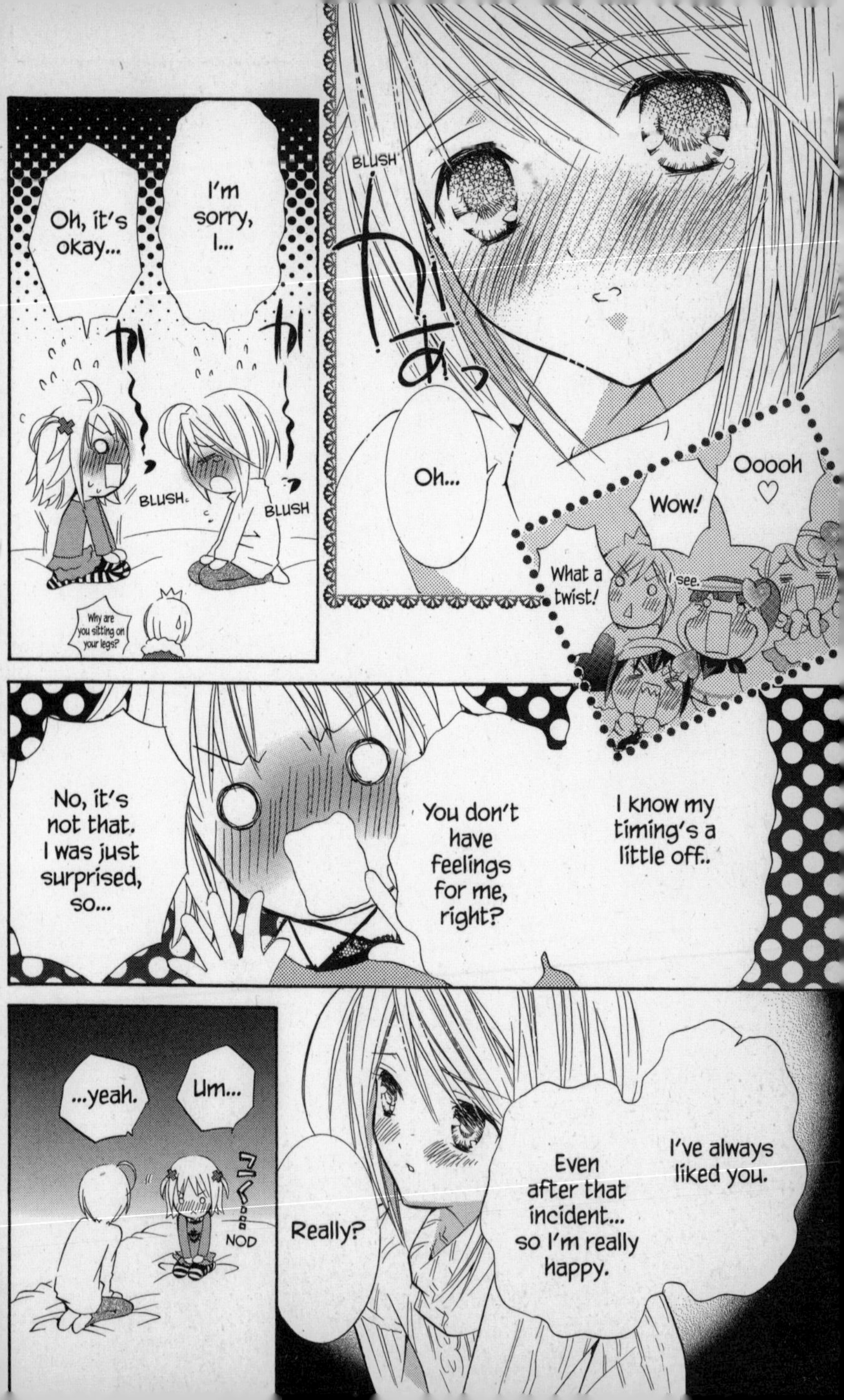
BLUSH
かあっ
Oh...
Ooooh ♡
Wow!
I see.
What a twist!
I'm sorry, I...
Oh, it's okay...
かー
かー
BLUSH
BLUSH
Why are you sitting on your legs?
I know my timing's a little off..
You don't have feelings for me, right?
No, it's not that. I was just surprised, so...
I've always liked you.
Even after that incident... so I'm really happy.
Really?
Um...
...yeah.
コク
NOD

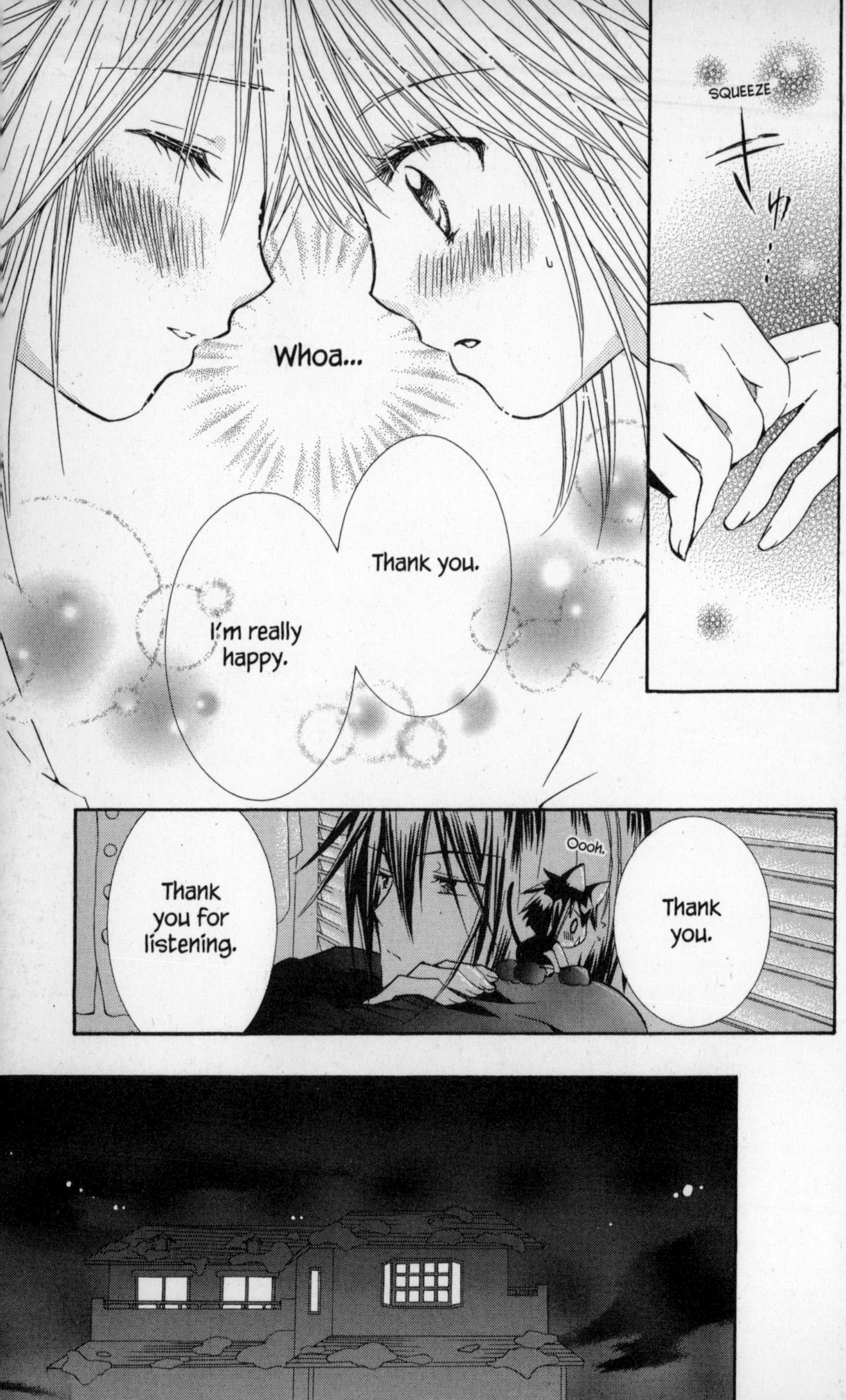
SQUEEZE
Whoa...
Thank you.
I'm really happy.
Oooh.
Thank you.
Thank you for listening.

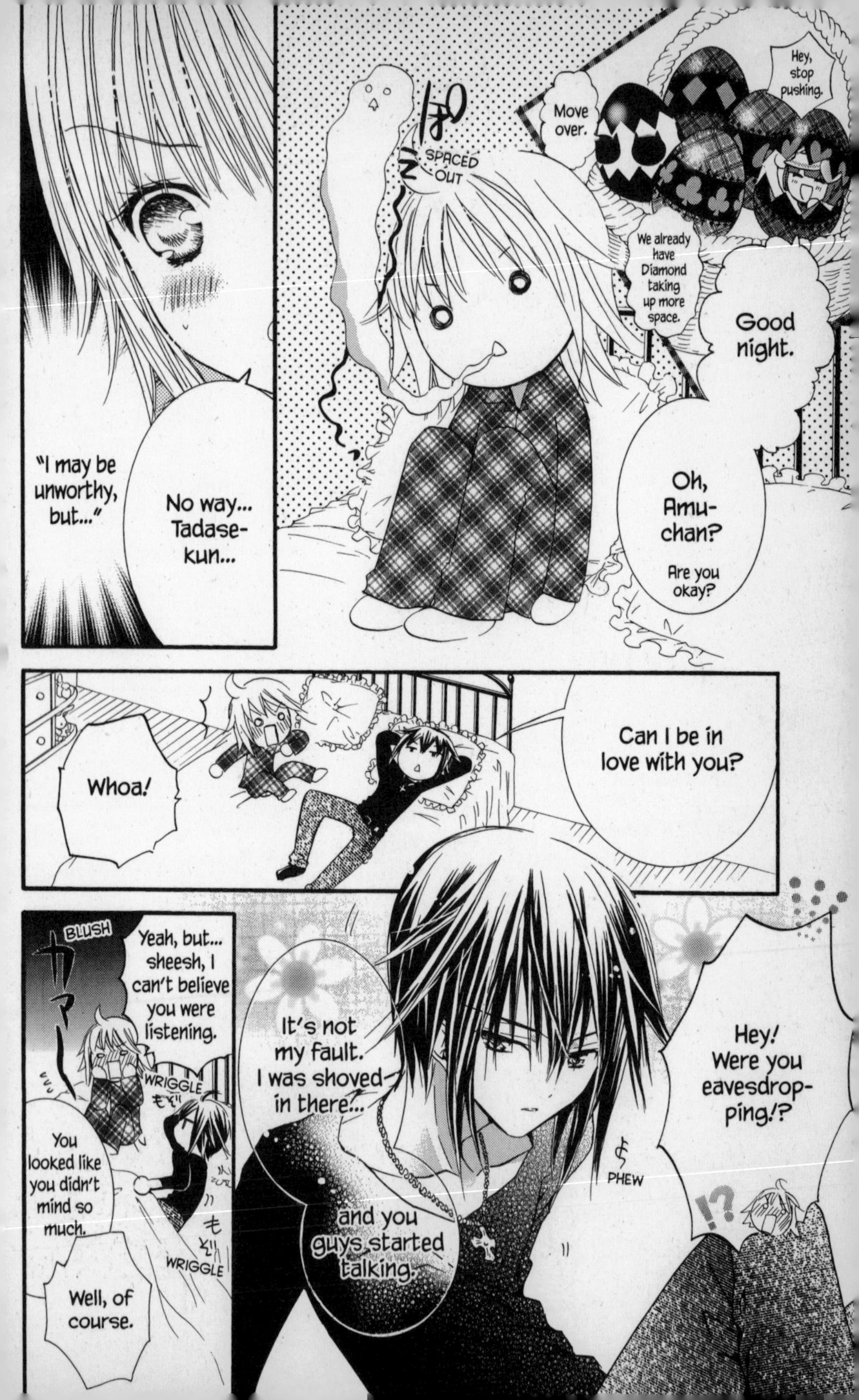

Hey, stop pushing.
Move over.
We already have Diamond taking up more space.
Good night.
SPACED OUT
Oh, Amu-chan? Are you okay?
No way... Tadase-kun...
"I may be unworthy, but..."
Can I be in love with you?
Whoa!
Hey! Were you eavesdropping!?
!?
PHEW
It's not my fault. I was shoved in there...
and you guys started talking.
BLUSH
Yeah, but... sheesh, I can't believe you were listening.
WRIGGLE
You looked like you didn't mind so much.
WRIGGLE
Well, of course.

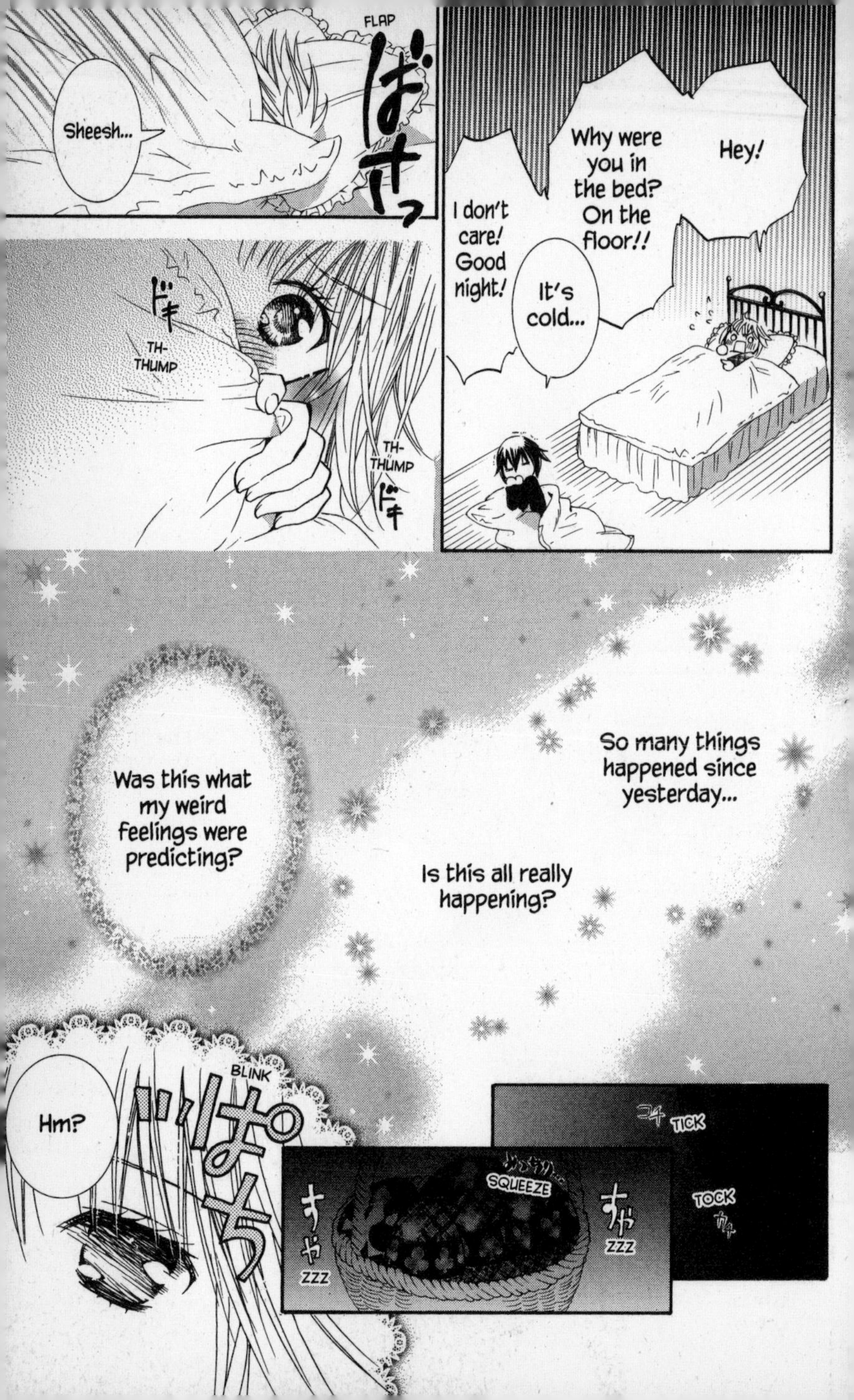
Hey!
Why were you in the bed? On the floor!!
It's cold...
I don't care! Good night!
FLAP
Sheesh...
ドキ
TH-THUMP
TH-THUMP
ドキ
So many things happened since yesterday...
Is this all really happening?
Was this what my weird feelings were predicting?
TICK
TOCK
ZZZ
SQUEEZE
ZZZ
BLINK
Hm?

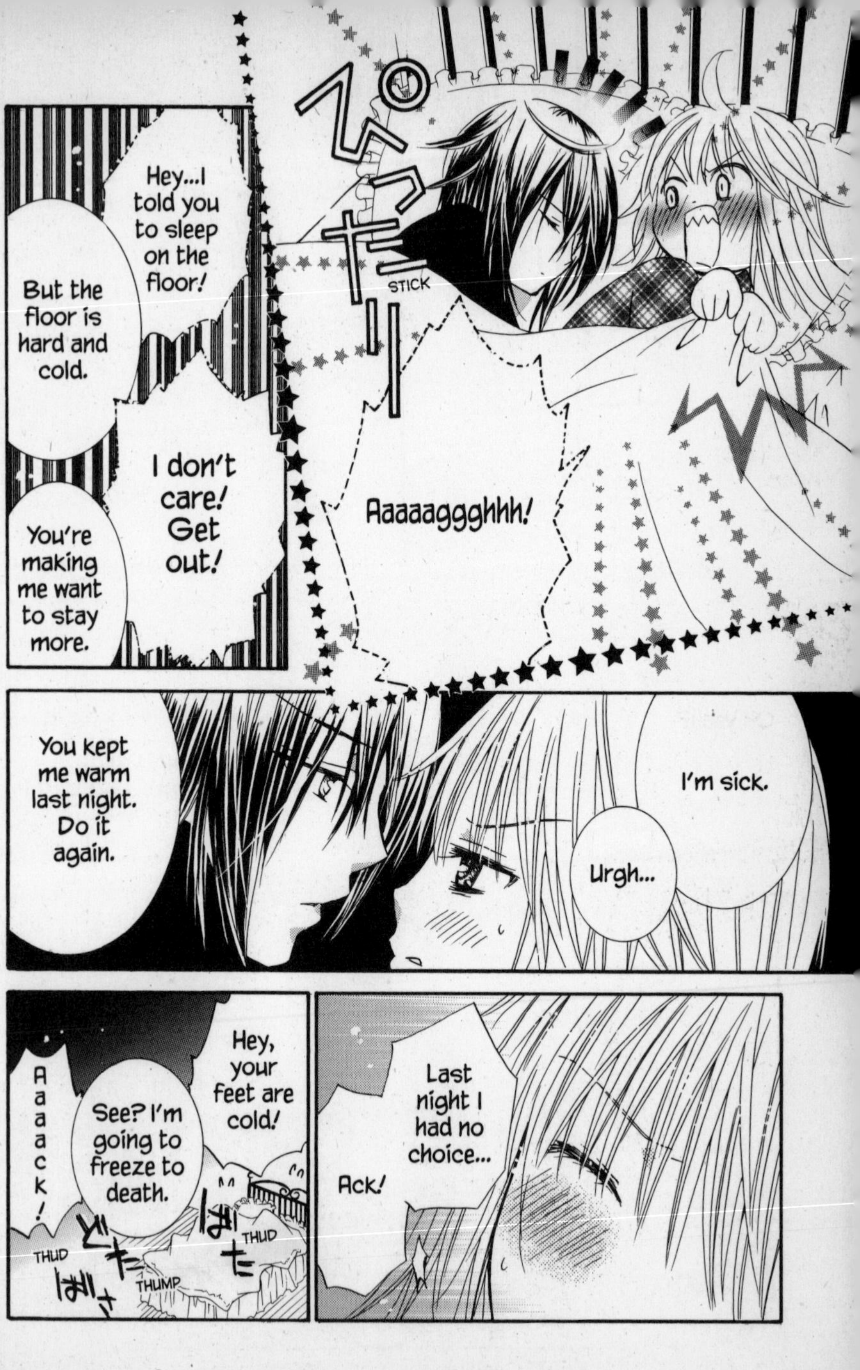
ぺったー
STICK
Aaaaaggghhh!
Hey...I told you to sleep on the floor!
But the floor is hard and cold.
I don't care! Get out!
You're making me want to stay more.
I'm sick.
Urgh...
You kept me warm last night. Do it again.
Last night I had no choice...
Ack!
Hey, your feet are cold!
See? I'm going to freeze to death.
Aaaack!
THUD
THUD
THUMP

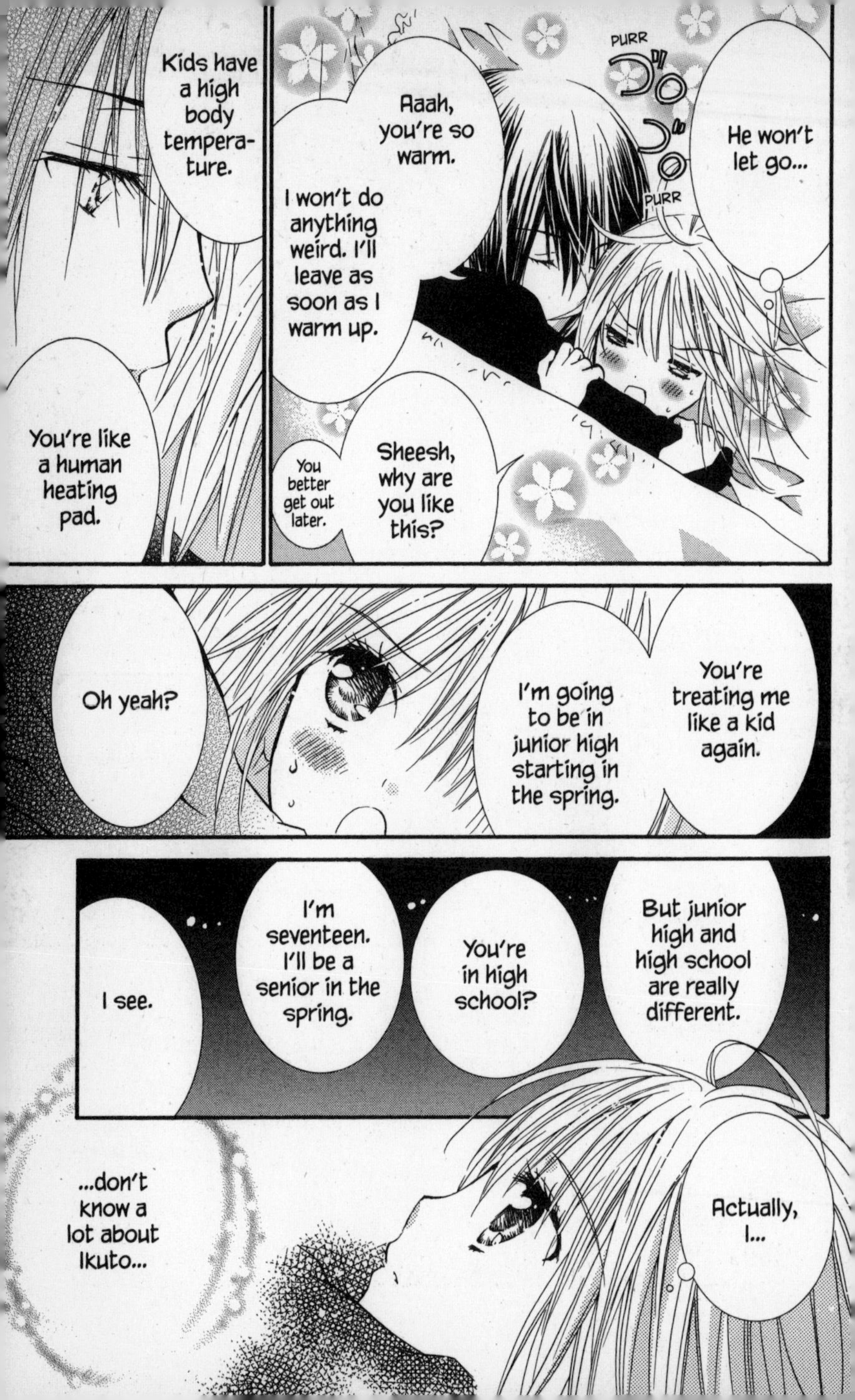
PURR
PURR
He won't let go...
Aaah, you're so warm.
I won't do anything weird. I'll leave as soon as I warm up.
Sheesh, why are you like this?
You better get out later.
Kids have a high body tempera-ture.
You're like a human heating pad.
You're treating me like a kid again.
I'm going to be in junior high starting in the spring.
Oh yeah?
But junior high and high school are really different.
You're in high school?
I'm seventeen. I'll be a senior in the spring.
I see.
Actually, I...
...don't know a lot about Ikuto...

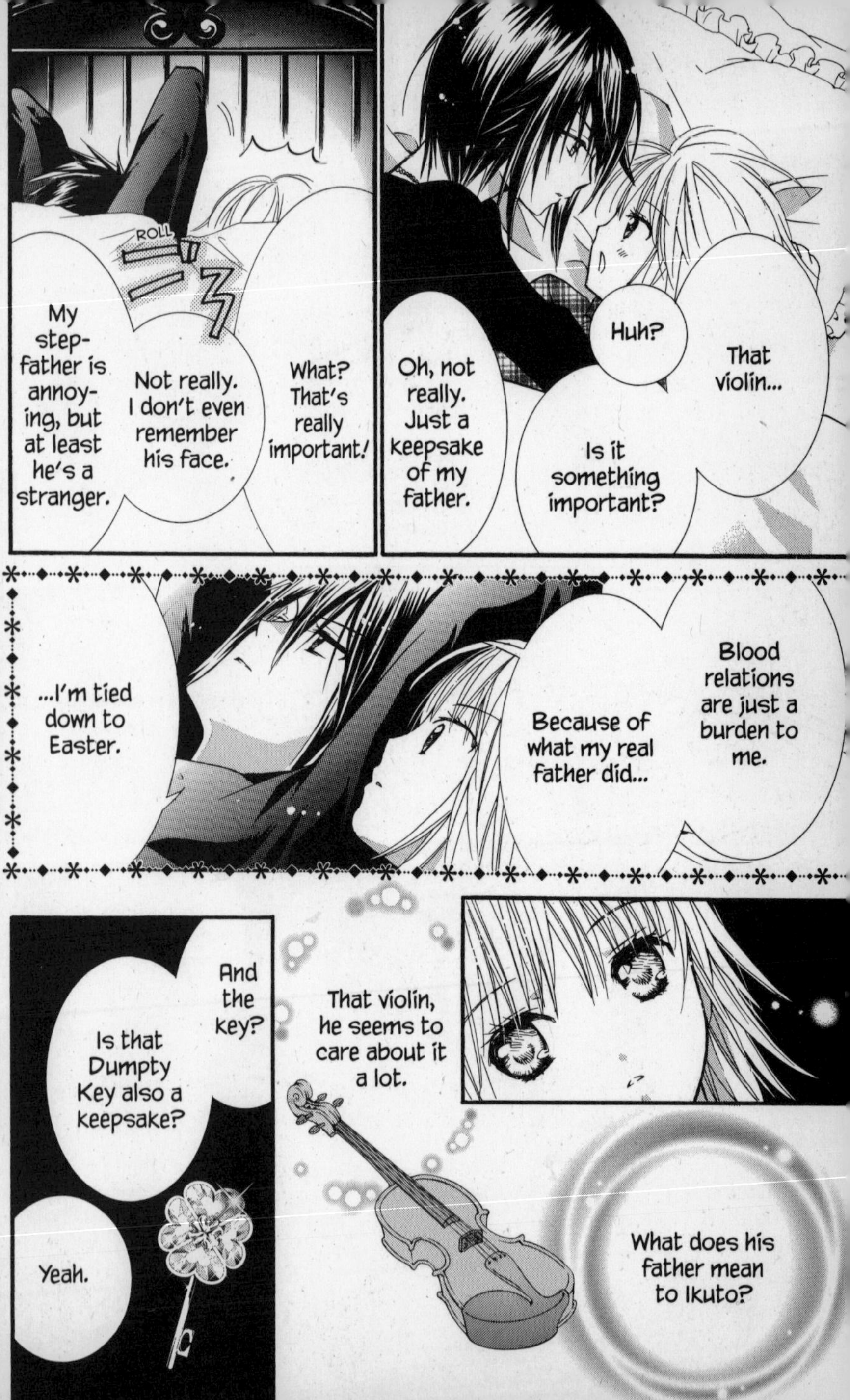

That violin...
Huh?
Is it something important?
Oh, not really. Just a keepsake of my father.
What? That's really important!
Not really. I don't even remember his face.
ROLL
My stepfather is annoying, but at least he's a stranger.
Blood relations are just a burden to me.
Because of what my real father did...
...I'm tied down to Easter.
That violin, he seems to care about it a lot.
What does his father mean to Ikuto?
And the key?
Is that Dumpty Key also a keepsake?
Yeah.

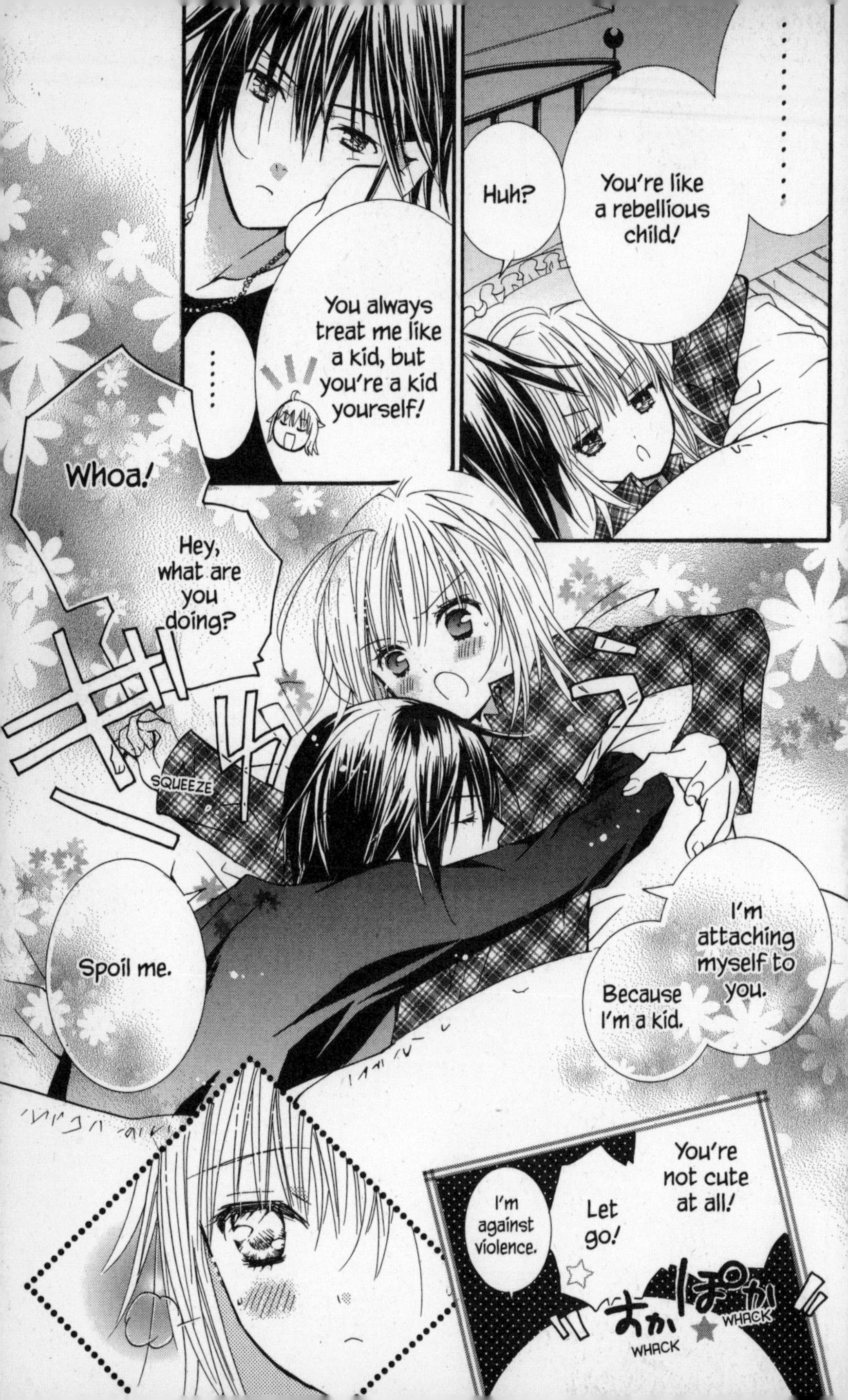
......
You're like a rebellious child!
Huh?
You always treat me like a kid, but you're a kid yourself!
......
Whoa!
Hey, what are you doing?
SQUEEZE
I'm attaching myself to you.
Because I'm a kid.
Spoil me.
You're not cute at all!
Let go!
I'm against violence.
WHACK
WHACK

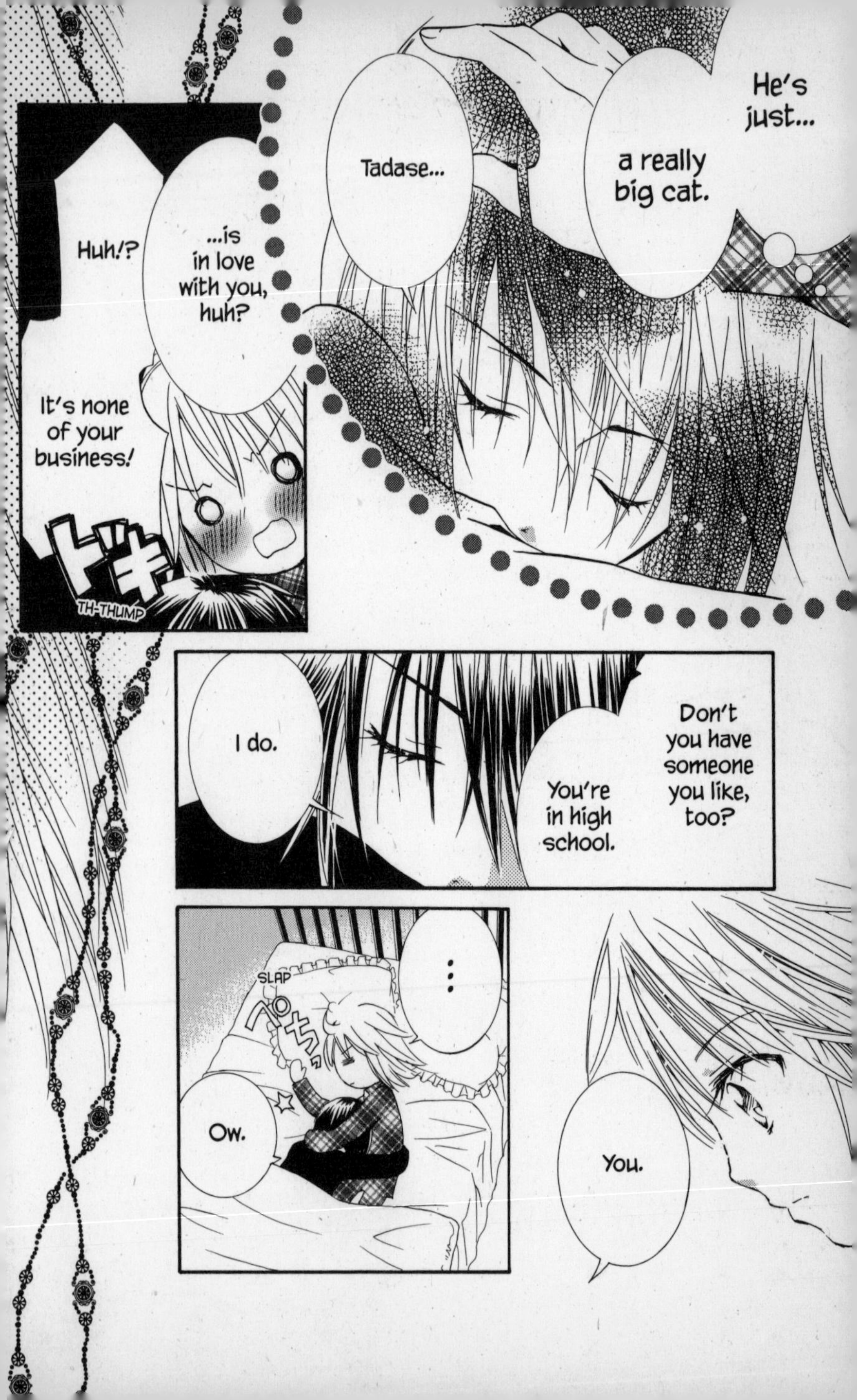
He's just...
a really big cat.
Tadase...
...is in love with you, huh?
Huh!?
It's none of your business!
TH-THUMP
Don't you have someone you like, too?
You're in high school.
I do.
You.
...
SLAP
Ow.

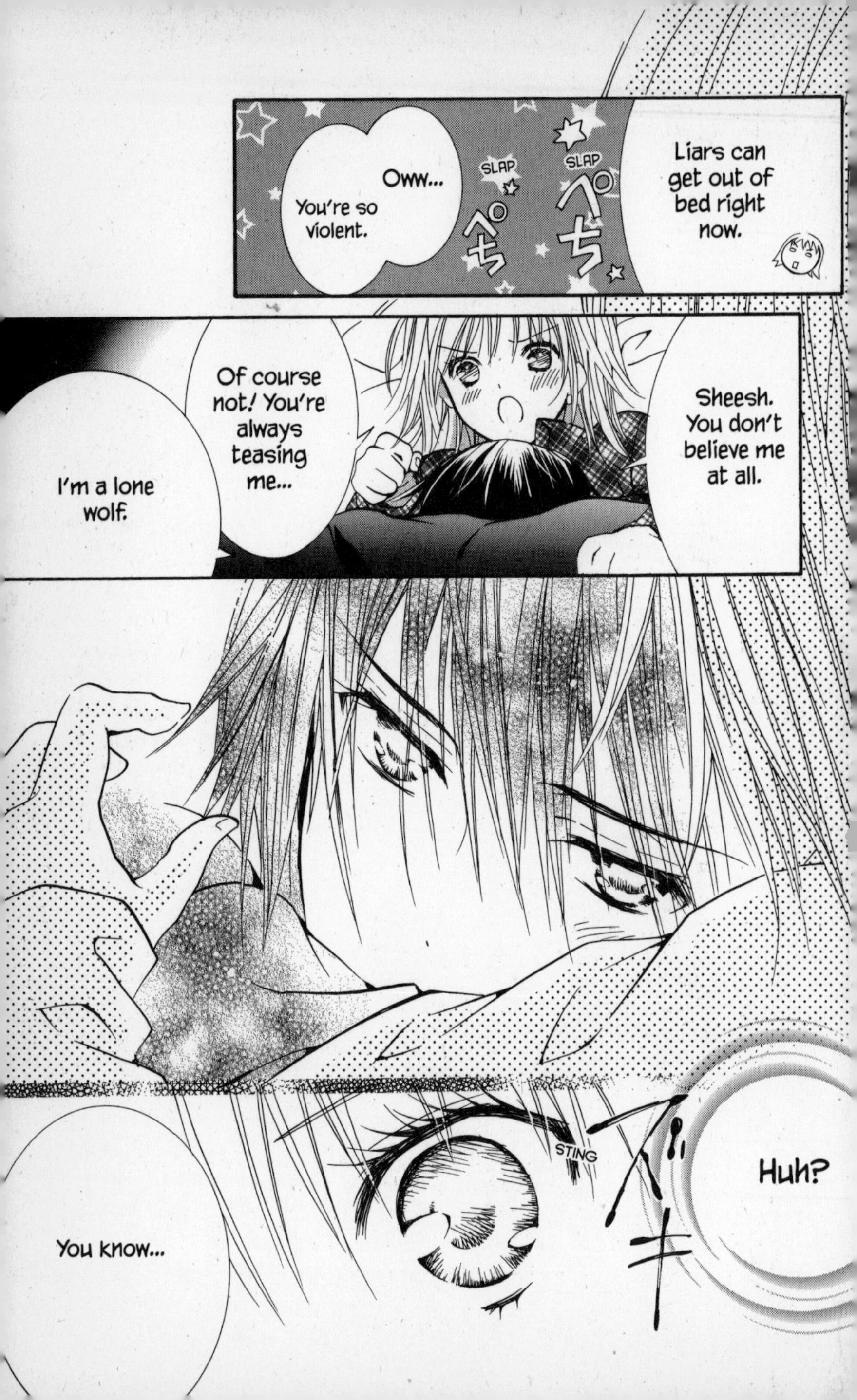
Liars can get out of bed right now.
SLAP
ぺち
SLAP
ぺち
Oww... You're so violent.
Sheesh. You don't believe me at all.
Of course not! You're always teasing me...
I'm a lone wolf.
Huh?
STING
You know...

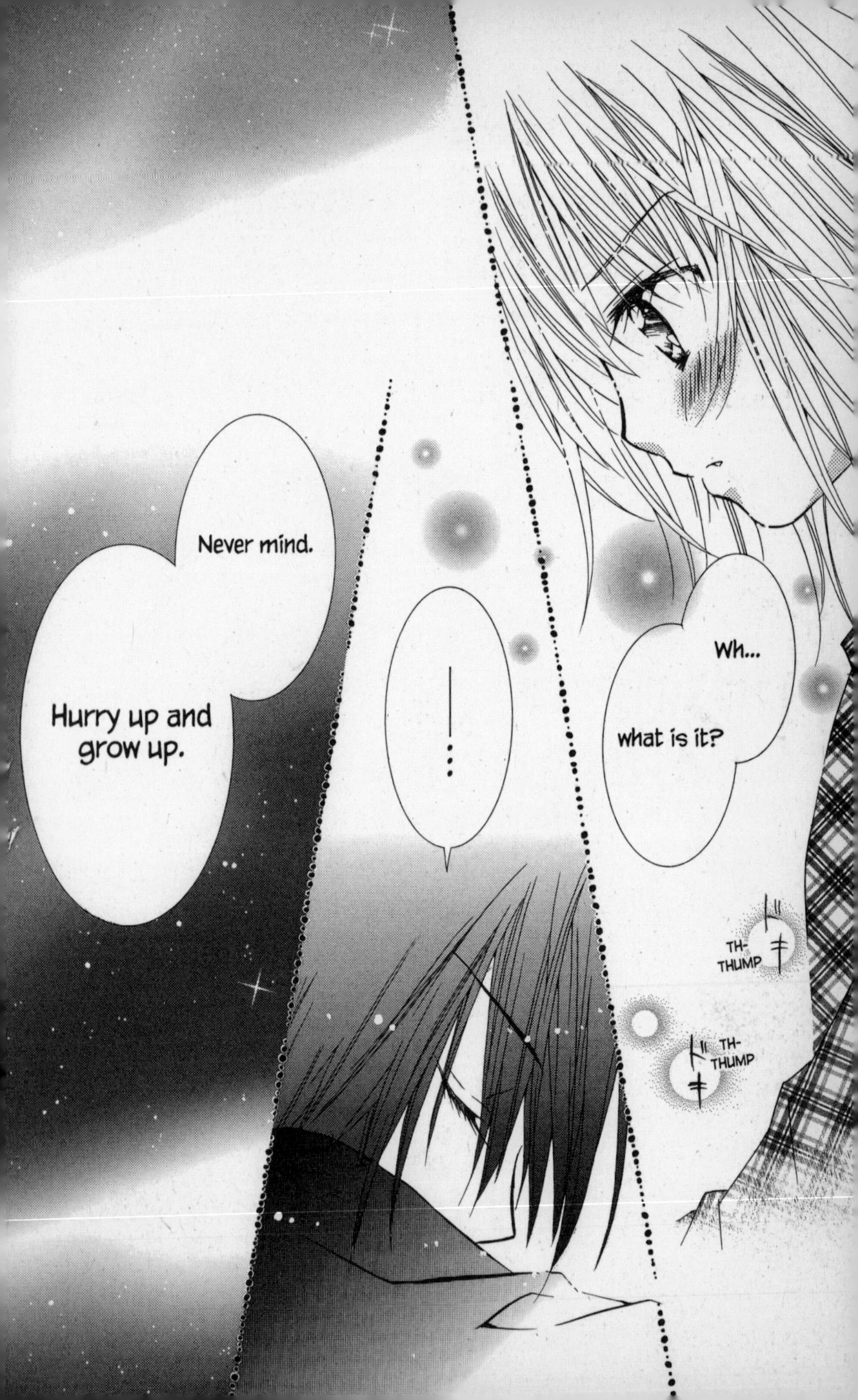
Wh... what is it?
TH-THUMP
TH-THUMP
—!
Never mind.
Hurry up and grow up.

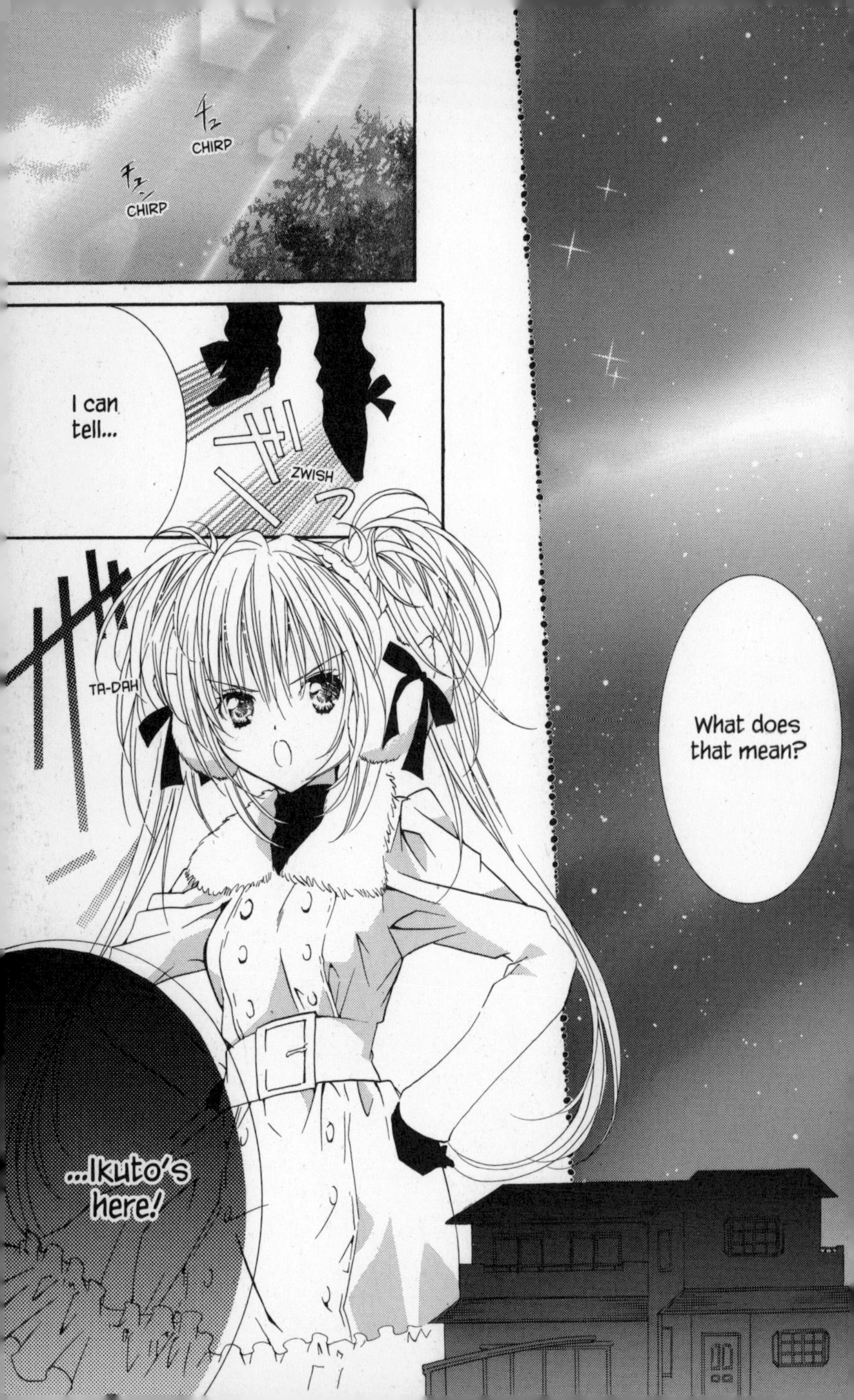

What does that mean?
CHIRP
CHIRP
I can tell...
ZWISH
TA-DAH
...Ikuto's here!

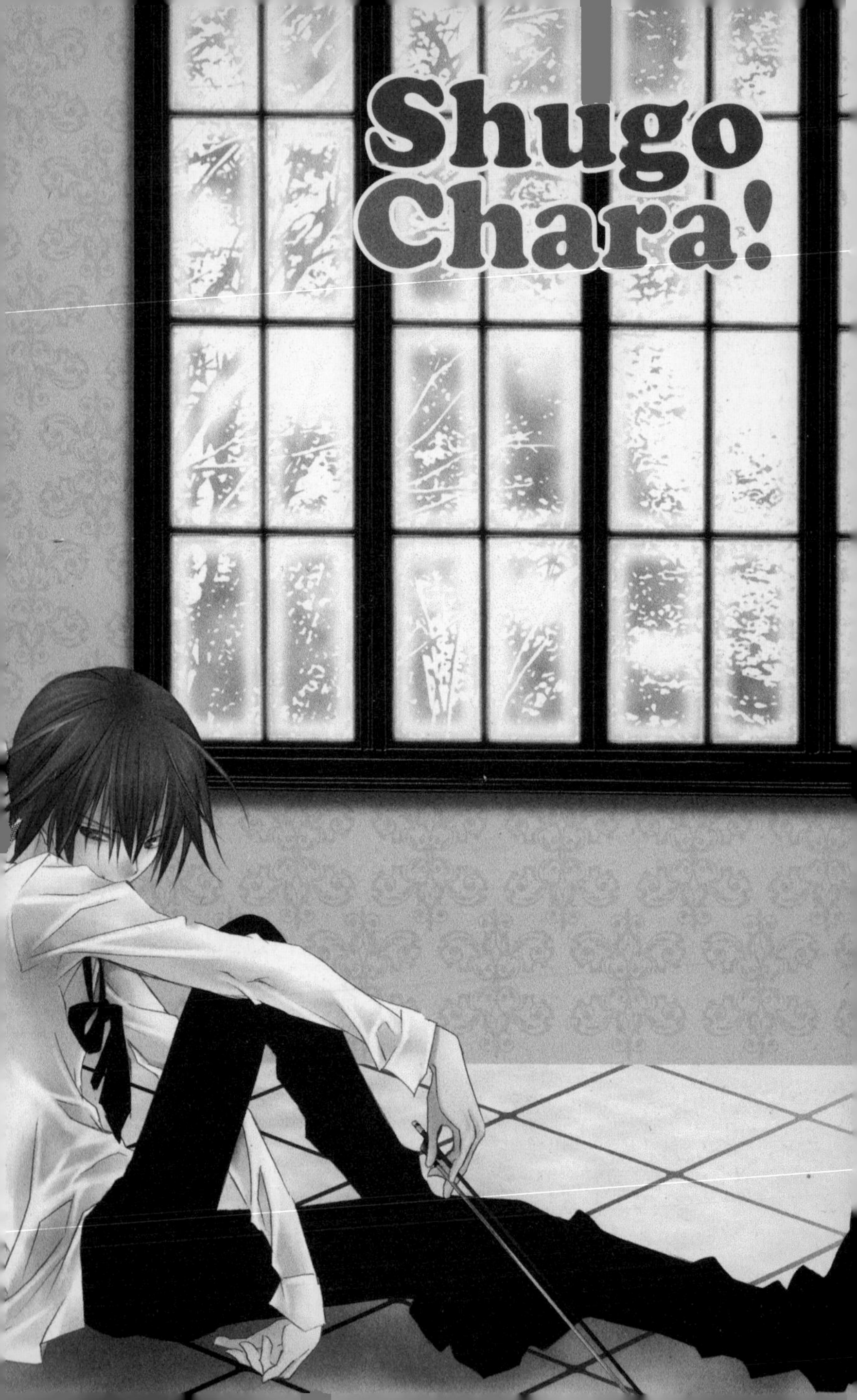
Shugo
Chara!

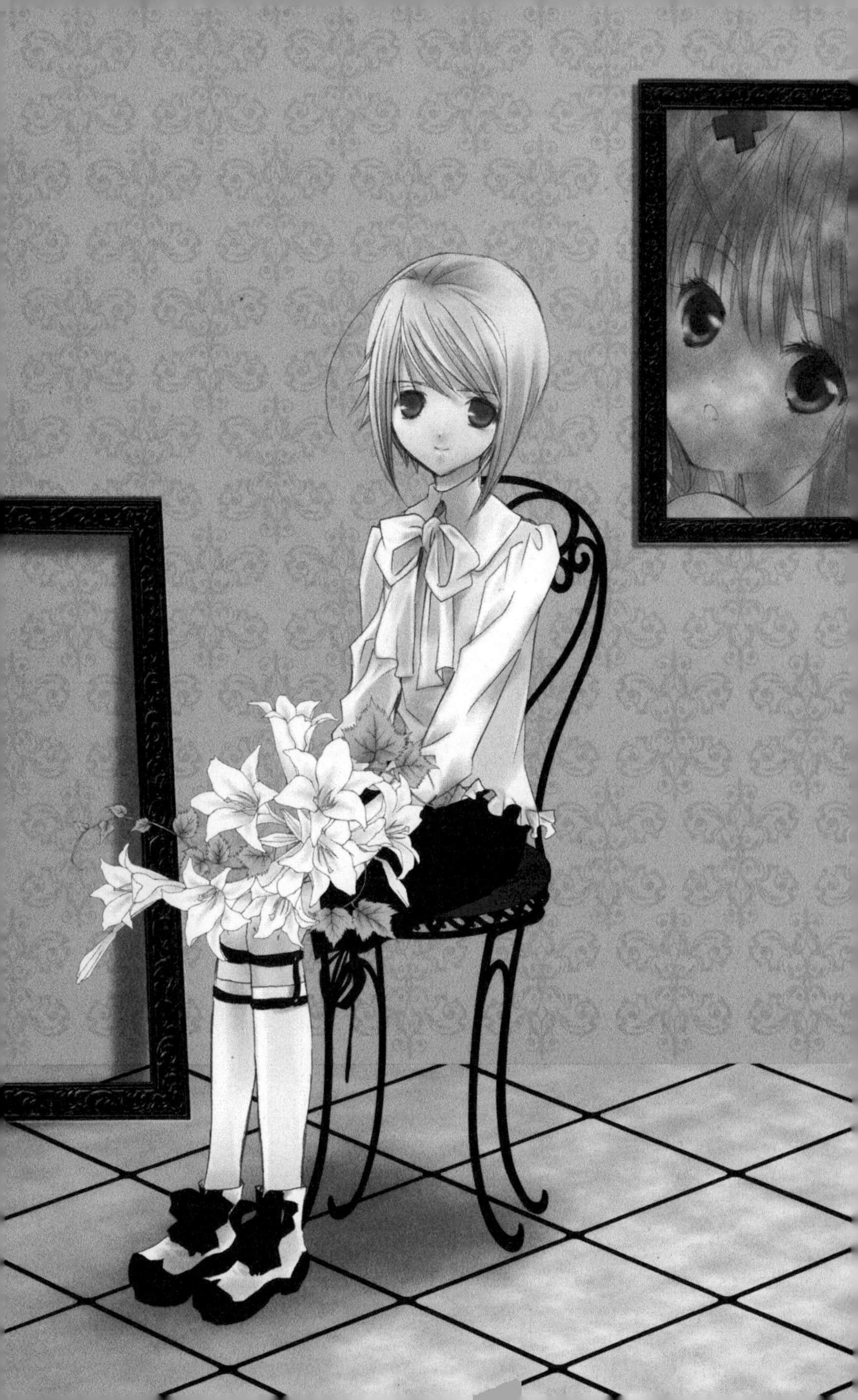

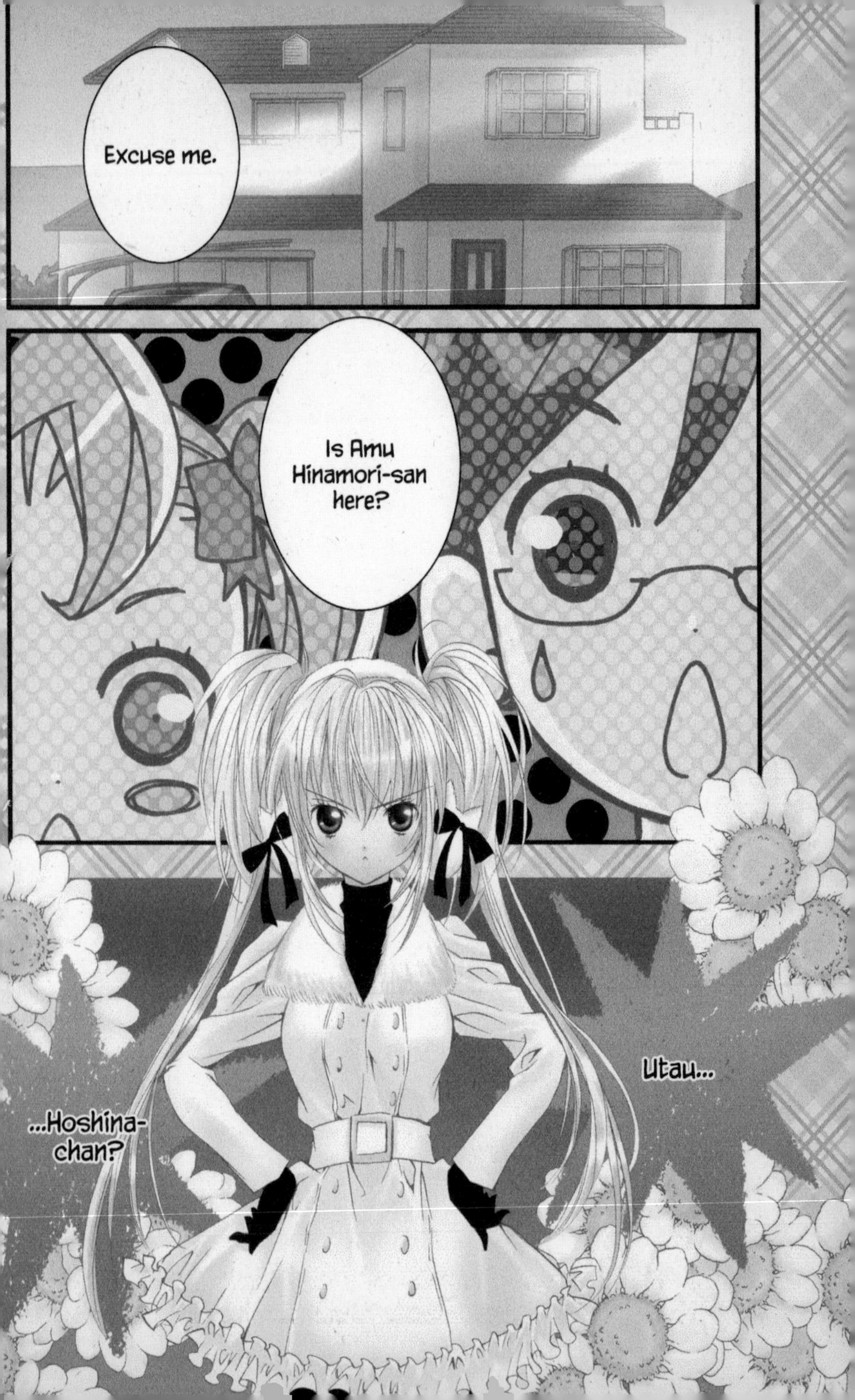
Excuse me.
Is Amu Hinamori-san here?
Utau...
...Hoshina-chan?

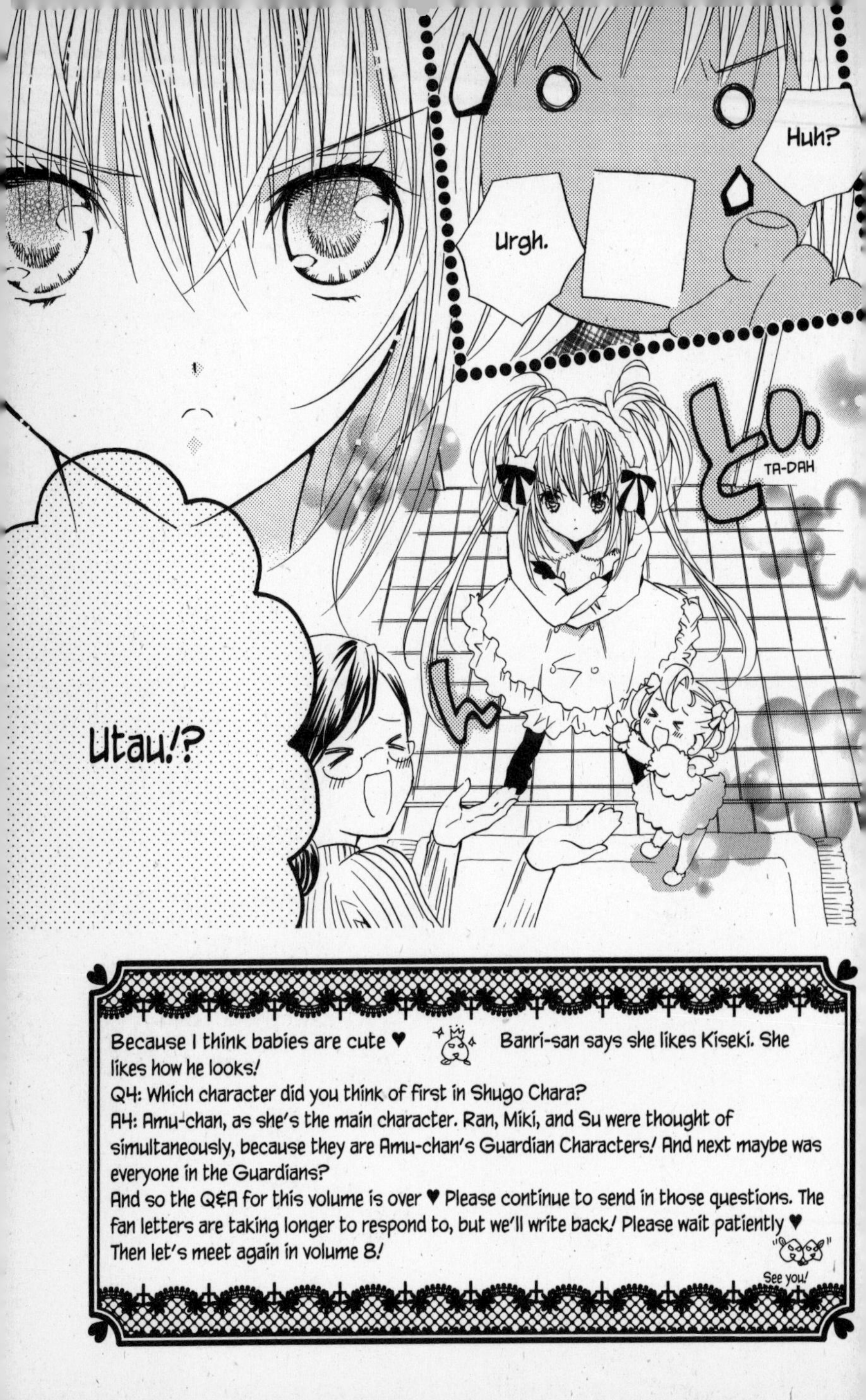
Huh?
Urgh.
TA-DAH
Utau!?

Because I think babies are cute ♥ Banri-san says she likes Kiseki. She likes how he looks!

Q4: Which character did you think of first in Shugo Chara?

A4: Amu-chan, as she's the main character. Ran, Miki, and Su were thought of simultaneously, because they are Amu-chan's Guardian Characters! And next maybe was everyone in the Guardians?

And so the Q&A for this volume is over ♥ Please continue to send in those questions. The fan letters are taking longer to respond to, but we'll write back! Please wait patiently ♥

Then let's meet again in volume 8!

See you!

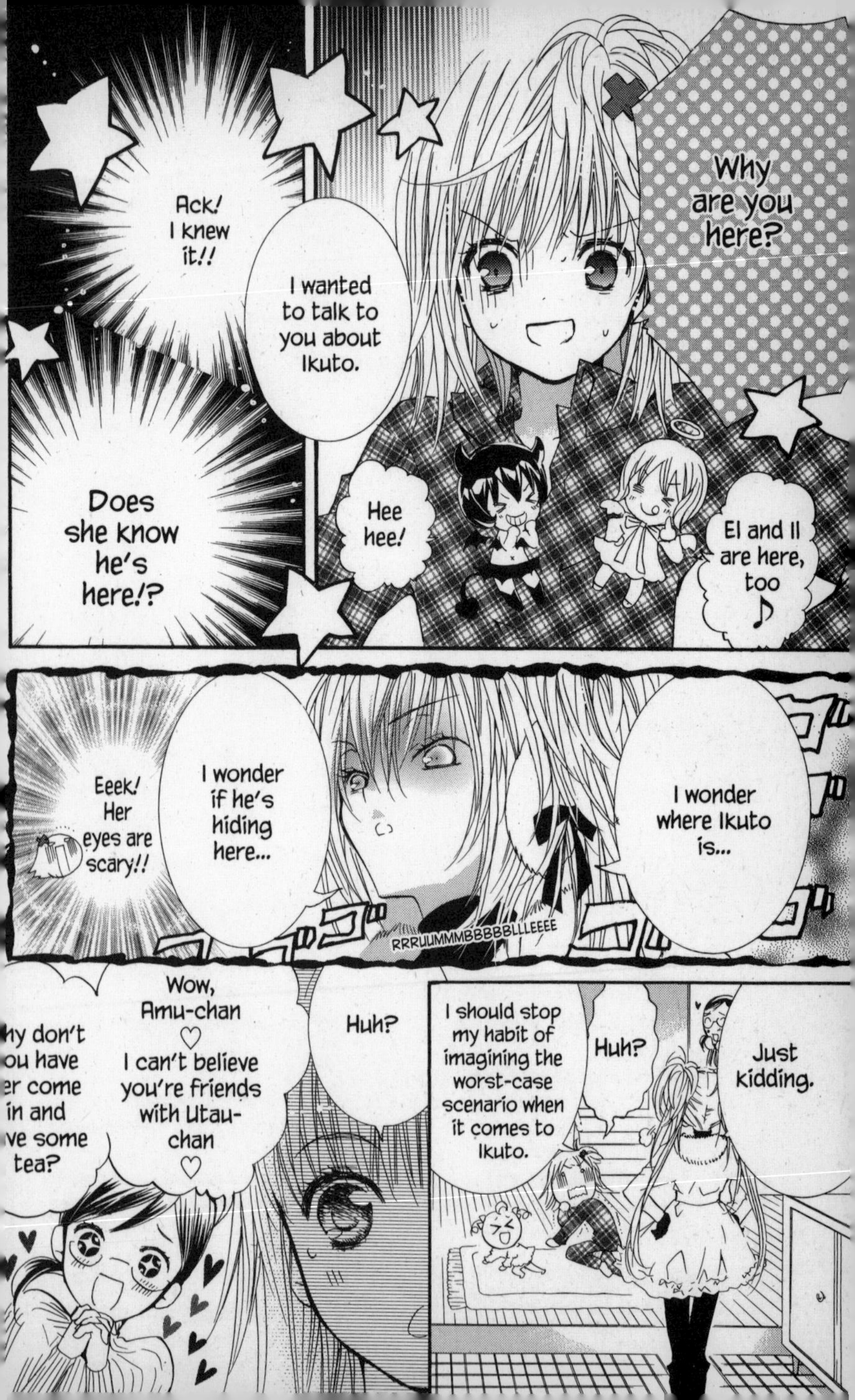
Why are you here?
I wanted to talk to you about Ikuto.
El and Il are here, too ♪
Hee hee!
Ack! I knew it!!
Does she know he's here!?
I wonder where Ikuto is...
I wonder if he's hiding here...
Eeek! Her eyes are scary!!
RRRUUMMMBBBBBLLLEEEE
Just kidding.
Huh?
I should stop my habit of imagining the worst-case scenario when it comes to Ikuto.
Huh?
Wow, Amu-chan ♡ I can't believe you're friends with Utau-chan ♡
hy don't ou have er come in and ve some tea?

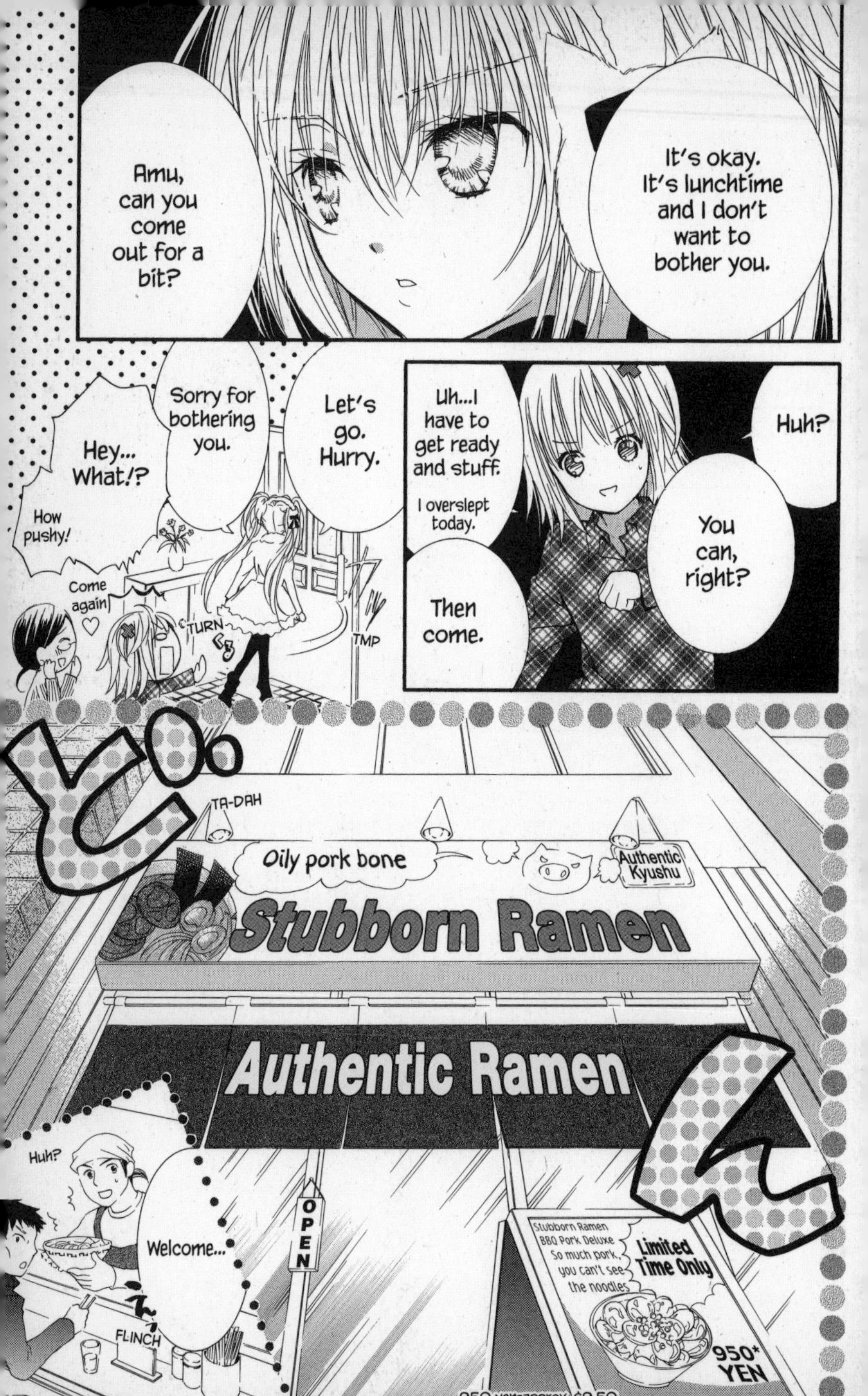
It's okay. It's lunchtime and I don't want to bother you.
Amu, can you come out for a bit?
Huh?
You can, right?
Uh...I have to get ready and stuff.
I overslept today.
Then come.
Let's go. Hurry.
TMP
Sorry for bothering you.
Hey... What!?
How pushy!
TURN
Come again ♡
Authentic Kyushu
Oily pork bone
TA-DAH
Stubborn Ramen
Authentic Ramen
Stubborn Ramen BBQ Pork Deluxe So much pork, you can't see the noodles
Limited Time Only
950* YEN
OPEN
Welcome...
Huh?
FLINCH

950 yen=approx. $9.50

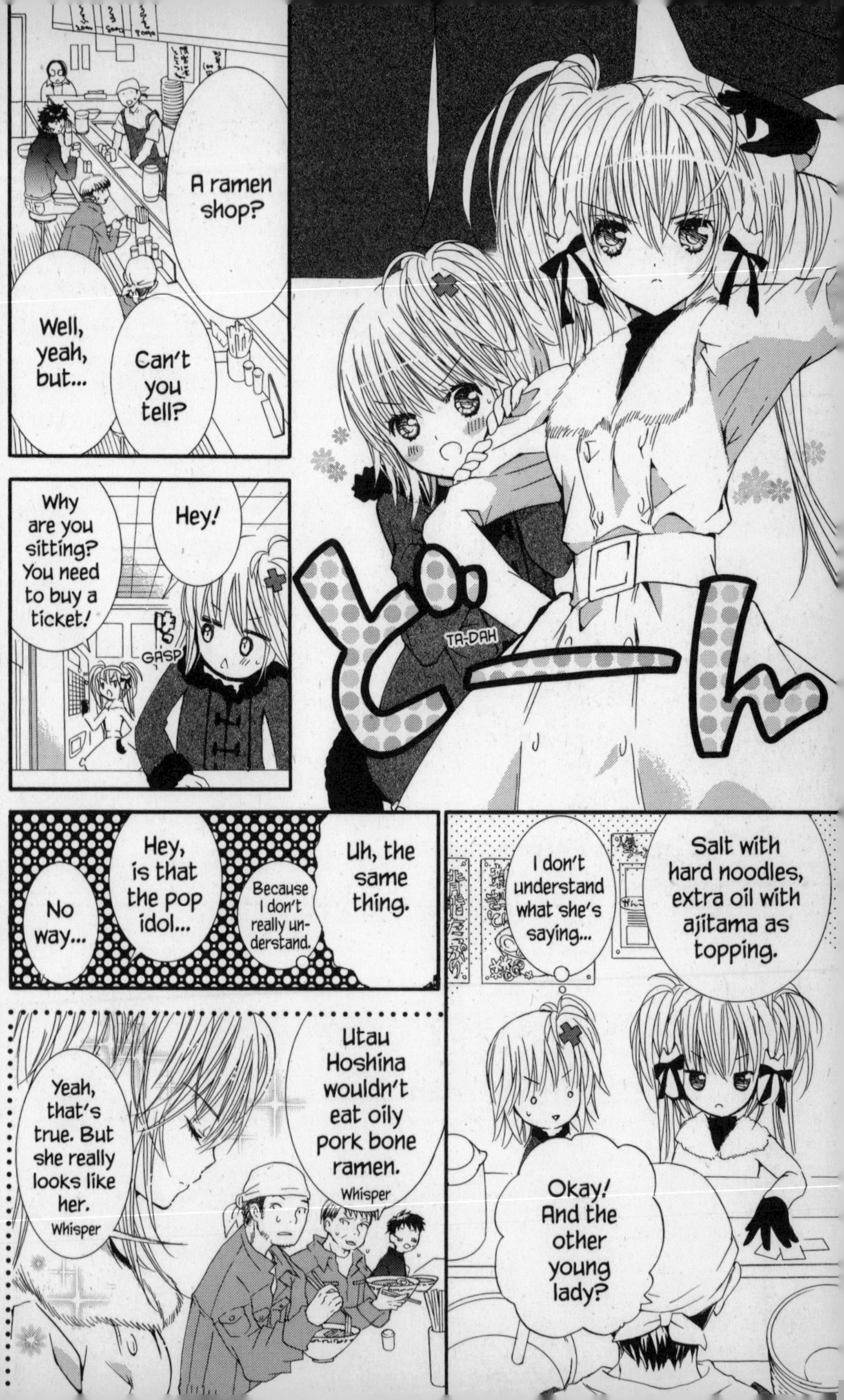

TA-DAH
A ramen shop?
Can't you tell?
Well, yeah, but...
Hey!
Why are you sitting? You need to buy a ticket!
GASP
Salt with hard noodles, extra oil with ajitama as topping.
I don't understand what she's saying...
Okay! And the other young lady?
Uh, the same thing.
Because I don't really un-derstand.
Hey, is that the pop idol...
No way...
Utau Hoshina wouldn't eat oily pork bone ramen.
Whisper
Yeah, that's true. But she really looks like her.
Whisper

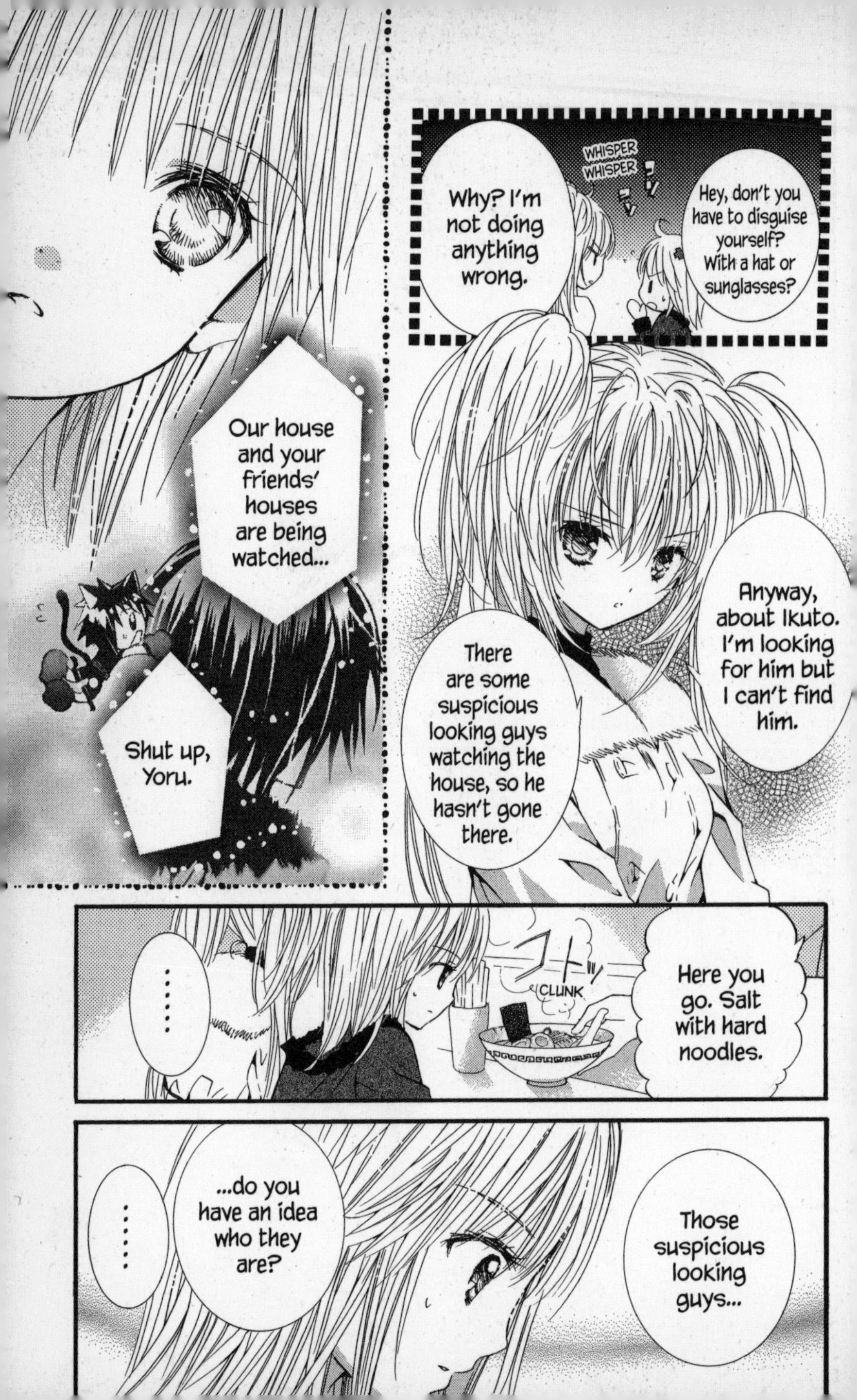
WHISPER WHISPER
Hey, don't you have to disguise yourself? With a hat or sunglasses?
Why? I'm not doing anything wrong.
Anyway, about Ikuto. I'm looking for him but I can't find him.
There are some suspicious looking guys watching the house, so he hasn't gone there.
Our house and your friends' houses are being watched...
Shut up, Yoru.
Here you go. Salt with hard noodles.
CLUNK
......
Those suspicious looking guys...
...do you have an idea who they are?
......

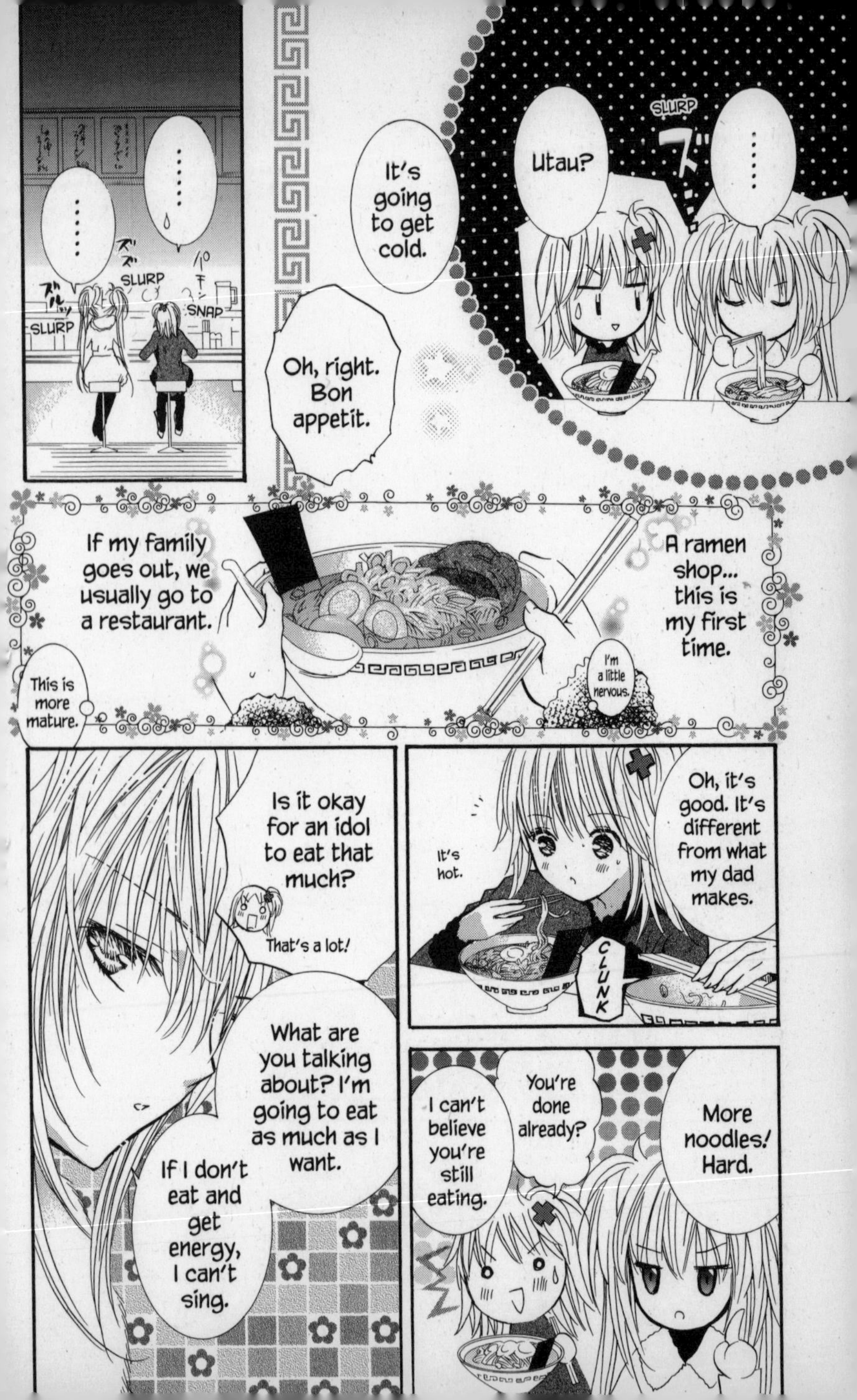
......
SLURP
Utau?
It's going to get cold.
Oh, right. Bon appetit.
......
......
SLURP
SNAP
SLURP
A ramen shop... this is my first time.
I'm a little nervous.
If my family goes out, we usually go to a restaurant.
This is more mature.
Oh, it's good. It's different from what my dad makes.
It's hot.
CLUNK
More noodles! Hard.
You're done already?
I can't believe you're still eating.
Is it okay for an idol to eat that much?
That's a lot!
What are you talking about? I'm going to eat as much as I want.
If I don't eat and get energy, I can't sing.

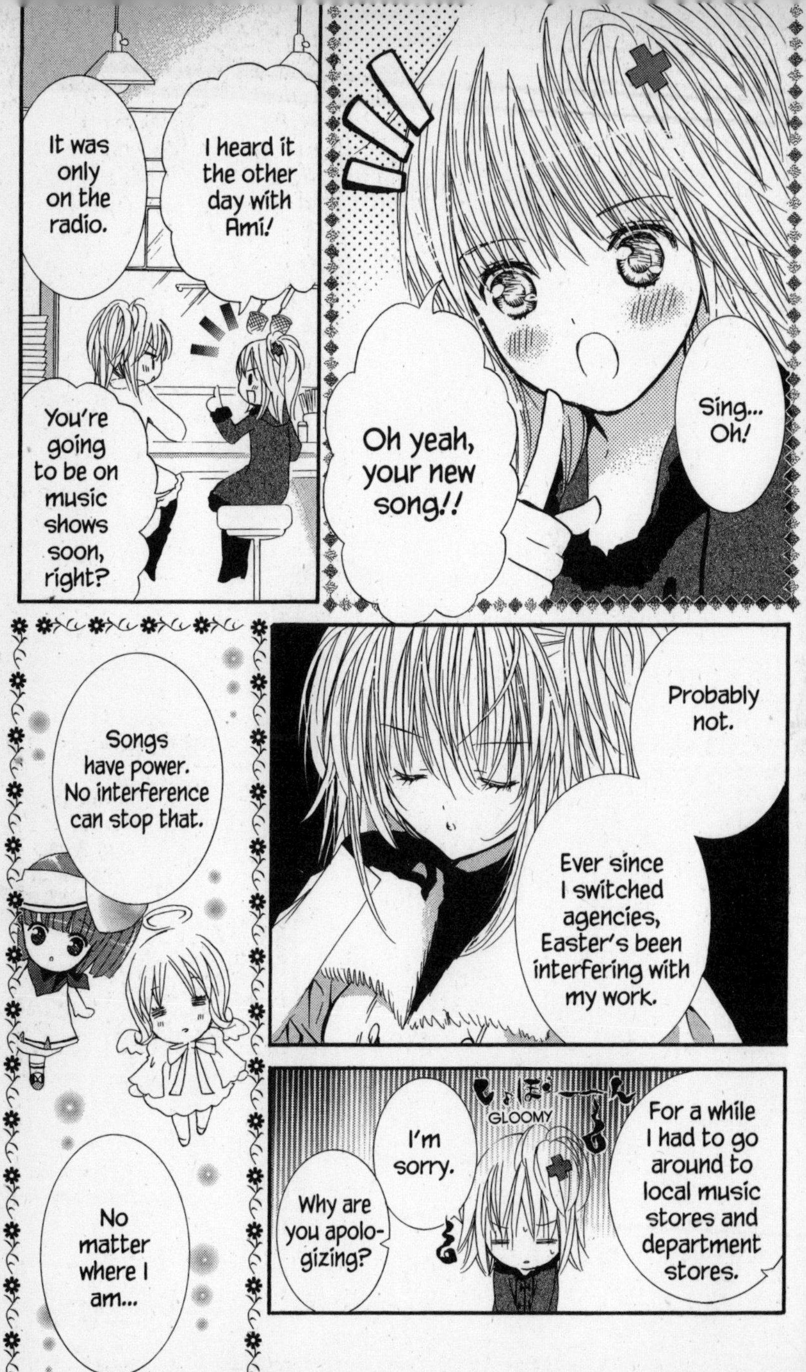

Sing... Oh!
Oh yeah, your new song!!
I heard it the other day with Ami!
It was only on the radio.
You're going to be on music shows soon, right?
Probably not.
Ever since I switched agencies, Easter's been interfering with my work.
For a while I had to go around to local music stores and department stores.
GLOOMY
I'm sorry.
Why are you apologizing?
Songs have power. No interference can stop that.
No matter where I am...

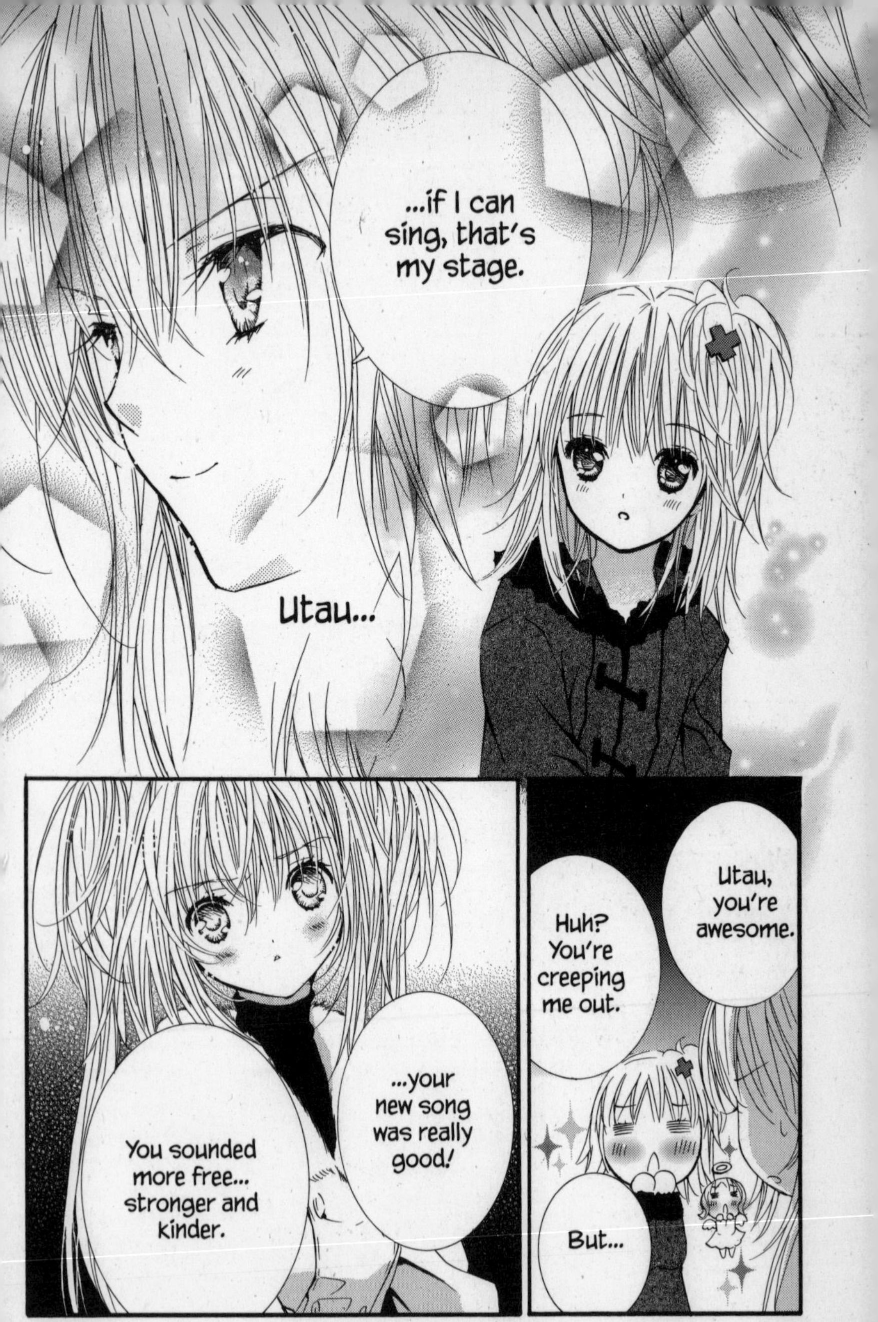
...if I can sing, that's my stage.
Utau...
Utau, you're awesome.
Huh? You're creeping me out.
But...
...your new song was really good!
You sounded more free... stronger and kinder.

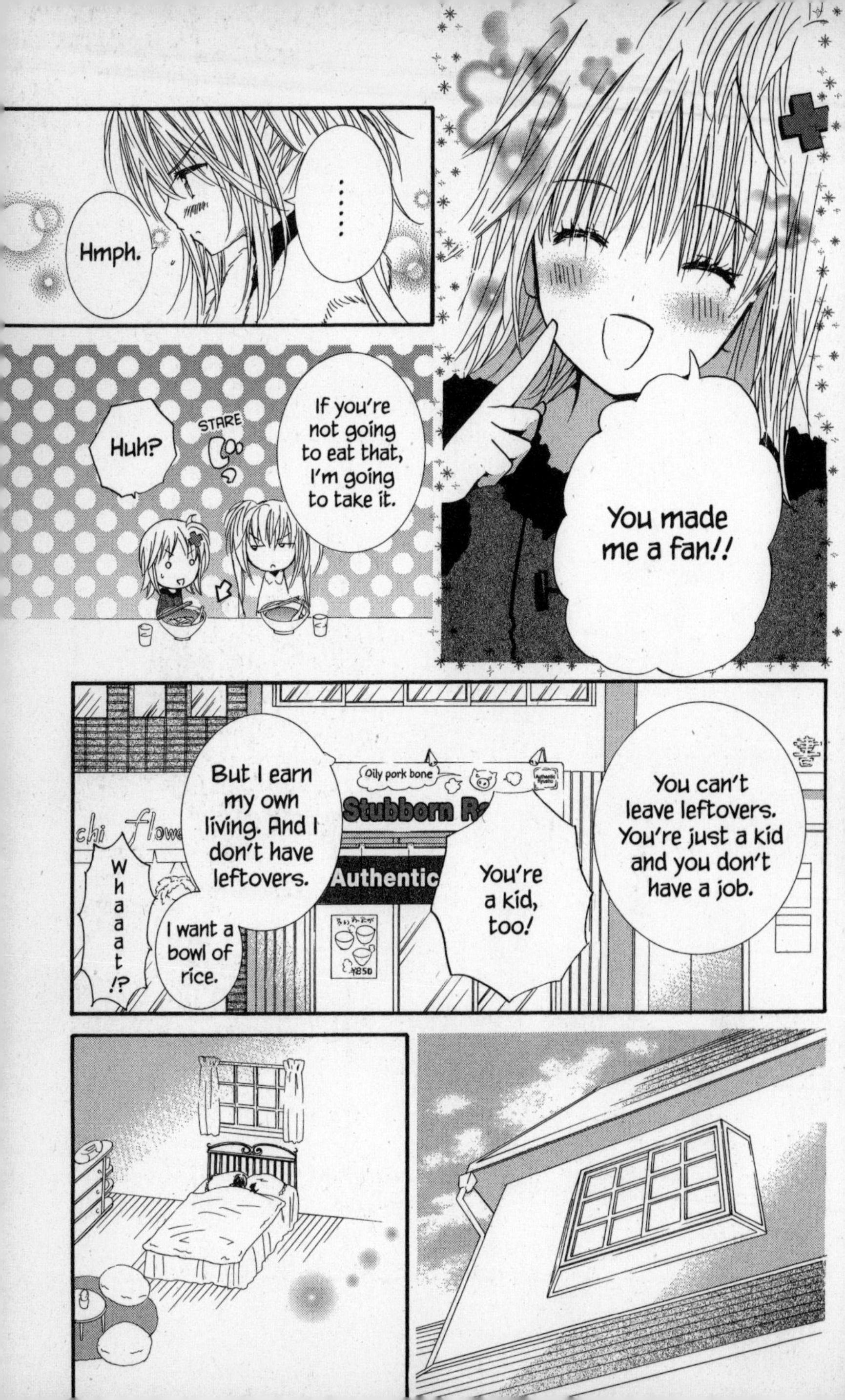
You made me a fan!!
......
Hmph.
If you're not going to eat that, I'm going to take it.
STARE
Huh?
You can't leave leftovers. You're just a kid and you don't have a job.
You're a kid, too!
Oily pork bone
Stubborn Ra
Authentic
But I earn my own living. And I don't have leftovers.
I want a bowl of rice.
Whaaaat!?

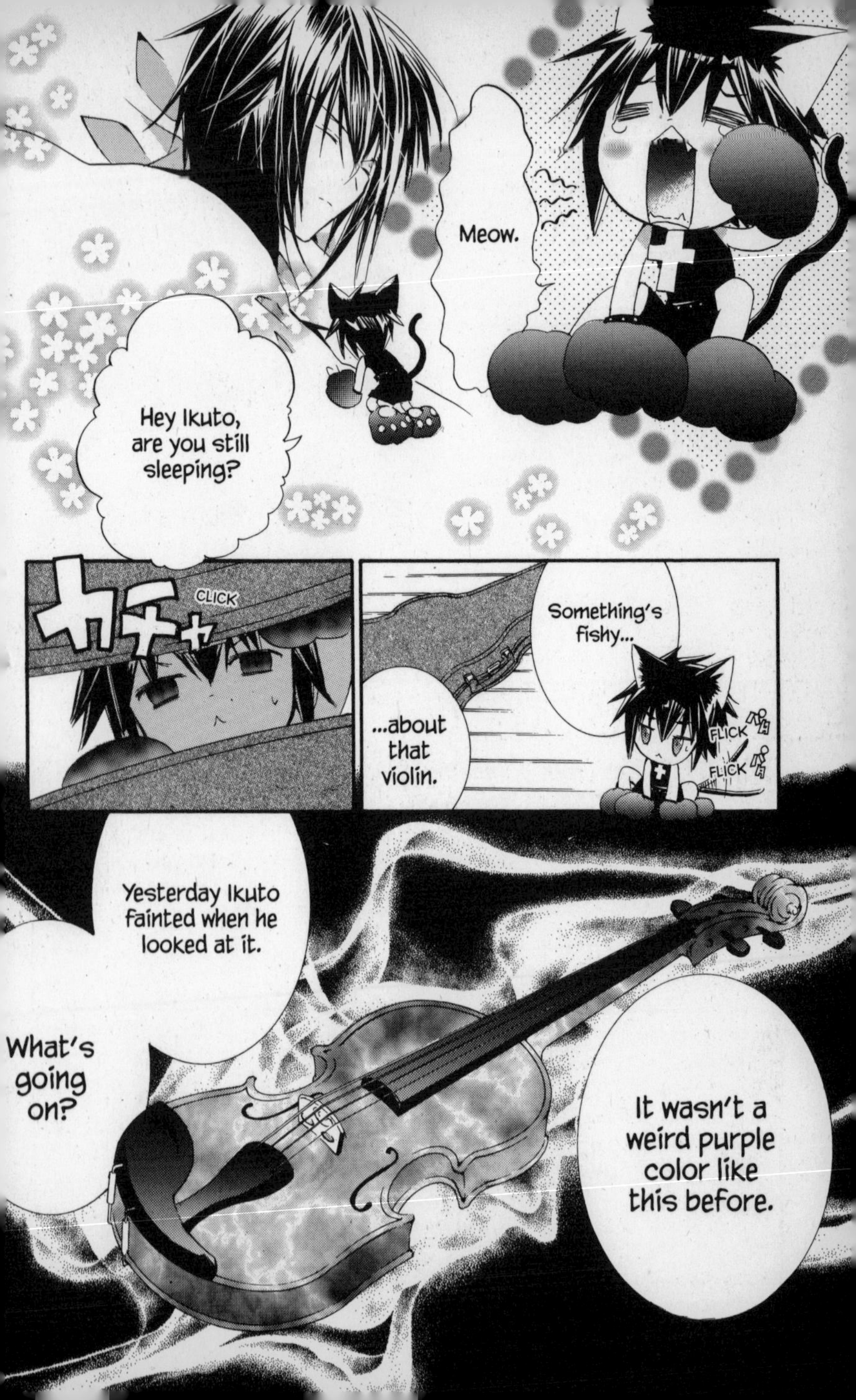

Meow.
Hey Ikuto, are you still sleeping?
Something's fishy...
...about that violin.
FLICK
FLICK
CLICK
Yesterday Ikuto fainted when he looked at it.
It wasn't a weird purple color like this before.
What's going on?

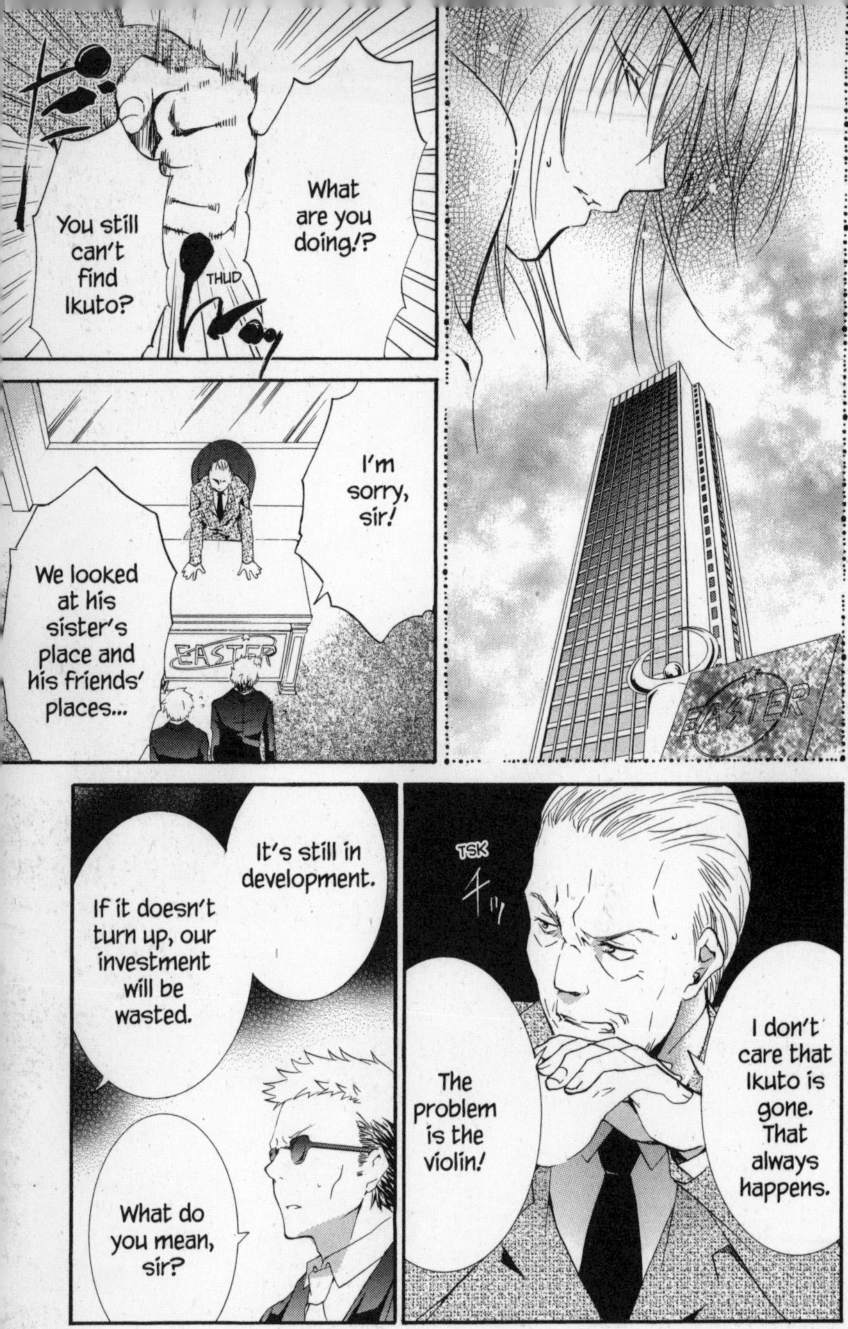
What are you doing!?
You still can't find Ikuto?
THUD
I'm sorry, sir!
We looked at his sister's place and his friends' places...
TSK
I don't care that Ikuto is gone. That always happens.
The problem is the violin!
It's still in development.
If it doesn't turn up, our investment will be wasted.
What do you mean, sir?

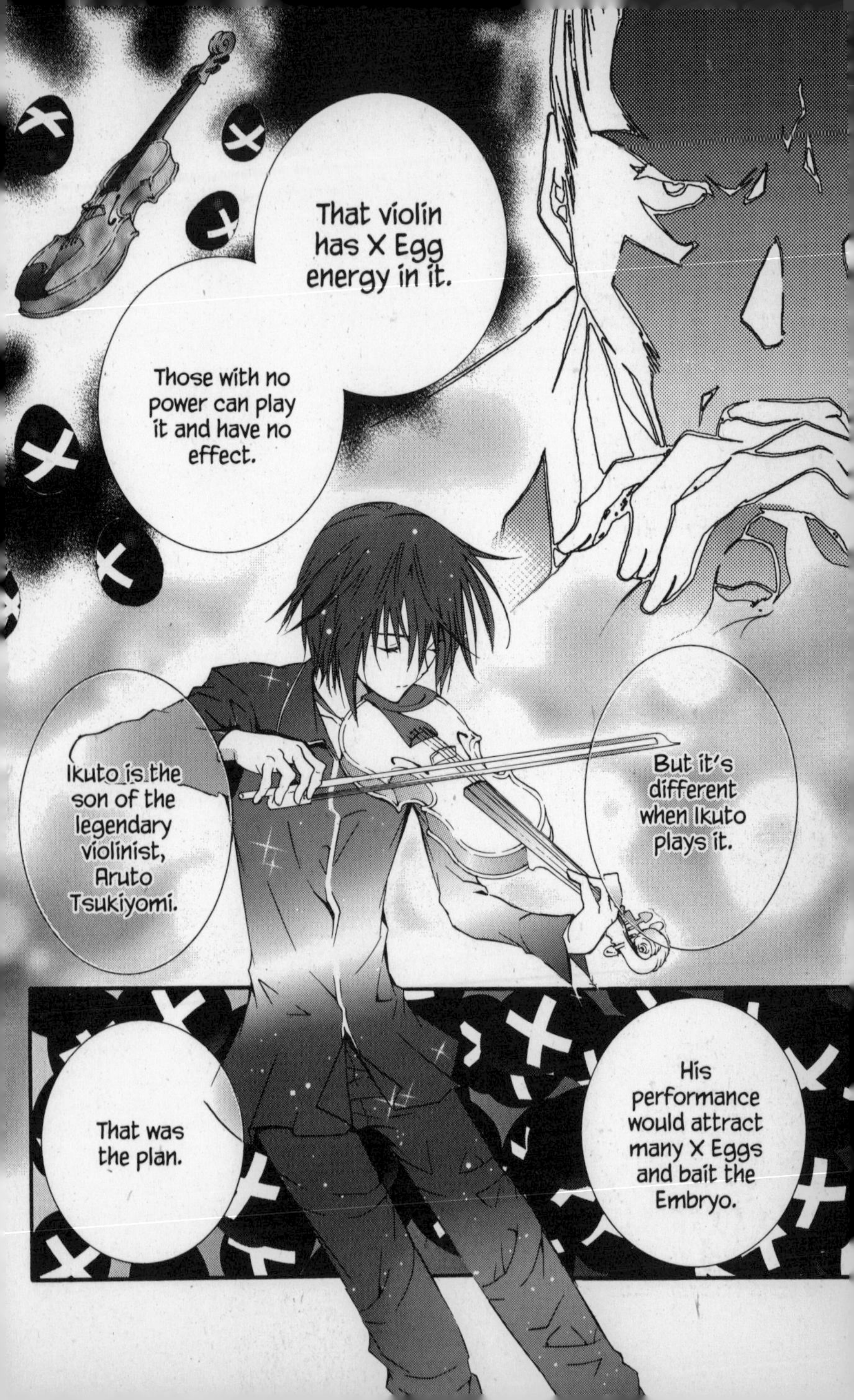
That violin has X Egg energy in it.
Those with no power can play it and have no effect.
But it's different when Ikuto plays it.
Ikuto is the son of the legendary violinist, Aruto Tsukiyomi.
His performance would attract many X Eggs and bait the Embryo.
That was the plan.

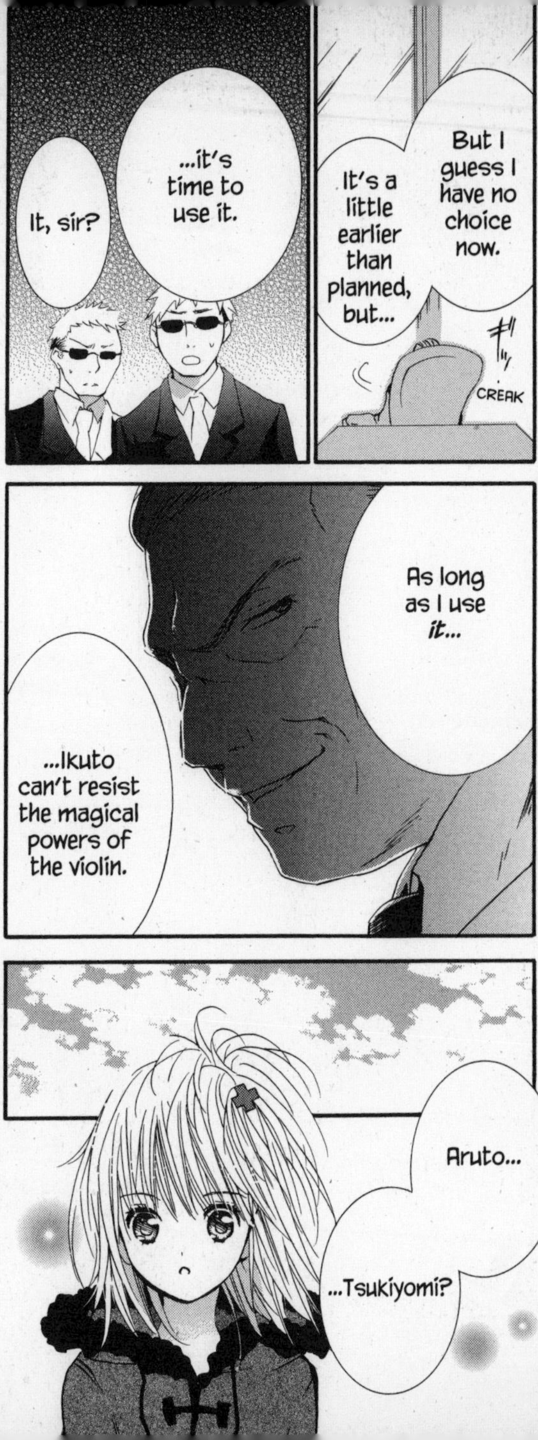
But I guess I have no choice now.
It's a little earlier than planned, but...
CREAK
...it's time to use it.
It, sir?
As long as I use *it*...
...Ikuto can't resist the magical powers of the violin.
Aruto...
...Tsukiyomi?

character profile

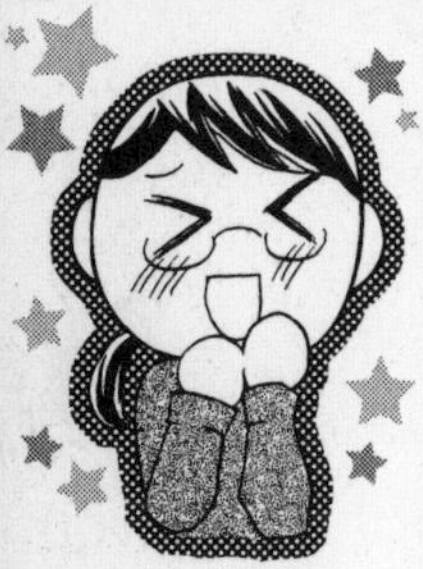

Midori Hinamori

Birthday: 12/27
Blood Type: A
Sign: Capricorn

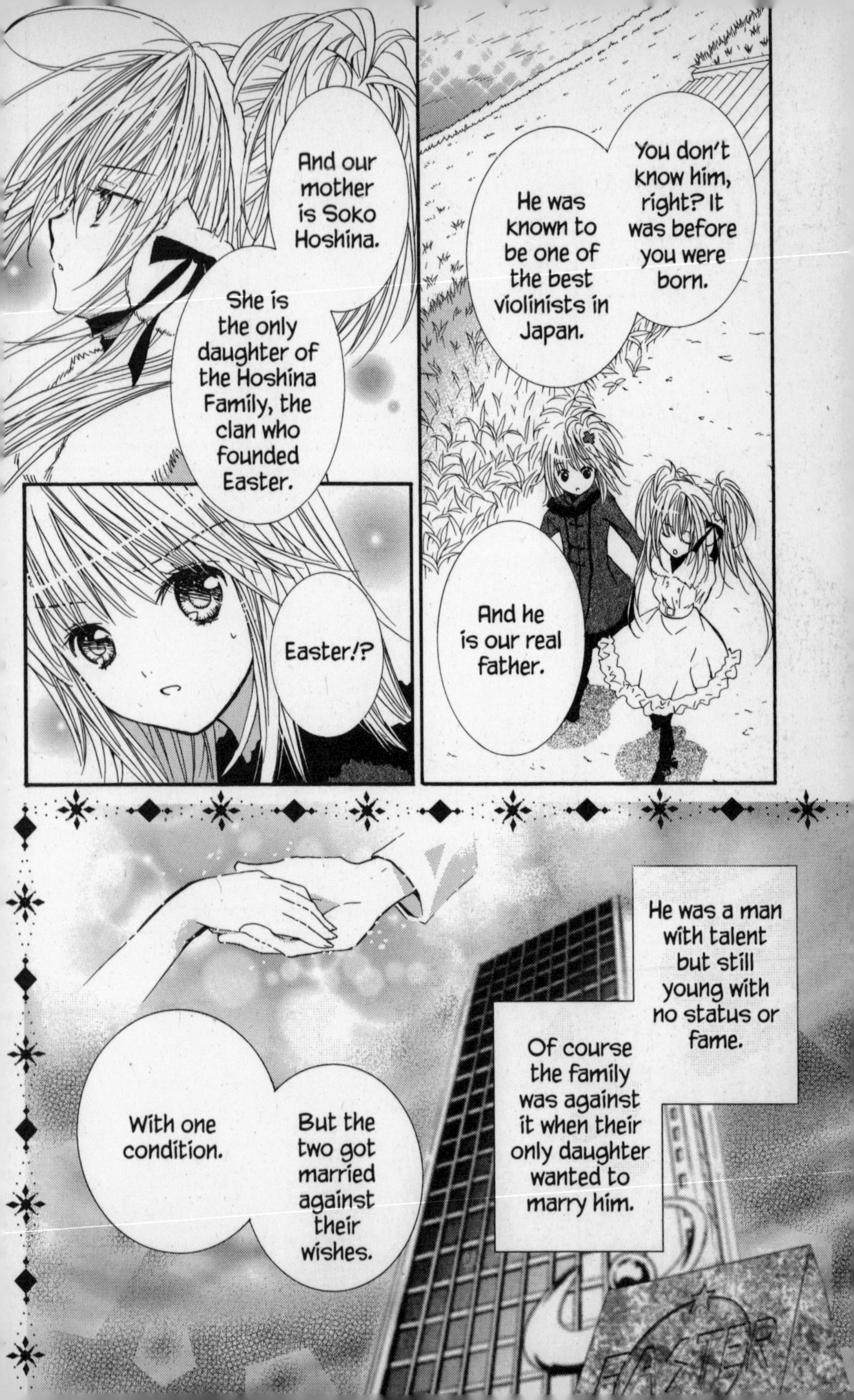
You don't know him, right? It was before you were born.
He was known to be one of the best violinists in Japan.
And he is our real father.
And our mother is Soko Hoshina.
She is the only daughter of the Hoshina Family, the clan who founded Easter.
Easter!?
He was a man with talent but still young with no status or fame.
Of course the family was against it when their only daughter wanted to marry him.
But the two got married against their wishes.
With one condition.

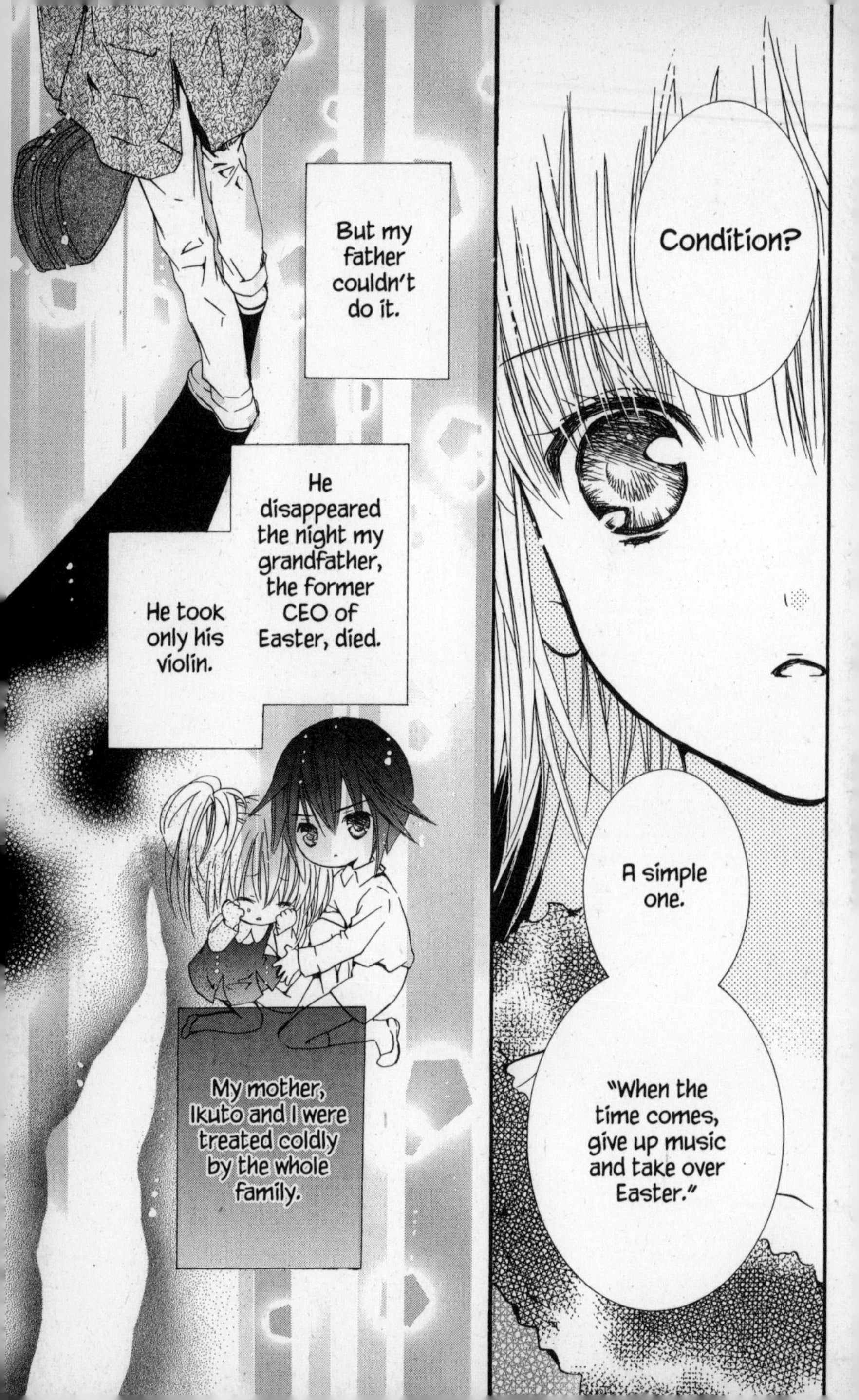
Condition?
A simple one.
"When the time comes, give up music and take over Easter."
But my father couldn't do it.
He disappeared the night my grandfather, the former CEO of Easter, died.
He took only his violin.
My mother, Ikuto and I were treated coldly by the whole family.

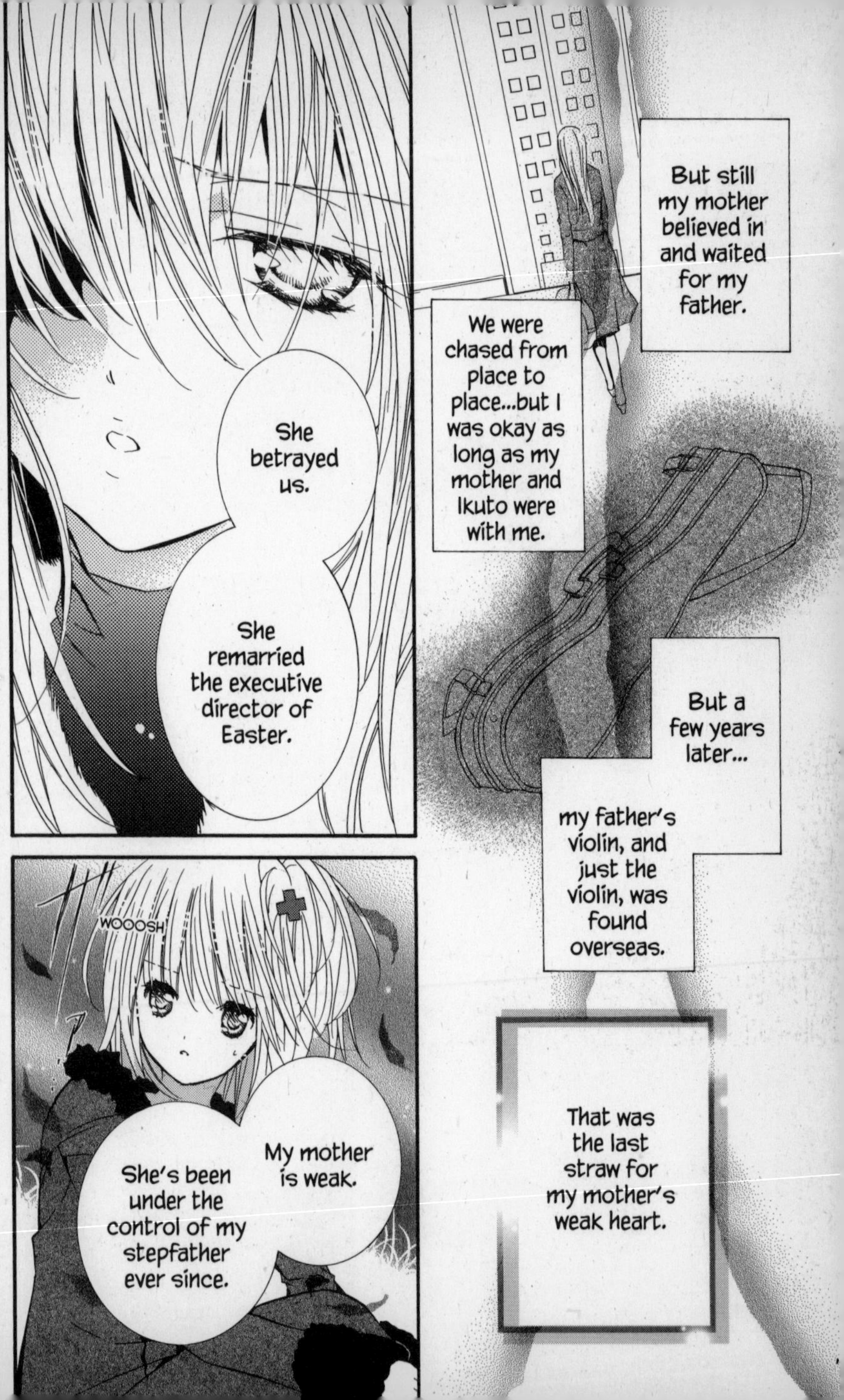
But still my mother believed in and waited for my father.
We were chased from place to place...but I was okay as long as my mother and Ikuto were with me.
But a few years later...
my father's violin, and just the violin, was found overseas.
That was the last straw for my mother's weak heart.
She betrayed us.
She remarried the executive director of Easter.
WOOOSH
My mother is weak.
She's been under the control of my stepfather ever since.

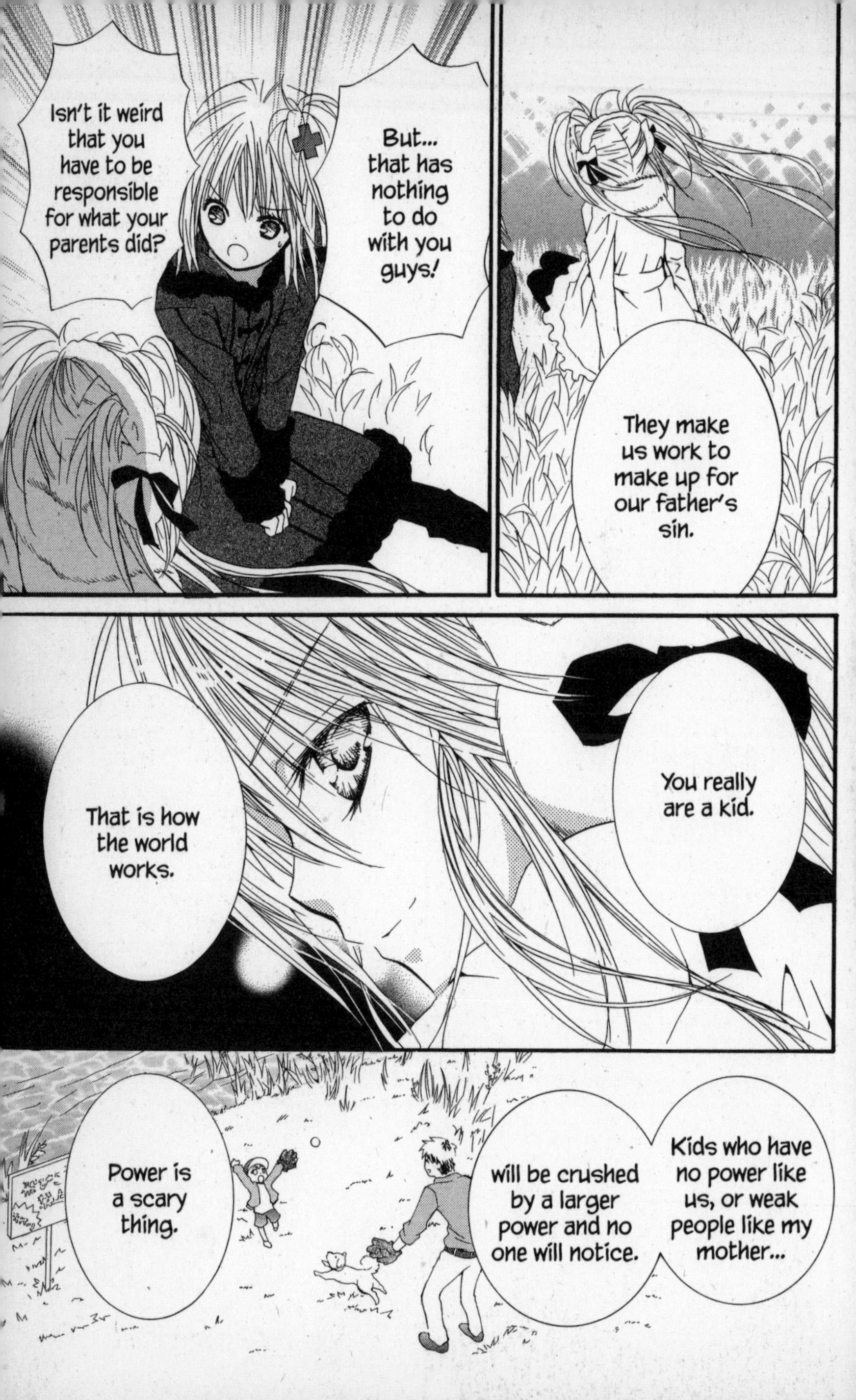
They make us work to make up for our father's sin.
But... that has nothing to do with you guys!
Isn't it weird that you have to be responsible for what your parents did?
You really are a kid.
That is how the world works.
Kids who have no power like us, or weak people like my mother...
will be crushed by a larger power and no one will notice.
Power is a scary thing.

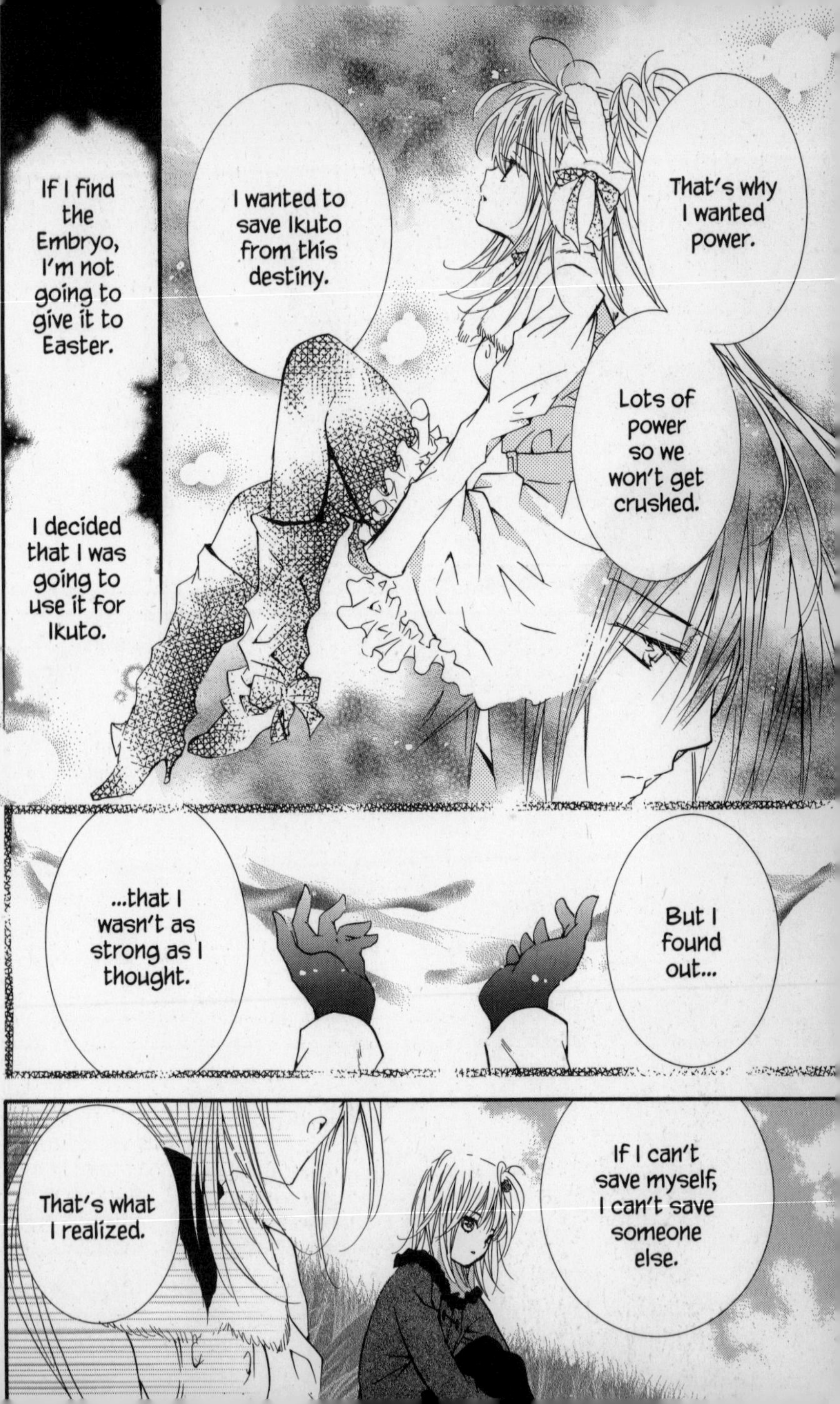
That's why I wanted power.
Lots of power so we won't get crushed.
I wanted to save Ikuto from this destiny.
If I find the Embryo, I'm not going to give it to Easter.
I decided that I was going to use it for Ikuto.
But I found out...
...that I wasn't as strong as I thought.
If I can't save myself, I can't save someone else.
That's what I realized.

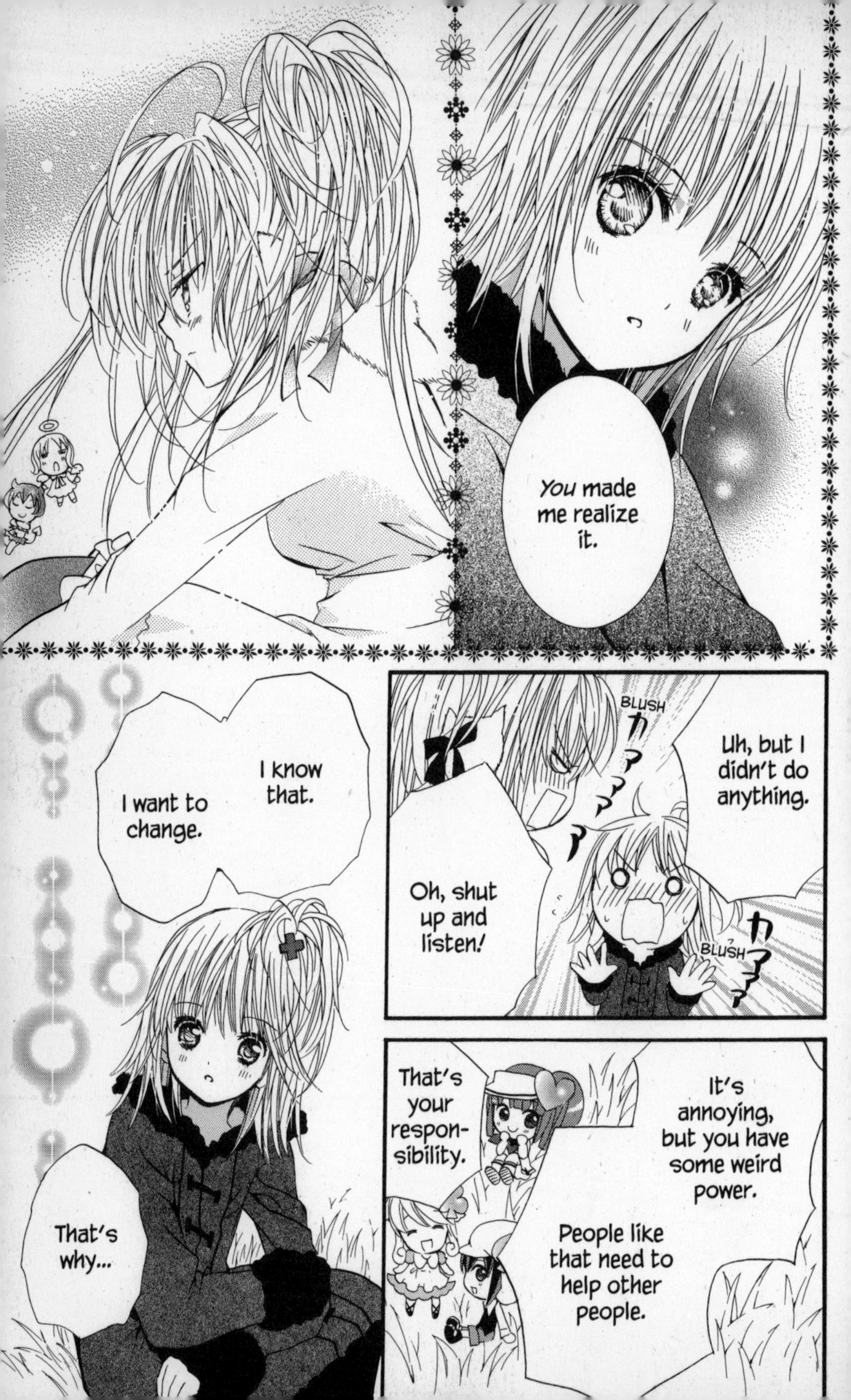
You made me realize it.
BLUSH
Uh, but I didn't do anything.
Oh, shut up and listen!
BLUSH
It's annoying, but you have some weird power.
People like that need to help other people.
That's your respon-sibility.
I know that.
I want to change.
That's why...

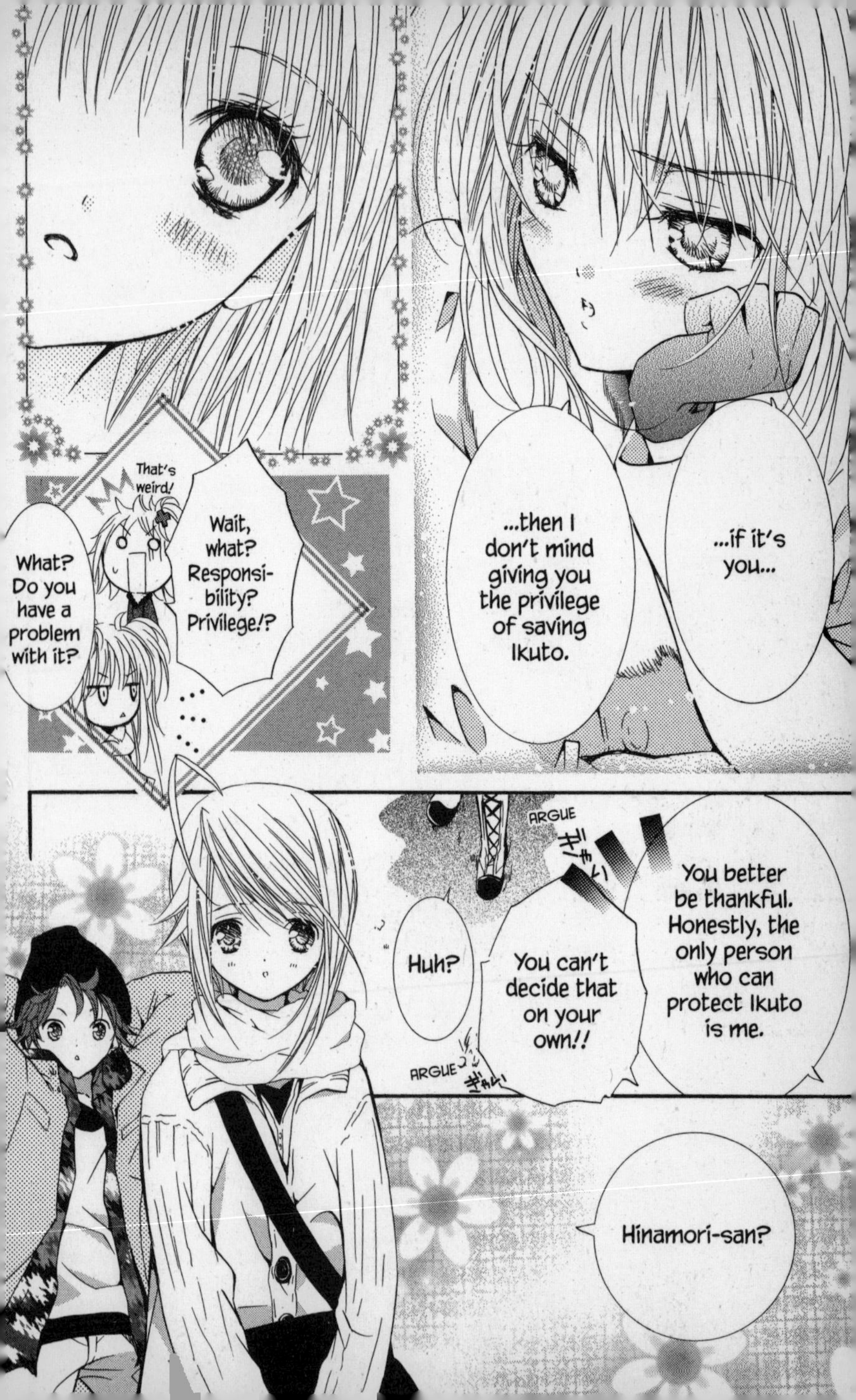
...if it's you...
...then I don't mind giving you the privilege of saving Ikuto.
Wait, what? Responsi-bility? Privilege!?
That's weird!
What? Do you have a problem with it?
You better be thankful. Honestly, the only person who can protect Ikuto is me.
ARGUE
You can't decide that on your own!!
ARGUE
Huh?
Hinamori-san?

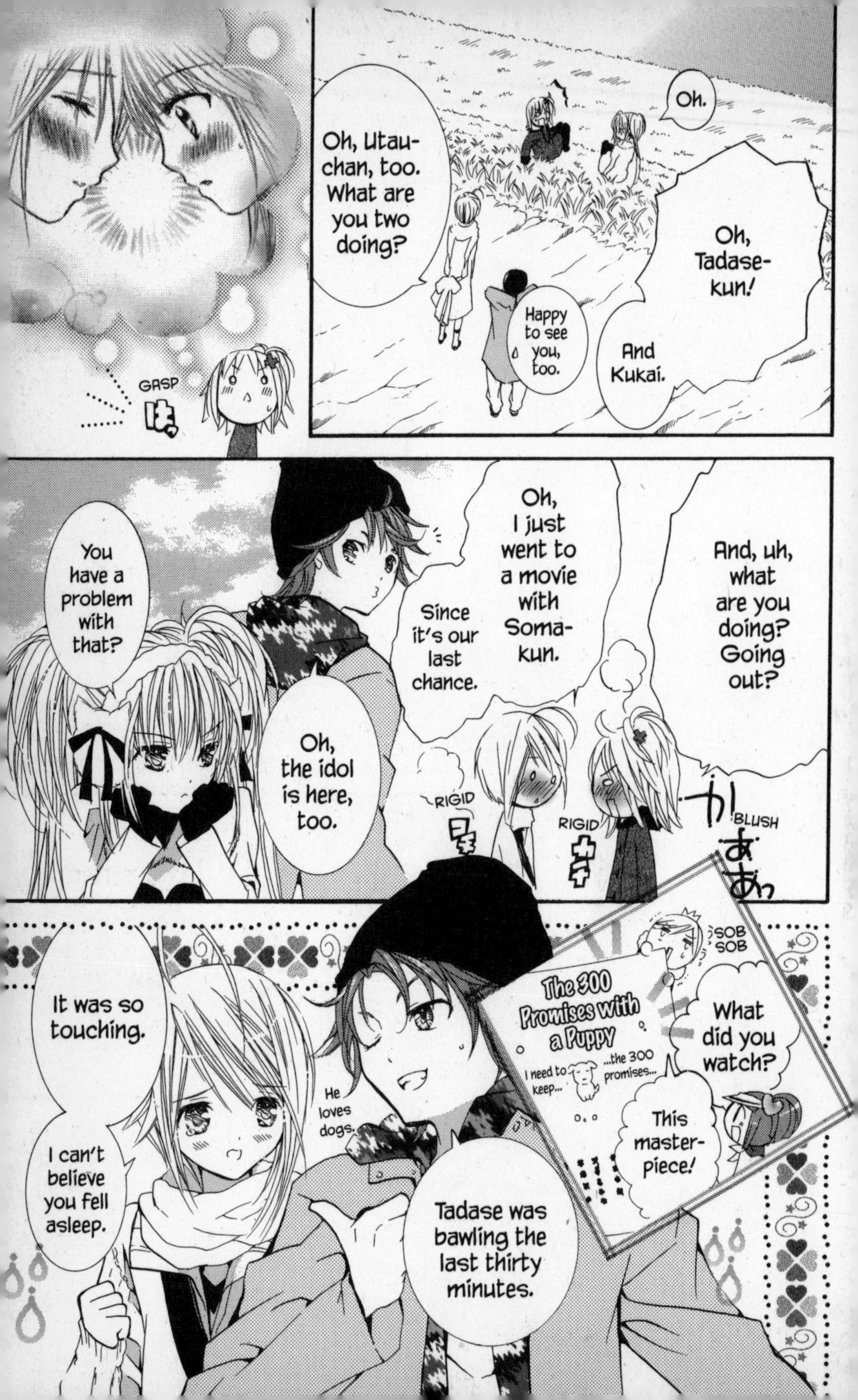

Oh.
Oh, Tadase-kun!
And Kukai.
Happy to see you, too.
Oh, Utau-chan, too. What are you two doing?
GASP
はっ
And, uh, what are you doing? Going out?
BLUSH
RIGID
RIGID
Oh, I just went to a movie with Soma-kun.
Since it's our last chance.
Oh, the idol is here, too.
You have a problem with that?
What did you watch?
SOB SOB
This masterpiece!
The 300 Promises with a Puppy
I need to keep...
...the 300 promises...
Tadase was bawling the last thirty minutes.
He loves dogs.
It was so touching.
I can't believe you fell asleep.

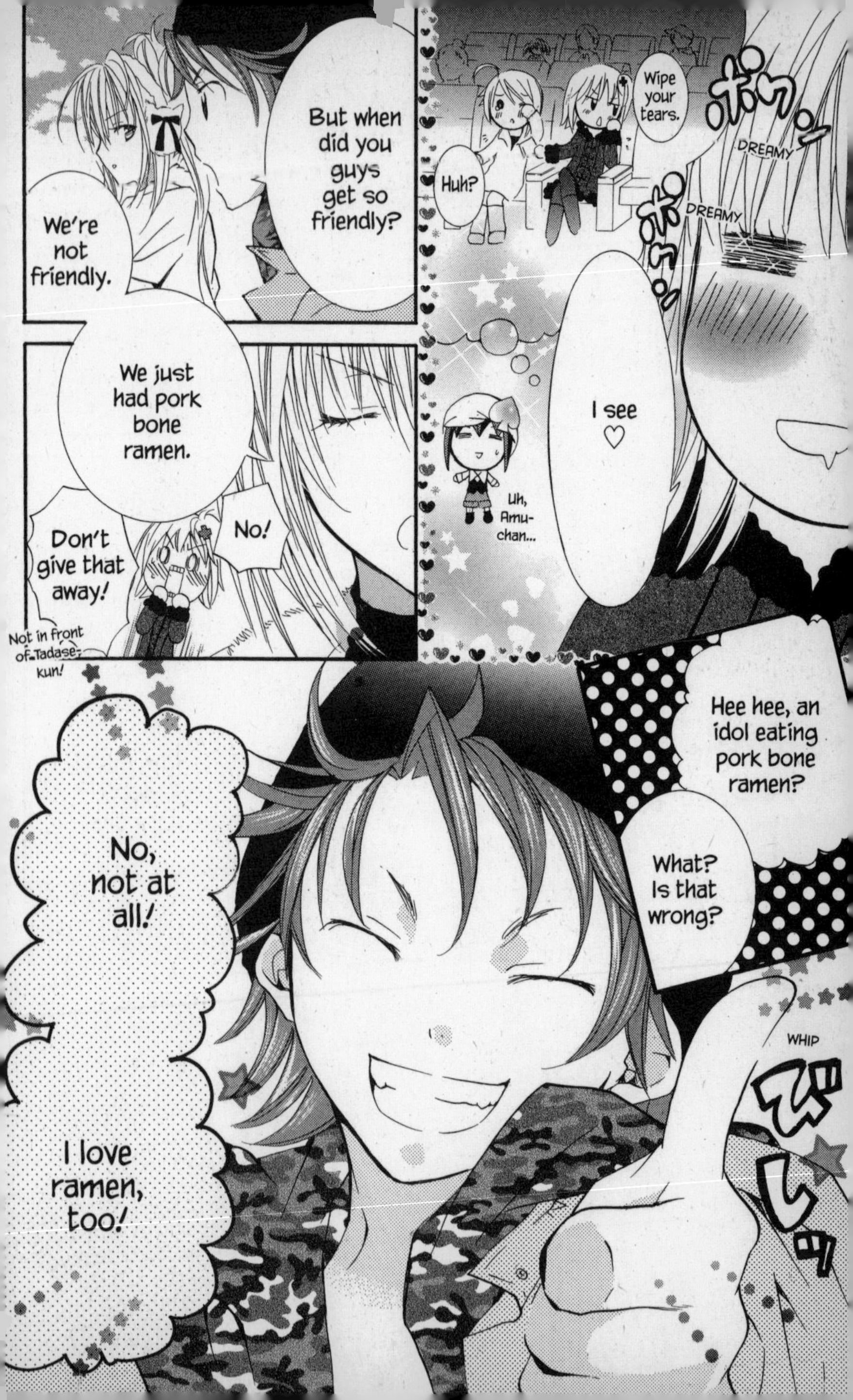
Wipe your tears.
Huh?
DREAMY
DREAMY
I see ♡
Uh, Amu-chan...
But when did you guys get so friendly?
We're not friendly.
We just had pork bone ramen.
No!
Don't give that away!
Not in front of Tadase-kun!
Hee hee, an idol eating pork bone ramen?
What? Is that wrong?
WHIP
No, not at all!
I love ramen, too!

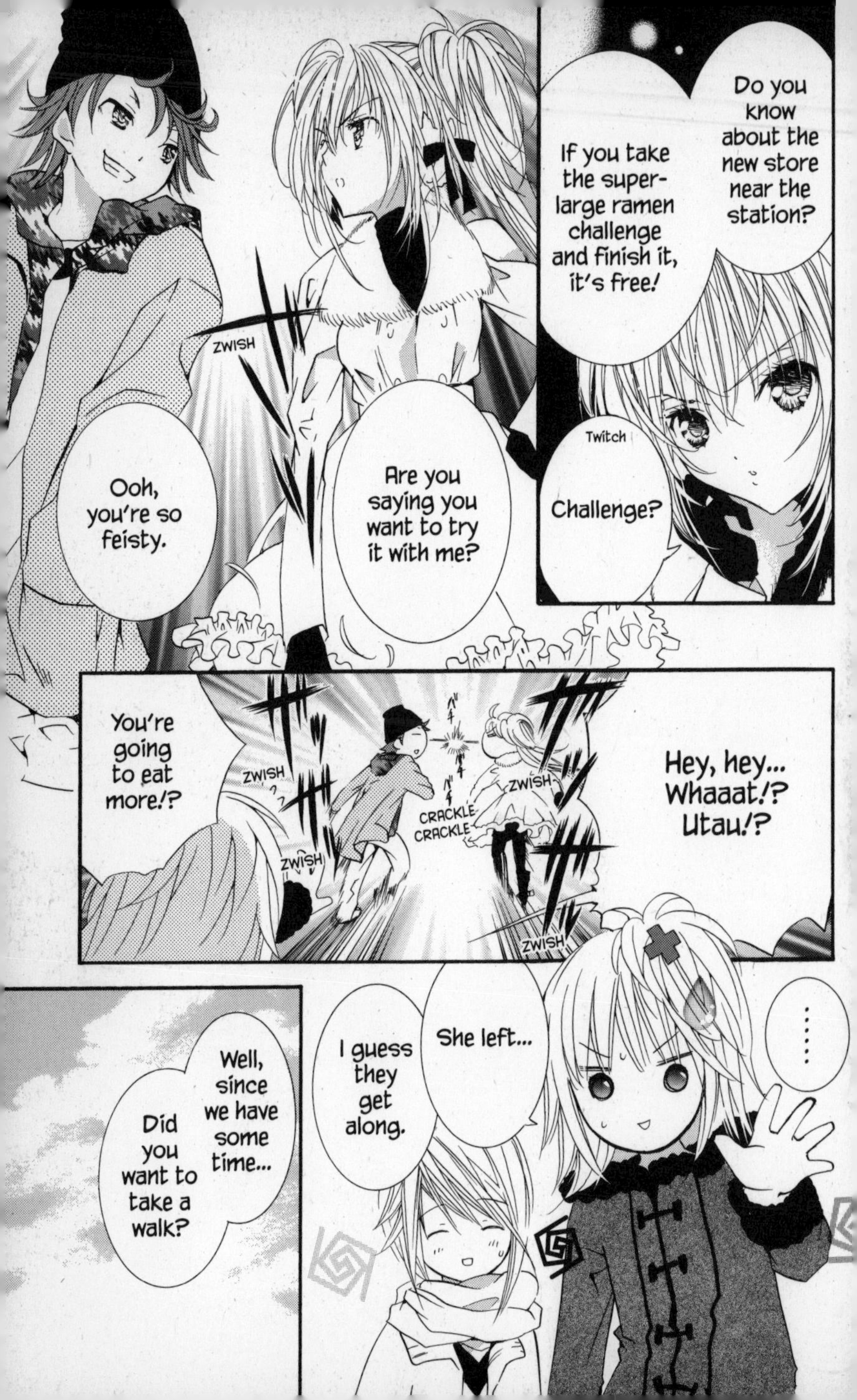
Do you know about the new store near the station?
If you take the super-large ramen challenge and finish it, it's free!
Twitch
Challenge?
ZWISH
Are you saying you want to try it with me?
Ooh, you're so feisty.
Hey, hey... Whaaat!? Utau!?
ZWISH
CRACKLE CRACKLE
ZWISH
ZWISH
You're going to eat more!?
ZWISH
......
She left...
I guess they get along.
Well, since we have some time...
Did you want to take a walk?

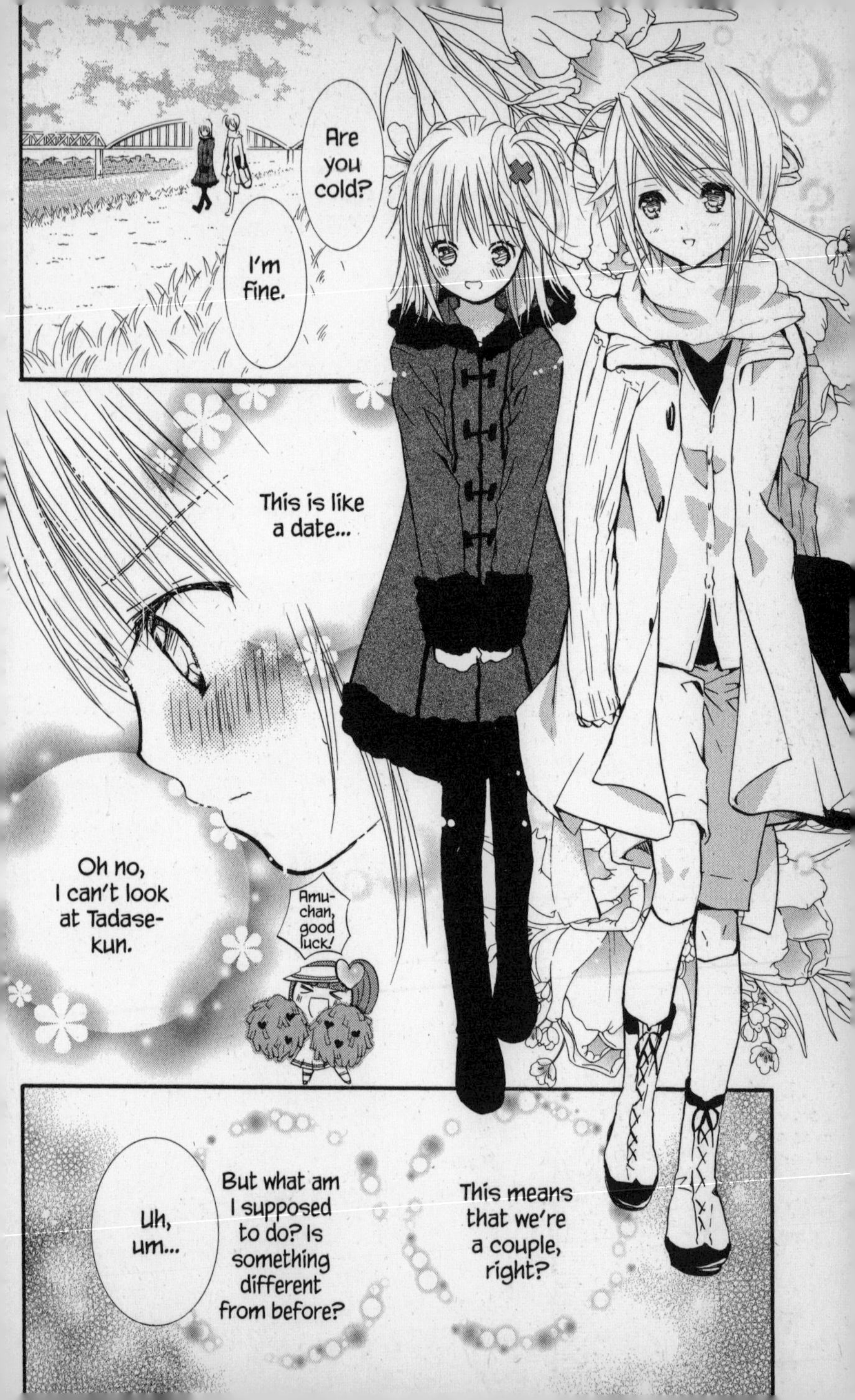
Are you cold?
I'm fine.
This is like a date...
Amu-chan, good luck!
Oh no, I can't look at Tadase-kun.
This means that we're a couple, right?
But what am I supposed to do? Is something different from before?
Uh, um...

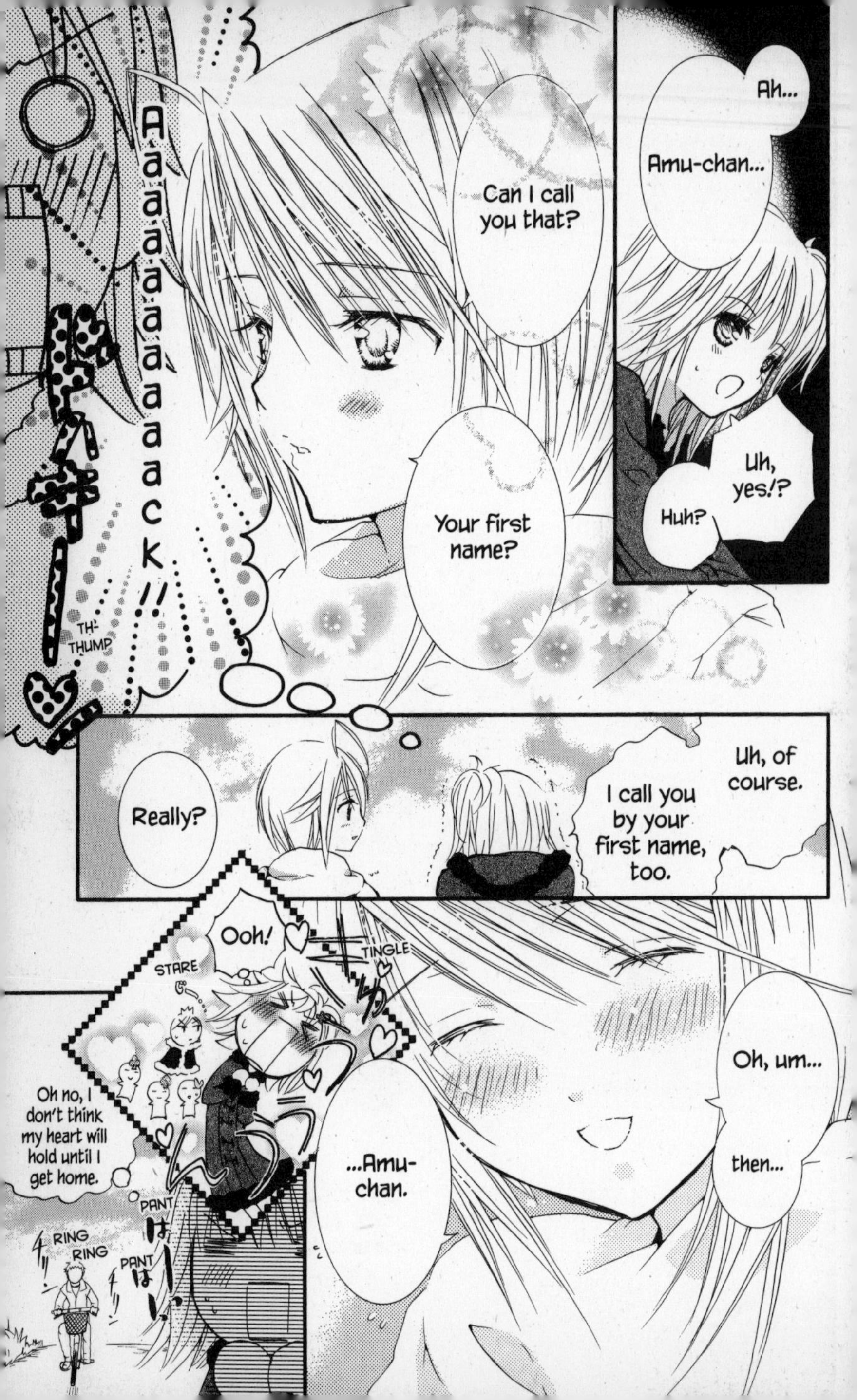
Ah...
Amu-chan...
Uh, yes!?
Huh?
Can I call you that?
Your first name?
Aaaaaaaaaaaack!!
TH-THUMP
Uh, of course.
I call you by your first name, too.
Really?
Oh, um...
then...
...Amu-chan.
Ooh!
TINGLE
STARE
Oh no, I don't think my heart will hold until I get home.
PANT
PANT
RING
RING

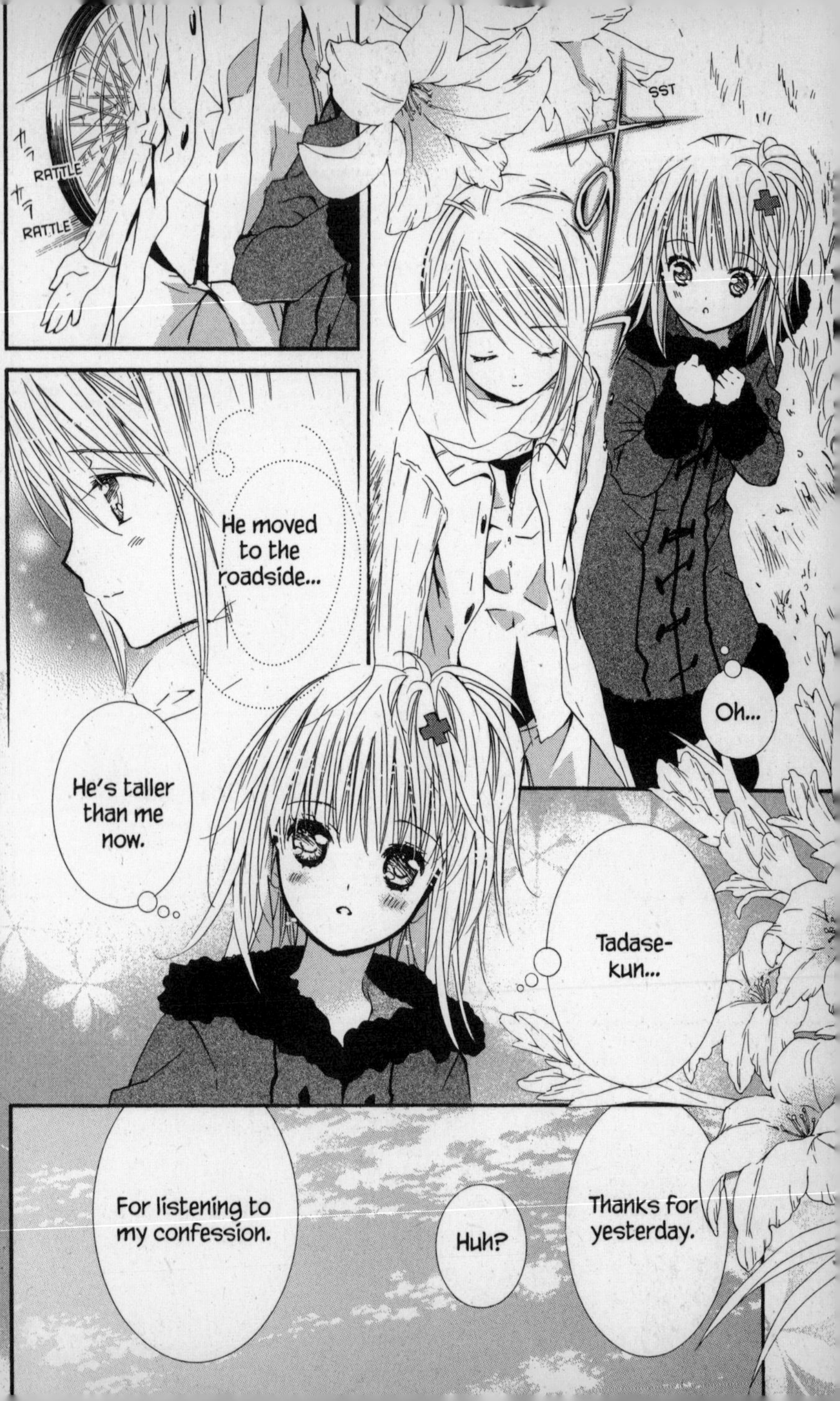
SST
Oh...
カラ
RATTLE
カラ
RATTLE
He moved to the roadside...
He's taller than me now.
Tadase-kun...
Thanks for yesterday.
Huh?
For listening to my confession.

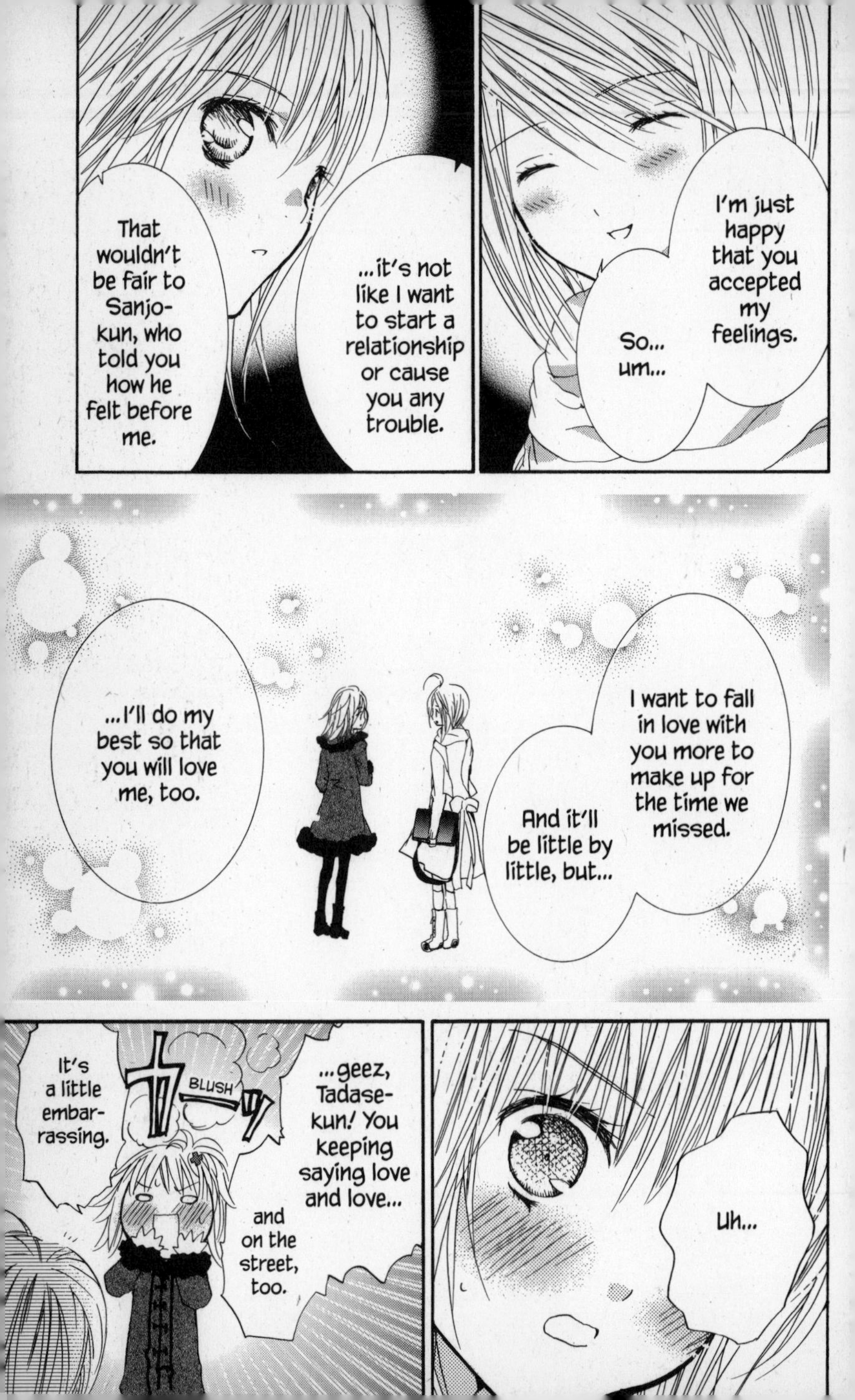
I'm just happy that you accepted my feelings.
So... um...
...it's not like I want to start a relationship or cause you any trouble.
That wouldn't be fair to Sanjo-kun, who told you how he felt before me.
I want to fall in love with you more to make up for the time we missed.
And it'll be little by little, but...
...I'll do my best so that you will love me, too.
Uh...
BLUSH
...geez, Tadase-kun! You keeping saying love and love...
and on the street, too.
It's a little embarrassing.

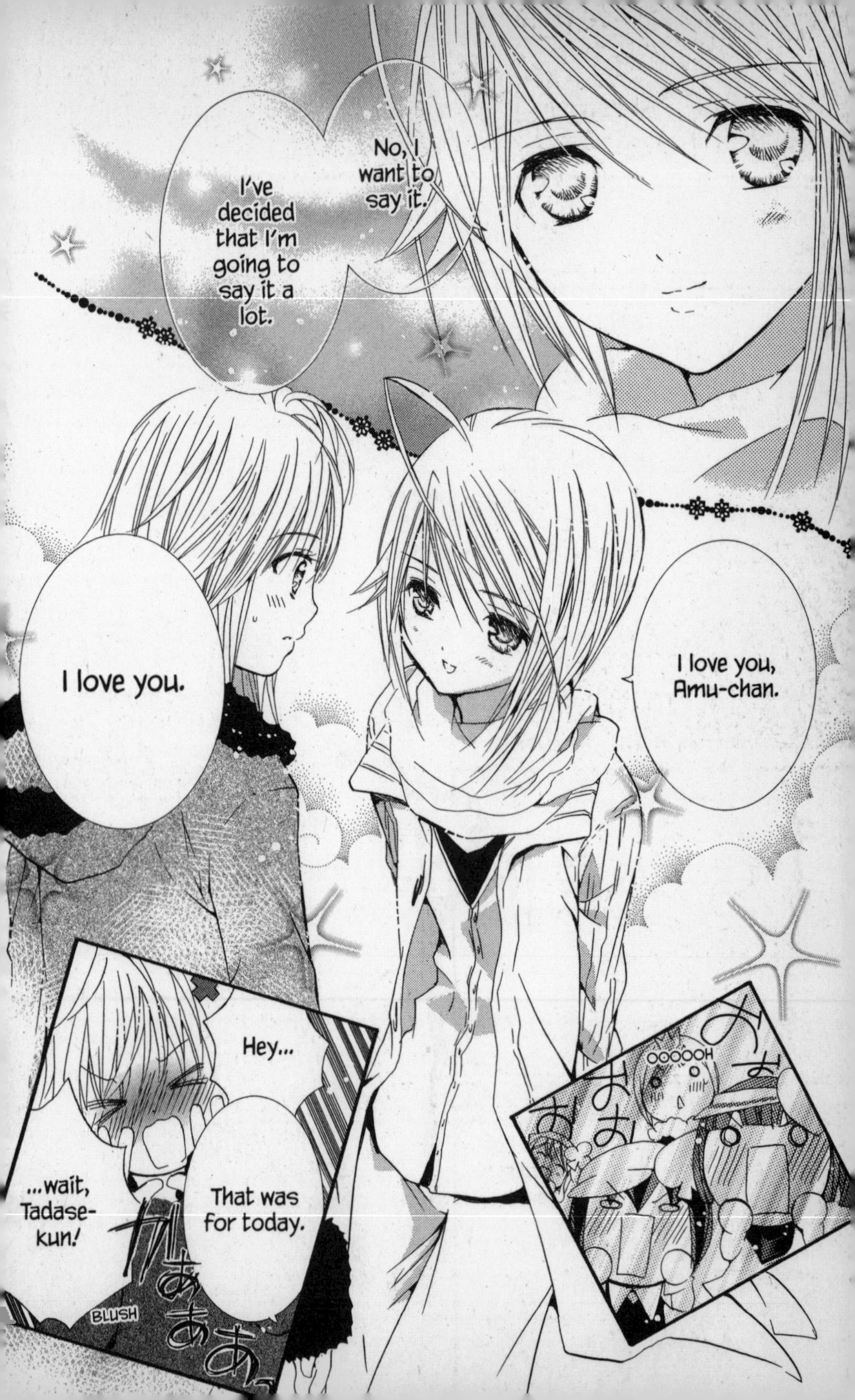
No, I want to say it.
I've decided that I'm going to say it a lot.
I love you, Amu-chan.
I love you.
OOOOOH
Hey...
That was for today.
...wait, Tadase-kun!
BLUSH

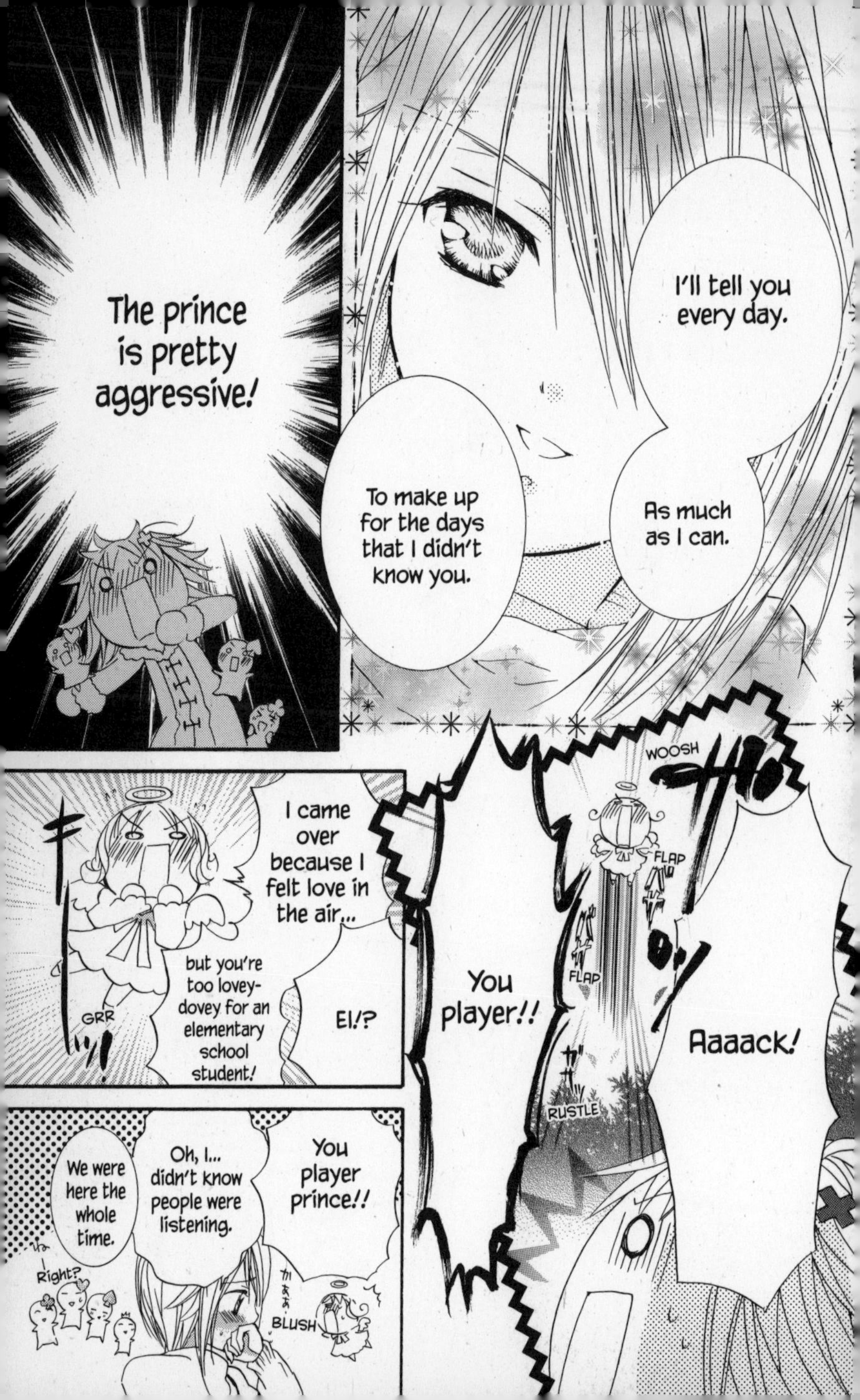
I'll tell you every day.
As much as I can.
To make up for the days that I didn't know you.
The prince is pretty aggressive!
WOOSH
Aaaack!
FLAP
FLAP
You player!!
RUSTLE
I came over because I felt love in the air...
El!?
but you're too lovey-dovey for an elementary school student!
GRR
You player prince!!
Oh, I... didn't know people were listening.
We were here the whole time.
Right?
BLUSH

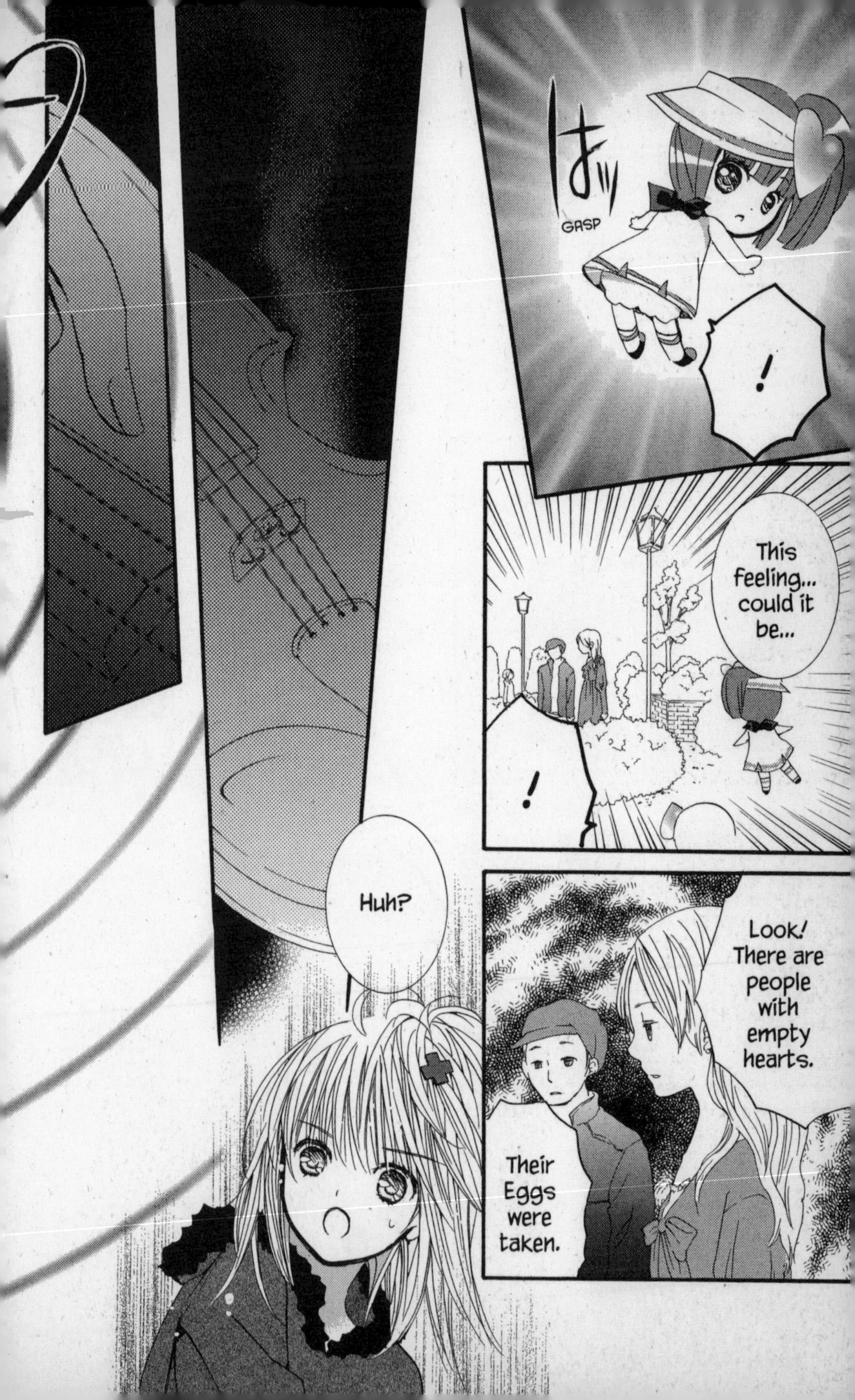
はッ
GASP
!
This feeling... could it be...
!
Look! There are people with empty hearts.
Their Eggs were taken.
Huh?

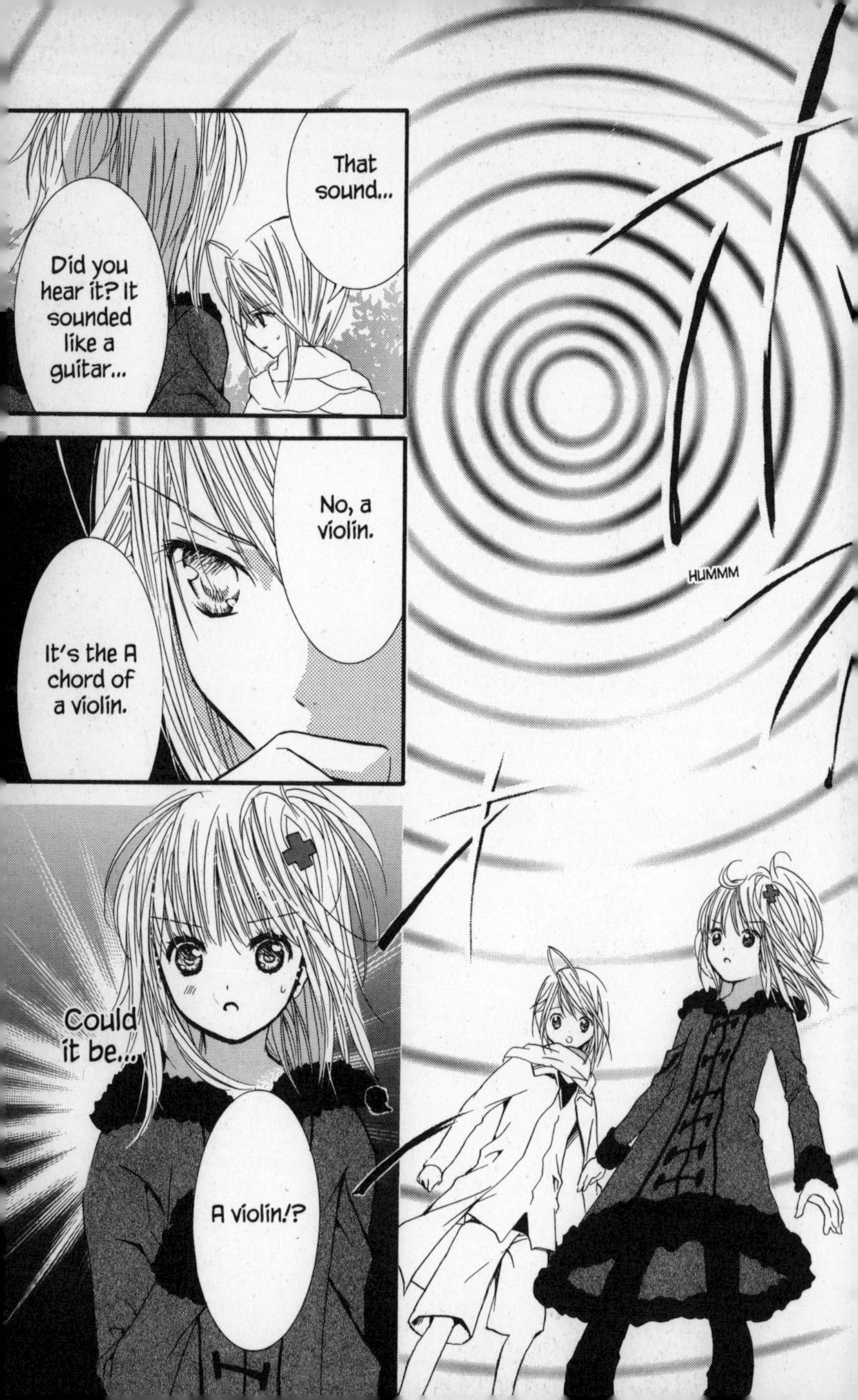
HUMMM
That sound...
Did you hear it? It sounded like a guitar...
No, a violin.
It's the A chord of a violin.
Could it be...
A violin!?

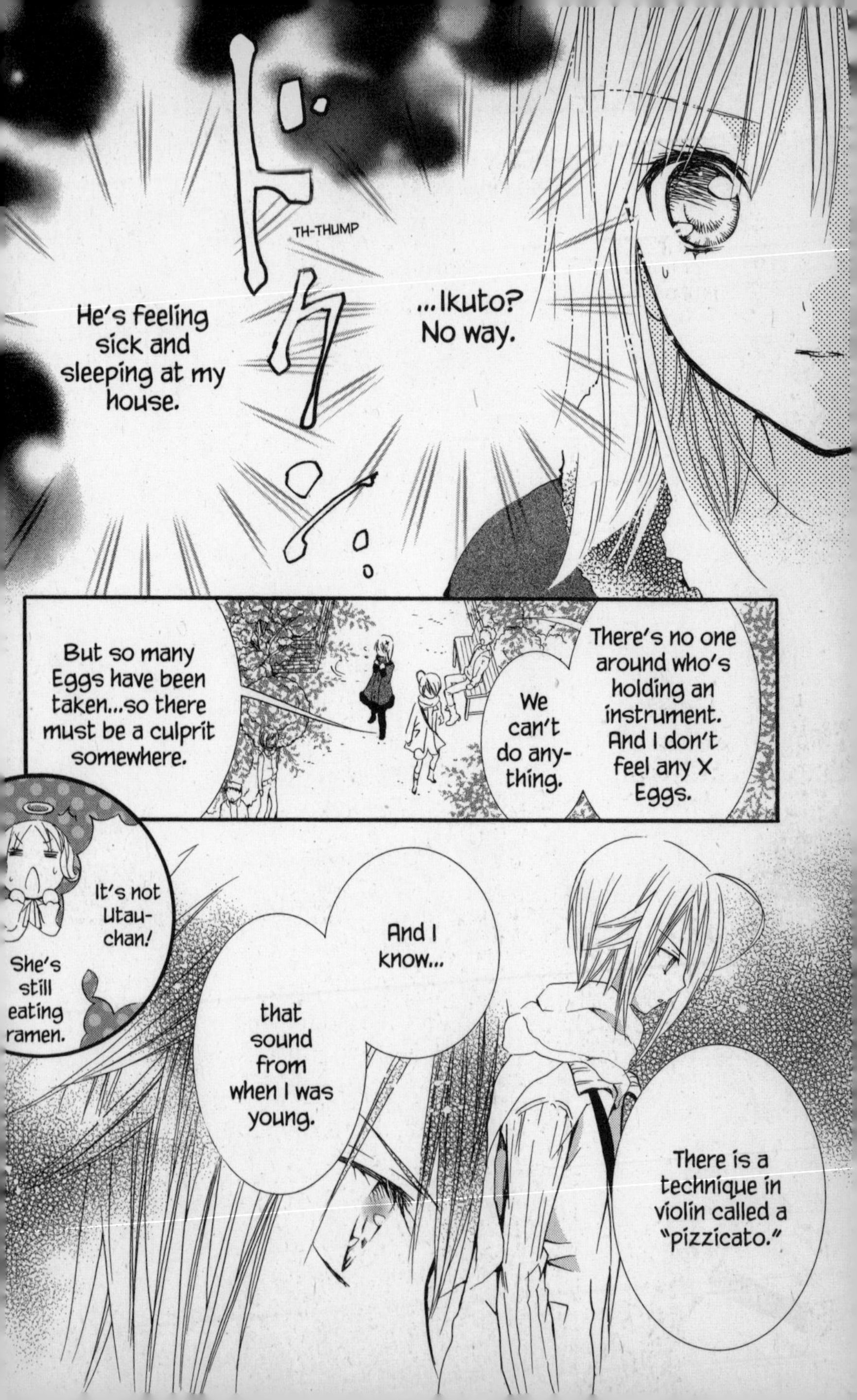
TH-THUMP
...Ikuto? No way.
He's feeling sick and sleeping at my house.
There's no one around who's holding an instrument. And I don't feel any X Eggs.
We can't do anything.
But so many Eggs have been taken...so there must be a culprit somewhere.
There is a technique in violin called a "pizzicato."
And I know...
that sound from when I was young.
It's not Utau-chan!
She's still eating ramen.

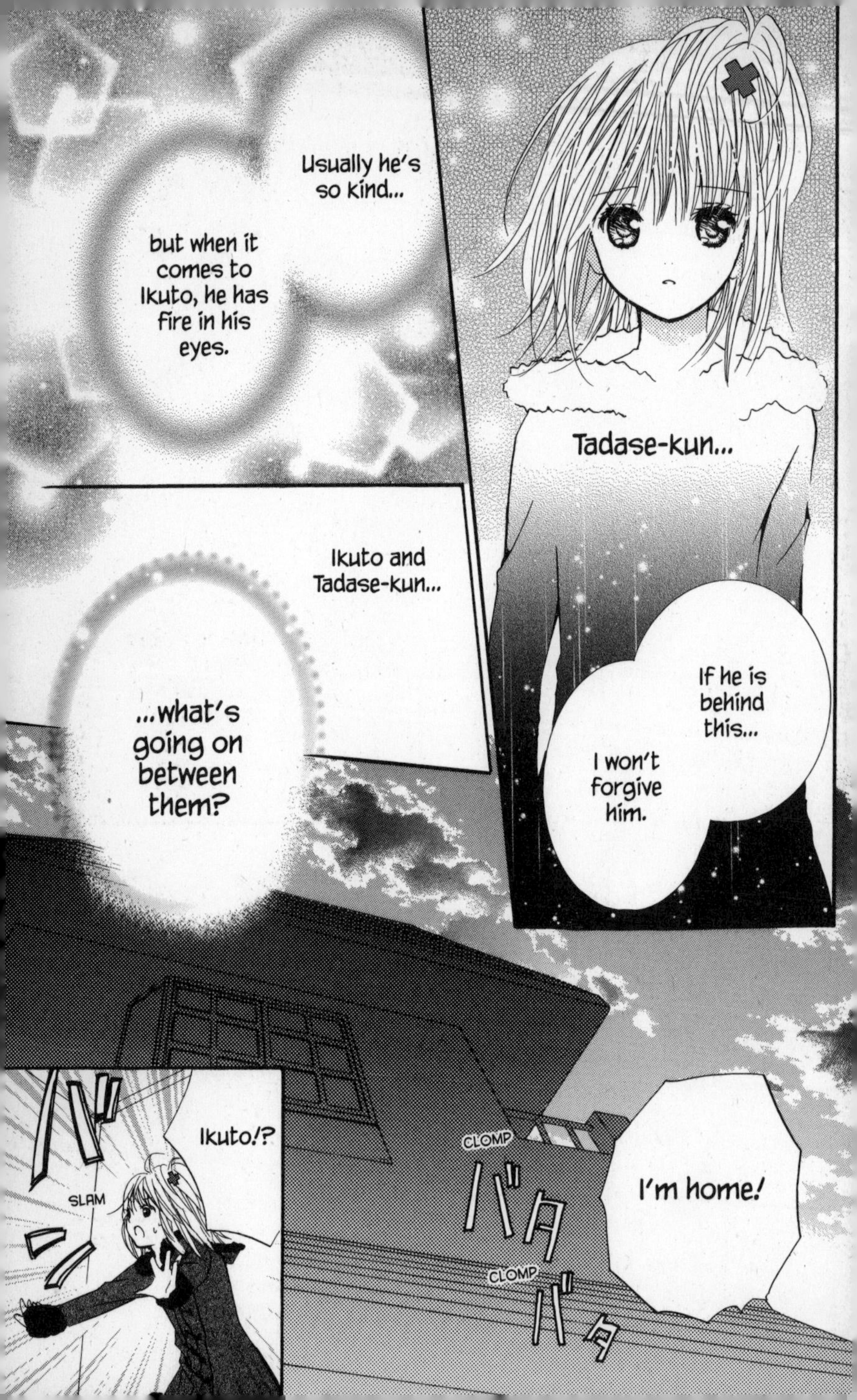

Tadase-kun...
If he is behind this...
I won't forgive him.
Usually he's so kind...
but when it comes to Ikuto, he has fire in his eyes.
Ikuto and Tadase-kun...
...what's going on between them?
CLOMP
CLOMP
I'm home!
Ikuto!?
SLAM

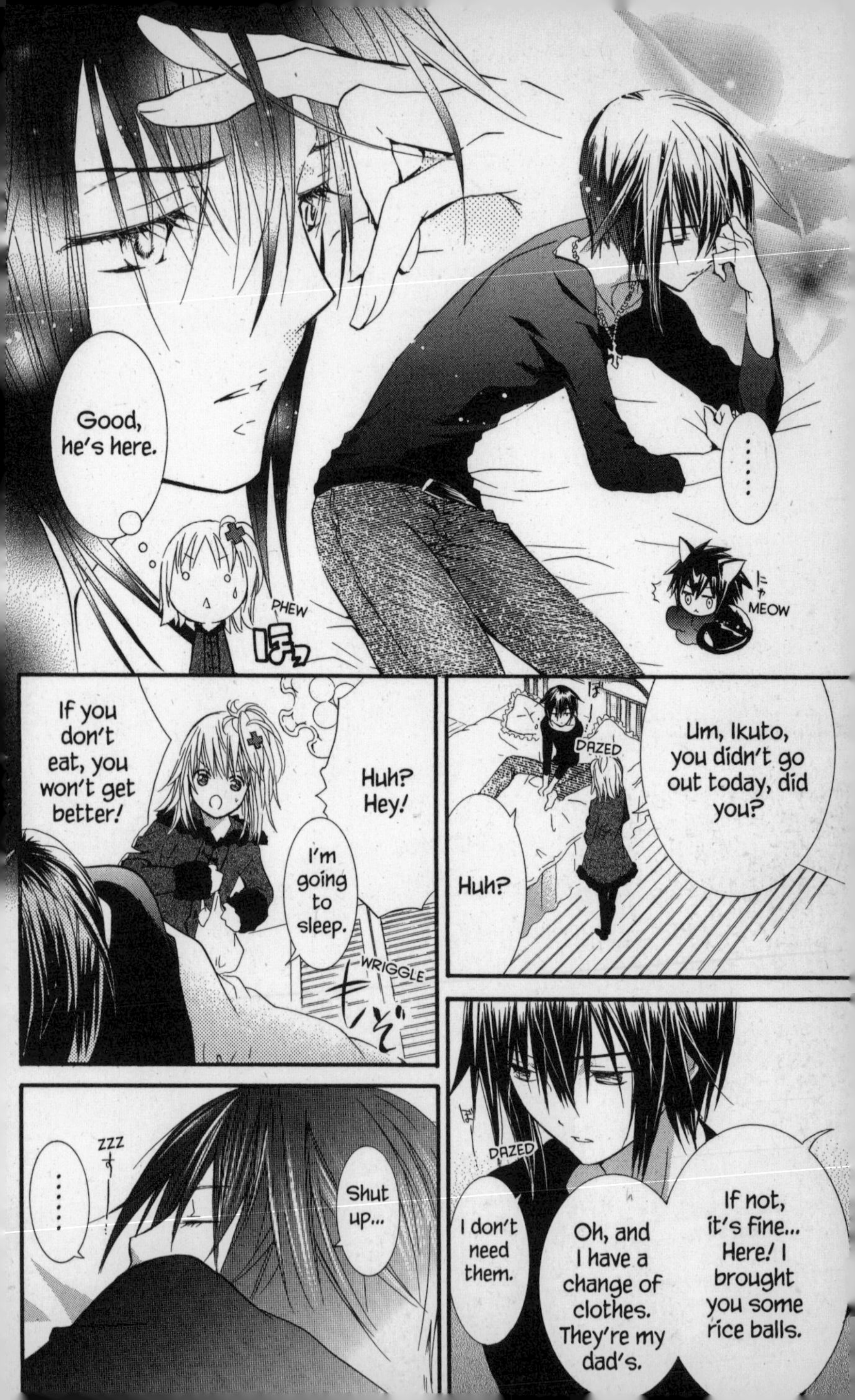
......
MEOW
Good, he's here.
PHEW
Um, Ikuto, you didn't go out today, did you?
DAZED
Huh?
Huh? Hey!
I'm going to sleep.
If you don't eat, you won't get better!
WRIGGLE
If not, it's fine... Here! I brought you some rice balls.
Oh, and I have a change of clothes. They're my dad's.
I don't need them.
DAZED
Shut up...
ZZZ
......

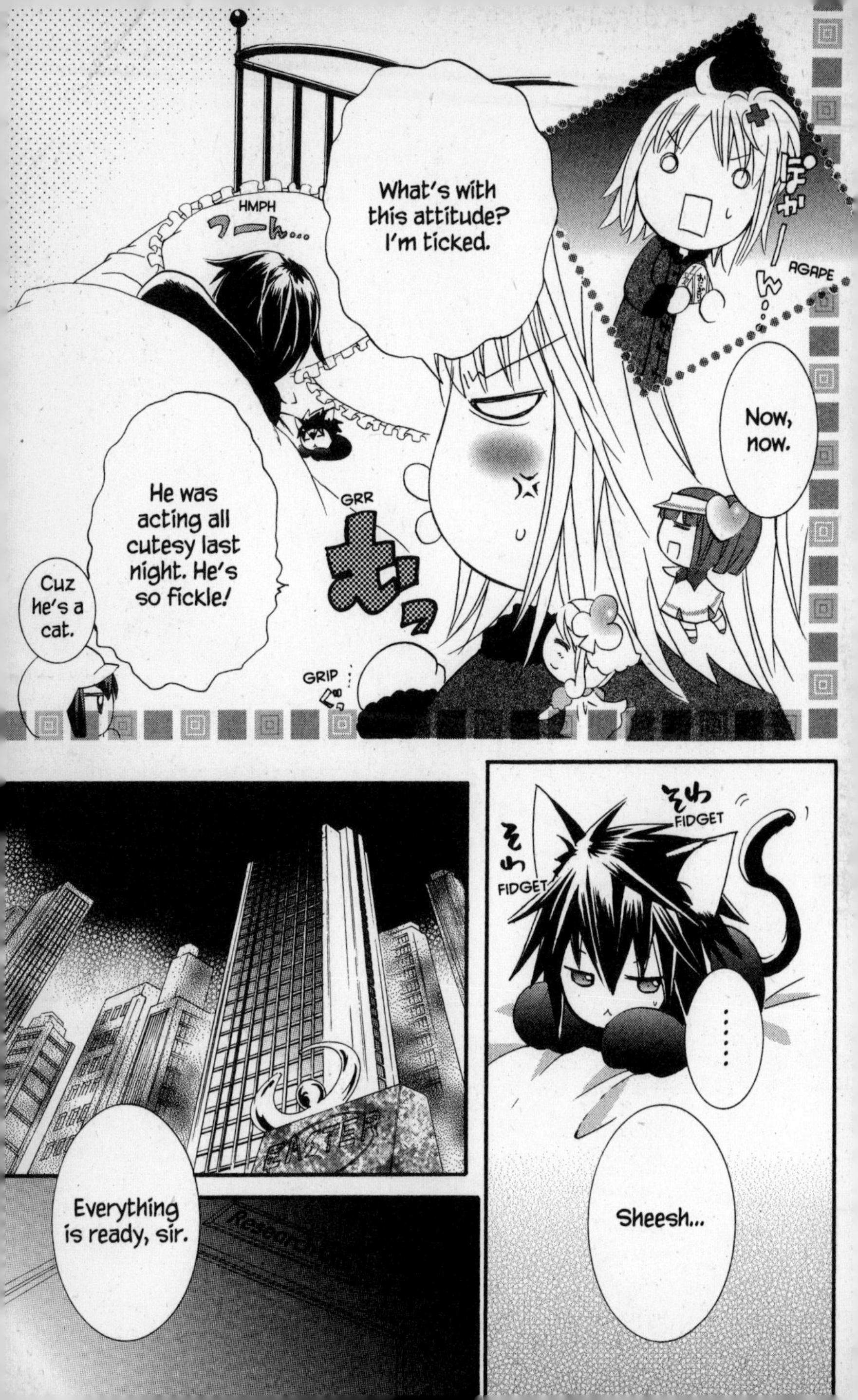
What's with this attitude? I'm ticked.
AGAPE
Now, now.
HMPH
GRR
He was acting all cutesy last night. He's so fickle!
Cuz he's a cat.
GRIP
FIDGET
FIDGET
......
Sheesh...
Everything is ready, sir.

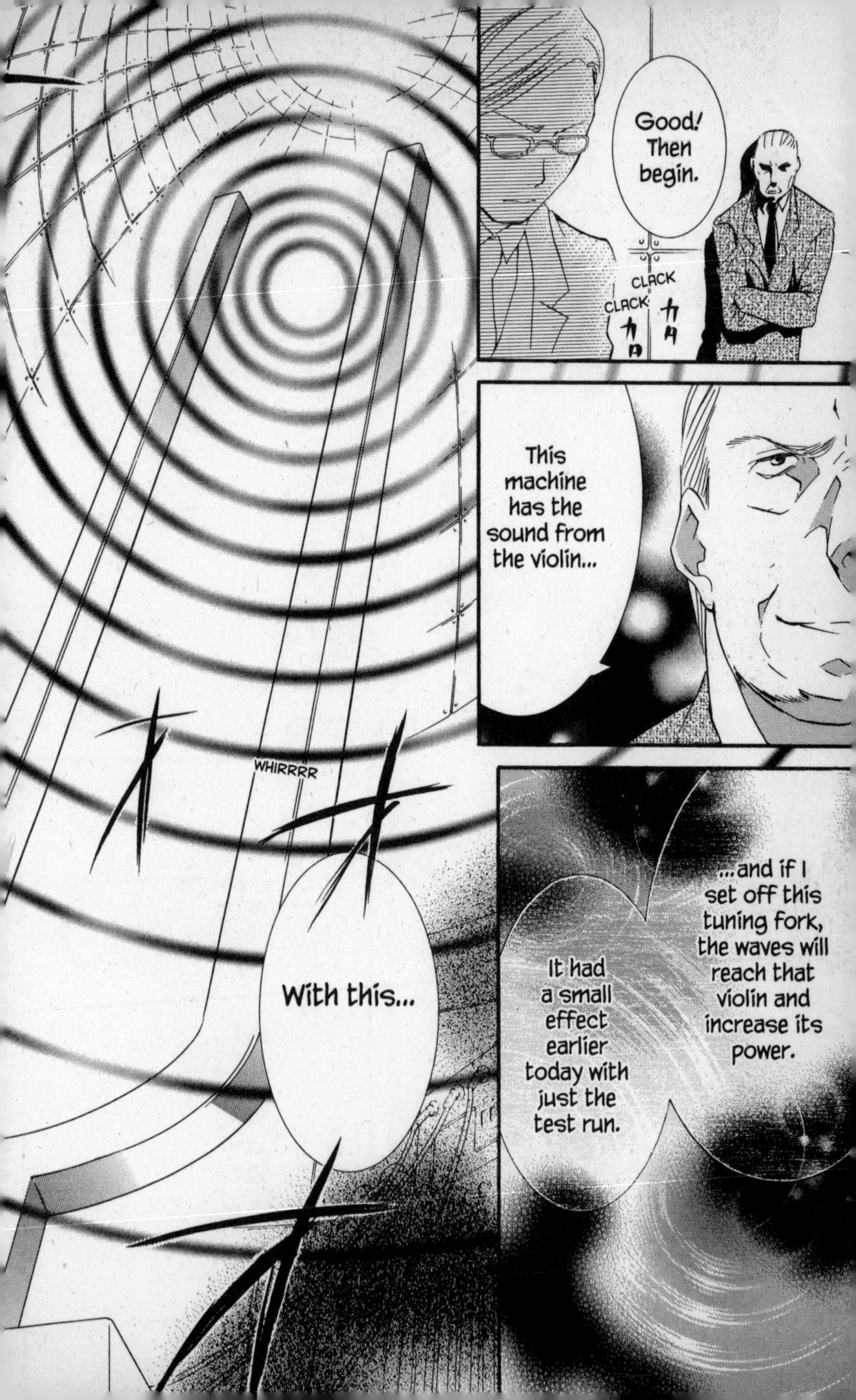
Good! Then begin.
CLACK
CLACK
This machine has the sound from the violin...
...and if I set off this tuning fork, the waves will reach that violin and increase its power.
It had a small effect earlier today with just the test run.
WHIRRRR
With this...

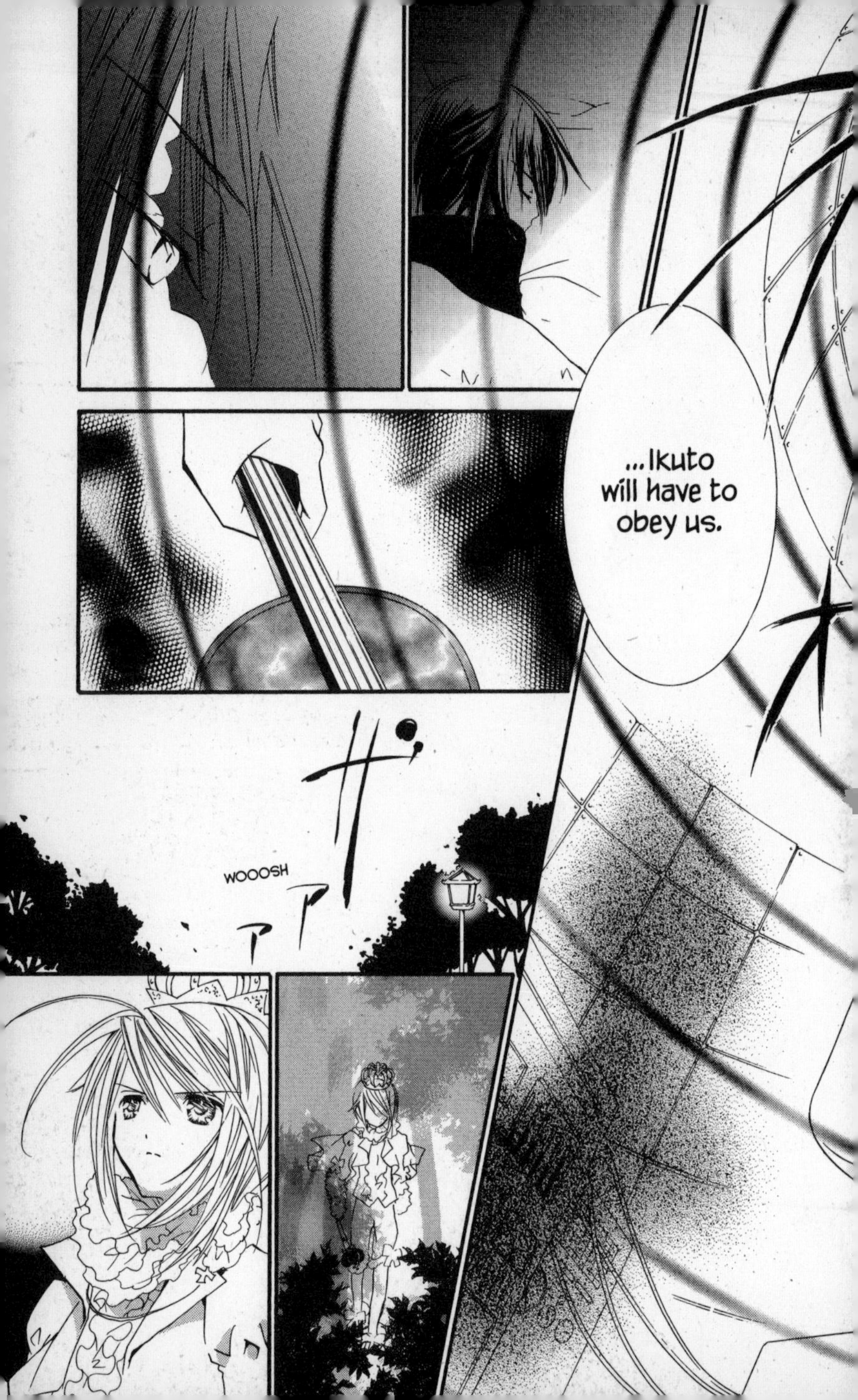
...Ikuto will have to obey us.
WOOOSH

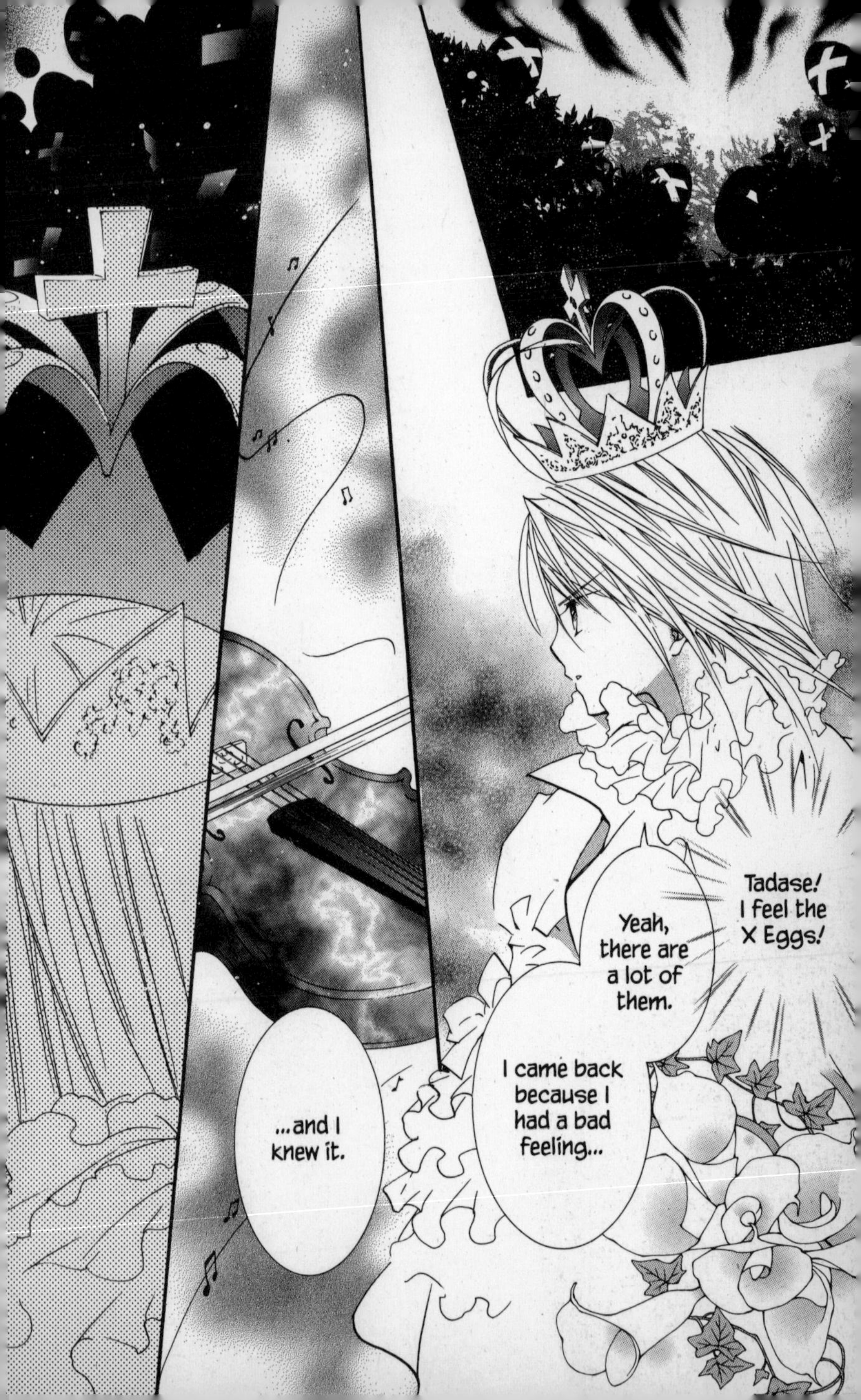
Tadase! I feel the X Eggs!
Yeah, there are a lot of them.
I came back because I had a bad feeling...
...and I knew it.

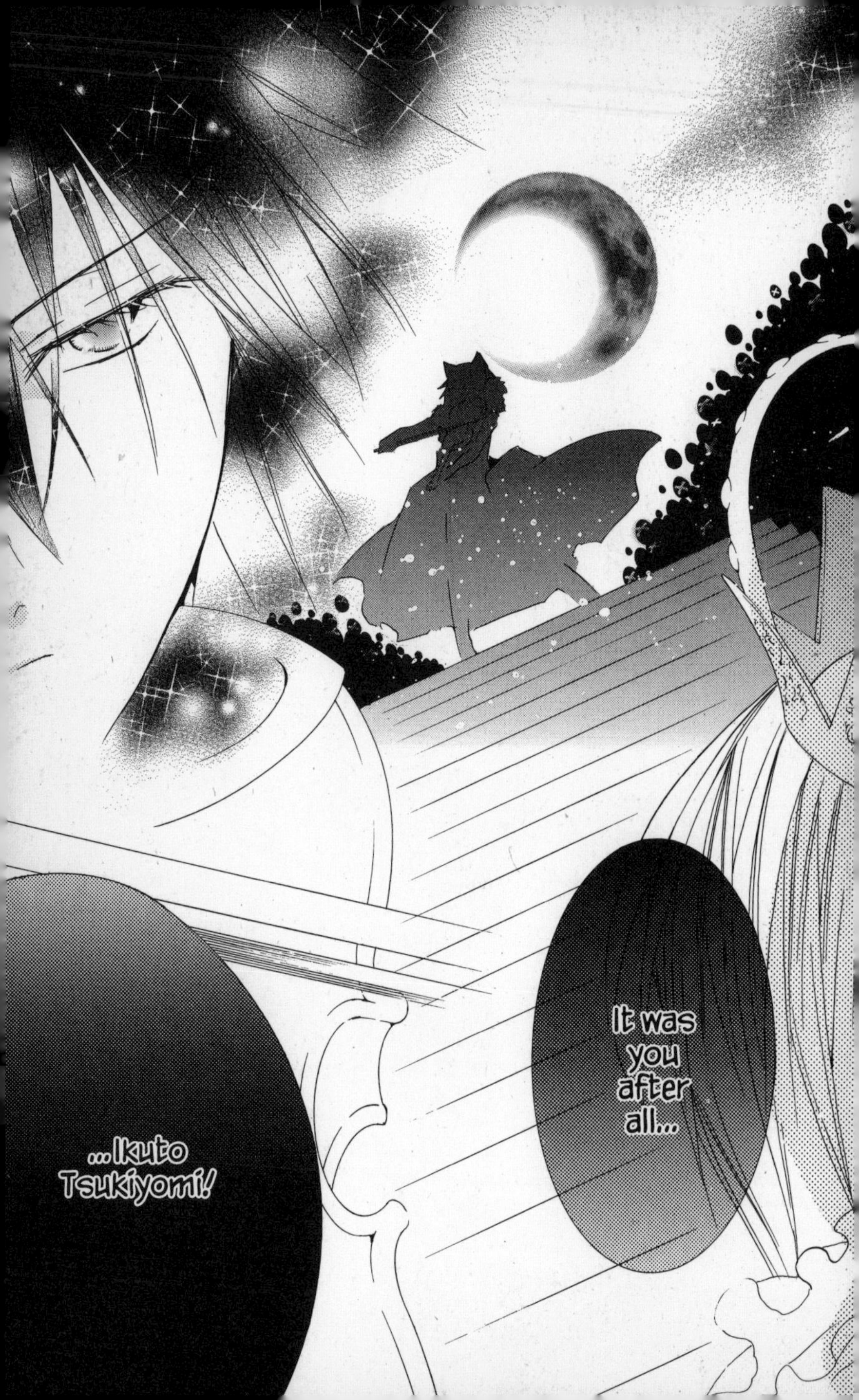
It was you after all...
...Ikuto Tsukiyomi!

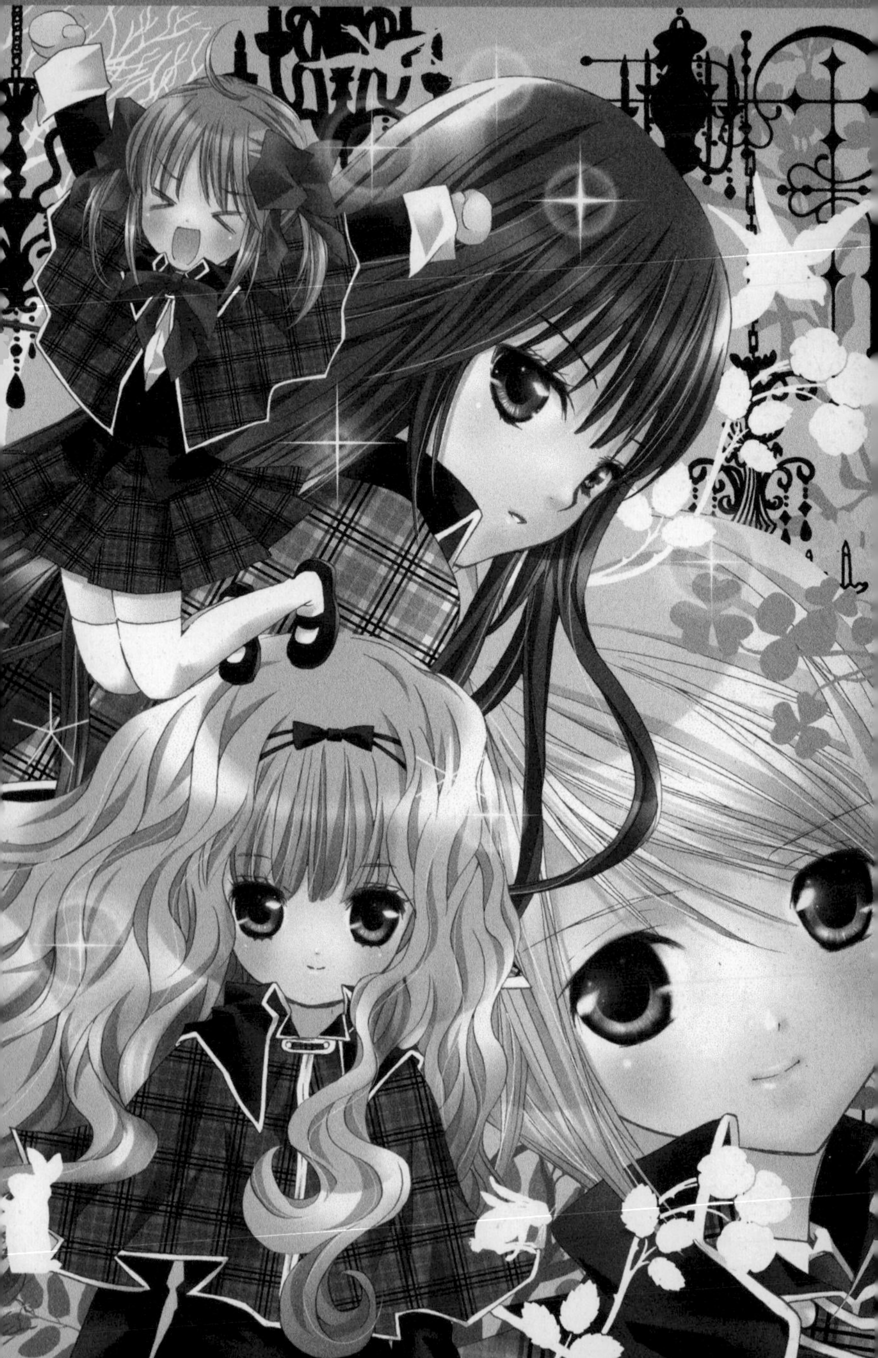

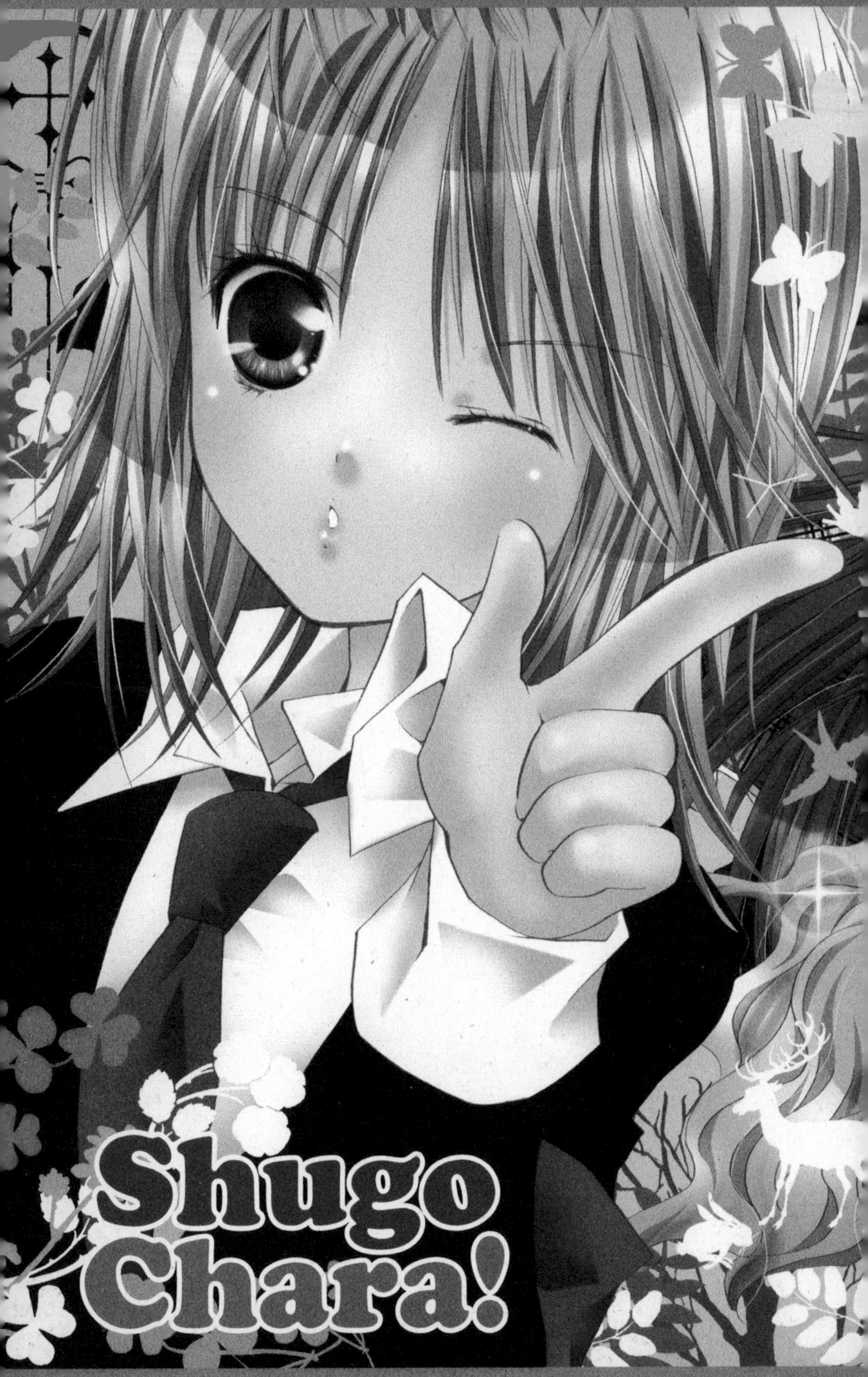
Shugo Chara!

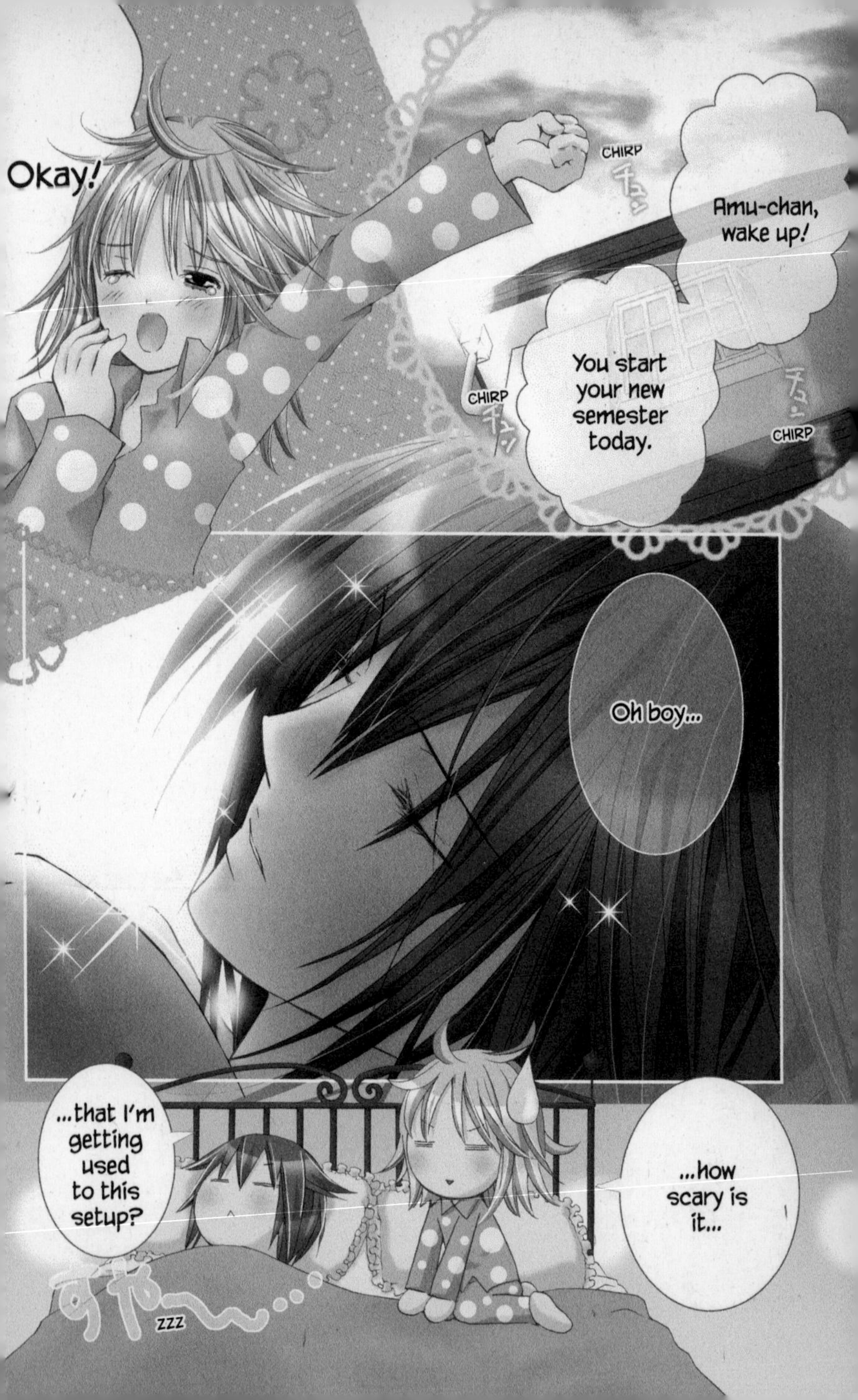
Amu-chan, wake up!
CHIRP
You start your new semester today.
CHIRP
CHIRP
Okay!
Oh boy...
...how scary is it...
...that I'm getting used to this setup?
ZZZ

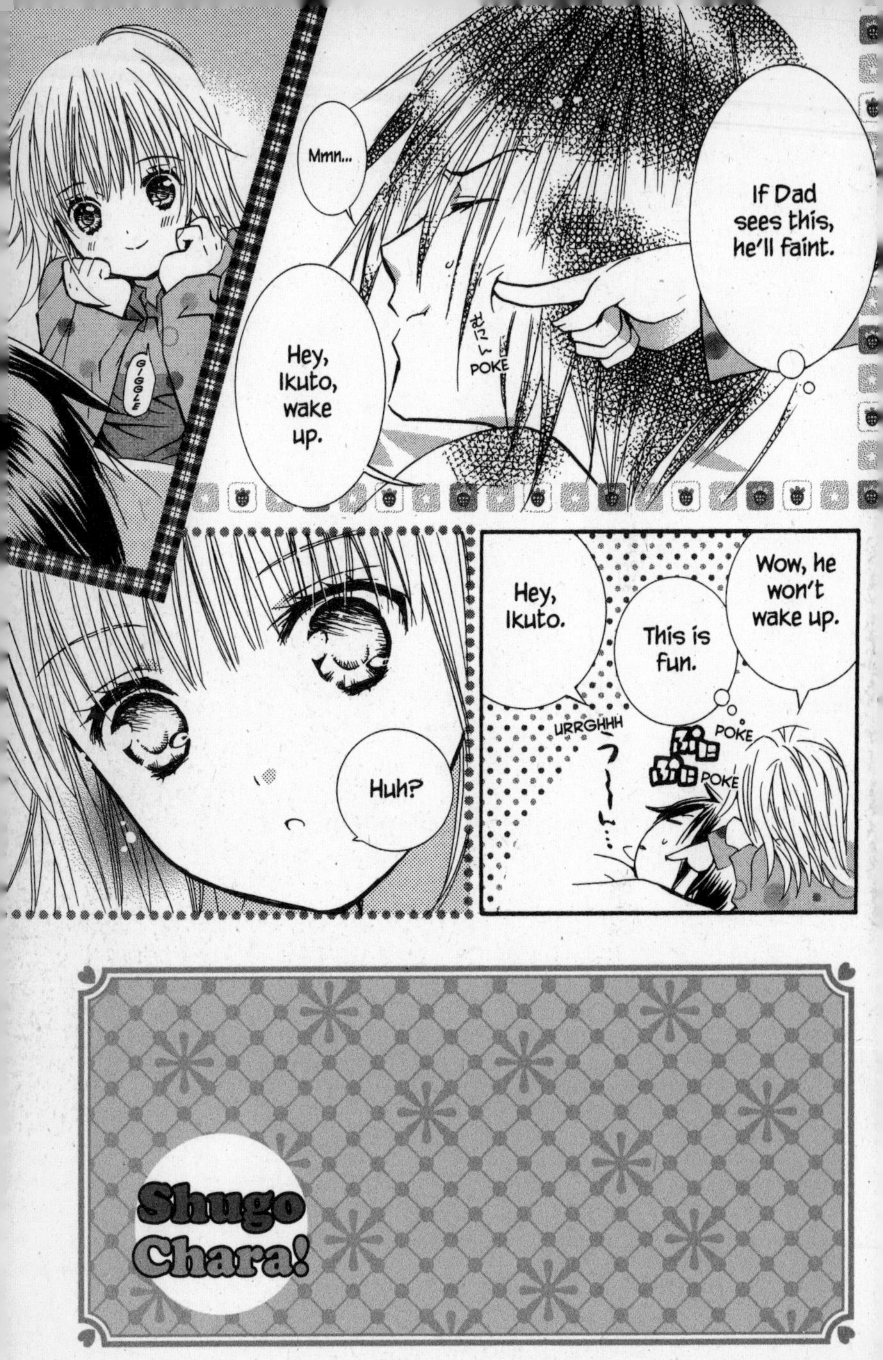
If Dad sees this, he'll faint.
Mmn...
POKE
Hey, Ikuto, wake up.
GIGGLE
Wow, he won't wake up.
This is fun.
Hey, Ikuto.
POKE
POKE
URRGHHH
Huh?

Shugo Chara!

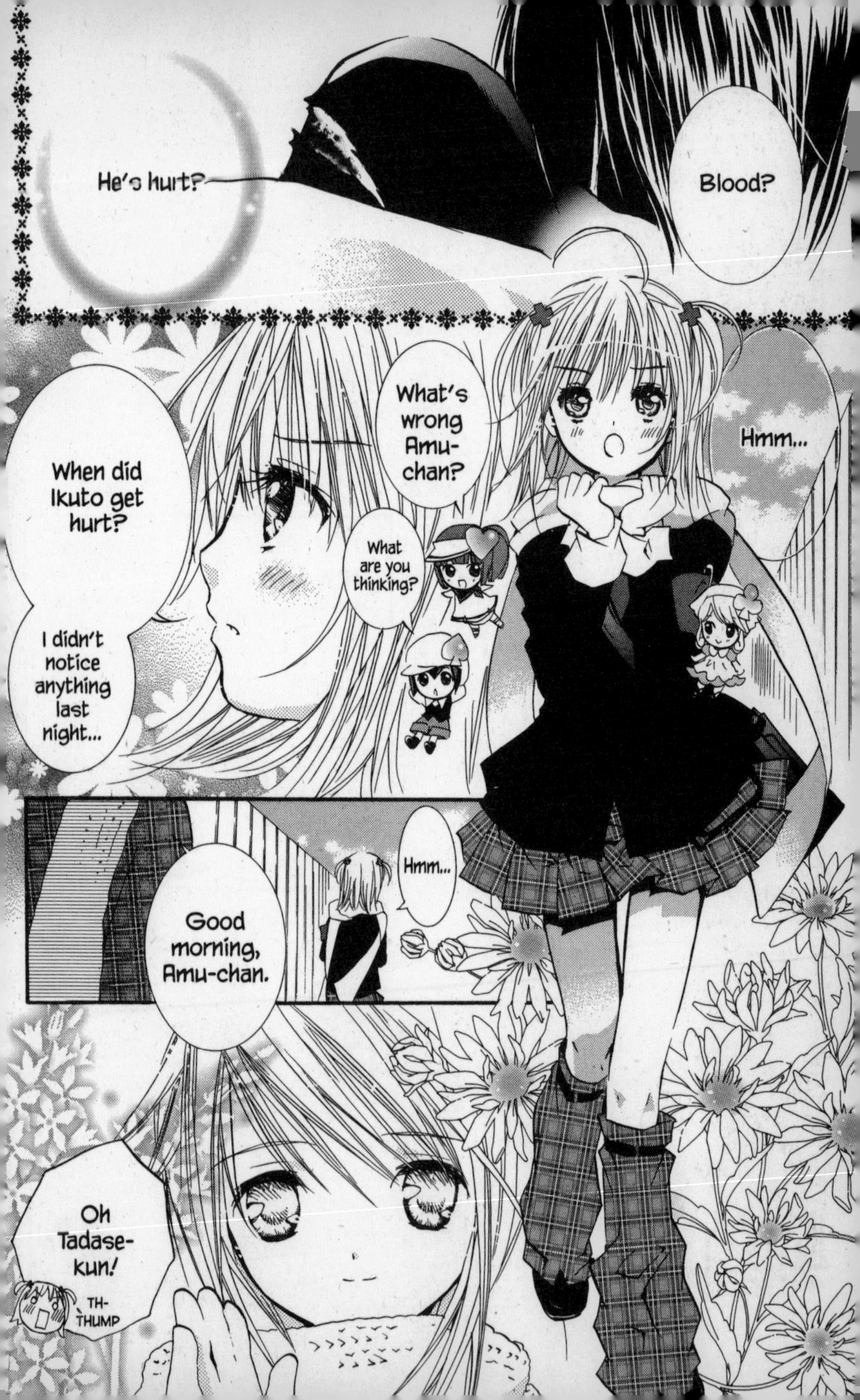
Blood?
He's hurt?
Hmm...
What's wrong Amu-chan?
What are you thinking?
When did Ikuto get hurt?
I didn't notice anything last night...
Hmm...
Good morning, Amu-chan.
Oh Tadase-kun!
TH-THUMP

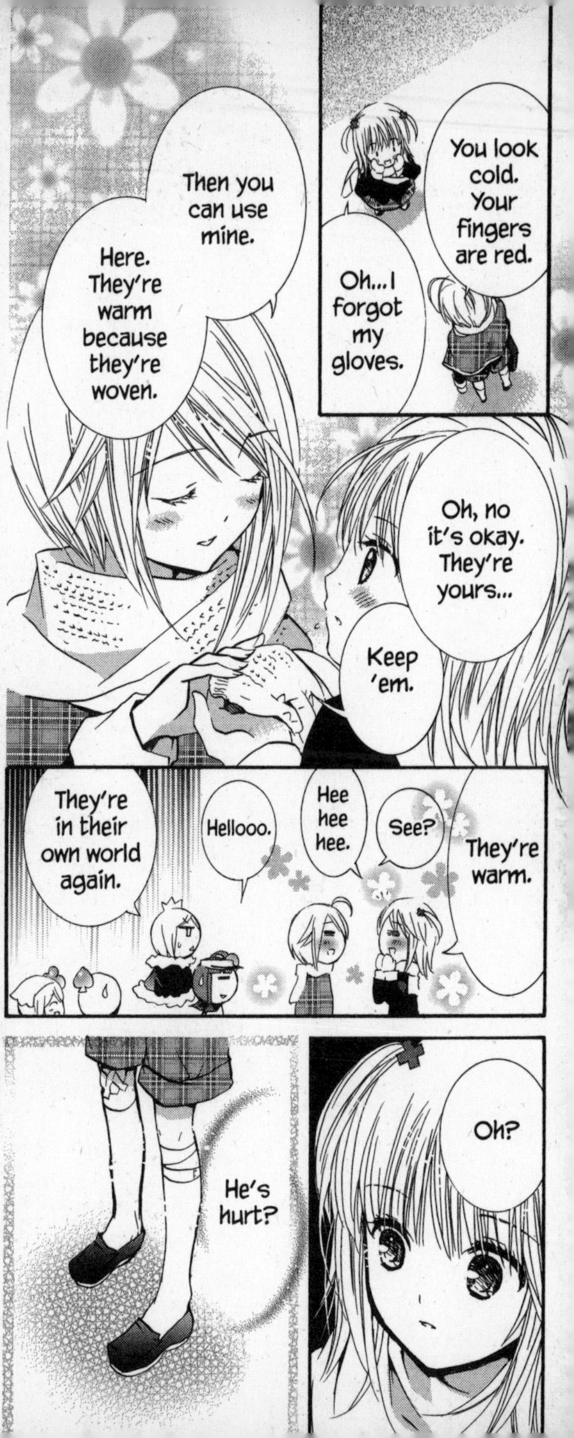
You look cold. Your fingers are red.
Oh...I forgot my gloves.
Then you can use mine.
Here. They're warm because they're woven.
Oh, no it's okay. They're yours...
Keep 'em.
They're warm.
See?
Hee hee hee.
Hellooo.
They're in their own world again.
Oh?
He's hurt?

character profile

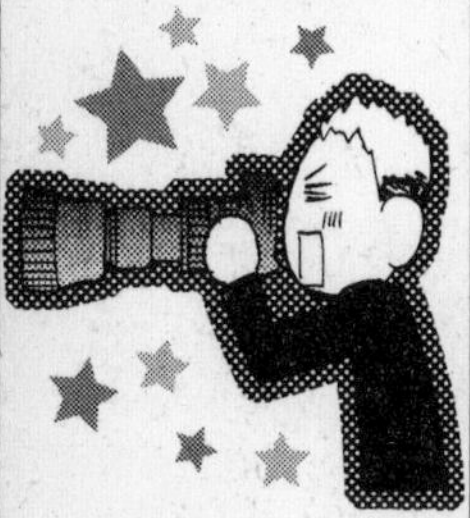

Tsumugu Hinamori

Birthday: 2/20
Blood Type: 0
Sign: Pisces

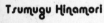

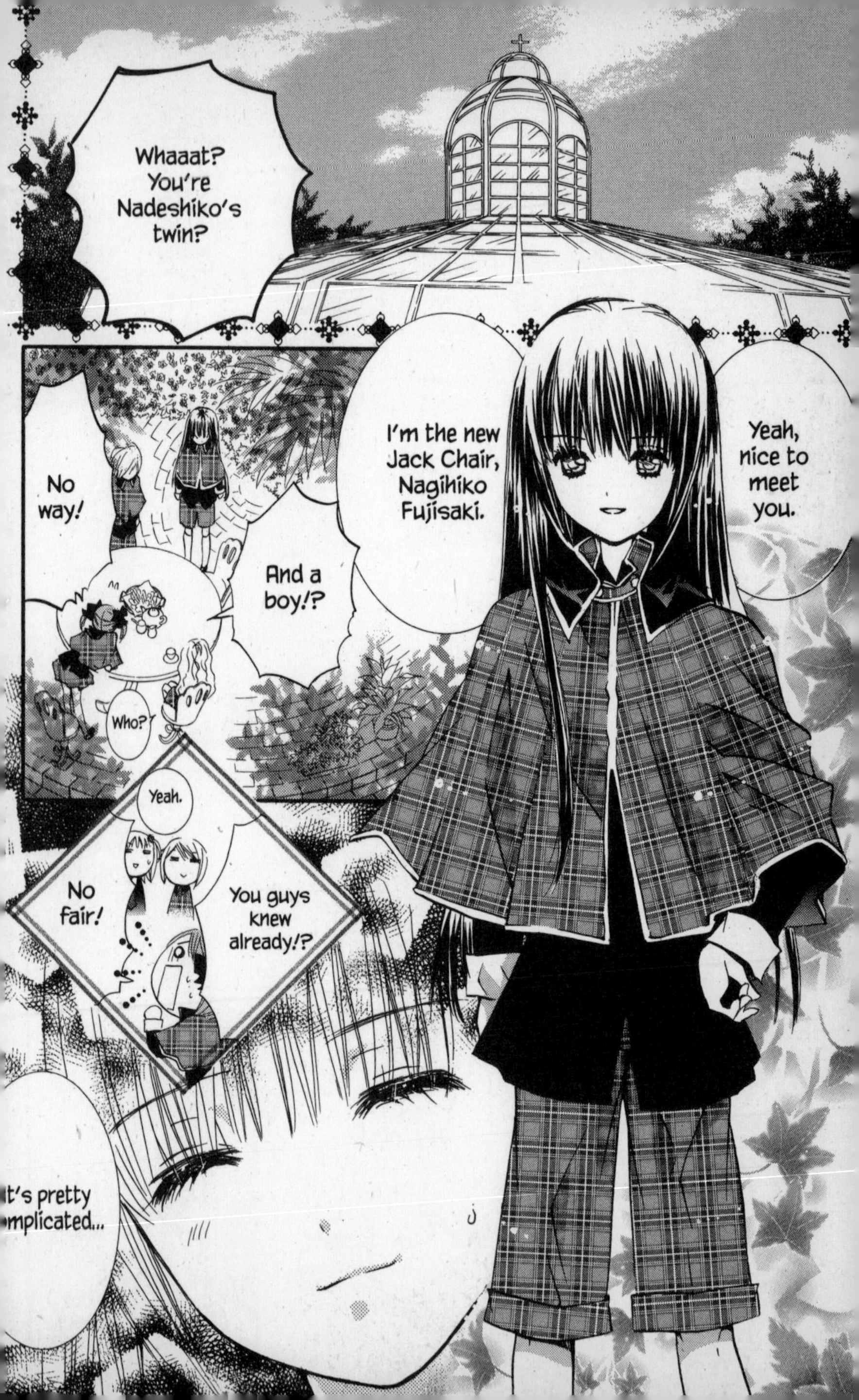
Whaaat? You're Nadeshiko's twin?
Yeah, nice to meet you.
I'm the new Jack Chair, Nagihiko Fujisaki.
And a boy!?
No way!
Who?
Yeah.
You guys knew already!?
No fair!
t's pretty mplicated...

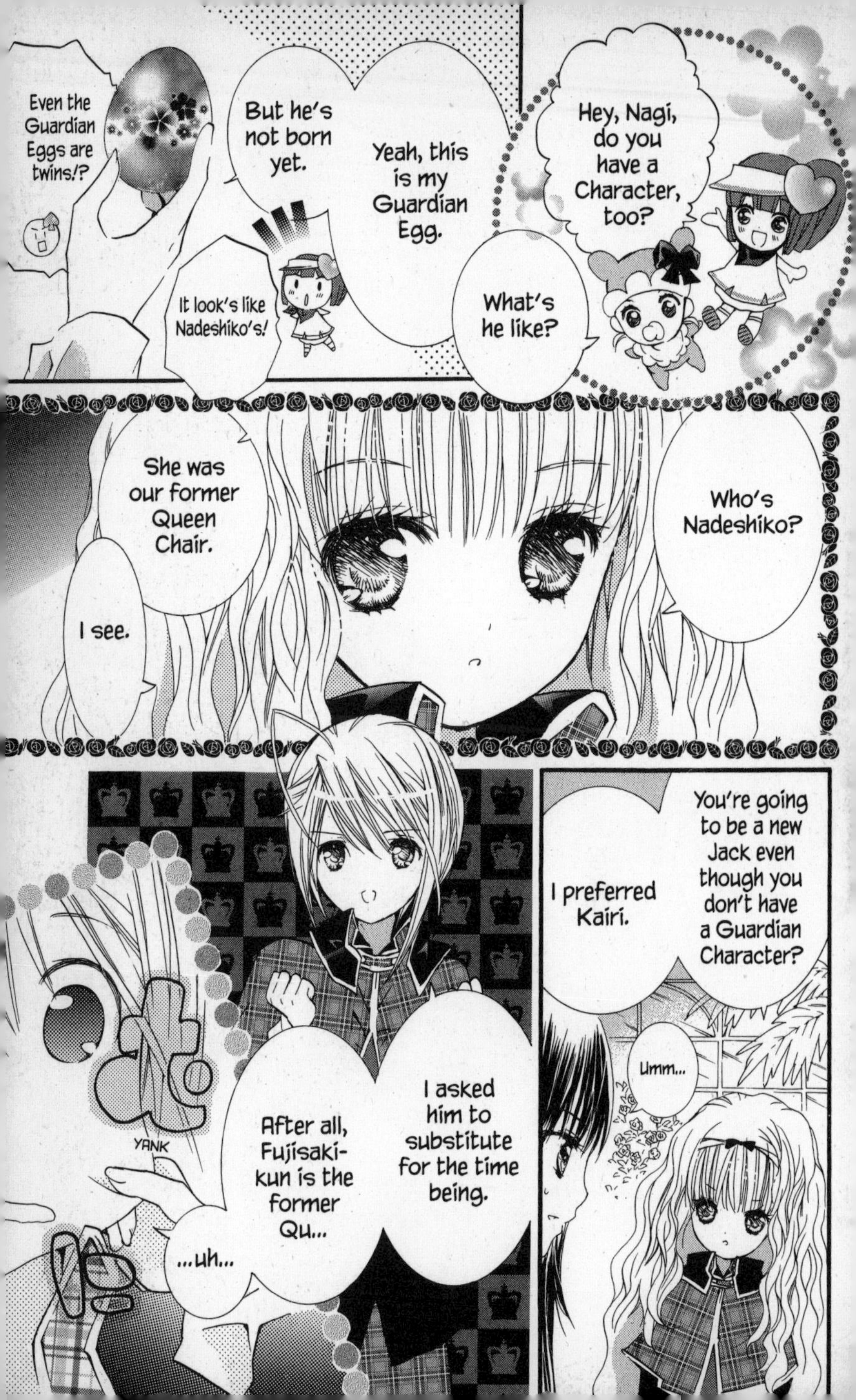
Hey, Nagi, do you have a Character, too?
What's he like?
Yeah, this is my Guardian Egg.
But he's not born yet.
It look's like Nadeshiko's!
Even the Guardian Eggs are twins!?
Who's Nadeshiko?
She was our former Queen Chair.
I see.
You're going to be a new Jack even though you don't have a Guardian Character?
I preferred Kairi.
Umm...
I asked him to substitute for the time being.
After all, Fujisaki-kun is the former Qu...
...uh...
YANK

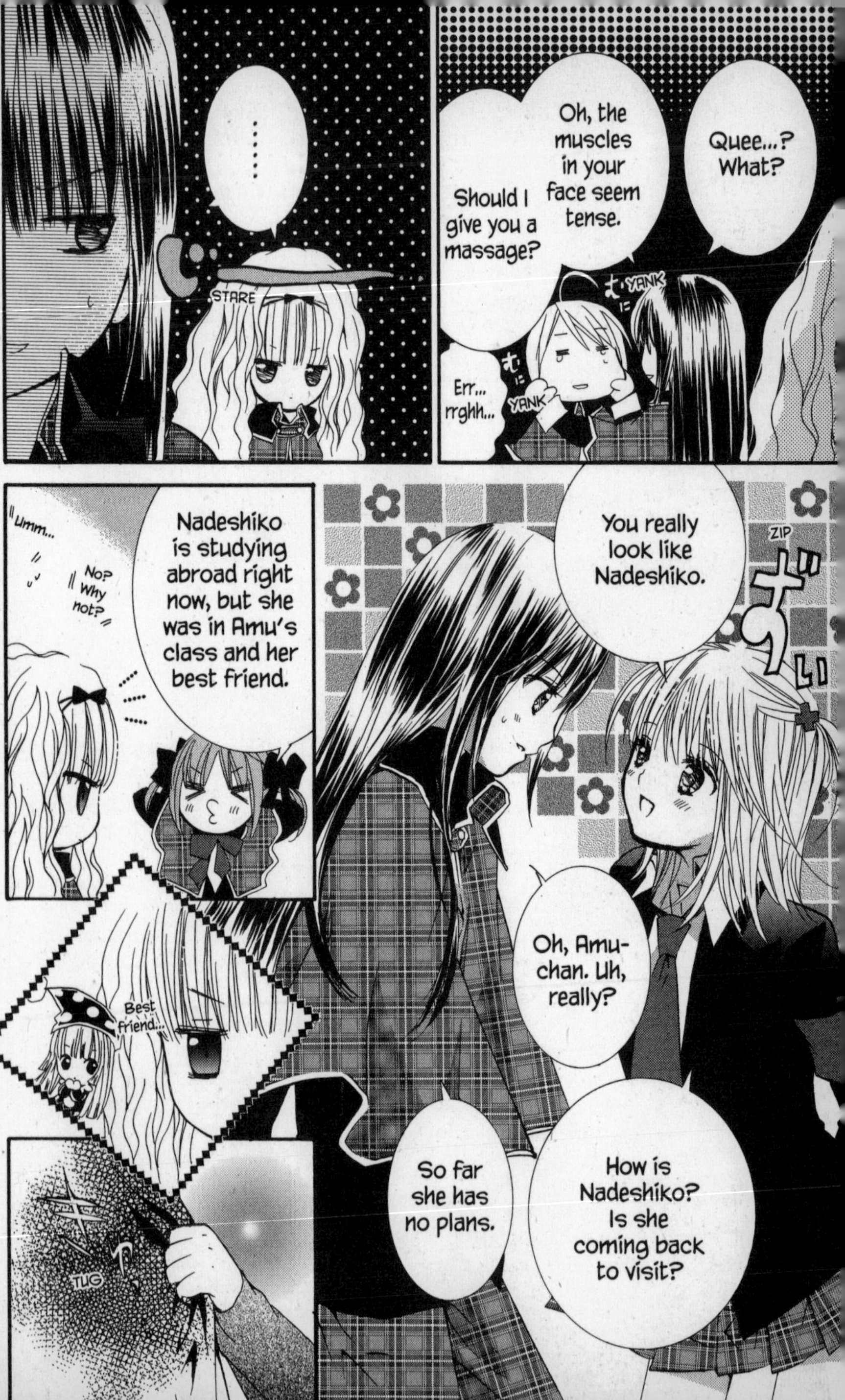
Quee...? What?
Oh, the muscles in your face seem tense.
Should I give you a massage?
YANK
Err... rrghh...
YANK
......
STARE
You really look like Nadeshiko.
ZIP
Nadeshiko is studying abroad right now, but she was in Amu's class and her best friend.
Umm...
No? Why not?
.....
Best friend...
Oh, Amu-chan. Uh, really?
How is Nadeshiko? Is she coming back to visit?
So far she has no plans.
TUG

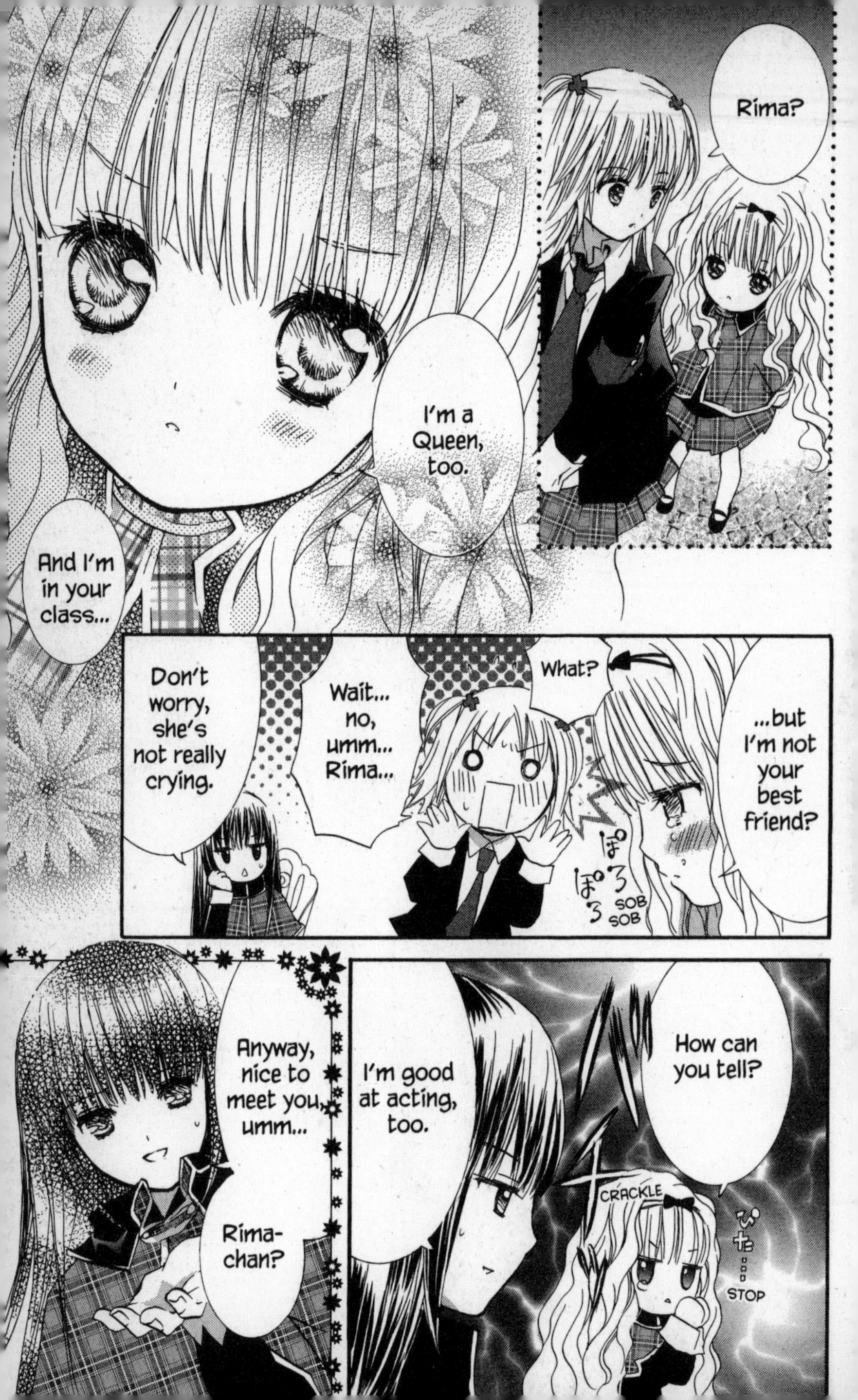
Rima?
I'm a Queen, too.
And I'm in your class...
...but I'm not your best friend?
What?
ぽろぽろ
SOB SOB
Wait... no, umm... Rima...
Don't worry, she's not really crying.
How can you tell?
CRACKLE
ぴた
STOP
I'm good at acting, too.
Anyway, nice to meet you, umm...
Rima-chan?

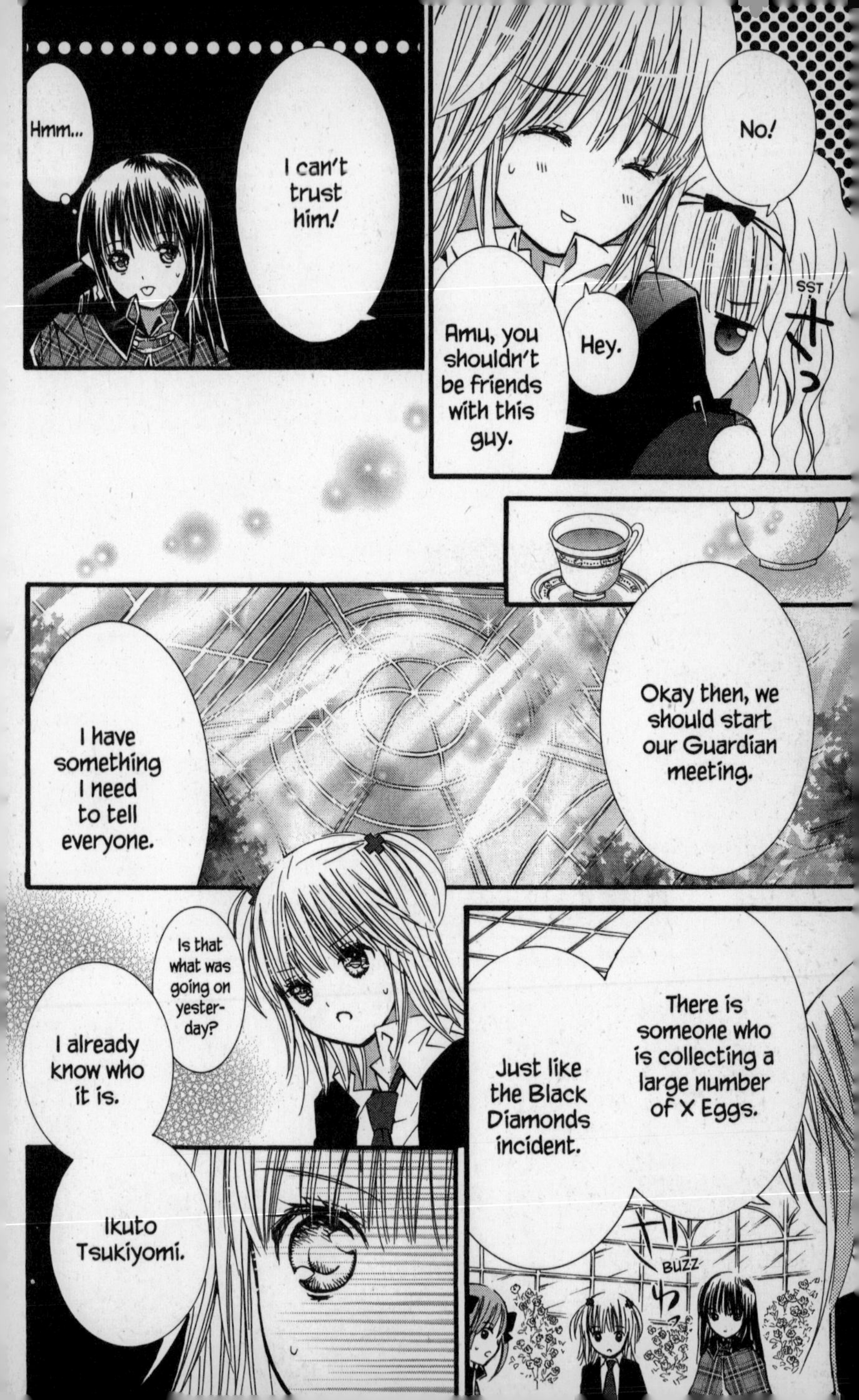
No!
SST
Hey.
Amu, you shouldn't be friends with this guy.
I can't trust him!
Hmm...
Okay then, we should start our Guardian meeting.
I have something I need to tell everyone.
There is someone who is collecting a large number of X Eggs.
Just like the Black Diamonds incident.
BUZZ
Is that what was going on yester-day?
I already know who it is.
Ikuto Tsukiyomi.

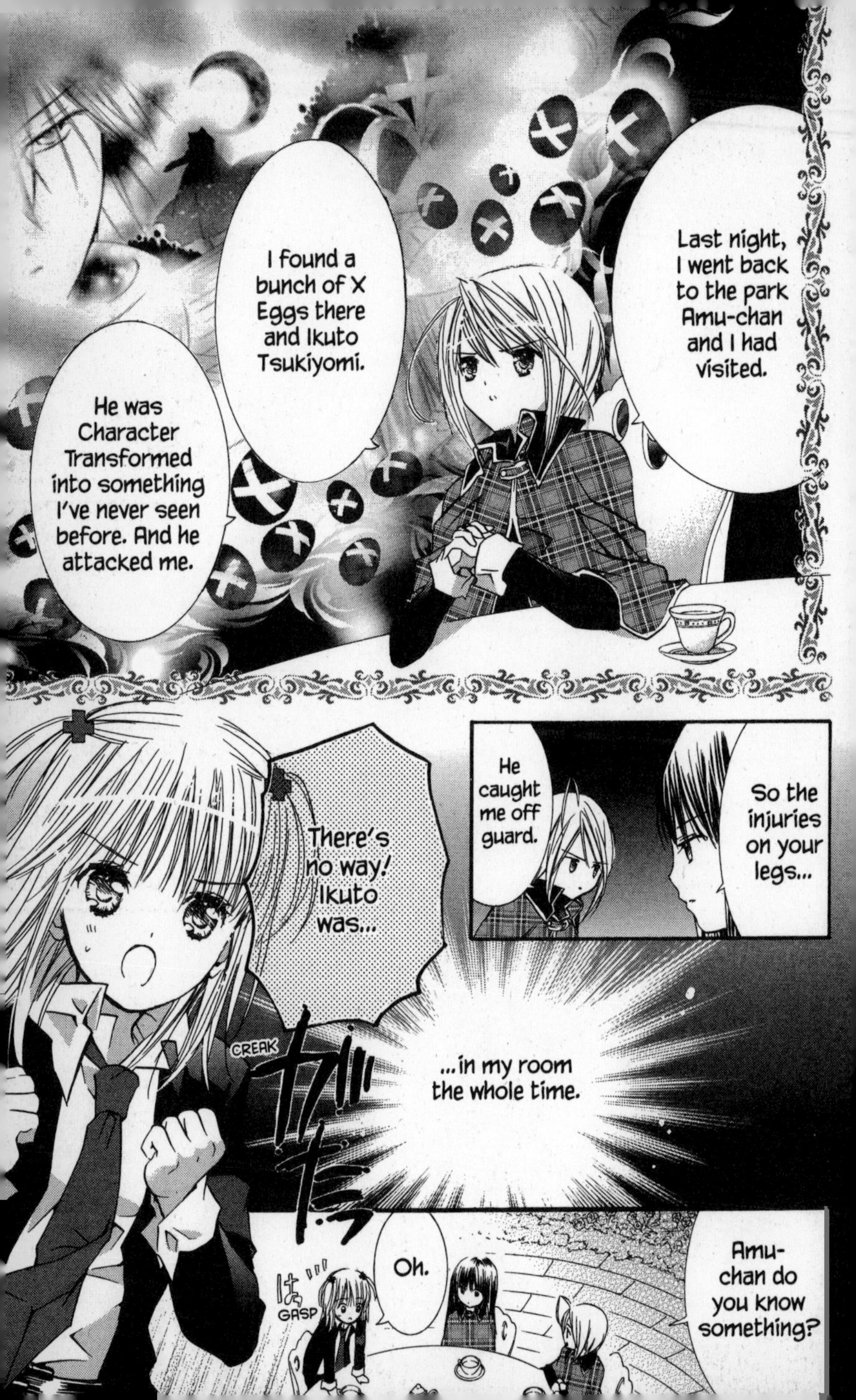
Last night, I went back to the park Amu-chan and I had visited.
I found a bunch of X Eggs there and Ikuto Tsukiyomi.
He was Character Transformed into something I've never seen before. And he attacked me.
So the injuries on your legs...
He caught me off guard.
There's no way! Ikuto was...
CREAK
...in my room the whole time.
Amu-chan do you know something?
Oh.
GASP

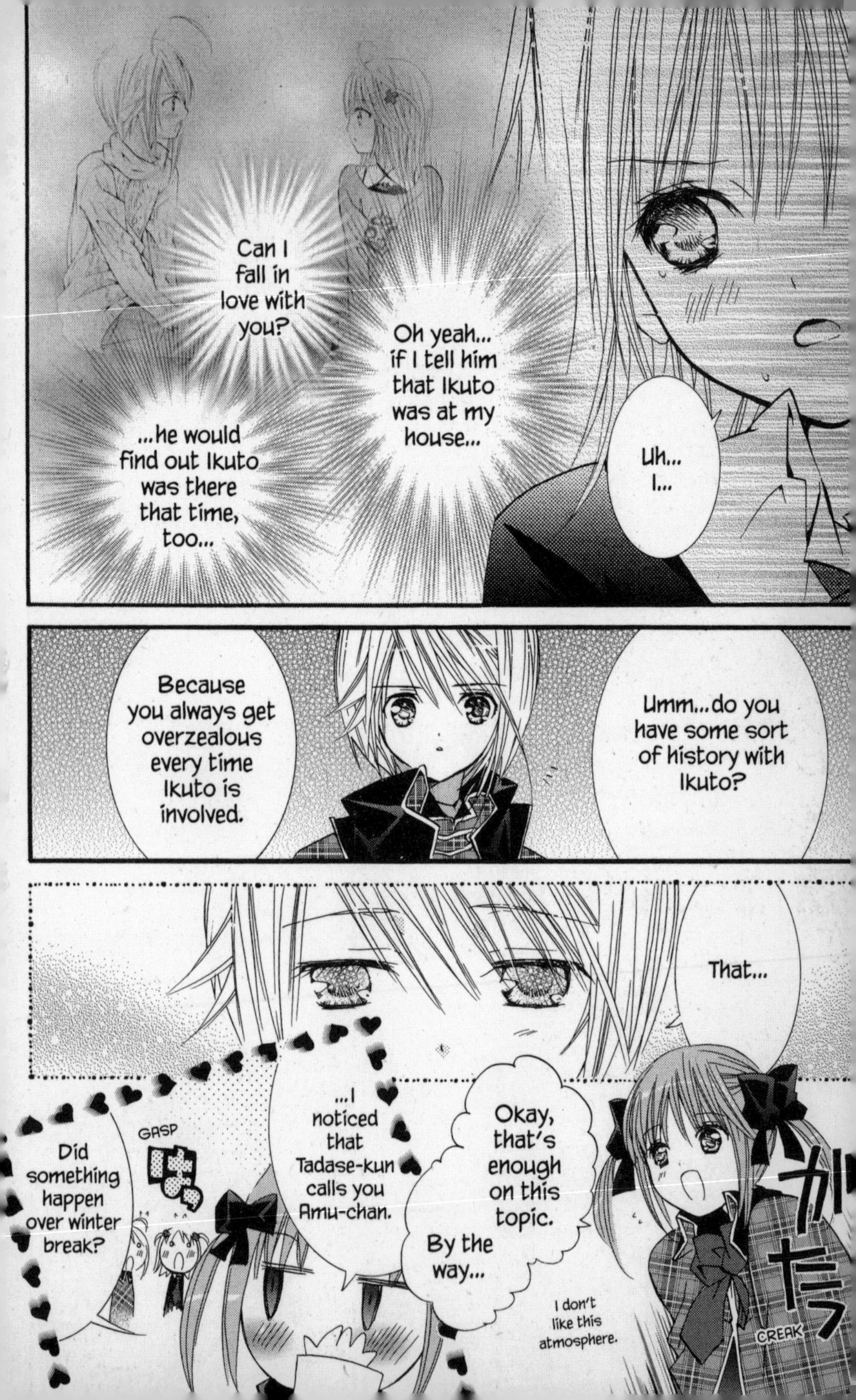
Uh... I...
Oh yeah... if I tell him that Ikuto was at my house...
Can I fall in love with you?
...he would find out Ikuto was there that time, too...
Umm...do you have some sort of history with Ikuto?
Because you always get overzealous every time Ikuto is involved.
That...
CREAK
Okay, that's enough on this topic.
By the way...
I don't like this atmosphere.
...I noticed that Tadase-kun calls you Amu-chan.
GASP
Did something happen over winter break?

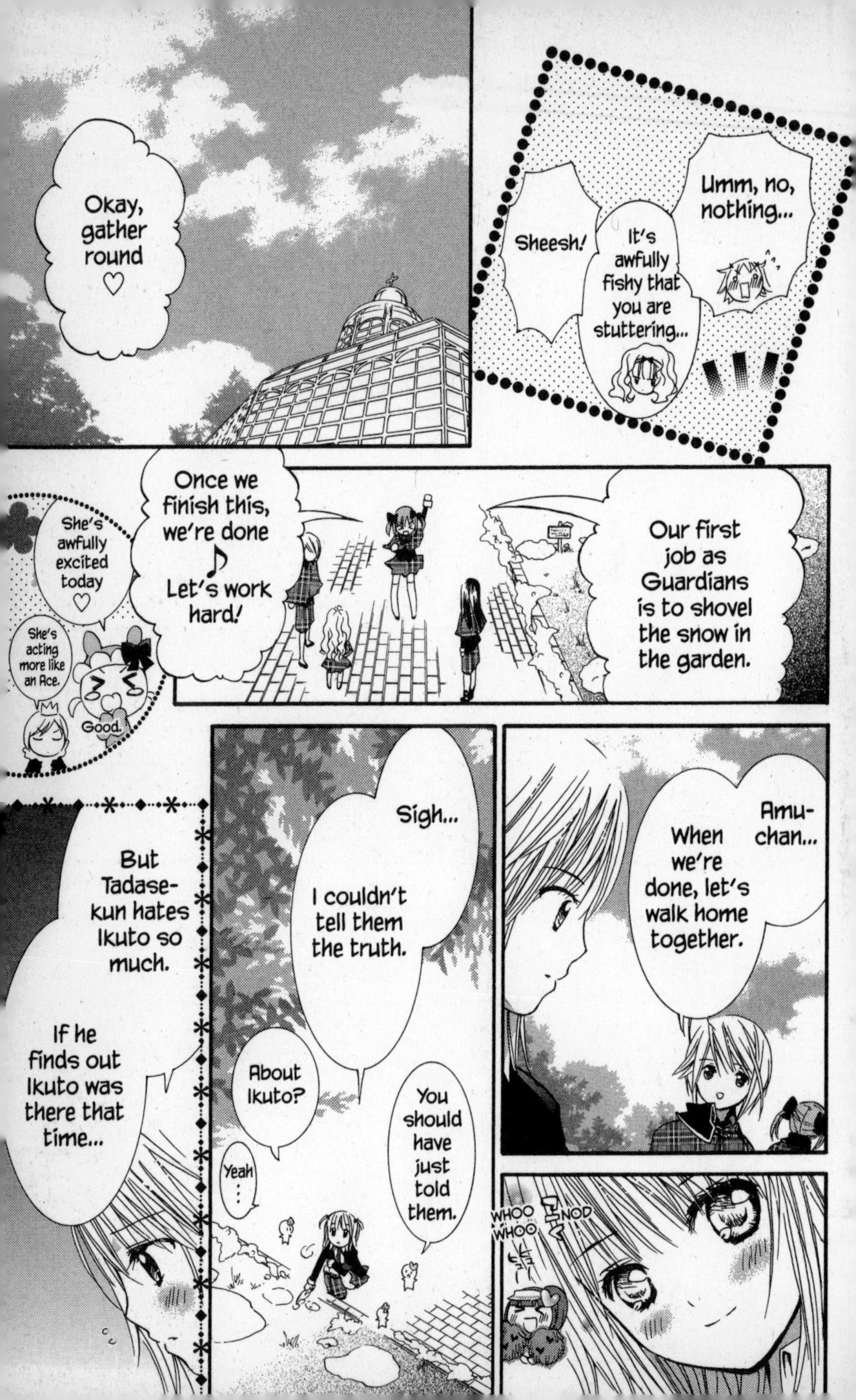

Umm, no, nothing...
It's awfully fishy that you are stuttering...
Sheesh!
Okay, gather round ♡
Our first job as Guardians is to shovel the snow in the garden.
Once we finish this, we're done ♪ Let's work hard!
She's awfully excited today ♡
She's acting more like an Ace.
Good.
Amu-chan... When we're done, let's walk home together.
WHOO WHOO
NOD
Sigh...
I couldn't tell them the truth.
You should have just told them.
About Ikuto?
Yeah...
But Tadase-kun hates Ikuto so much.
If he finds out Ikuto was there that time...

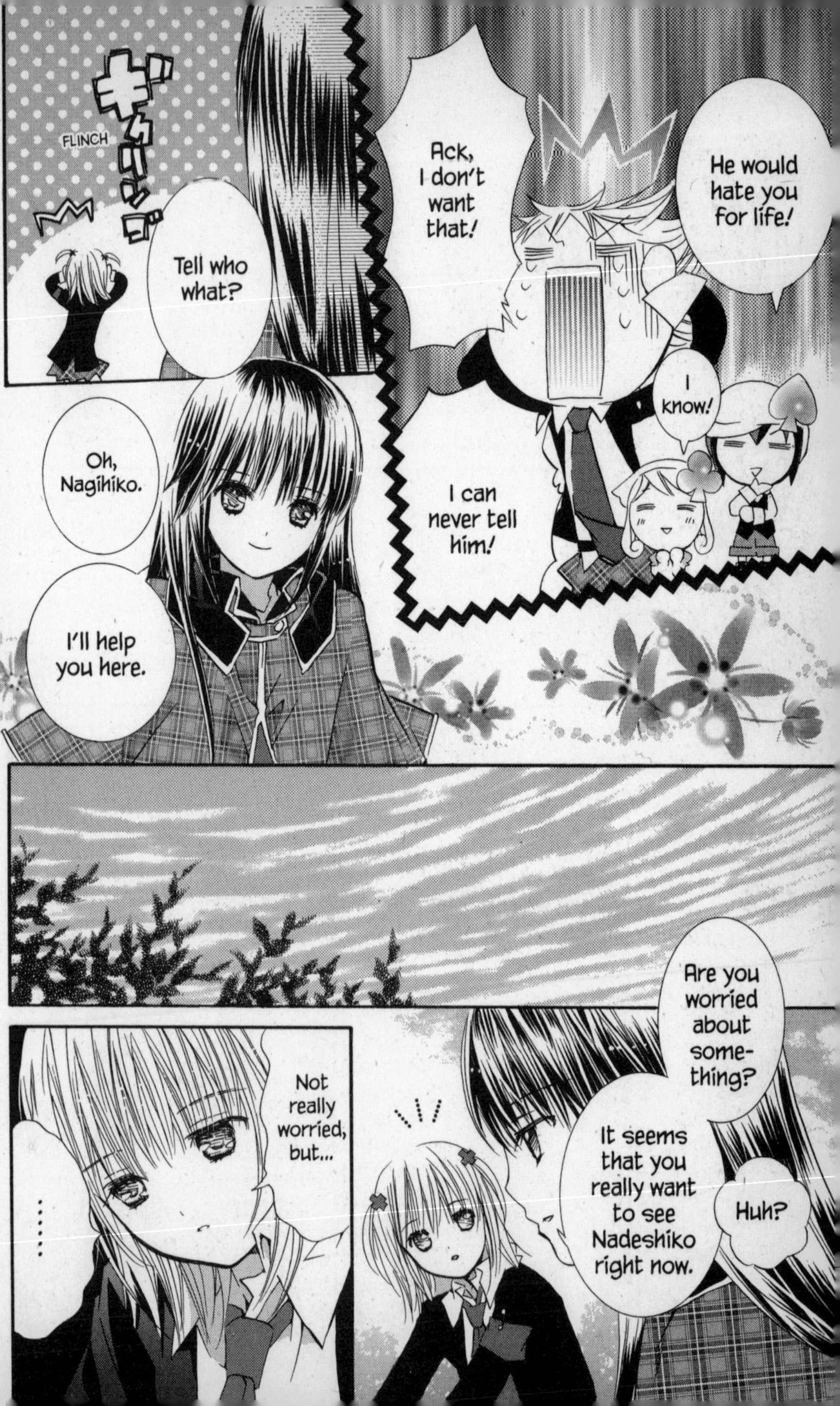
He would hate you for life!
Ack, I don't want that!
I know!
I can never tell him!
FLINCH
Tell who what?
Oh, Nagihiko.
I'll help you here.
Are you worried about some-thing?
Huh?
It seems that you really want to see Nadeshiko right now.
Not really worried, but...
......

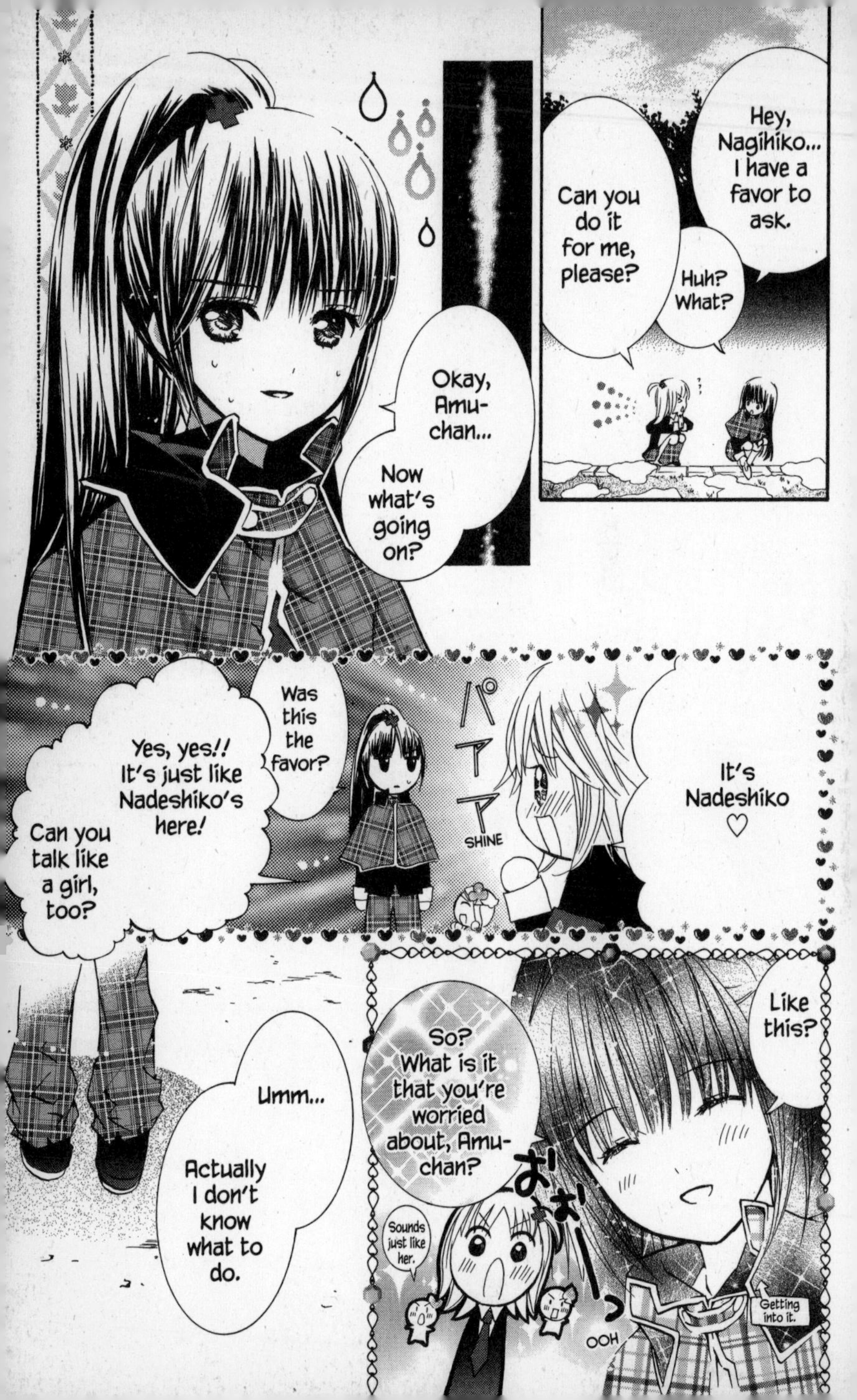
Hey, Nagihiko... I have a favor to ask.
Huh? What?
Can you do it for me, please?
Okay, Amu-chan...
Now what's going on?
It's Nadeshiko ♡
SHINE
Was this the favor?
Yes, yes!! It's just like Nadeshiko's here!
Can you talk like a girl, too?
Like this?
So? What is it that you're worried about, Amu-chan?
Getting into it.
Sounds just like her.
OOH
Umm...
Actually I don't know what to do.

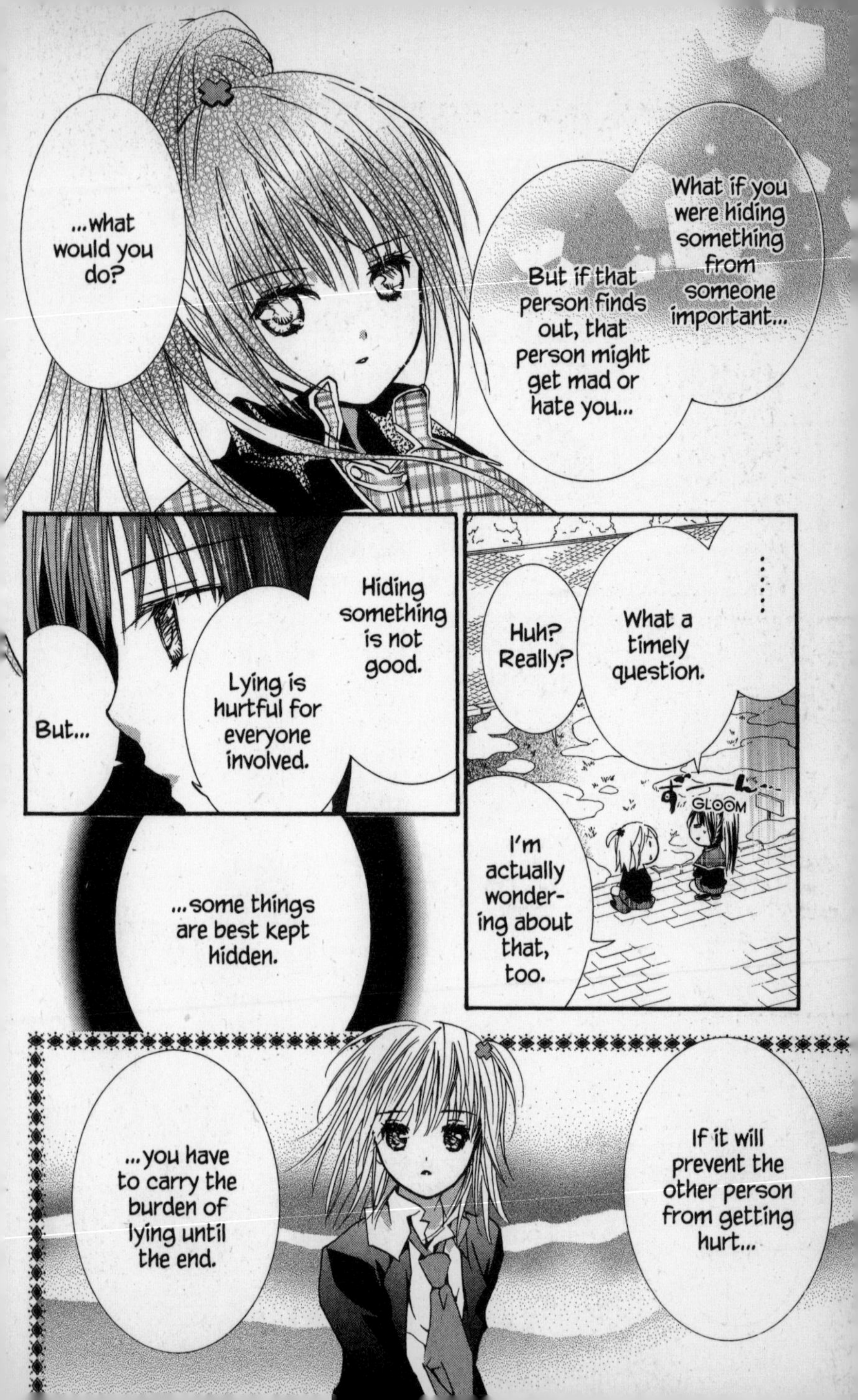
What if you were hiding something from someone important...
But if that person finds out, that person might get mad or hate you...
...what would you do?
......
What a timely question.
Huh? Really?
I'm actually wondering about that, too.
GLOOM
Hiding something is not good.
Lying is hurtful for everyone involved.
But...
...some things are best kept hidden.
If it will prevent the other person from getting hurt...
...you have to carry the burden of lying until the end.

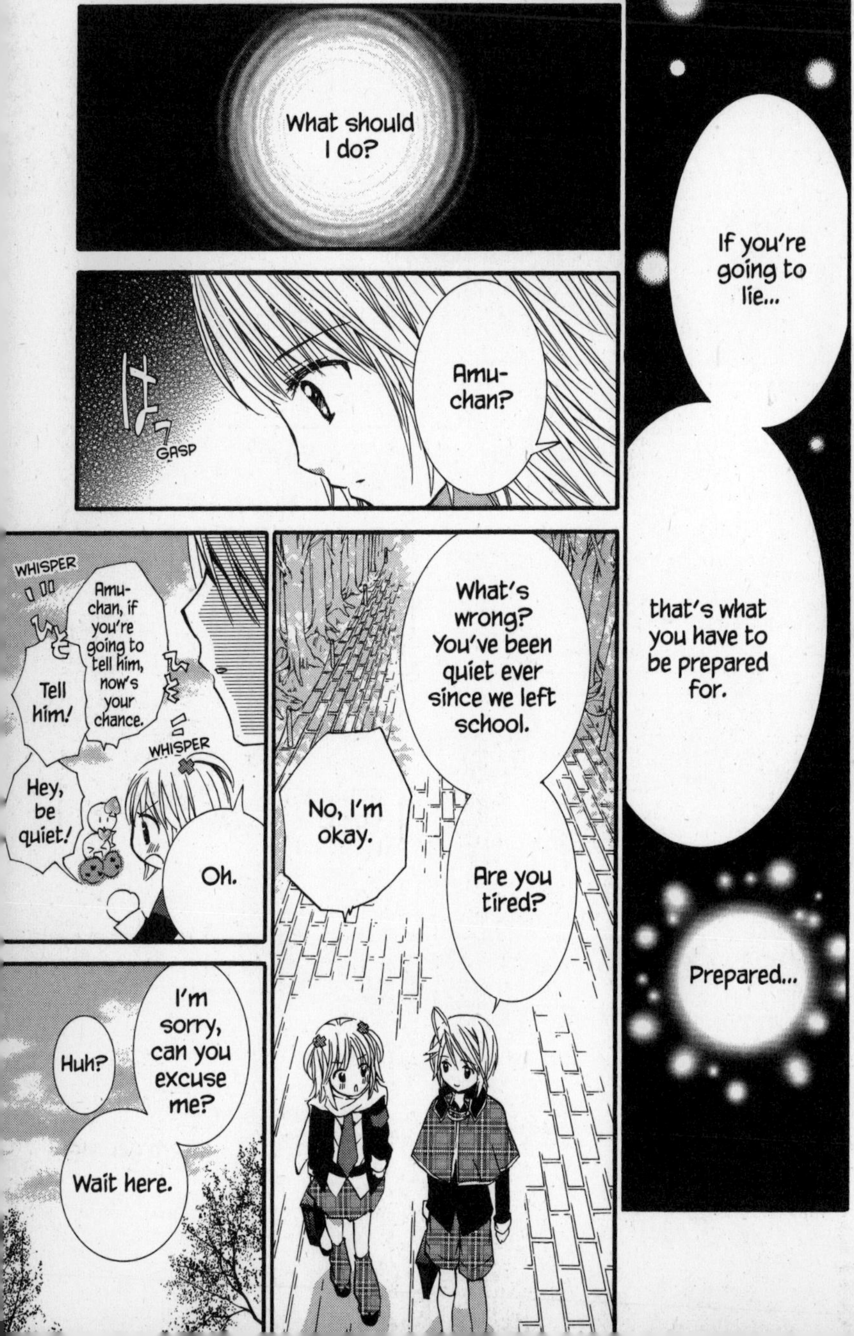
If you're going to lie...
that's what you have to be prepared for.
Prepared...
What should I do?
GASP
Amu-chan?
What's wrong? You've been quiet ever since we left school.
No, I'm okay.
Are you tired?
WHISPER
Amu-chan, if you're going to tell him, now's your chance.
Tell him!
WHISPER
Hey, be quiet!
Oh.
I'm sorry, can you excuse me?
Huh?
Wait here.

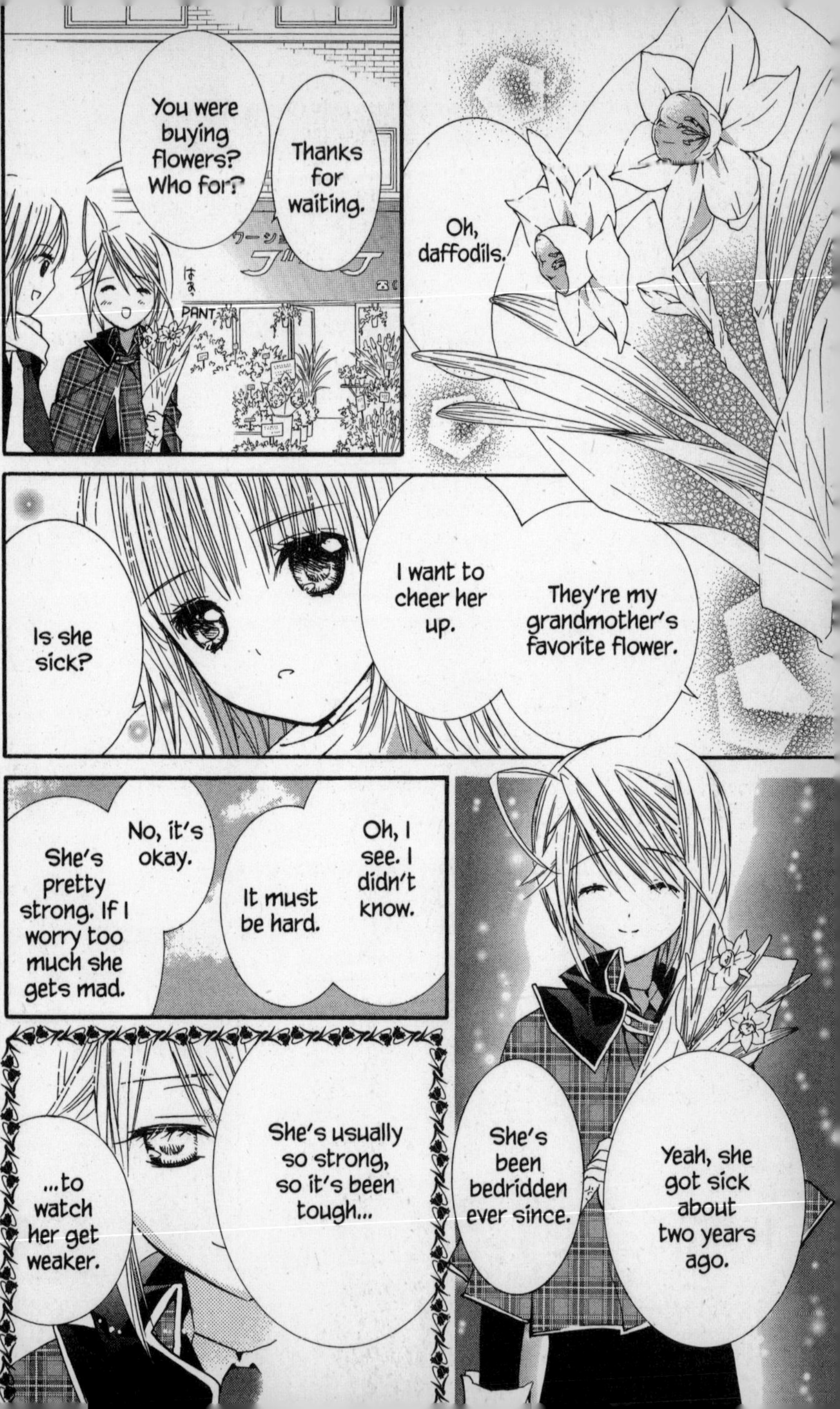
Thanks for waiting.
You were buying flowers? Who for?
PANT
Oh, daffodils.
They're my grandmother's favorite flower.
I want to cheer her up.
Is she sick?
Yeah, she got sick about two years ago.
She's been bedridden ever since.
Oh, I see. I didn't know.
It must be hard.
No, it's okay.
She's pretty strong. If I worry too much she gets mad.
She's usually so strong, so it's been tough...
...to watch her get weaker.

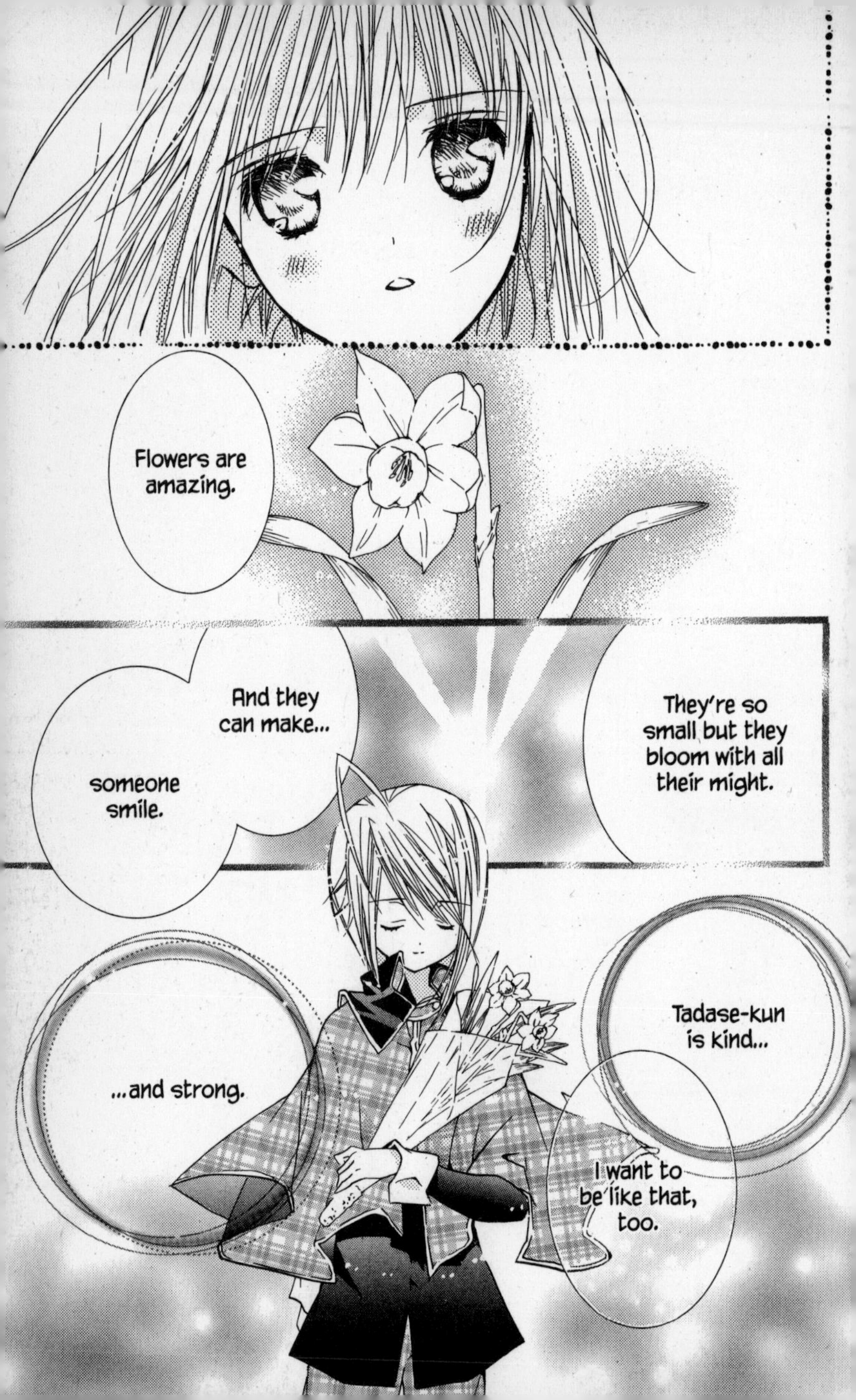
Flowers are amazing.
They're so small but they bloom with all their might.
And they can make...
someone smile.
Tadase-kun is kind...
...and strong.
I want to be like that, too.

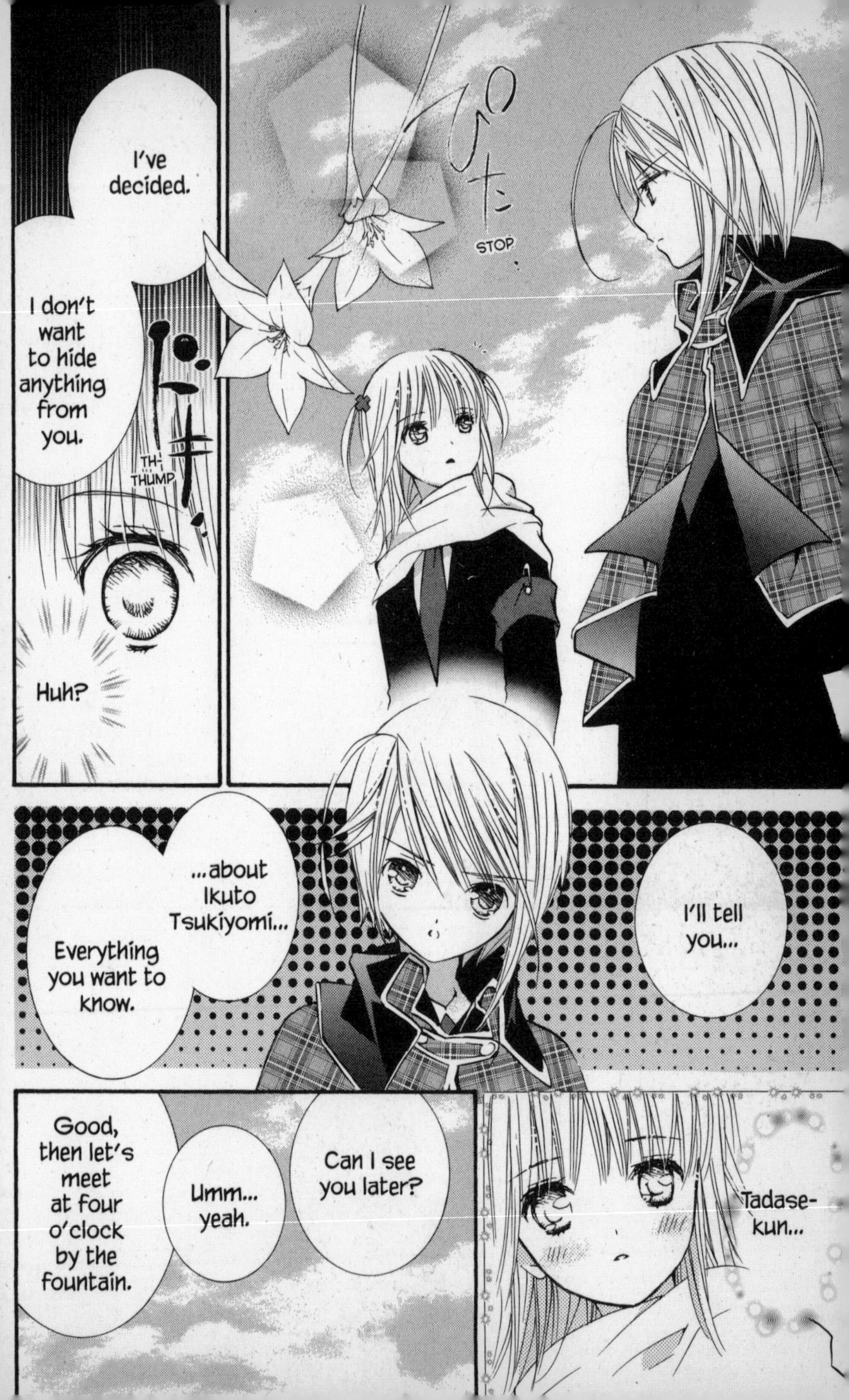
STOP
I've decided.
I don't want to hide anything from you.
TH-THUMP
Huh?
I'll tell you...
...about Ikuto Tsukiyomi...
Everything you want to know.
Tadase-kun...
Can I see you later?
Umm... yeah.
Good, then let's meet at four o'clock by the fountain.

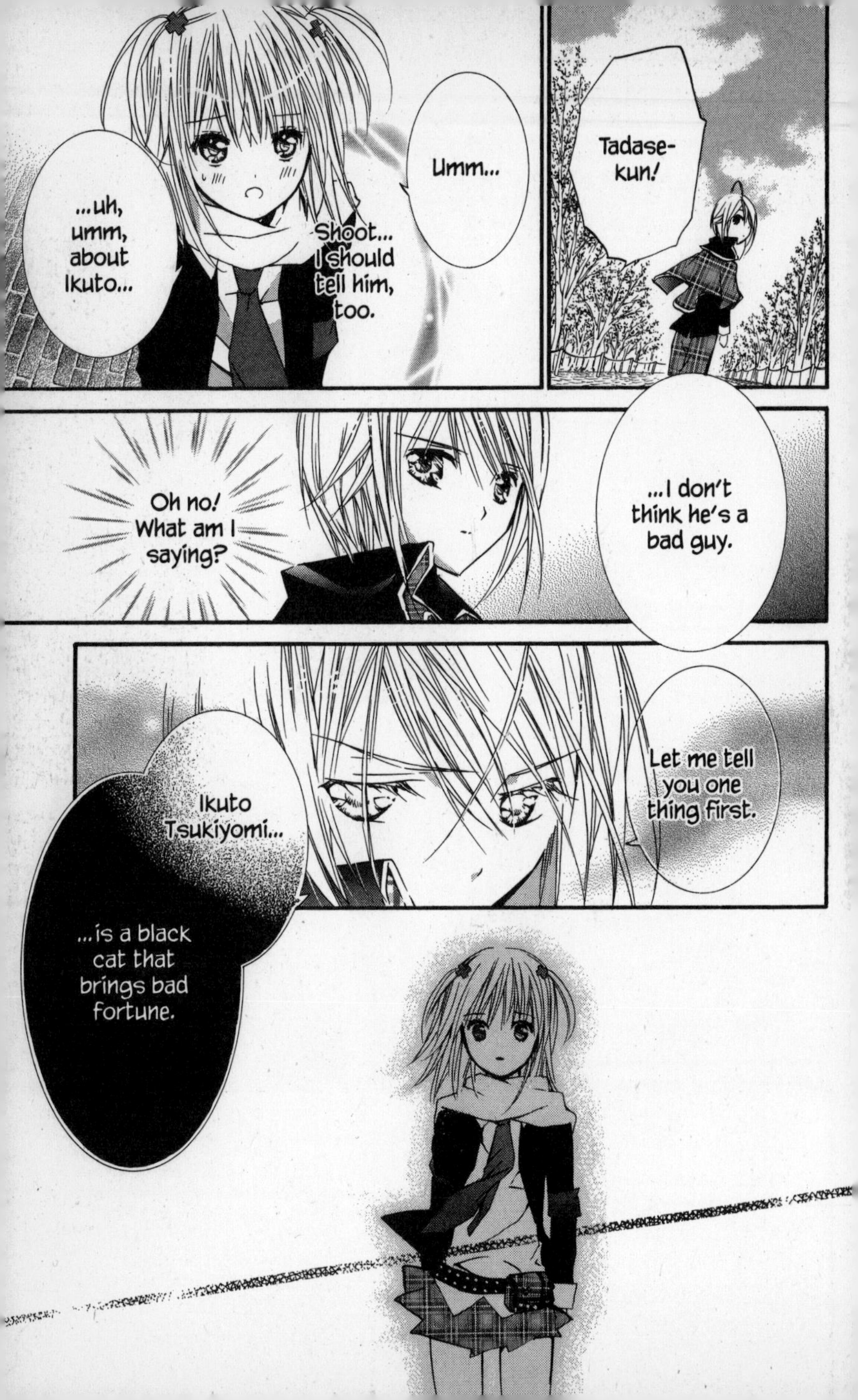
Tadase-kun!
Umm...
Shoot... I should tell him, too.
...uh, umm, about Ikuto...
...I don't think he's a bad guy.
Oh no! What am I saying?
Let me tell you one thing first.
Ikuto Tsukiyomi...
...is a black cat that brings bad fortune.

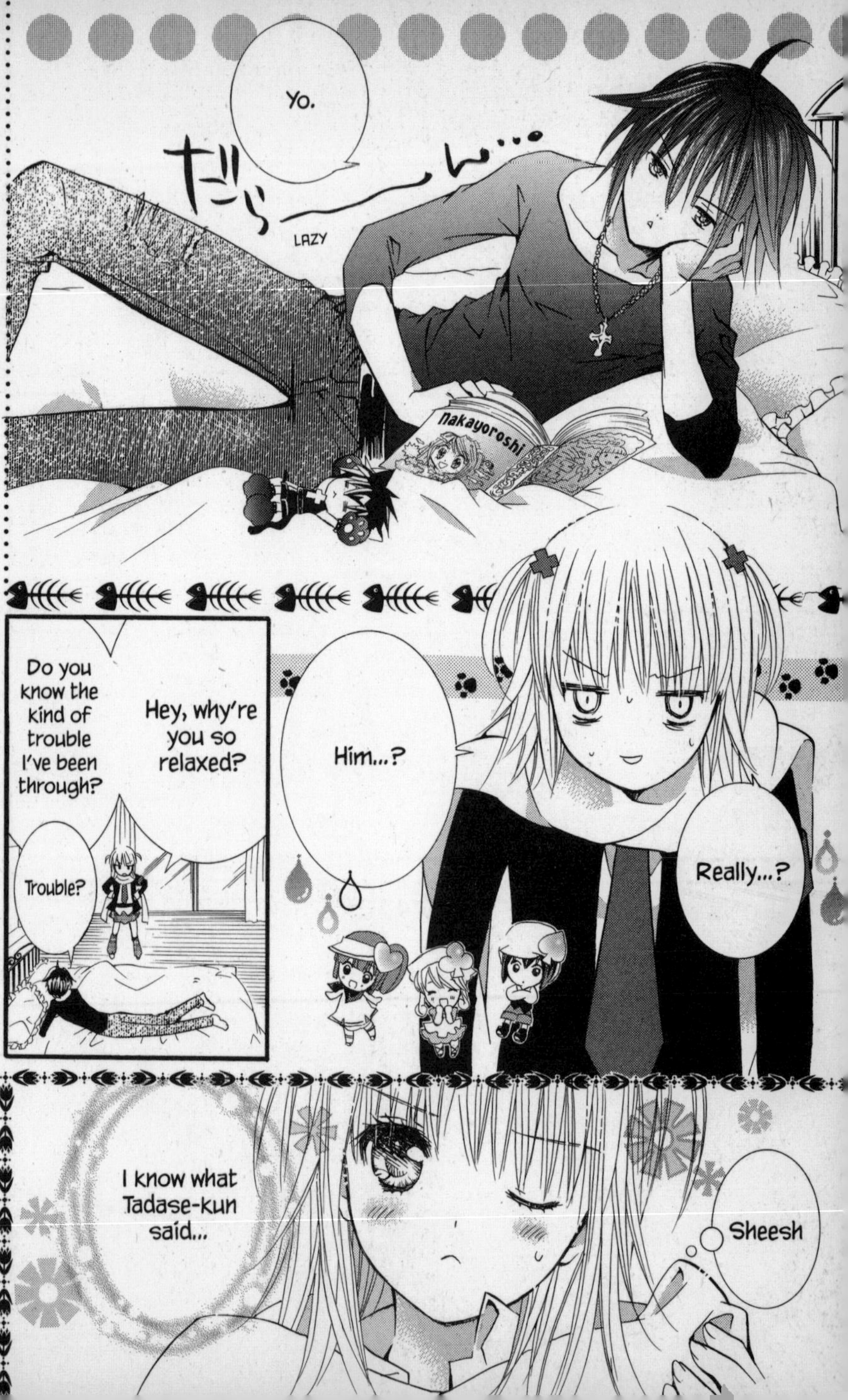

Yo.
だら——ん…
LAZY
Him...?
Really...?
Hey, why're you so relaxed?
Do you know the kind of trouble I've been through?
Trouble?
Sheesh
I know what Tadase-kun said...
Nakayoroshi

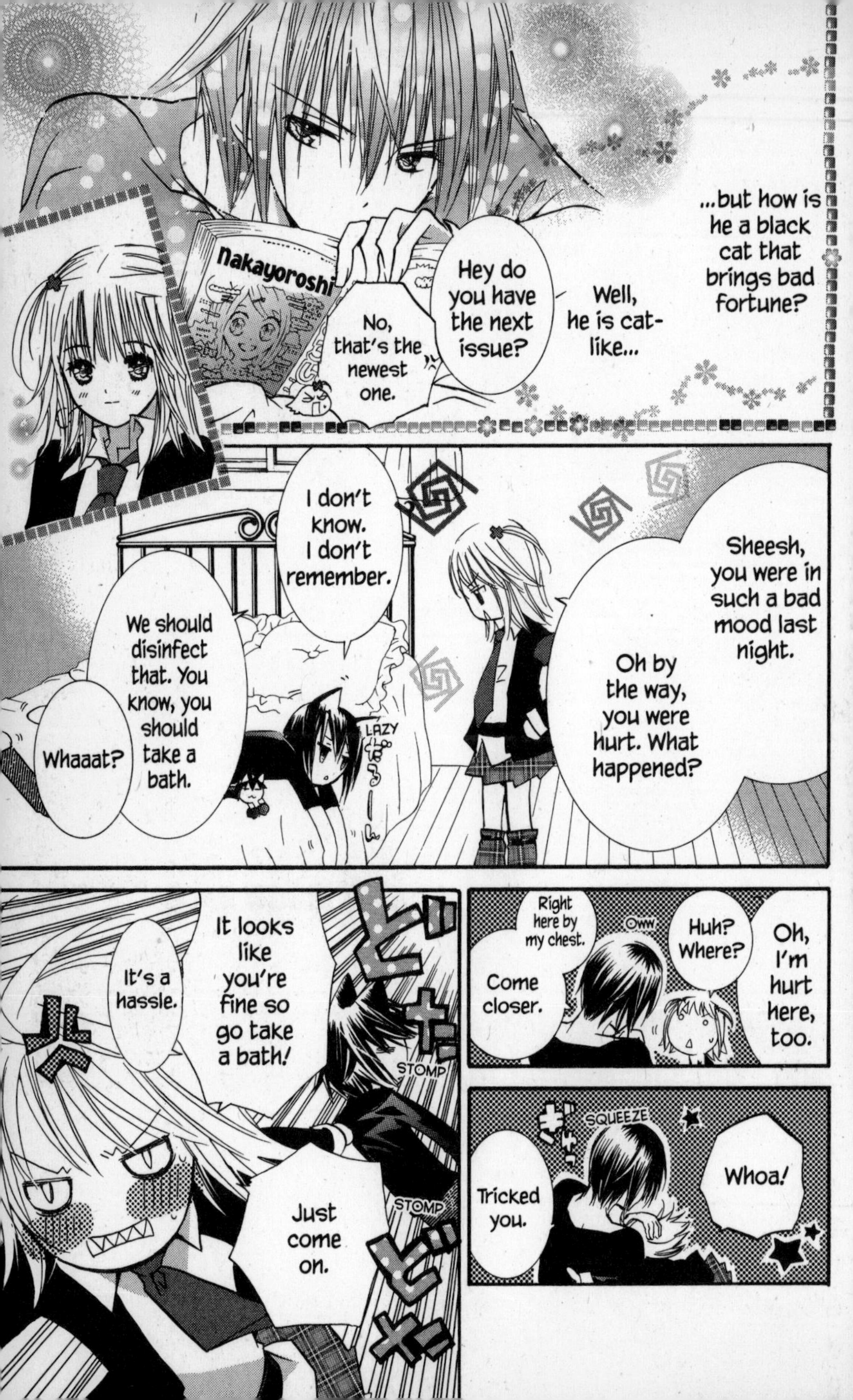
...but how is he a black cat that brings bad fortune?
Well, he is cat-like...
Hey do you have the next issue?
Nakayoroshi
No, that's the newest one.
Sheesh, you were in such a bad mood last night.
Oh by the way, you were hurt. What happened?
I don't know. I don't remember.
We should disinfect that. You know, you should take a bath.
LAZY
Whaaat?
Oh, I'm hurt here, too.
Huh? Where?
OWW
Right here by my chest.
Come closer.
Whoa!
SQUEEZE
Tricked you.
It looks like you're fine so go take a bath!
It's a hassle.
STOMP
Just come on.
STOMP

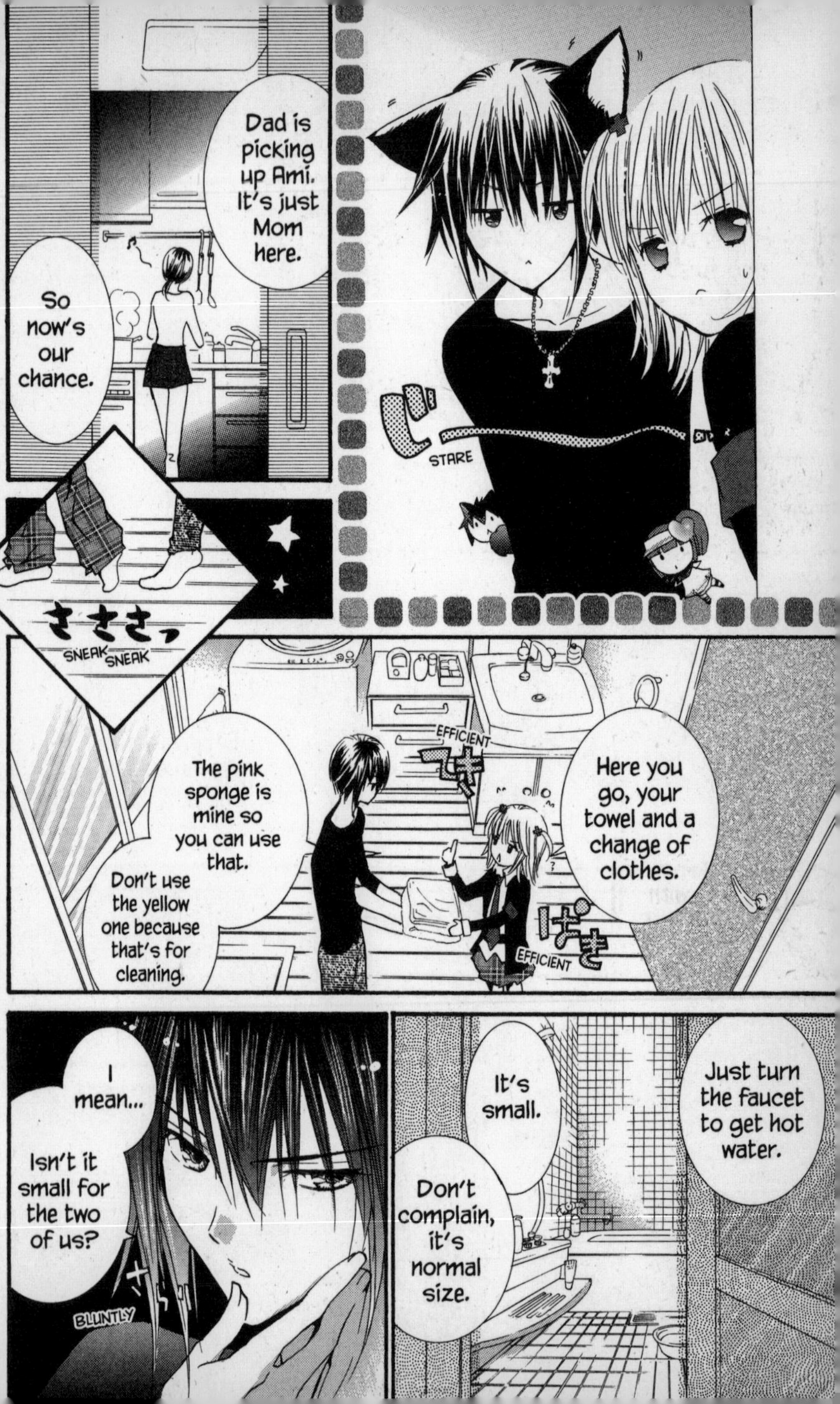
じ
STARE
Dad is picking up Ami. It's just Mom here.
So now's our chance.
さささっ
SNEAK SNEAK
Here you go, your towel and a change of clothes.
てき
EFFICIENT
The pink sponge is mine so you can use that.
ぱき
EFFICIENT
Don't use the yellow one because that's for cleaning.
Just turn the faucet to get hot water.
It's small.
Don't complain, it's normal size.
I mean...
Isn't it small for the two of us?
BLUNTLY

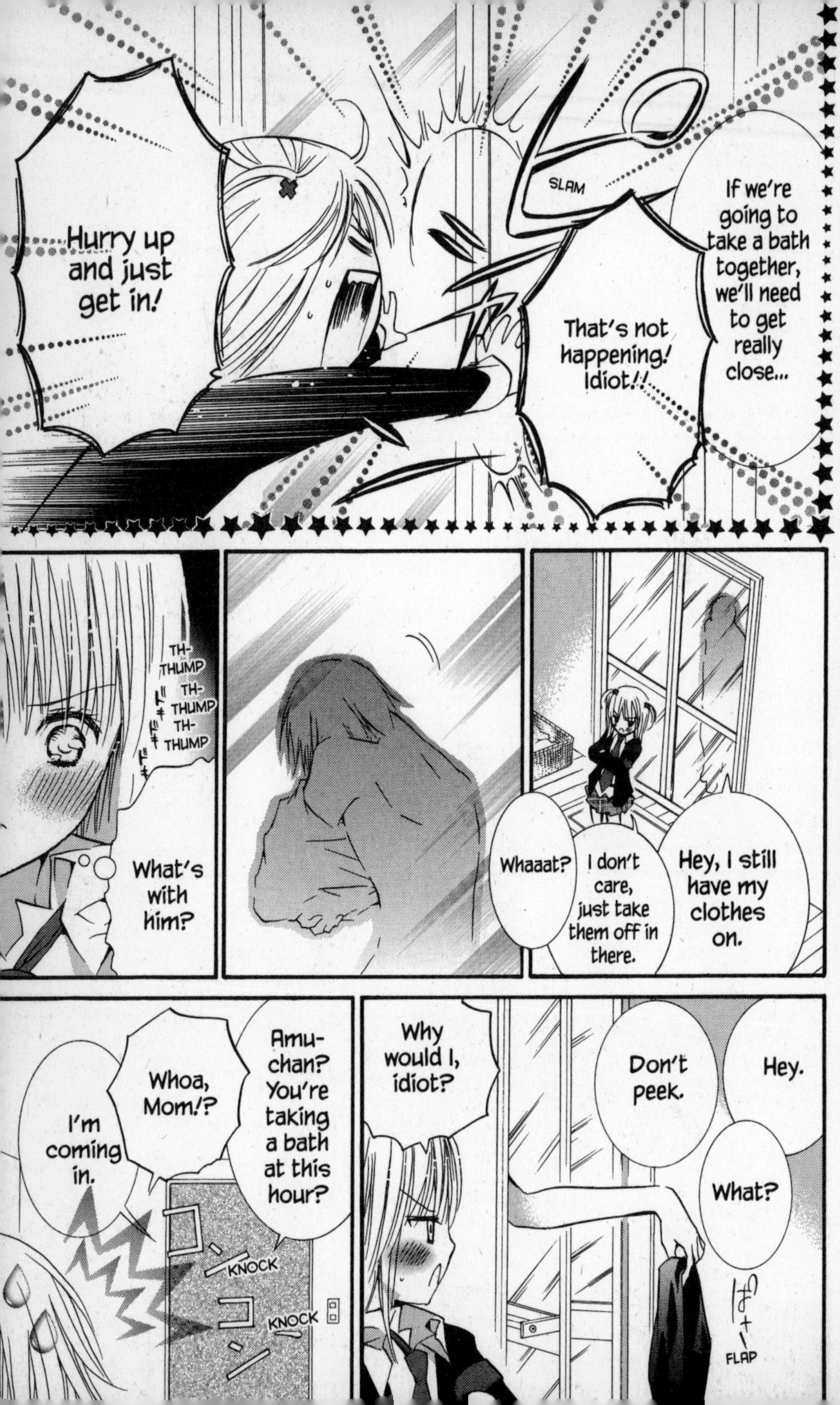
If we're going to take a bath together, we'll need to get really close...
SLAM
That's not happening! Idiot!!
Hurry up and just get in!
Hey, I still have my clothes on.
I don't care, just take them off in there.
Whaaat?
TH-THUMP
TH-THUMP
TH-THUMP
What's with him?
Hey.
Don't peek.
What?
Why would I, idiot?
FLAP
Amu-chan? You're taking a bath at this hour?
KNOCK
KNOCK
Whoa, Mom!?
I'm coming in.

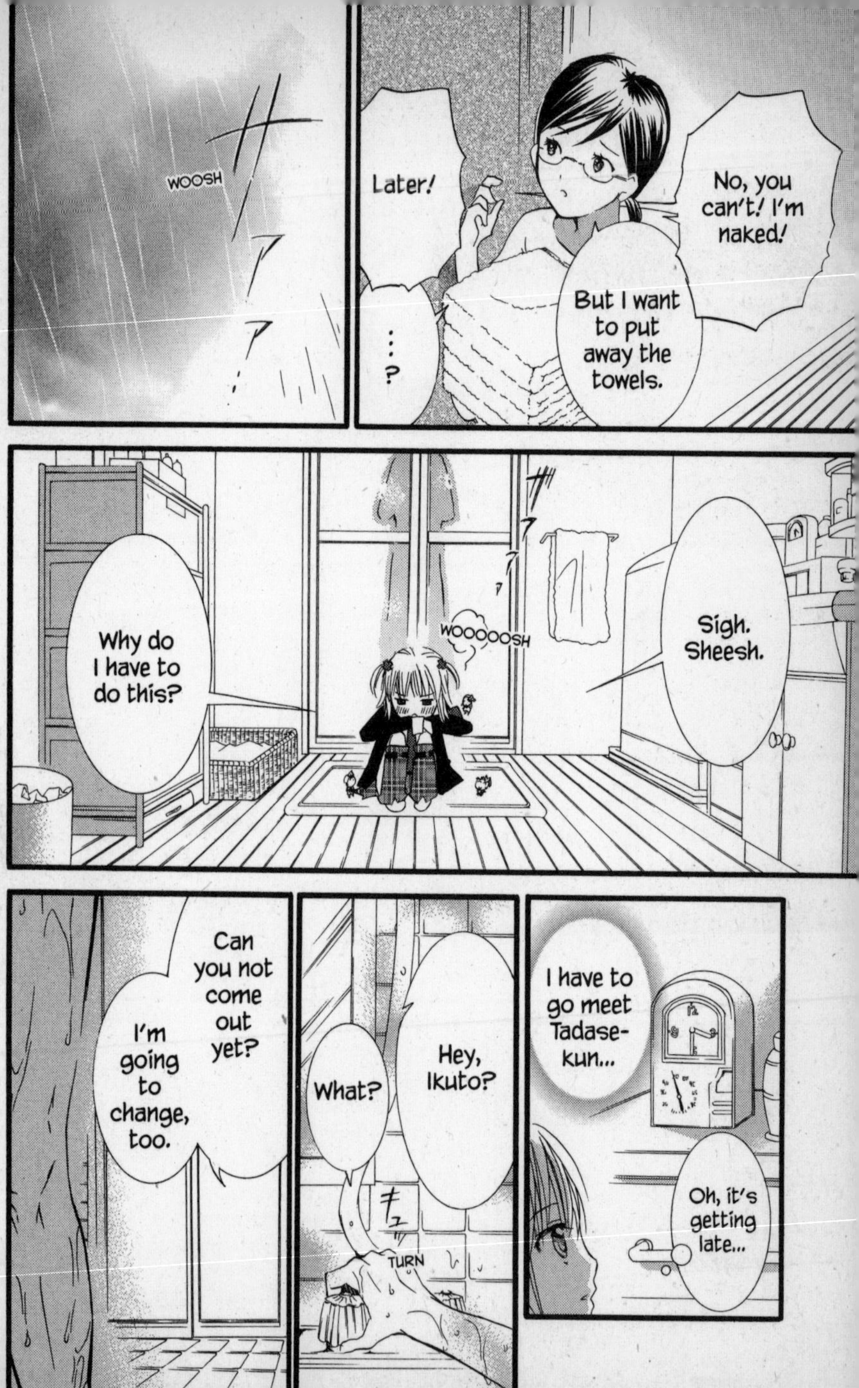
No, you can't! I'm naked!
But I want to put away the towels.
Later!
...?
WOOSH
Sigh. Sheesh.
WOOOOOSH
Why do I have to do this?
I have to go meet Tadase-kun...
Oh, it's getting late...
Hey, Ikuto?
What?
TURN
Can you not come out yet?
I'm going to change, too.

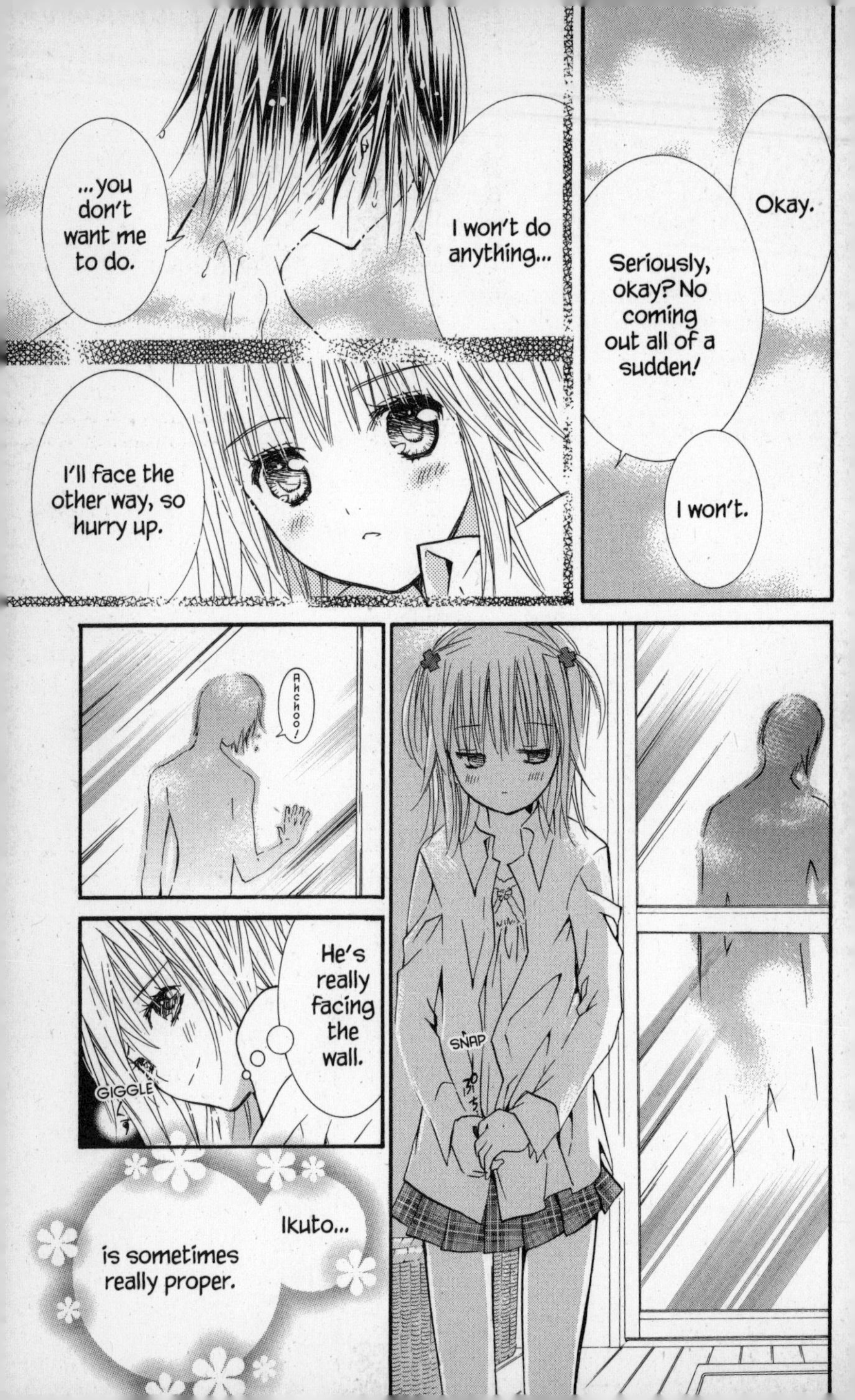
Okay.
Seriously, okay? No coming out all of a sudden!
I won't.
I won't do anything...
...you don't want me to do.
I'll face the other way, so hurry up.
SNAP
Ahchoo!
He's really facing the wall.
GIGGLE
Ikuto...
is sometimes really proper.

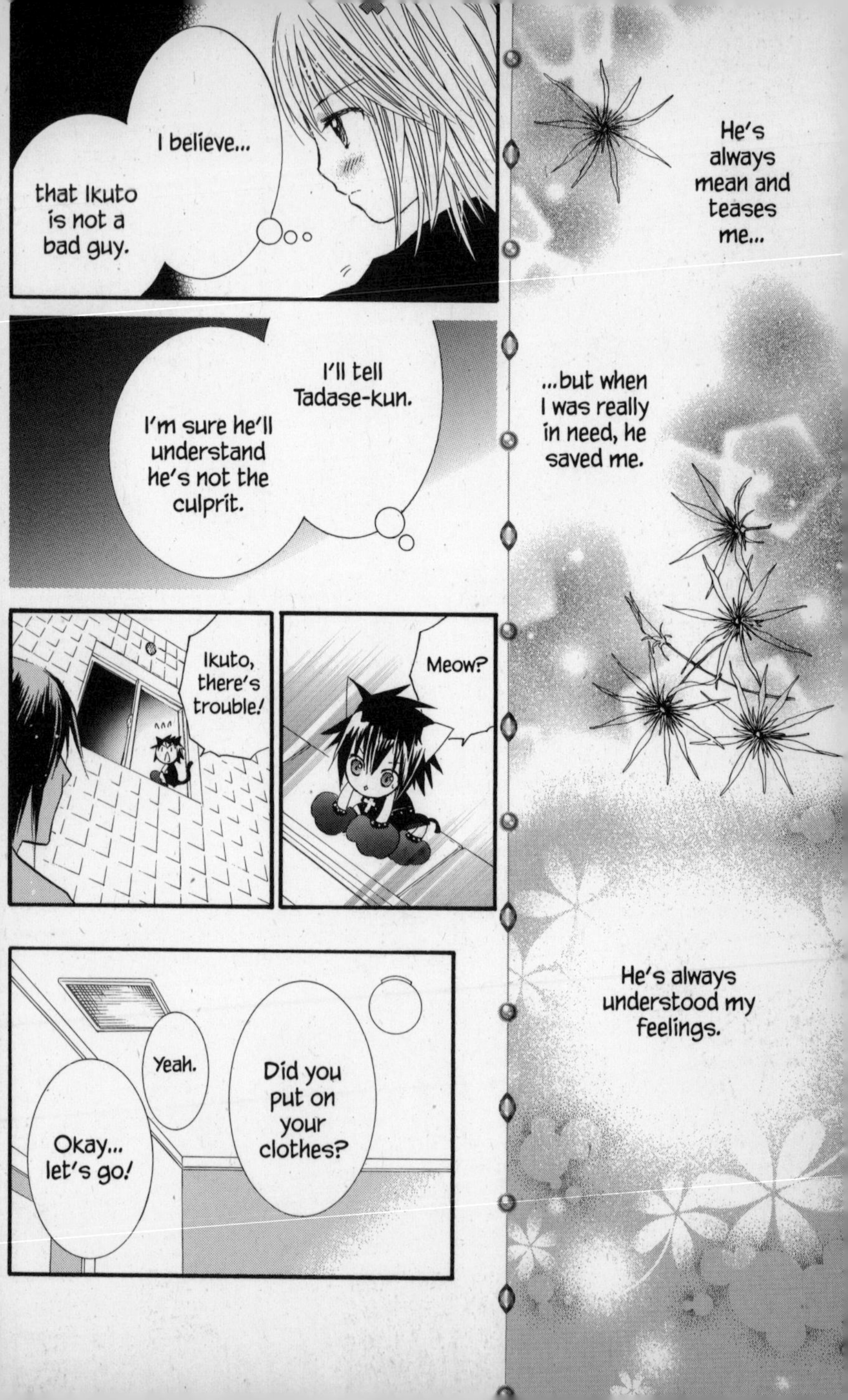
He's always mean and teases me...
...but when I was really in need, he saved me.
He's always understood my feelings.
I believe...
that Ikuto is not a bad guy.
I'll tell Tadase-kun.
I'm sure he'll understand he's not the culprit.
Meow?
Ikuto, there's trouble!
Did you put on your clothes?
Yeah.
Okay... let's go!

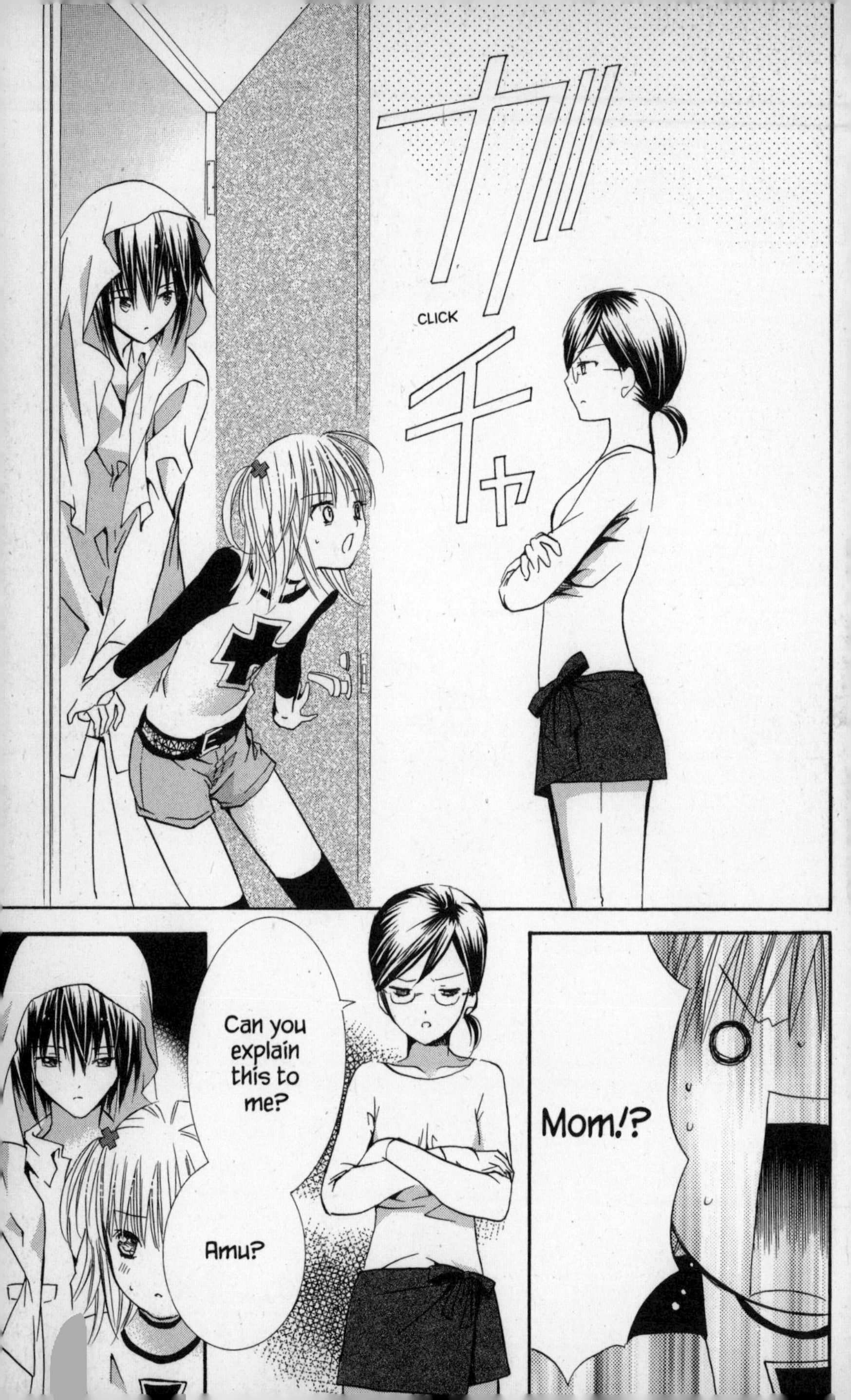
カチャ
CLICK
Mom!?
Can you explain this to me?
Amu?

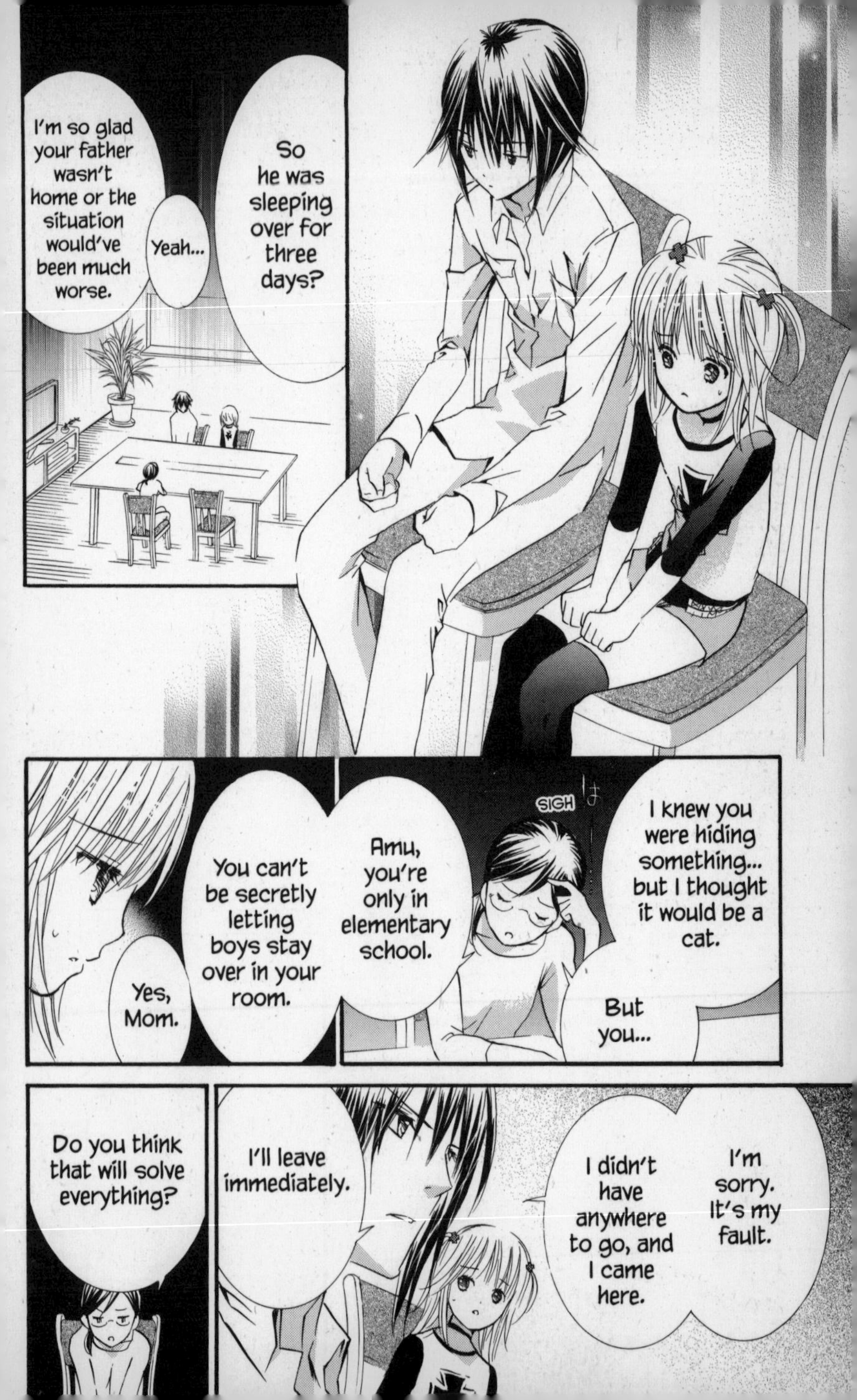
So he was sleeping over for three days?
Yeah...
I'm so glad your father wasn't home or the situation would've been much worse.
SIGH
I knew you were hiding something... but I thought it would be a cat.
But you...
Amu, you're only in elementary school.
You can't be secretly letting boys stay over in your room.
Yes, Mom.
I'm sorry. It's my fault.
I didn't have anywhere to go, and I came here.
I'll leave immediately.
Do you think that will solve everything?

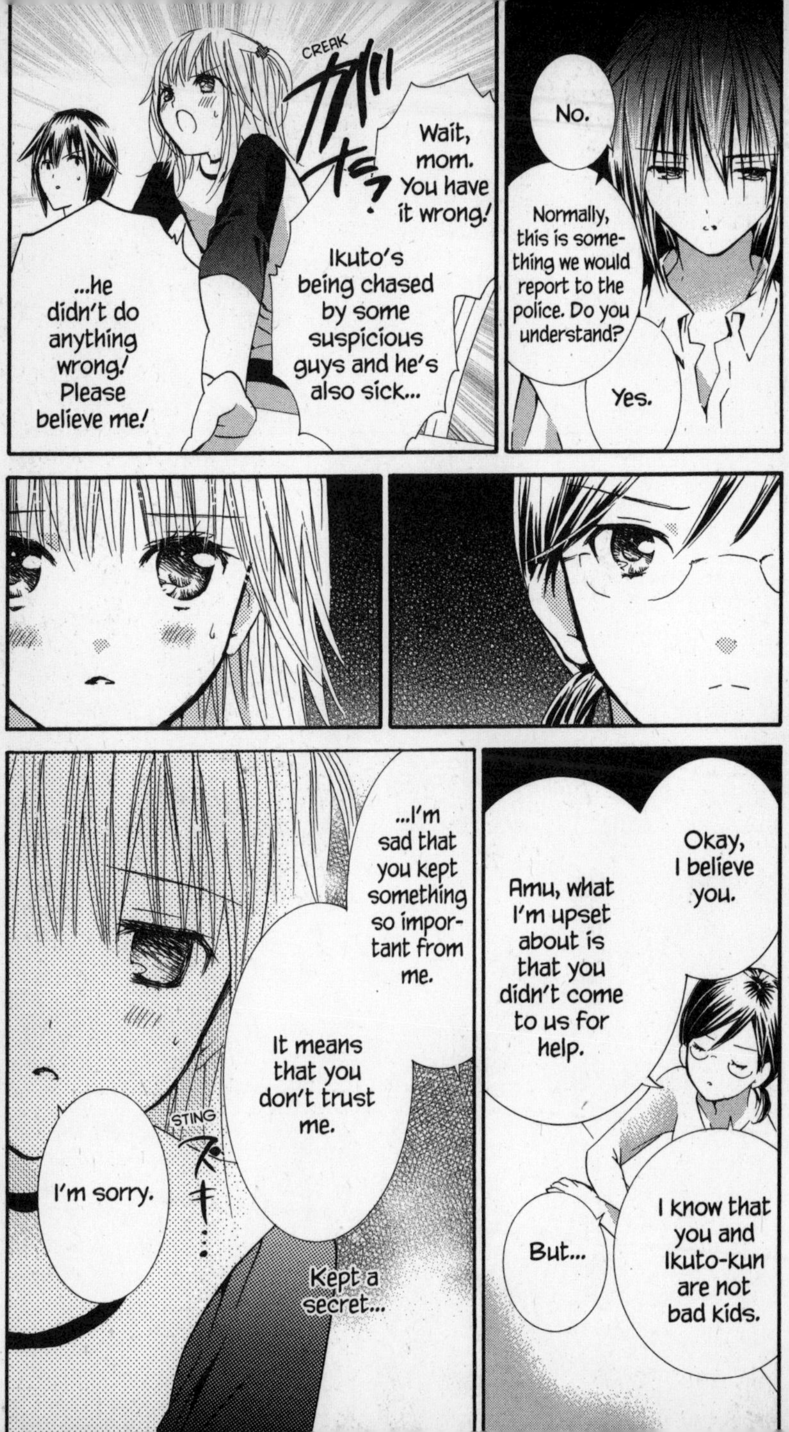
No.
Normally, this is something we would report to the police. Do you understand?
Yes.
CREAK
Wait, mom. You have it wrong!
Ikuto's being chased by some suspicious guys and he's also sick...
...he didn't do anything wrong! Please believe me!
Okay, I believe you.
Amu, what I'm upset about is that you didn't come to us for help.
I know that you and Ikuto-kun are not bad kids.
But...
...I'm sad that you kept something so important from me.
It means that you don't trust me.
STING
Kept a secret...
I'm sorry.

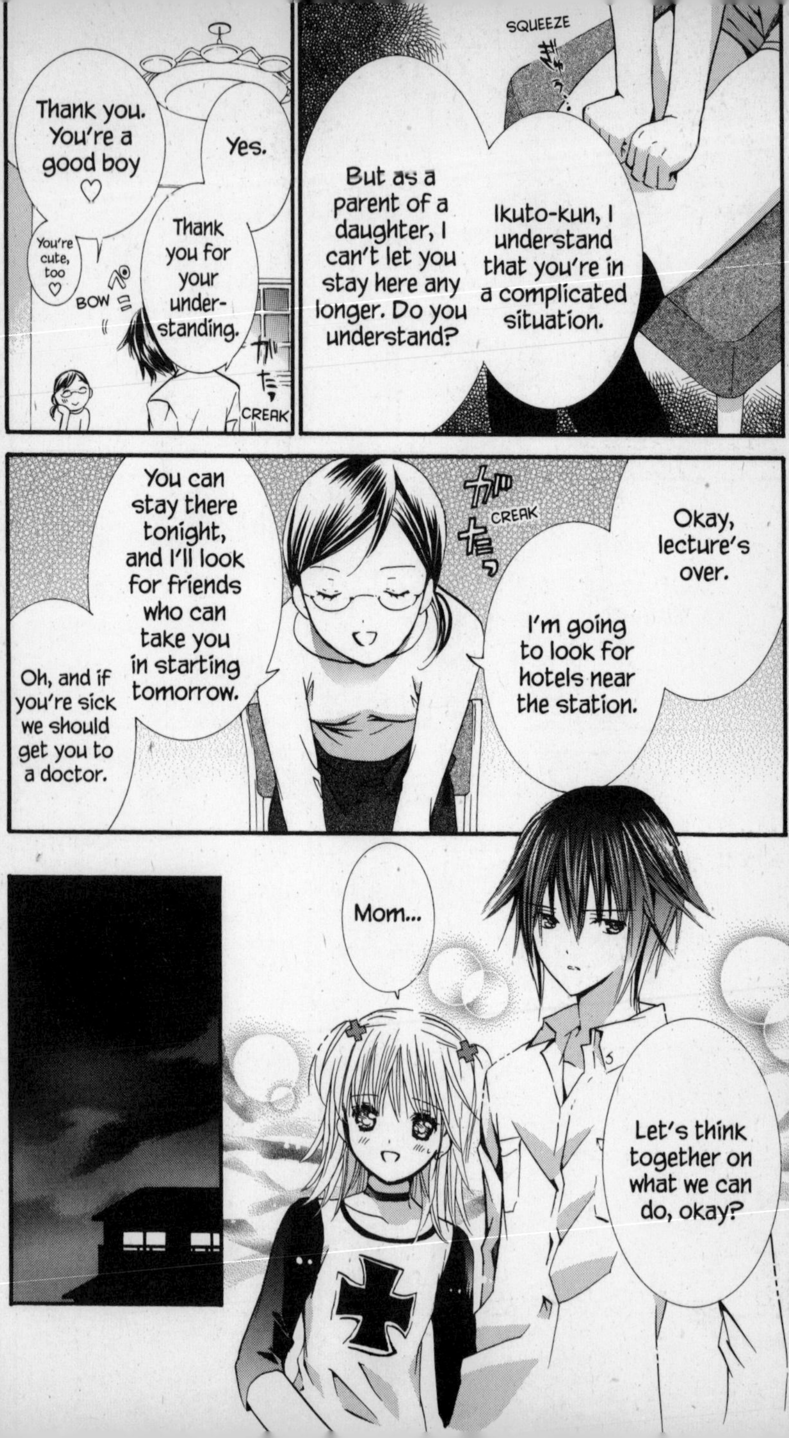
SQUEEZE
Ikuto-kun, I understand that you're in a complicated situation.
But as a parent of a daughter, I can't let you stay here any longer. Do you understand?
Yes.
Thank you for your under-standing.
Thank you. You're a good boy ♡
You're cute, too ♡
BOW
CREAK
CREAK
Okay, lecture's over.
I'm going to look for hotels near the station.
You can stay there tonight, and I'll look for friends who can take you in starting tomorrow.
Oh, and if you're sick we should get you to a doctor.
Mom...
Let's think together on what we can do, okay?

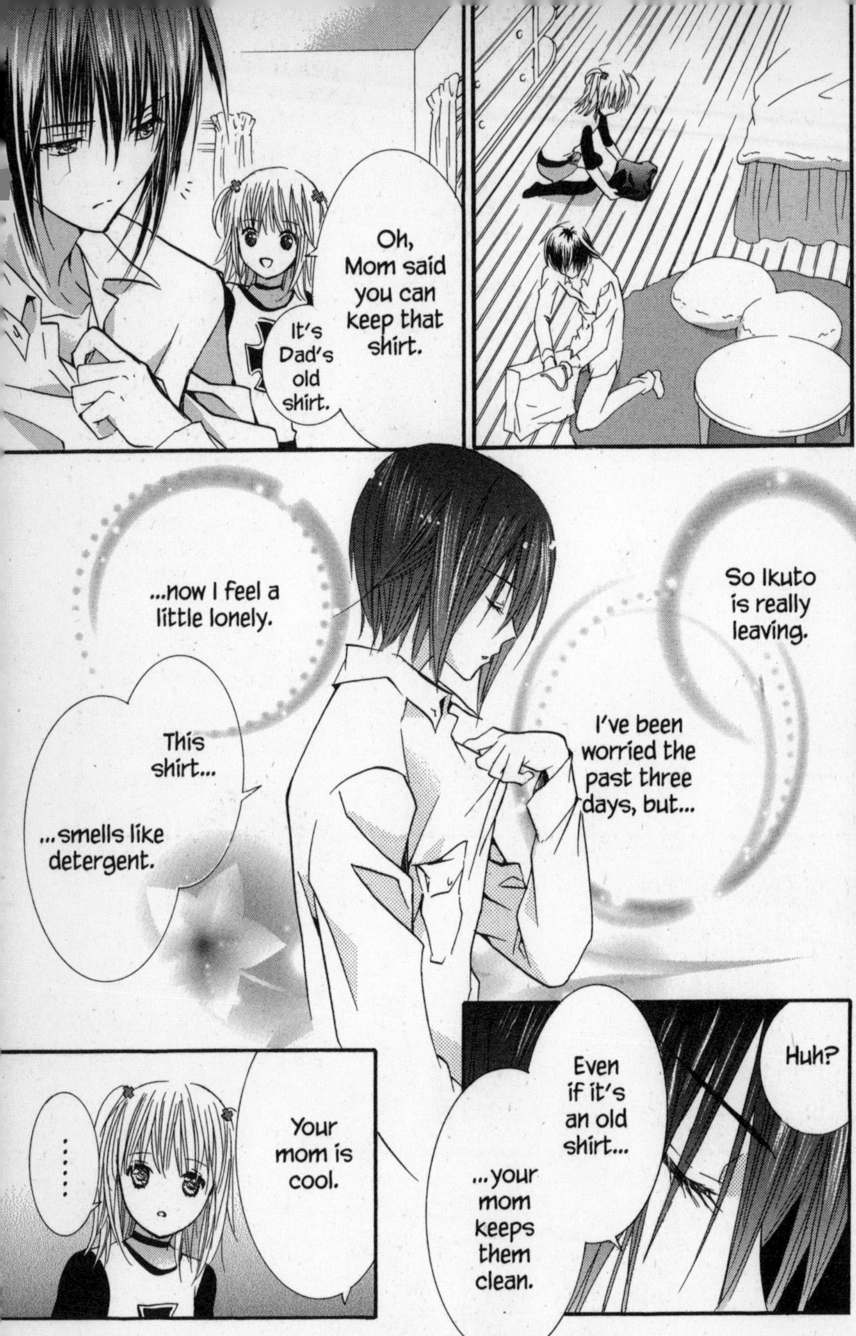
Oh, Mom said you can keep that shirt.
It's Dad's old shirt.
So Ikuto is really leaving.
I've been worried the past three days, but...
...now I feel a little lonely.
This shirt...
...smells like detergent.
Huh?
Even if it's an old shirt...
...your mom keeps them clean.
Your mom is cool.
......

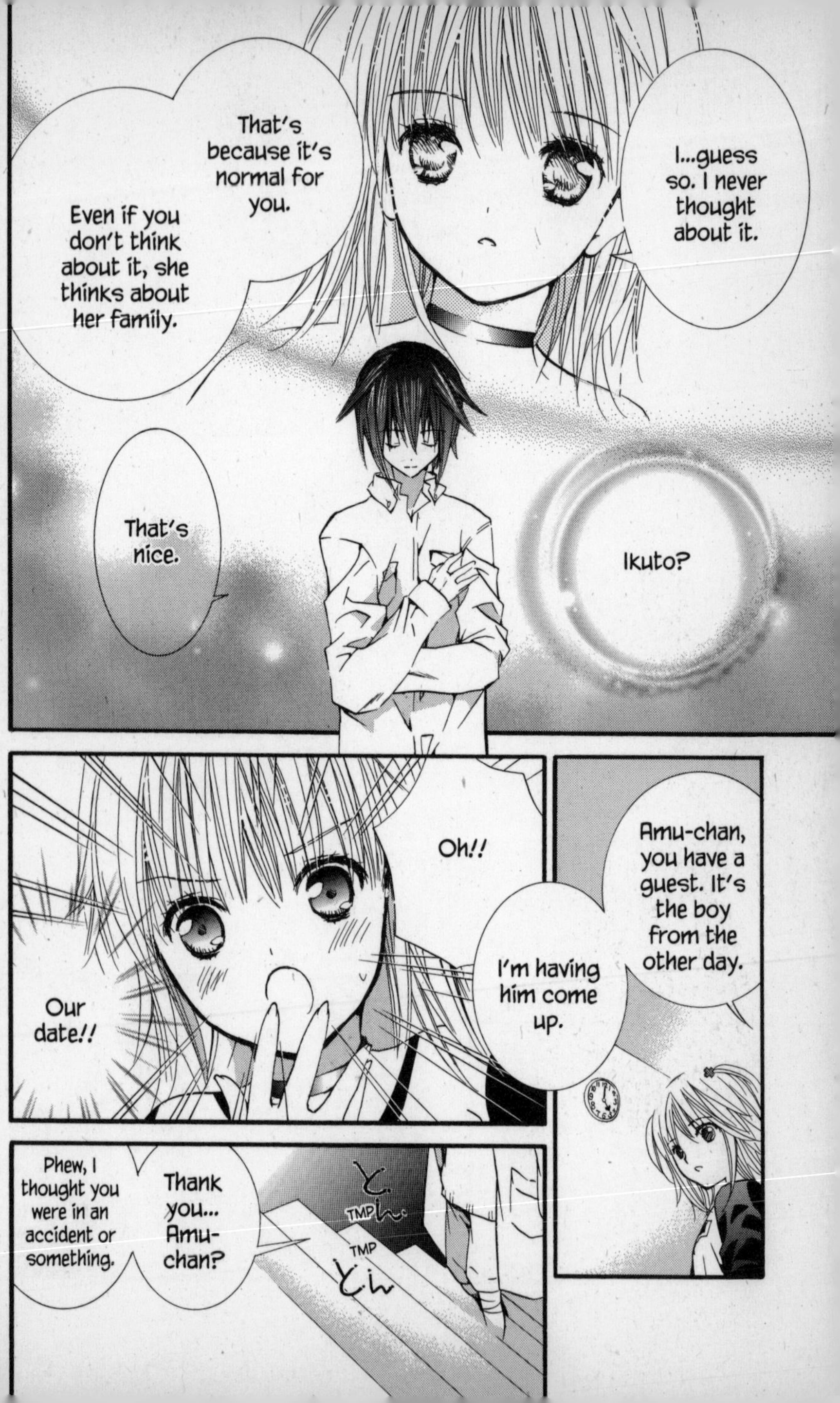

I...guess so. I never thought about it.
That's because it's normal for you.
Even if you don't think about it, she thinks about her family.
Ikuto?
That's nice.
Amu-chan, you have a guest. It's the boy from the other day.
I'm having him come up.
Oh!!
Our date!!
TMP
TMP
Thank you... Amu-chan?
Phew, I thought you were in an accident or something.

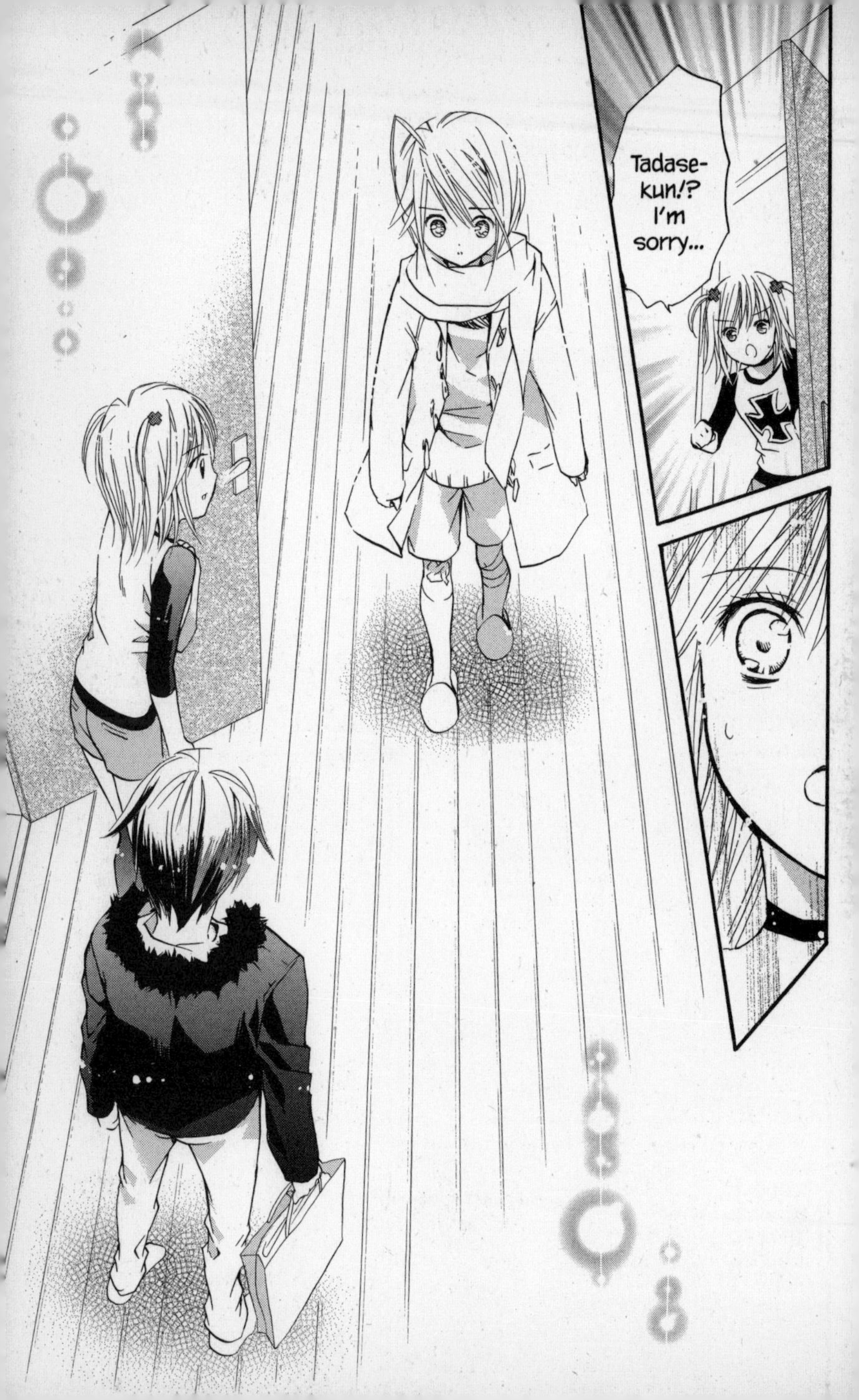
Tadase-kun!? I'm sorry...

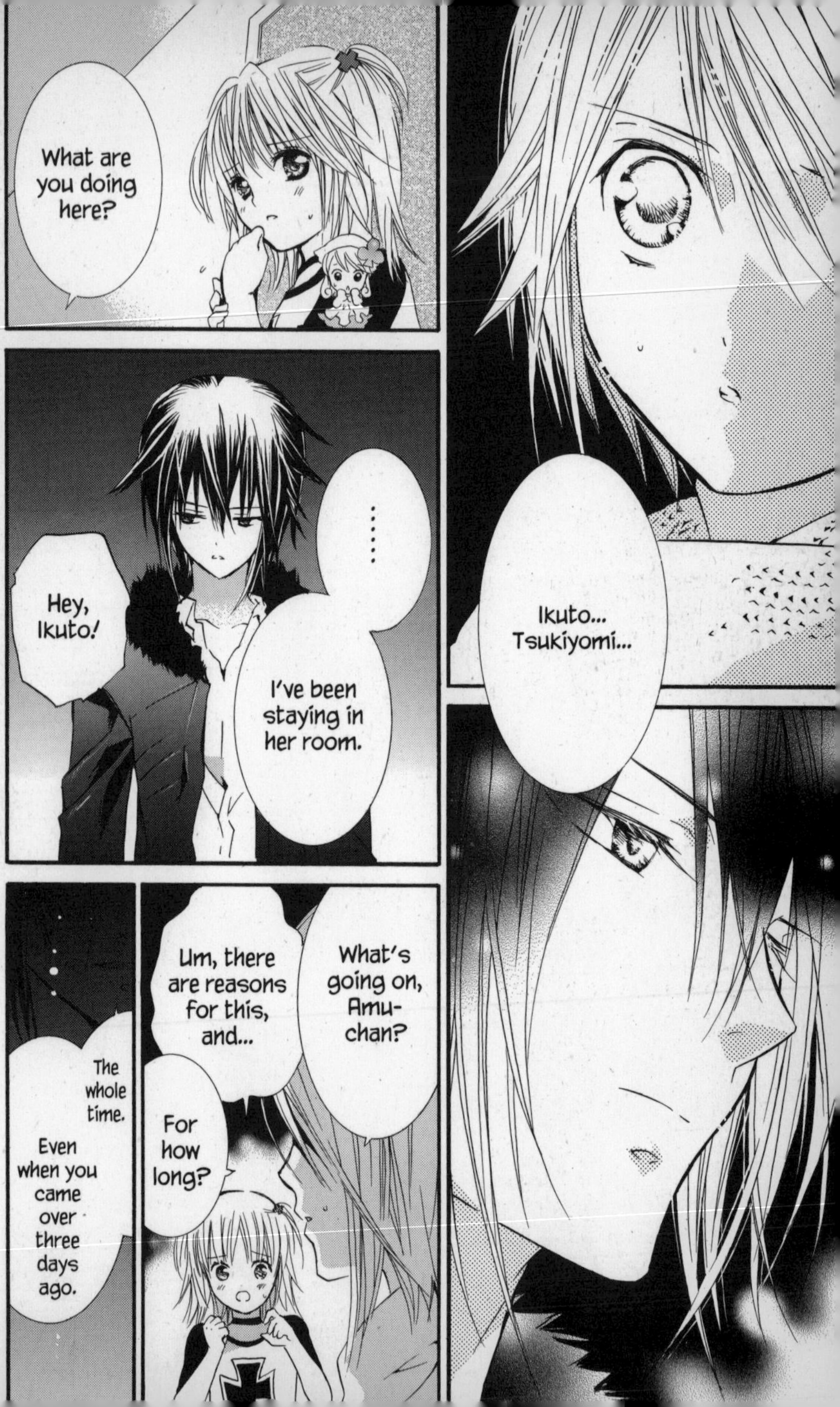
Ikuto... Tsukiyomi...
What are you doing here?
.....
I've been staying in her room.
Hey, Ikuto!
What's going on, Amu-chan?
Um, there are reasons for this, and...
For how long?
The whole time.
Even when you came over three days ago.

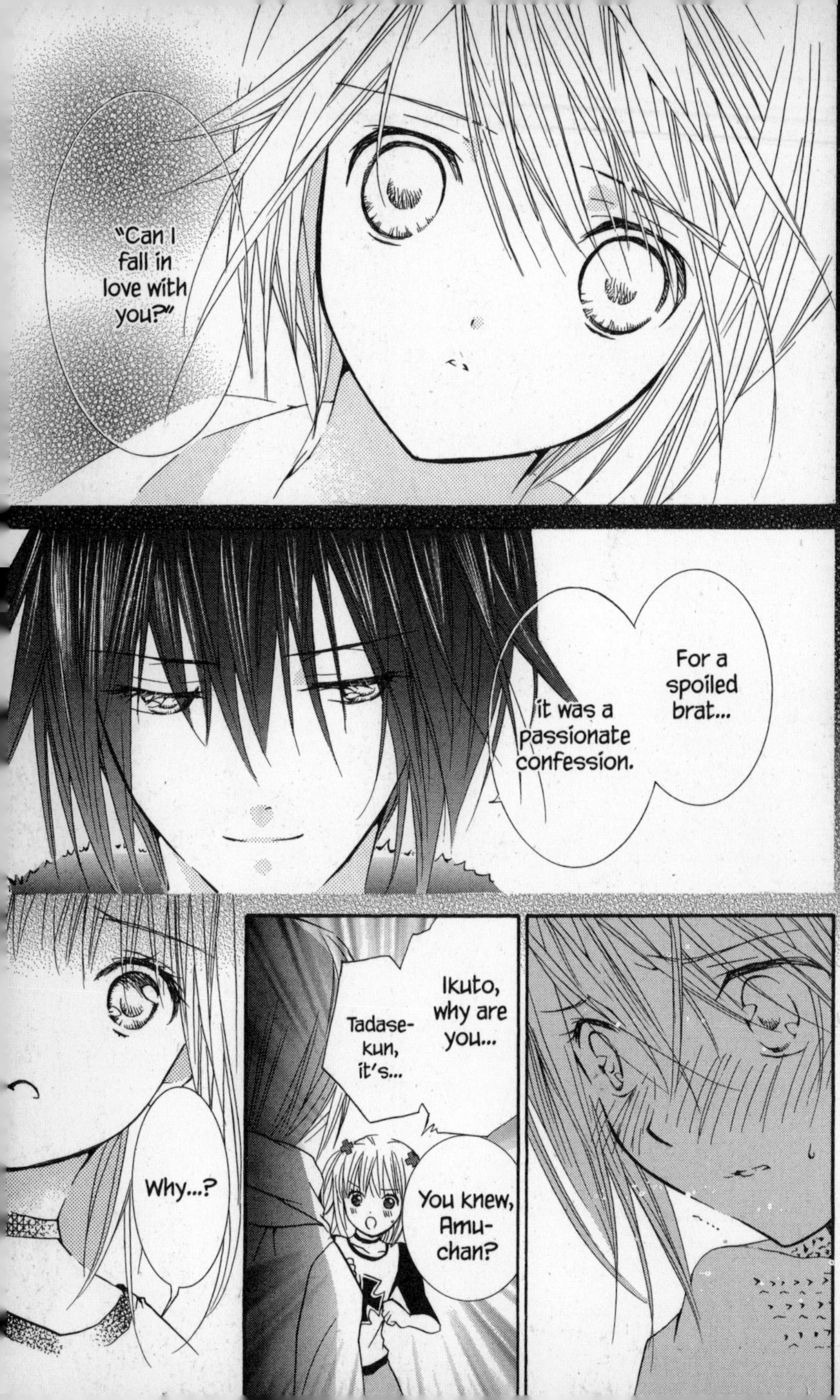
"Can I fall in love with you?"
For a spoiled brat...
it was a passionate confession.
Ikuto, why are you...
Tadase-kun, it's...
You knew, Amu-chan?
Why...?

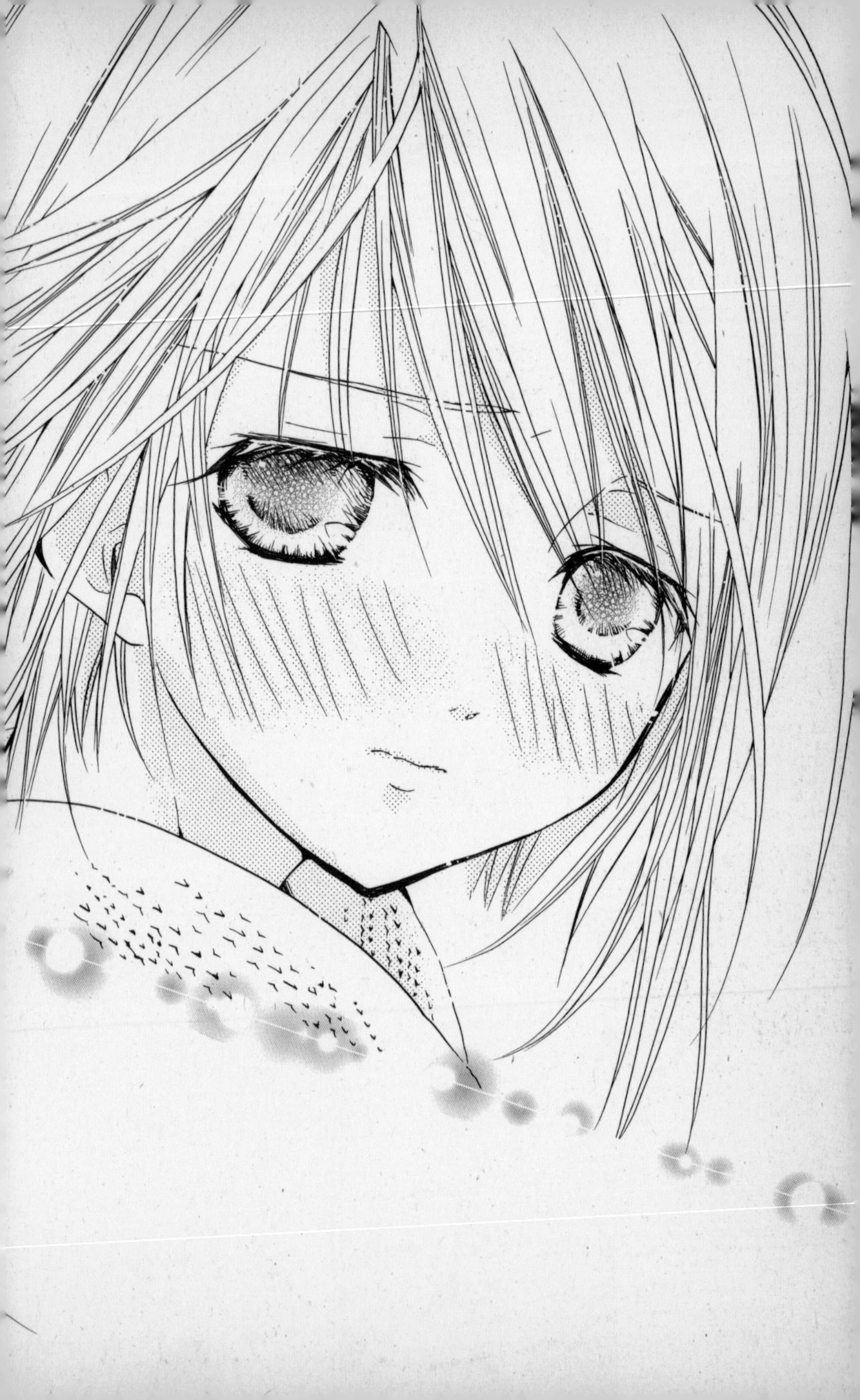

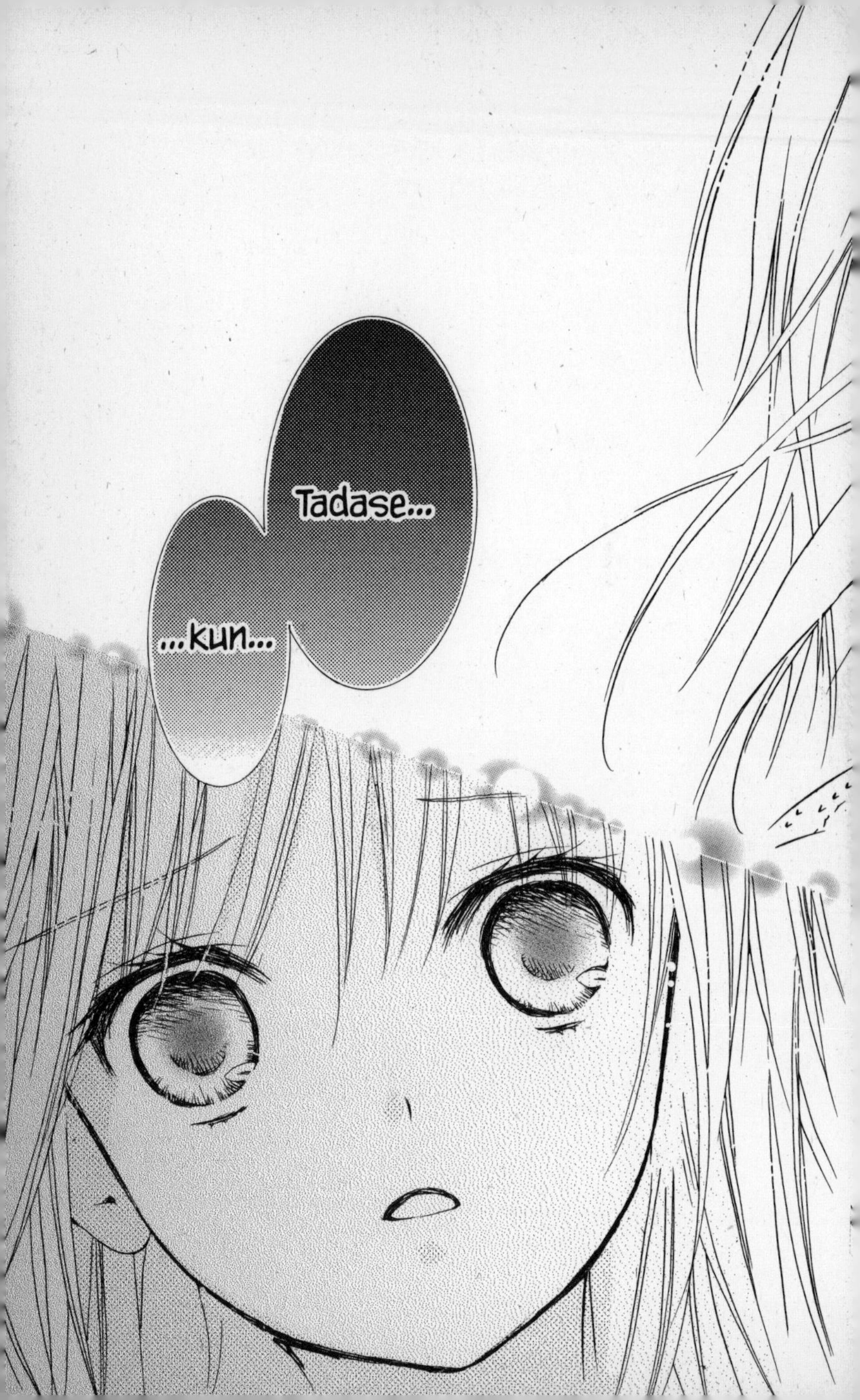
Tadase...
...kun...

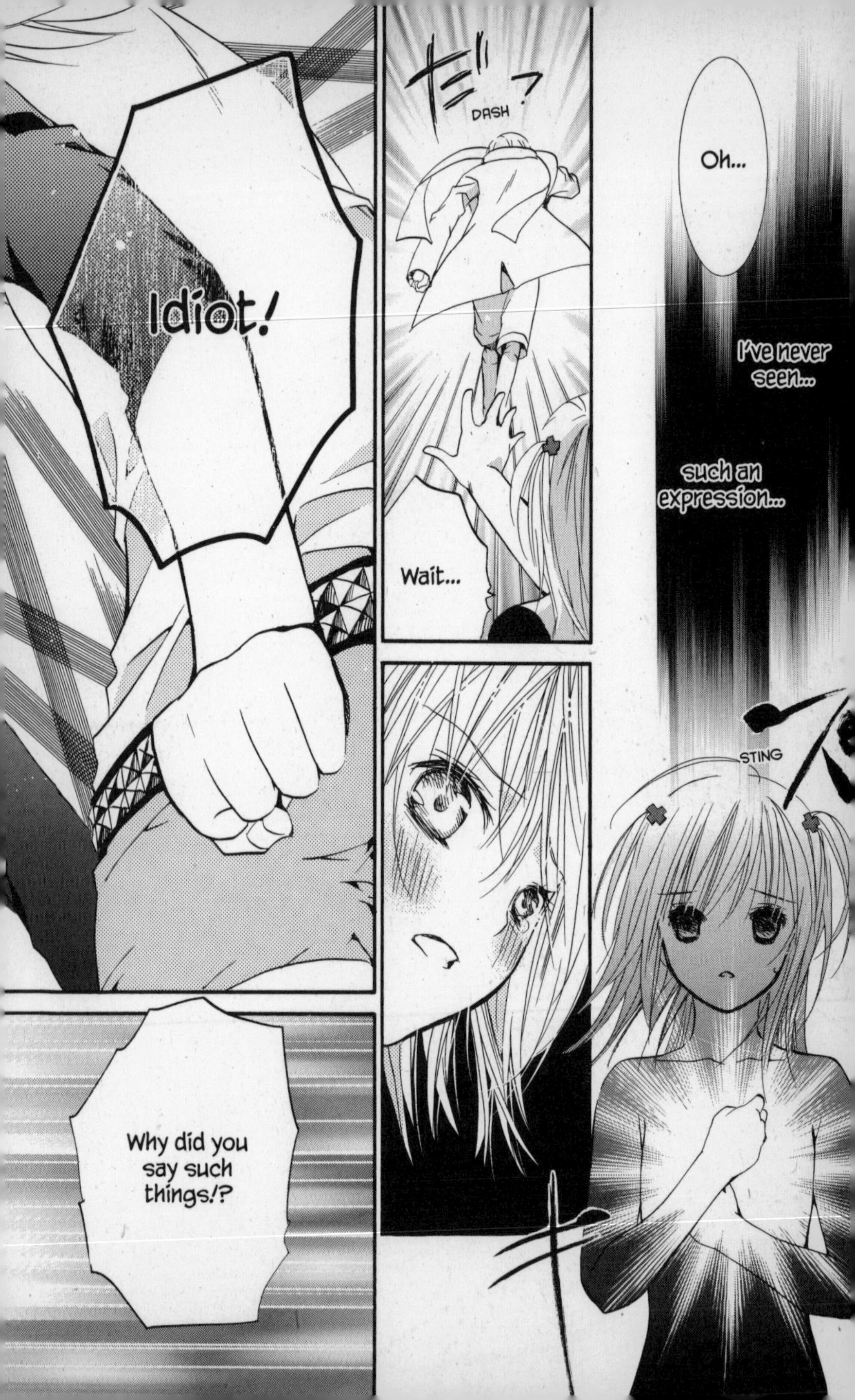
Oh...
I've never seen...
such an expression...
STING
DASH
Wait...
Idiot!
Why did you say such things!?

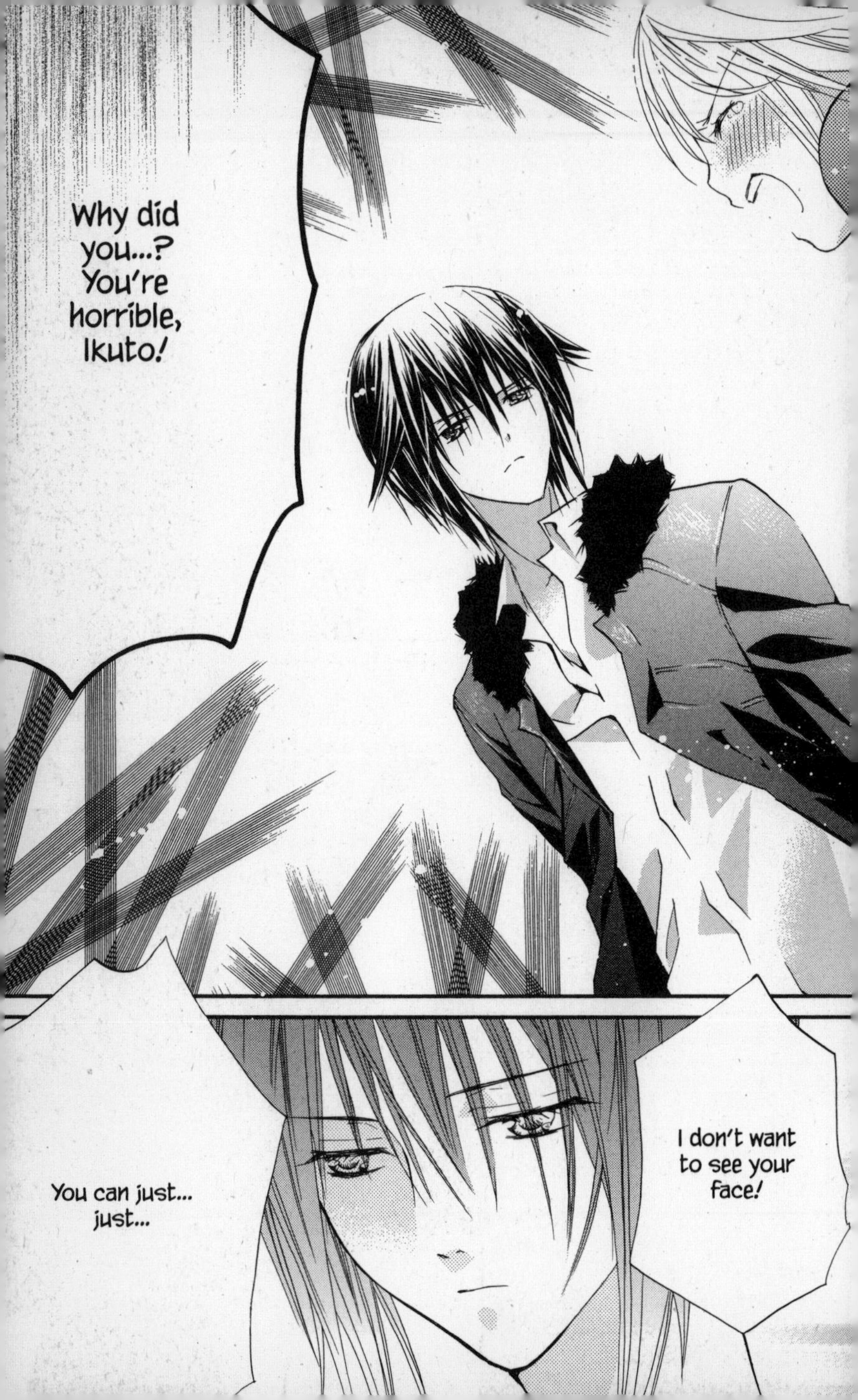
Why did you...? You're horrible, Ikuto!
I don't want to see your face!
You can just... just...

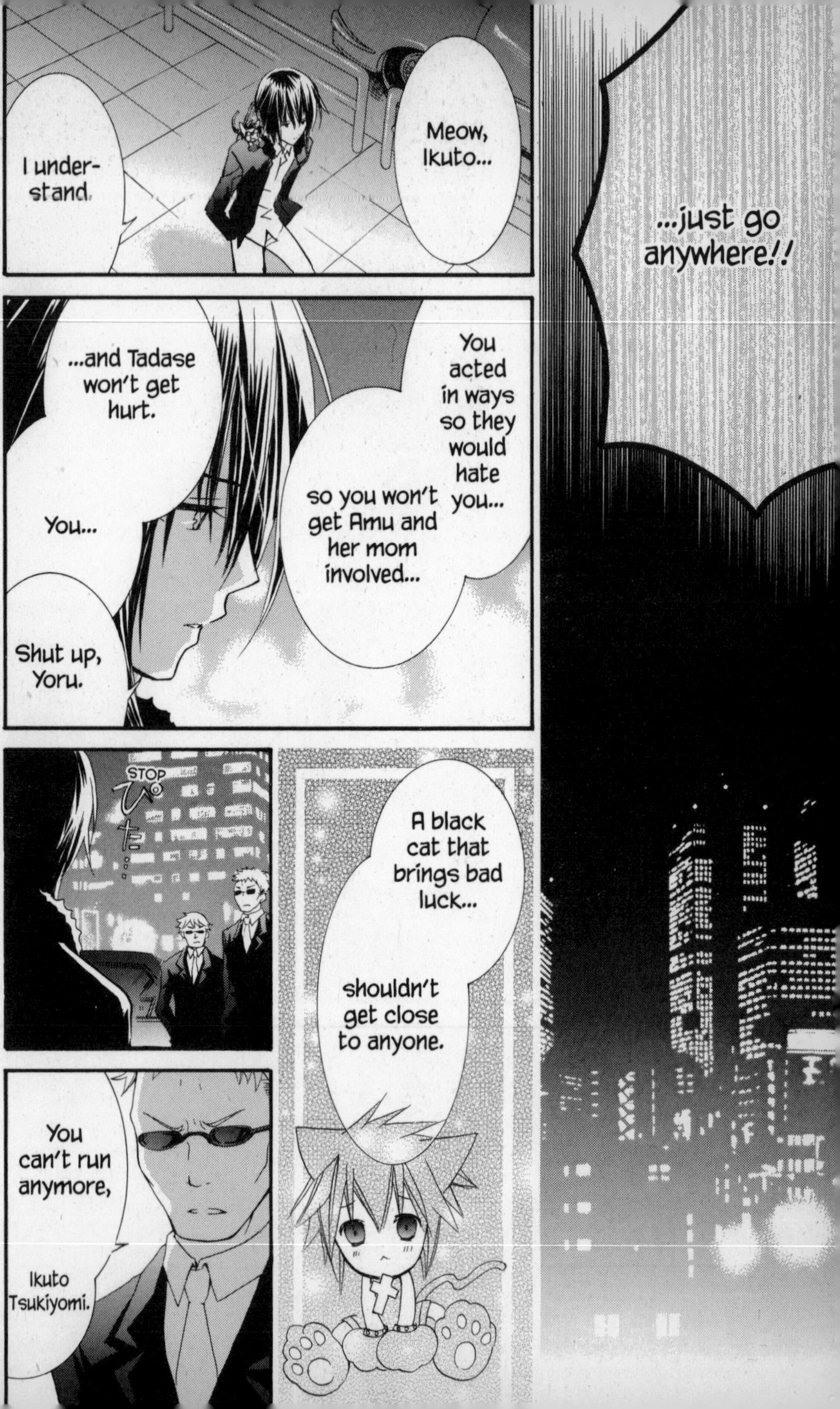
...just go anywhere!!
Meow, Ikuto...
I under-stand.
You acted in ways so they would hate you...
so you won't get Amu and her mom involved...
...and Tadase won't get hurt.
You...
Shut up, Yoru.
A black cat that brings bad luck...
shouldn't get close to anyone.
STOP
You can't run anymore,
Ikuto Tsukiyomi.

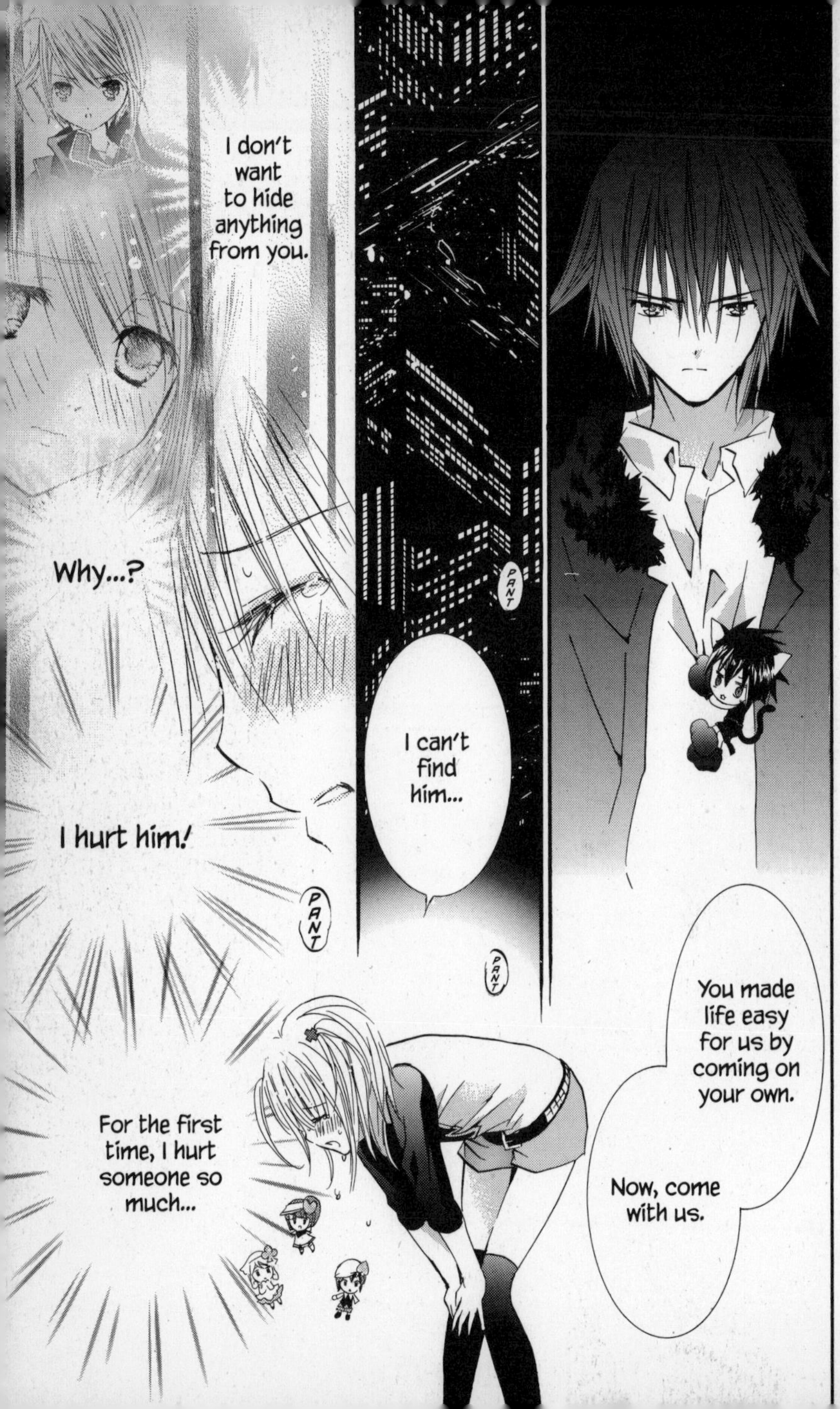
PANT
I can't find him...
PANT
I don't want to hide anything from you.
Why...?
I hurt him!
PANT
You made life easy for us by coming on your own.
Now, come with us.
For the first time, I hurt someone so much...

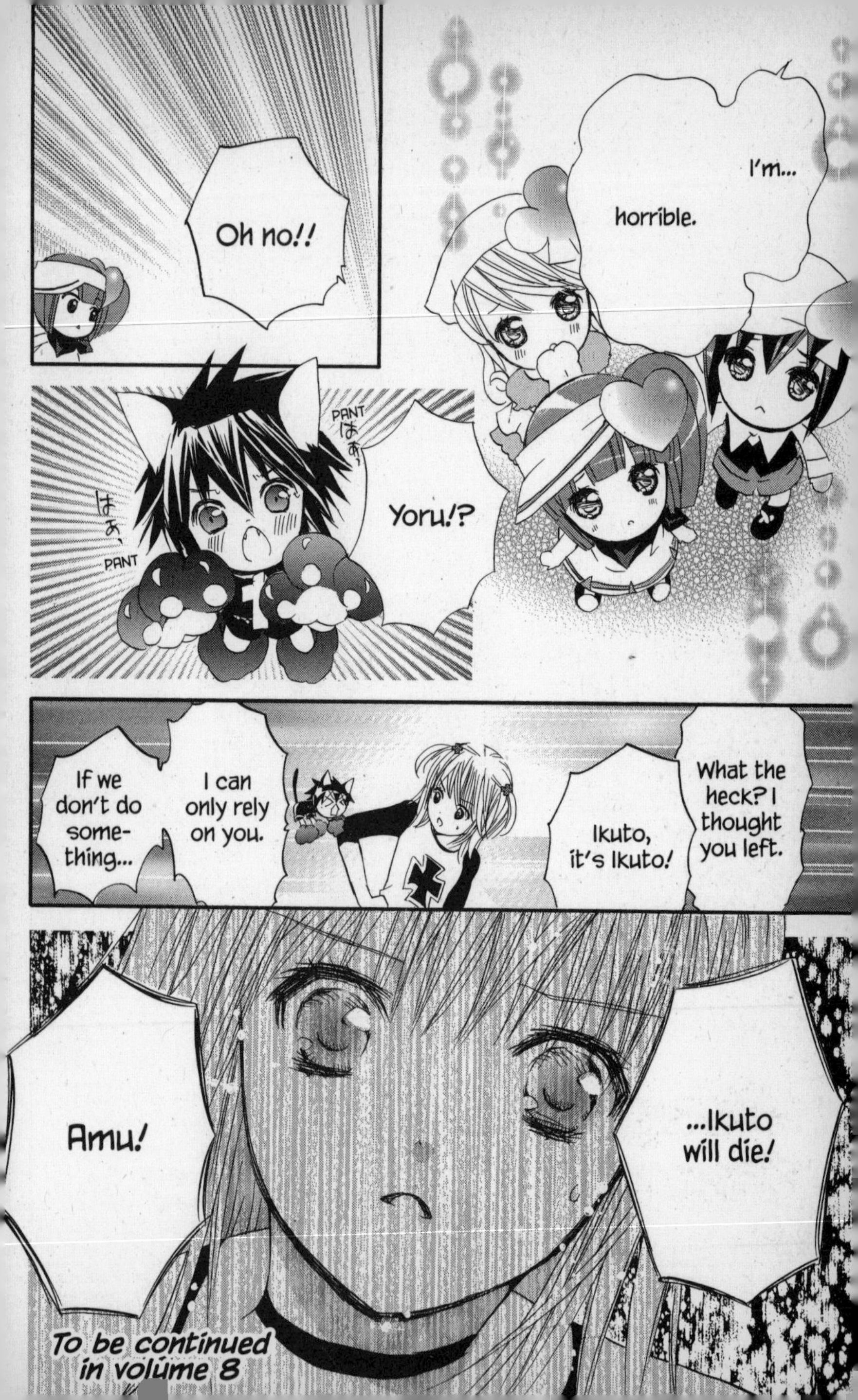
I'm...
horrible.
Oh no!!
PANT はぁっ
Yoru!?
はぁ PANT
What the heck? I thought you left.
Ikuto, it's Ikuto!
I can only rely on you.
If we don't do something...
...Ikuto will die!
Amu!
To be continued in volume 8

Shugo Chara!

About the Creators

PEACH-PIT:
Banri Sendo was born on June 7th. Shibuko
Ebara was born on June 21st. They are a
pair of Gemini manga artists who work
together. Sendo likes to eat sweets, and
Ebara likes to eat spicy stuff.

"Thank you to everyone who has supported us. We won the
Kodansha Manga Award. Thank you for reading!" —PEACH-PIT

Translation Notes

Japanese is a tricky language for most Westerners, and translation is often more art than science. For your edification and reading pleasure, here are notes on some of the places where we could have gone in a different direction in our translation of the work, or where a Japanese cultural reference is used.

Kotatsu, page 8

A *kotatsu* is a table with a blanket over it and a heat generator attached to it. It's used to keep one's feet warm.

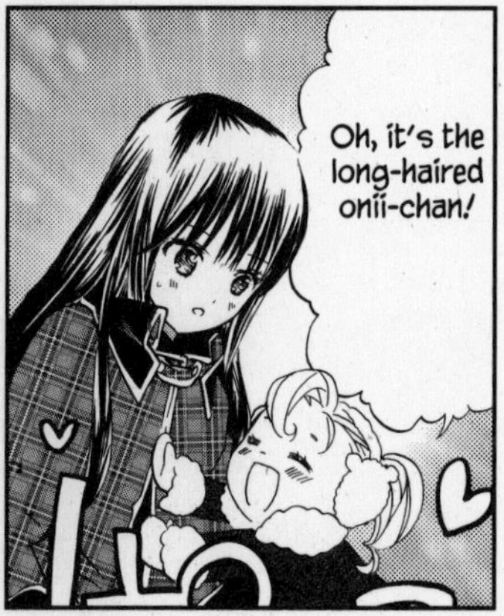
Oh, it's the long-haired onii-chan!

Onii-chan, page 31

Onii-chan is a Japanese honorific for "big brother."

Taiyaki, page 70

A *taiyaki* is a Japanese snack made with batter and usually filled with red beans. It's shaped like a fish and can also be filled with various other things including cream, custard or chocolate.

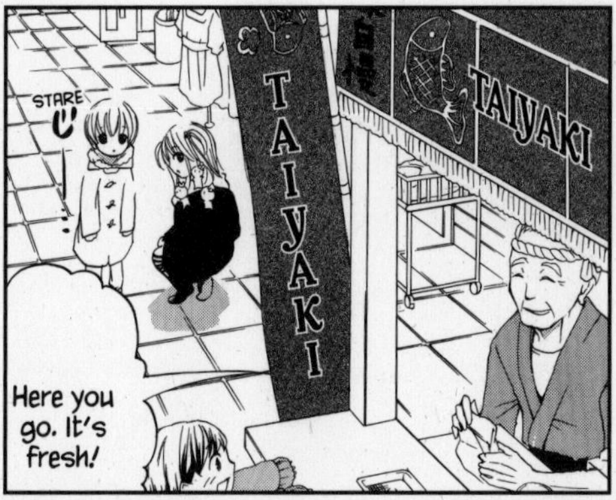
TAIYAKI
TAIYAKI
STARE
Here you go. It's fresh!

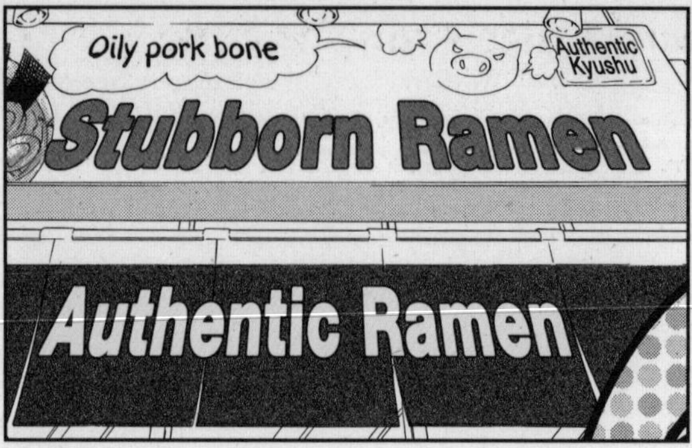
Oily pork bone
Authentic Kyushu
Stubborn Ramen
Authentic Ramen

Kyushu, page 107

Kyushu is the third largest island in Japan. It is known for its pork bone ramen.

Ajitama, page 108

Ajitama means "flavored eggs," which are boiled eggs soaked in a sauce. Usually the sauce is made out of soy sauce, rice wine, and water.

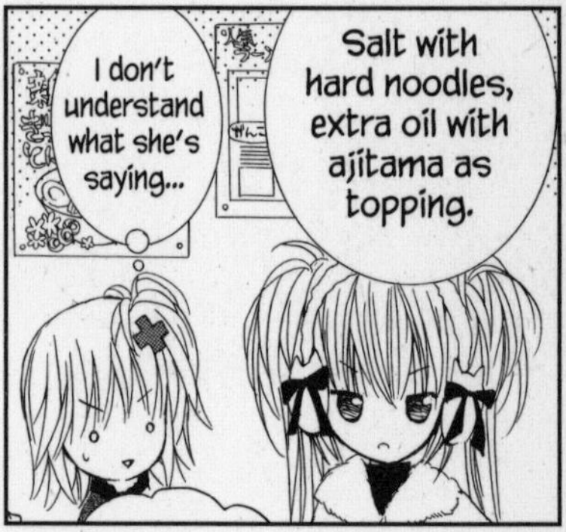
Salt with hard noodles, extra oil with ajitama as topping.
I don't understand what she's saying...

Preview of *Shugo Chara!* volume 8

We're pleased to present you a preview from volume 8. Please check our
website (www.kodanshacomics.com) for more information. For now you'll have
to make do with Japanese!

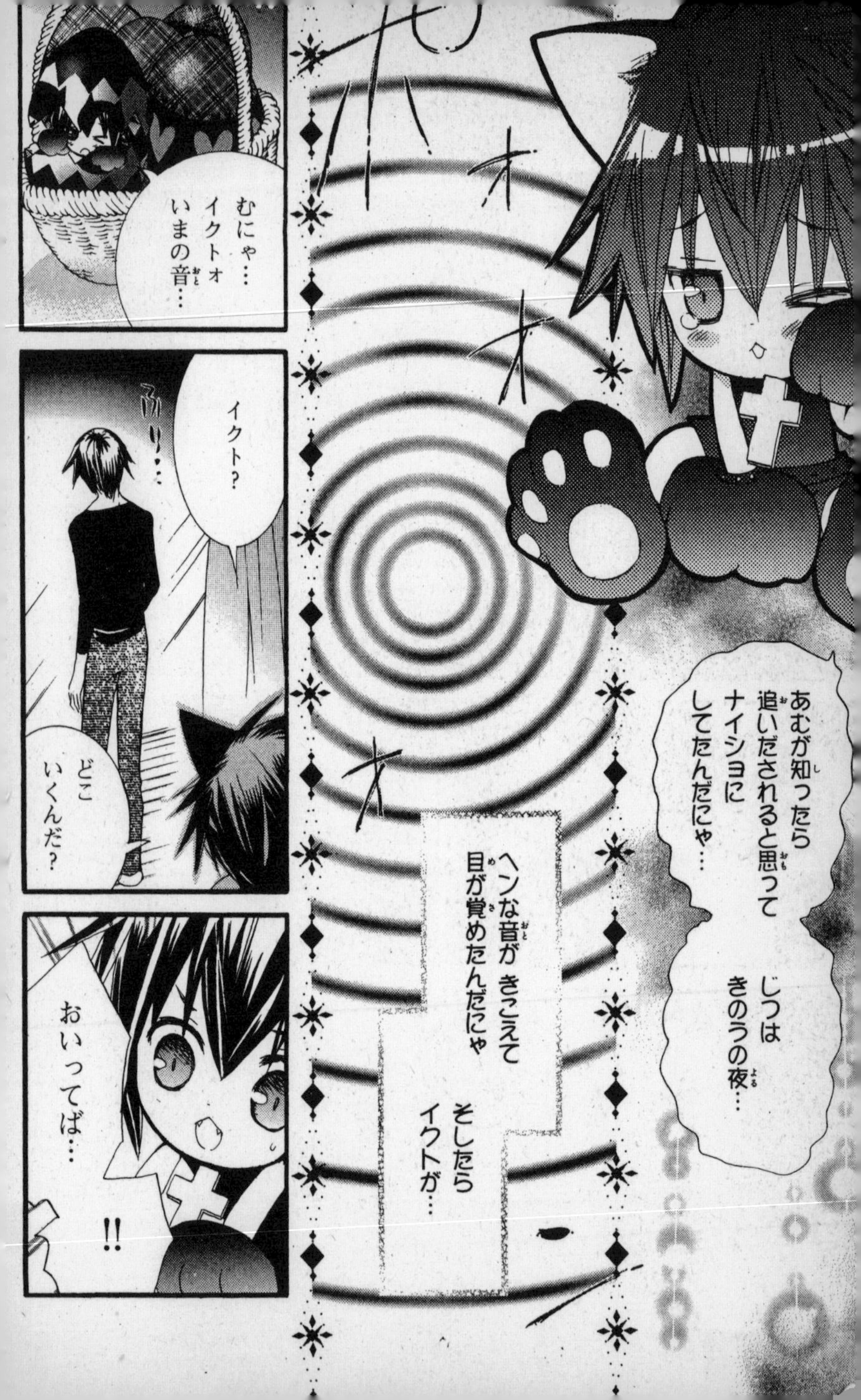
じつは
きのうの夜…
あむが知ったら
追いだされると思って
ナイショに
してたんだにゃ…
ヘンな音がきこえて
目が覚めたんだにゃ
そしたら
イクトが…
むにゃ…
イクトォ
いまの音…
イクト?
ふい…
どこ
いくんだ?
おいってば…
!!

むらさきのバイオリン!?

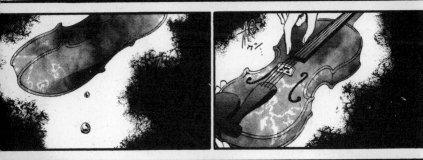

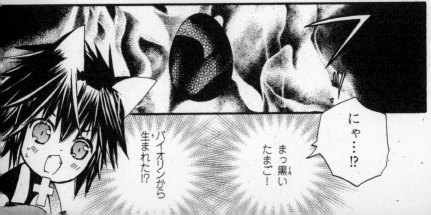

にゃ…!?

まっ黒いたまご！

バイオリンから生まれた!?

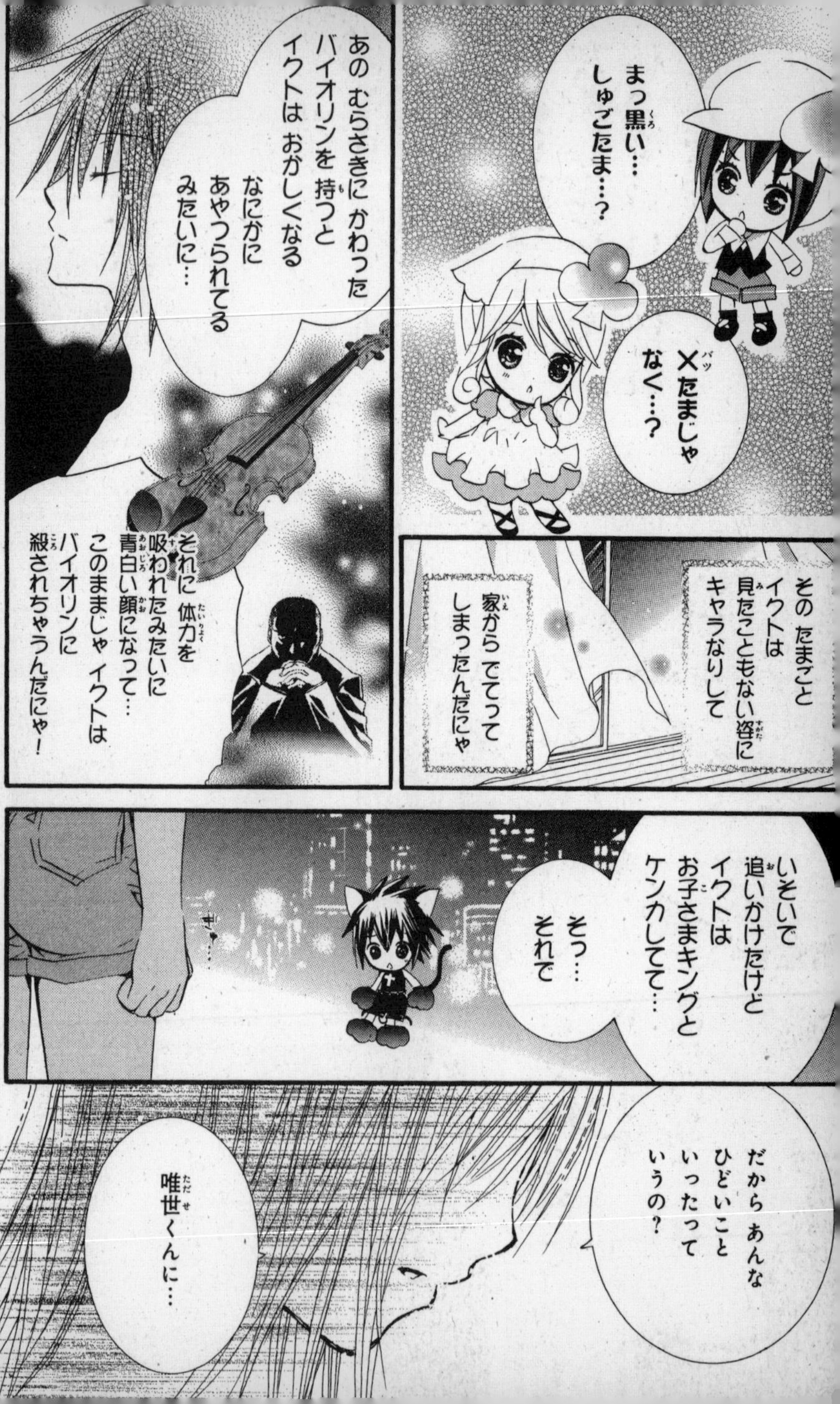
まっ黒い…しゅごたま…？
×たまじゃなく…？
そのたまごと イクトは 見たこともない姿に キャラなりして
家から でてって しまったんだにゃ
あの むらさきに かわった バイオリンを 持つと イクトは おかしくなる
なにかに あやつられてる みたいに…
それに 体力を 吸われたみたいに 青白い顔になって… このままじゃ イクトは バイオリンに 殺されちゃうんだにゃ！
いそいで 追いかけたけど イクトは お子さまキングと ケンカしてて…
そっ… それで
だから あんな ひどいこと いったって いうの？
唯世くんに…

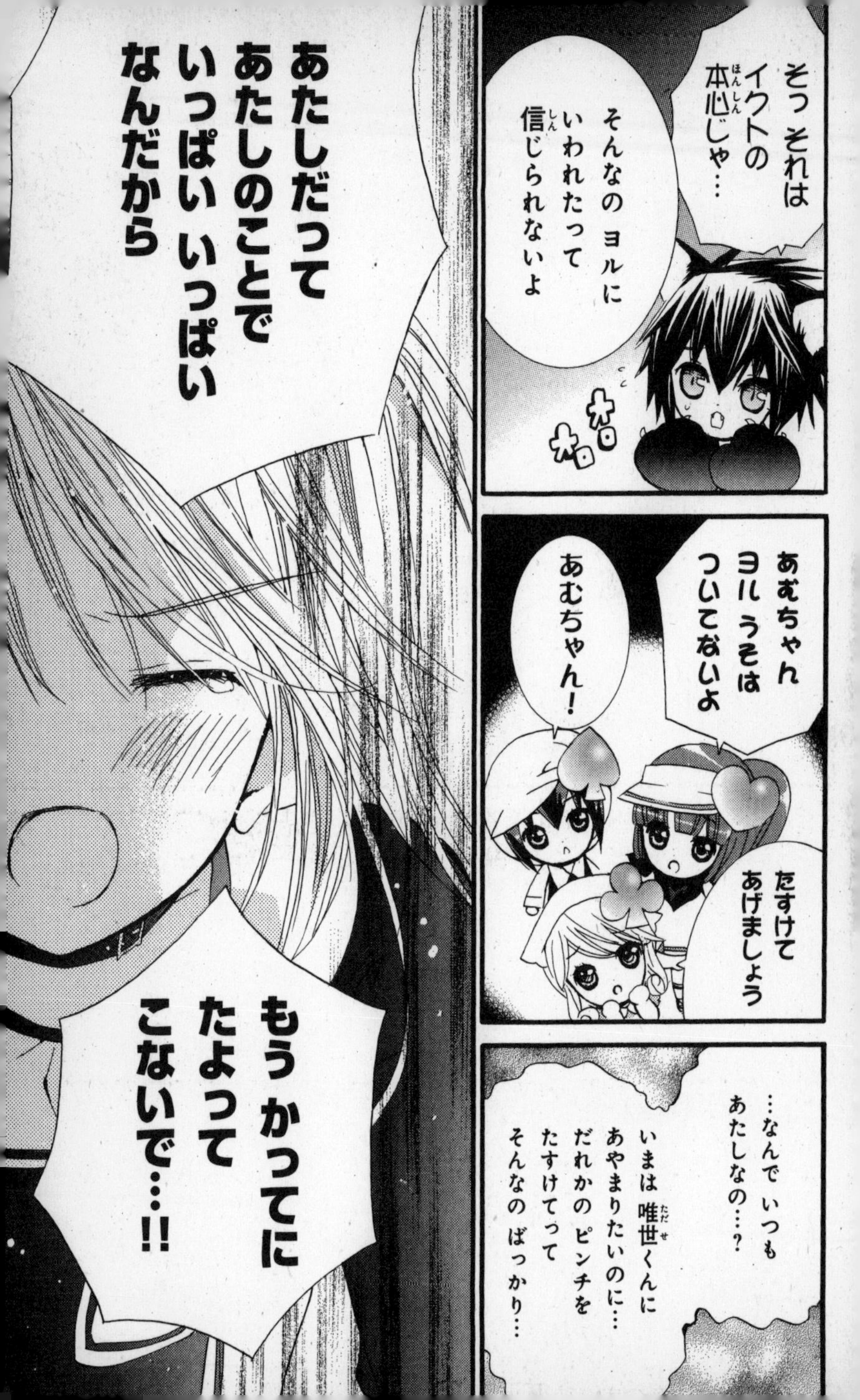
そっ それは イクトの 本心じゃ…
そんなの ヨルに いわれたって 信じられないよ
オロ オロ
あむちゃん ヨル うそは ついてないよ
あむちゃん！
たすけて あげましょう
…なんで いつも あたしなの…？
いまは 唯世くんに あやまりたいのに… だれかの ピンチを たすけてって そんなの ばっかり…
あたしだって あたしのことで いっぱい いっぱい なんだから
もう かってに たよって こないで…!!

TOMARE!

[STOP!]

You're going the wrong way!

Manga is a completely
different type of reading
experience.

To start at the *beginning,*
go to the *end*!

That's right! Authentic manga is read the traditional Japanese way—from right to left. Exactly the *opposite* of how American books are read. It's easy to follow: Just go to the other end of the book, and read each page—and each panel—from right side to left side, starting at the top right. Now you're experiencing manga as it was meant to be!